Casting Her Own Shadow

ELEANOR ROOSEVELT AND THE SHAPING OF POSTWAR LIBERALISM

Casting Her Own Shadow

ELEANOR ROOSEVELT

AND THE SHAPING OF

POSTWAR LIBERALISM

■

Allida M. Black

COLUMBIA UNIVERSITY PRESS

New York

Inclusion of many of the photographs in this book was made possible by the generous contribution of an anonymous donor.

Columbia University Press
New York   Chichester, West Sussex
Copyright (c) 1996 Columbia University Press
All rights reserved
Library of Congress Cataloging-in-Publication Data
    Black, Allida M.
        Casting her own shadow : Eleanor Roosevelt and the shaping of
    Postwar liberalism / Allida M. Black. — Casebound ed.
        p. cm.
    Includes bibliographical references and index.
    ISBN 0-231-10404-9   PA ISBN 0-231-10405-7
    1. Roosevelt, Eleanor, 1884-1962—Influence. 2. Liberalism—
    United States—History—20th century. I. Title.
    E807.1.R48B53 1996
    973.917'092—dc20   95-23500
                                                        CIP

Printed in the United States of America
c 10 9 8 7 6 5 4 3 2 1
p 10 9 8 7 6 5 4 3 2 1

■

For
Leo Paul Ribuffo
Jennie Mayes Crumbaugh

Franklin's death ended a period in history and
now in its wake for lots of us who lived in his shadow
periods come and we have to start again under our
own momentum and wonder what we can achieve.

Eleanor Roosevelt
To Lorena Hickok
April 19, 1945

Staying aloof is not a solution. It is a cowardly evasion.

Eleanor Roosevelt
Tomorrow Is Now, 1963

Contents

ACKNOWLEDGMENTS *XI*

INTRODUCTION: CASTING HER OWN SHADOW *1*

One
Learning To Be Independent: ER as Democratic Activist
7

Two
Coming into Her Own: ER as First Lady
23

Three
Holding Truman Accountable: Full and Fair
Employment at Just Wages
51

Four
Championing Civil Rights: From Patience to Protest
85

Five
Confronting the Vital Center: Civil Liberties in War and Peace
151

Six
Challenging the Party: John Kennedy and the Election of 1960
177

CONCLUSION: IN THE SHADOW OF ER *199*

NOTES *205*

BIBLIOGRAPHY *255*

INDEX *273*

ACKNOWLEDGMENTS

One of the hardest parts of submitting the manuscript is finding accurate descriptions for all those colleagues, friends, and archivists who helped me reconstruct and reinterpret Eleanor Roosevelt's life. So many historians and friends read drafts, listened to stories, helped track down leads, shared information, and challenged me to provocative debate that I often feel their names should accompany mine as author. These written thanks cannot convey the gratitude I have for their support nor express the respect I have for them as friends.

With a unique blend of sarcasm and affection, Leo Ribuffo taught me to think historically and to write with conviction and clarity. As the director of an earlier version of this manuscript, he set exacting standards from which he never wavered. A demanding mentor, he took the time to become a valued friend. Thirty years ago, in a different classroom, Jennie Mayes Crumbaugh challenged me to reach, to argue, and to dare. Together they not only showed me new ways to see the world but taught me the tools I needed to change it. I thank them.

Linda Lear and Gail Savage also read the manuscript in entirety. Our conversations about women, aging, power, and politics helped me interpret

Acknowledgments

ER's growing independence and appreciate the nuance of biography and the value of friendship.

Fiery debates with Ed Berkowitz, Guy Alchon, and Michael Barton about the limits of liberalism clarified my assessment of ER's influence while thoughtful conversations with Bill Becker about national economic policy reaffirmed my commitment to ER's vision.

Blanche Wiesen Cook scrutinized the manuscript, provided hours of unqualified support, shared sources, and took me to Tivoli on a hunt for ER's special tree—which was one of the greatest field trips of my life. Rather than succumbing to professional territorial disputes, Cook proclaimed that if ER was big enough for the world, she certainly could handle two biographers.

I also benefitted from the wise and thorough reading of Geoffrey Smith, who encouraged me to let the stories speak for themselves, to put ER in the center of power, and to attack conventional interpretations.

Comments made by Joan Hoff-Wilson, Jean Baker, and Judy Sealander on the portions of manuscript I presented to the Society of Historians of American Foreign Relations, the Social Science History Association, and the American Association for Voluntary Action strengthened my argument. Lewis Gould also skillfully edited an earlier discussion of the Marian Anderson affair, which appeared in *Presidential Studies Quarterly.*

Three young scholars shared with me documents they had collected during their own research. I am very grateful to Rose Gladney for sharing correspondence she found between ER and Lillian Smith; to Ben Koeppel for notes he found by Ralph Bunche describing his two-hour 1940 White House interview with ER; and to Bernard Unti for correspondence and minutes regarding ER's relationship with SCEF and Anne and Carl Braden.

Two grants from the Franklin and Eleanor Roosevelt Institute helped finance my four-year study at the Franklin D. Roosevelt Presidential Library. Frances Seeber and her archival staff set the standard by which all archivists should be judged. Assistant Director Seeber always found time to listen to my hypotheses, track down sources from other collections, and interpret ER's often illegible scrawl. Lynn Bassanese, Karen Burtis, Beth Denier, John Ferris, Cheryl Griffith, Bob Parks, Mark Renovitch, Nancy Snedeker, and Ray Teichman made my time in the Library my most pleasurable research experience. Their unique combination of expertise and kindness make them the model for all archival staffs.

I am also grateful to John White of the Southern Historical Collection at the University of North Carolina at Chapel Hill and to Ronald Grele and Alice Rwabzaire of the Oral History Research Office of Columbia

University for making my quick sojourns to their stacks so effective. I appreciate ORHO's permission to cite their interviews with Anna Roosevelt Halstead, Jonathan Daniels, Virginia Durr, Harry Hopkins, Gardner Jackson, Herbert Lehman, Thurgood Marshall, Frances Perkins, Eleanor Roosevelt, Bayard Rustin, Henry Wallace, and Aubrey Williams. I also thank the SHC for allowing me to cite the papers of Frank Porter Graham, Evans C. Johnson, and Allard K. Lowenstein as well as Southern Oral History Program interviews with Jessie Daniel Ames, Jonathan W. Daniels, Virginia Foster Durr, Alexander Heard, Calvin and Elizabeth Kytle, Hilda Worthington Smith, Olive Matthews Stone, George Stoney, Adolphine Fletcher Terry, and Louise Young.

John Howard, Susan Cimburek, and Nancy Beck Young expeditiously tackled my obscure archival requests from the Martin Luther King, Jr., Center for Non-Violent Social Change, the National Archives, and the Lyndon B. Johnson Presidential Library. Alycia Vibona, Linda Bouchey, Kate Canevari, Karen Casey, Kellie Casey, Susan Christoffersen, Reginia Lorenzo, Dianne McNeil, Eileen Rigothin, Shannon Sayles, and Mary Jane Zukushi graciously took time away from their own ER projects to help me make a final search for documents establishing ER's role in interning Japanese Americans. I look forward to seeing their work published.

Patricia Duane Lichtenberg and Angela Stultz of the Eleanor Roosevelt Center at Val-Kill deserve a special thanks for letting me ghost walk through the property when I needed more visual inspiration.

I also thank Arthur Schlesinger, Jr., Dorothy Height, and Conrad Lynn for making time in their very hectic schedules to meet with me. Mary Lasker and Anne Braden allowed me to read portions of their oral histories which had been closed for several years. Dale Wiehoff kindly agreed to present parts of chapter 5 to Alger Hiss.

Elizabeth Matheson graciously opened her North Carolina home to me during my trips to Chapel Hill, shared memories of conversations with her uncle, Frank Porter Graham, and carefully read the manuscript.

Debbie Rybicki handled my computer crises with unfailing good humor and efficiency.

Anna and Charles Black provided that special encouragement and unwavering optimism that only parents can provide. Ida May Armstrong, my 95-year-old aunt, who first told me about the Roosevelts, said "get it right and tell the truth."

For the past eleven years, I have been fortunate enough to be part of a community whose commitment to friendship, like their commitment to history, is exemplary. Charlene Bickford, Helen Veit, and Kenneth Bowling

Acknowledgments

applied the same discipline to ER that they applied to their own work on the First Federal Congress. Wendy Wolff shared her guest room and her knowledge of Democratic national campaigns and senatorial power plays with unfailing kindness. With great wit, expertise, and patience, they lived through this project with me.

Nina Seavey challenged me when my respect for ER threatened my historical judgment. Michael Weeks and Cyndy Donnell always kept me grounded. Gretchen Zimmerman and Frank Crumbaugh III gave me sanctuary and family. When funds ran out, Gaylord Neely took me to New York, gave me an unique opportunity to mix research and personal politics, and demanded that I follow all leads I could find. Her unique perceptions of life, struggle, and justice not only informed my research but strengthened me as an individual. Ellen Ratner opened doors with the Cold War left and at the White House. Kenneth Mannings, when he was not reading chapters or interceding on my behalf with the FBI, helped me comb the Schomberg Center for African-American Culture and the Library of Congress for photographs. Pillow Lee regaled me with her observations of New Deal and Cold War politics. Judy Beck not only "lived with the other woman" for four years, but helped track down elusive documents, proofed the manuscript and listened with grace and devotion to more ER stories than readers could possibly imagine. Doug Carl and Frank Crumbaugh, Jr., could not live to see this manuscript published. More than anyone, these men pushed me to do this and celebrated each discovery I made with sincere joy. I miss them. When party leaders disappointed her, ER turned to young Americans for inspiration and support. Rebecca Carl, Medora and Lydia Zimmerman-Crumbaugh, Sam Crumbaugh, Ian Lear-Nickum, Max and Samara Neely-Cohen, Eleanor Seavey, and Johanna Summerfield prove that her trust was well placed.

Alan M. Greenberg, of Integrity Indexing, prepared the index with great care. Leslie Bialler copyedited the manuscript. His fine sense of political nuance and grammatical clarity—combined with his cryptic observations on life, art, and politics—not only improved the book but also enlivened my e-mail.

Finally, I thank Kate Wittenberg. Her faith in this project sustained me when mine wavered. She is professional, astute, and fun—and a marvelous editor.

From queries regarding documentation to politics, from personal to political crises, from the Age of Reagan to the Age of Clinton, this group's attention never wavered. No one could have better friends.

Casting Her Own Shadow

ELEANOR ROOSEVELT

AND THE SHAPING OF

POSTWAR LIBERALISM

■

INTRODUCTION
Casting Her Own Shadow

Eleanor Roosevelt's political career did not end when her husband died. Indeed, her influence within the Democratic party and civil rights and other liberal reform organizations expanded during the last seventeen years of her life. She described this period, which began with FDR's death on April 12, 1945, and ended with her own death on November 7, 1962, as the time when she was "on my own." But this was also a time when the horrors of war had ripped liberalism away from its idealistic mooring in a perfectible human nature. Stunned by the Holocaust and the rise of totalitarianism, liberals struggled to balance their commitment to a more humane world against their new awareness of the darkness of human spirit. In a postwar world defined by opposites, they scrambled to redefine their place in American politics. Seeking a "fighting faith," they sought a tame politics "in an age of anxiety." Rejecting the anti-business sentiment they had embraced for half a century, they now argued liberals had more in common with business than they had with radical reformers. Now fearing the left as much as the right, they strove to promote what Arthur Schlesinger, Jr., has labeled "the vital center."[1]

ER, as she began to sign letters to FDR in 1909, disagreed with this approach. She did not see the world so simply. Liberal domestic reform faced a much more difficult choice than simply promoting anticommunist or noncommunist coalitions. Liberal international policy should see beyond the superficial juxtaposition of international accommodation with the Soviets and containment. While she agreed with Schlesinger that freedom must be "a fighting faith," she also believed that freedom must take risks or it would cease to be of any realistic value. Rather than yielding to those Reinhold Niebuhr labelled "the children of darkness," she worked to make sure that "the children of light" controlled the agenda. Comfortable with her own power, she remained uncomfortable with both consensus liberals and communist-front sympathizers. Treasuring democratic values, she opposed the politics of fear. Relieved that FDR's death freed her to pursue her own goals, ER nevertheless worried that FDR's death deprived liberals of the leadership they needed to humanize reform, to make America a more just democracy. And she worried that perhaps she did not have the expertise necessary to hold both the Democratic party and sympathetic Americans to the promises underpinning her reading of FDR's legacy. Indeed ER spent part of her last night in the White House discussing her fears with her dear friend Lorena Hickok, wondering not only how "to start again under our [her] momentum" but also what she could "achieve."[2]

Once freed from the constraints of the White House, ER eagerly expanded her career and unabashedly challenged both the Democratic party and American liberals to practice what they preached. Whether the issue was civil rights for African Americans, opposition to the House Un-American Activities Committee or Senator Joseph McCarthy, defending Alger Hiss, or questioning John Kennedy's character, ER continually asserted that civil liberties and civil rights were the cornerstones of American democracy.

Skillfully using a variety of forums, such as daily newspaper columns, monthly magazine articles, national lecture tours, and government and Democratic party appointments, ER challenged America and its political leaders to recognize hypocrisy and accept their civic responsibilities. Often this stance hurt ER financially. A few times it provoked assassination attempts. Other times, it angered American conservatives so intensely that the Ku Klux Klan placed a bounty on her head. More often it generated venomous press attacks against her character and her patriotism. Indeed, if some of the media objected to ER's activism while she was first lady, when she left the White House the attacks reached unforeseen proportions. Acutely aware of her public image, ER nevertheless continued to press for change—even if the change that she advocated offended friends, members of her own party, and high-ranking government officials—and, even if it placed her outside the vital center of American liberalism.

This book examines ER's efforts to push American liberalism to promote a more inclusive domestic policy agenda. It is not a comprehensive reconstruction of all the issues ER addressed during the Cold War. Rather, it analyzes her commitment to a society that might maximize employment at a fair wage, respect diversity, and tolerate dissent, and assesses her influence on Democratic leadership, party reformers, civil rights and civil liberties associations, and the American public.

While Blanche Cook brilliantly reconstructs ER's early life and Doris Kearns Goodwin explores ER's power within the wartime White House, no one depicts Eleanor Roosevelt as an accomplished political insider who developed a myriad of skills needed to articulate an increasingly liberal anti-racist agenda to a diverse and skeptical post-World War II public. This work begins to fill that void.

It is impossible to reconstruct in one brief tome a life as full and as complex as Eleanor Roosevelt's. I have left to the scholars more versed in psycho-history and psychological theory the opportunity to examine the emotional imbroglios of ER's life. And I encourage scholars to follow Cook's lead and reconstruct the influence that ER had as a feminist within public and private associations and use ER as a prism through which to examine the issues of human rights, containment, and nuclear disarmament. Instead, I deliberately chose to use a very traditional form, political history, to describe ER's nontraditional activities. Simply put, I am concerned with liberal politics, civil rights, and power. And Eleanor Roosevelt—as previous books fail to recognize—was the consummate liberal power broker.

Eleanor Roosevelt grew into power. Hers was neither an easy nor painless development. Indeed, her life before 1945 was marked by intensely private and public challenges. Some demands threatened ER's self-confidence, while others pushed her into unfamiliar arenas which demanded skills she never knew she possessed. The more she confronted the disappointments and set her own expectations, the more independent she became, the more she trusted her own abilities, and the more she wanted to achieve.

By mid-April 1945, when ER questioned what she could do "on my own," she could ease these doubts by remembering that at a time when she was under equally intense scrutiny she conquered her own fears and transcended the traditional helpmate role politicians and citizens prescribed for her. Just as she struggled to pursue goals that sometimes threatened her husband's political coalition, as America's foremost postwar liberal Eleanor Roosevelt could apply the lessons from her past to set a new course free from domestic political constraints. When confronted with this huge change in her life, when she no longer had to defer to her husband's office and priorities, she could rise to the challenge. She had now not only the opportunity "to start again," but the expertise necessary to build a legacy of her own.

ER's dissatisfaction with Harry Truman and Henry Wallace shaped her relentless efforts to shape their domestic economic policies. Convinced that he must have her support to hold the New Deal coalition together, Truman tried to appease ER by appointing her to the United Nations. Yet he soon learned that she was not so easily coopted. And he entered the election of 1948 without her endorsement. Wallace also underestimated ER. Disappointed as she was with the Democratic party in 1948, she refused to abandon the Democrats to promote a third party that was not sure of its membership or its principles. ER entered the era of Eisenhower committed to making the Democratic party less glued to the consensus agenda of price controls and fair deals and more supportive of racial justice and tolerant of political dissent.

ER gave unflinching support to the cause of civil rights for African Americans and her perception of racial justice grew as she aged. She was not a complacent supporter of civil rights. Her friendships with civil rights leaders and her experience chairing investigations of race riots, internment facilities, and violent segregationist backlashes continually exposed her to the brute fact of American racism. Her involvement with Democratic party leaders and liberal interest groups also revealed daily the superficial nature of liberal commitment to racial justice. Gradually she moved away from counselling patience and working within the system to supporting those activists who staged grand public events designed to force the political system to recognize the shallowness of its promises.

ER struggled simultaneously to support civil liberties. This proved a more difficult challenge. Plagued by her acquiescence to FDR's internment policies, ER spent the war years trying to balance her conscience against presidential dictates. By 1943, she worried that if America continued along its present political and economic path, it would win the war only to lose the peace. Once again uncomfortable with the stringent dictates of vital center liberalism, ER frequently opposed Cold War liberals who argued that communism had no place in American politics. Not only was she the first nationally prominent liberal to oppose Joseph McCarthy, she was also the only liberal to oppose from inception the House Un-American

Activities Committee and the Smith Act. Despite the rapidity with which Adlai Stevenson and other liberals deserted Alger Hiss after his conviction, ER refused to let her disappointment in Hiss's judgment dictate her reaction to it. Angry that Democrats had turned away from reform and embraced their own anti-communist rhetoric, she rebuked her party tersely, arguing that they could not "outconserve the Republicans."

The aging, impatient, and increasingly liberal ER confronted in the mid-1950s the young, pragmatic, and politically centrist John Kennedy. Discouraged by Stevenson's defeats in the 1952 and 1956 elections, ER approached the campaign of 1960 with mixed emotions. Convinced that the party needed a new bold vision to win the election and implement reform, ER nevertheless could not convince herself that Kennedy was the answer to the liberals' dilemma. His moderation on civil rights, his family association with McCarthy, his reliance on machine politics, and his father's conduct during World War II, only reinforced ER's opposition to his election. Yet Kennedy realized that he needed her support. Their relationship and the political aspirations of the young senator provide a useful prism through which to assess the aging ER's political clout.

Ultimately Eleanor Roosevelt exerted great influence on both the Democratic party and on America's attitude toward liberal reform. By the end of her life, she emerged as a skilled political insider who, as she aged, struggled to cope with a changing political world in which her influence declined. Resolute in her commitment to civil rights and civil liberties, ER sought to expand her influence by appealing, over the heads of party leaders, to the American public and reform organizations. Ever the democrat, ER entered the final years of her life worried that the nation may have forgotten its purpose and determined to resurrect the principles she believed essential to expand American democracy.

■

Chapter One

LEARNING TO BE INDEPENDENT
ER as Democratic Activist

For most of her early life, Eleanor Roosevelt lived in someone else's shadow. Her mother, Anna Hall Roosevelt, was one of New York society's most beautiful belles. Her teacher, Marie Souvestre, loomed larger than life over the Allenswood Academy, prodding an extremely shy Eleanor to develop her own opinions on world events. Her uncle, Theodore Roosevelt, transformed the presidency into a national bully pulpit. Her mother-in-law, Sara Delano Roosevelt, repeatedly undermined ER's maternal authority and always sided with her grandchildren against their mother. Her husband, Franklin Delano Roosevelt, charmed his way through New York politics and Washington social circles. And her friend and social secretary, the stylish Lucy Mercer, became one of the great loves of FDR's life.[1]

ER found it difficult to find a place of her own. She shared her home and her children with her mother-in-law. She shared her husband with gregarious New York bachelors and aspiring politicians. She had no retreat that was hers, no room in which to lock out the pressures of the outside world.

All that started to change in 1911. When Dutchess County voters elected her husband to the New York State Senate, FDR asked her to leave Hyde Park and to set up a home for the family in Albany. Eager to leave the ever-

of her mother-in-law, ER tackled the move with enthusi-
ne. "For the first time I was going to live on my own," she
six years later. "I had to stand on my own two feet. . . . I
.ependent. I was beginning to realize that something within
an individual."[2]

By the time FDR left Albany two years later to join the Wilson administration, ER began to view independence in both personal and political
terms. FDR had led the campaign against the Tammany Hall block in the
New York senate and an indignant ER watched in fascination as the
machine attacked its critics. "I [not only] realized that you might be a slave
and not a public servant if your bread and butter could be taken from you,"
she wrote after Tammany maliciously shut down a small opposition newspaper, but she also learned that "if you grew too fond of public life it might
exact compromises even if finances were not involved." Outraged that a
political machine could vindictively deprive its critics of the means to support themselves, ER lost a great deal of the naivete that characterized her
earlier attitude toward government. "That year taught me many things
about politics and started me thinking along lines that were completely
new." FDR agreed, later telling a friend, Albany "was the beginning of my
wife's political sagacity and co-operation."[3]

Consequently, when FDR was appointed assistant secretary of the Navy
in autumn 1913, ER knew most of the rules under which a political couple
operated. "I was really well schooled now. . . . I simply knew that what we
had to do we did, and that my job was to make it easy." "It" was whatever
needed to be done to complete a specific familial or political task. As ER
oversaw the Roosevelt transitions from Albany to Hyde Park to
Washington, coordinated the family's entrance into the proper social circles
for a junior Cabinet member, and evaluated FDR's administrative and
political experiences, her "considerable independence" increased as her
managerial expertise grew. When the threat of world war freed cabinet
wives from the obligatory social rounds, ER, with her commitment to settlement work, administrative skills, disdain for social small talk, and aversion to corrupt political machines, entered the war eager for new responsibilities.[4]

World War I gave ER an acceptable arena in which to challenge existing
social restrictions and the connections necessary to expedite reform.
Anxious to escape the confines of Washington high society, she threw herself into wartime relief with a zeal that amazed her family and her colleagues. Her fierce dedication to Navy Relief and the Red Cross canteen, as
exemplified by the day she refused to leave the canteen even though she had

cut her arm to the bone on the bread slicing machine, not only stunned soldiers and Washington officials but shocked ER as well. Moreover, even though she had never kept the family books, she devised the accounting system that tracked canteen expenses. She began to realize that she could contribute valuable service to projects that interested her and that her energies did not necessarily have to focus on her husband's political career. "The war," observed a friend, "pushed Eleanor Roosevelt into the first real work *outside her family* since she was married twelve years before."[5]

The family was not exempt from ER's new-found confidence. For the first time, she took sides in a family argument, rebuking her grandmother in the process. She understood how extensively her personality was changing. This dispute, ER later recalled, was her "first really outspoken declaration against the accepted standards in which I had spent my childhood and marked the fact that . . . an increasing ability to think for myself was changing my point of view."[6]

Emboldened by these experiences, ER began to respond to requests for a more public political role. When a Navy chaplain whom she had met through her Red Cross efforts asked her to visit shell-shocked sailors confined in St. Elizabeth's Hospital, the federal government's facility for the insane, she immediately accepted his invitation. Appalled by the quality of treatment the sailors received compared to that provided in other military medical facilities, as well as by the shortage of aides, supplies, and equipment available to all the St. Elizabeth's patients, ER urged her friend Secretary of the Interior Franklin Lane to visit the facility. When Lane declined to intervene, fearing allegations of preferential treatment for Navy enlistees, ER pressured him until he appointed a commission to investigate the institution. Reflecting on this experience in her autobiography, she wrote, "I became . . . more determined to try for certain ultimate objectives. I had gained a certain assurance as to my ability to run things, and the knowledge that there is joy in accomplishing good." Duty no longer had to be dull and tedious. She learned that independence could make her happy.[7]

The end of the war did not slow ER's pace or revise her new perspective on duty and independence. In June 1920, while vacationing with her children at Campobello, Josephus Daniels telegraphed her that FDR "was nominated unanimously for Vice-President" on the ticket with presidential nominee James M. Cox. Although both her grandmother and mother-in-law strongly believed that "a woman's place was not in the public eye" and pressured ER to respond to press inquiries through her social secretary, she developed a close working relationship with FDR's intimate adviser and press liaison, Louis Howe. Invigorated by Howe's support, ER threw herself into the election and enjoyed participating in the routine political decisions that daily confronted the ticket. She happily developed what she called "a certain adaptability to circumstances." By the end of the campaign, while other journalists aboard the Roosevelt campaign train played cards, Howe and ER could frequently be found huddled over paperwork, reviewing FDR's speeches, and discussing campaign protocol.[8]

When the Republican ticket of Warren G. Harding and Calvin Coolidge won the 1920 election, the Roosevelts returned to New York. While Eleanor Roosevelt considered her options, FDR practiced law and planned his next political move. Dreading "a winter of four days in New York with nothing but teas and luncheons and dinners to take up [her] time," ER "mapped out a schedule" in which she spent Monday through Thursday in New York City and the weekend in Hyde Park. She declined invitations to sit on the boards of organizations that wanted to exploit her name rather than use her energy, opting instead to join the Women's City Club, the National Consumers League, the Women's Division of the Democratic State Committee, and the New York chapters of the League of Women Voters and the Women's Trade Union League.[9]

Despite her labelling in *This I Remember* of the 1920s as a time of "private interlude," in the seven-year span between the onset of FDR's paralysis and his campaign for the New York governorship, Eleanor Roosevelt's political contributions and organizational sagacity made her one of New York's leading politicians. While still committed to democratic ideals, she recognized that ideology alone did not provide the votes and skills necessary to win elections. She quickly substituted a subdued realpolitik pragmatism for dilettante debates. Urging coworkers and fellow reformers to spend less time theorizing, she spent more time concentrating on what "exactly" could be done before the next meeting. Repeatedly she goaded women's and other reform groups to set realistic goals, prioritize their tasks, and delegate assignments. Her persistent pragmatism attracted attention within the party and women's political organizations. Soon the media publicized her clout, treating her as the "woman [of influence] who speaks her political mind."[10]

After working with attorney Elizabeth Read and her partner, educator and consumer activist Esther Lape, ER agreed to chair the League of Women Voters Legislative Affairs Committee and to represent the League on the Women's Joint Legislative Committee. Each week, Eleanor Roosevelt studied the *Congressional Record*, examined legislation and committee reports, interviewed members of Congress and the State Assembly, and met with League officers to discuss the information she gathered. Each month, she assembled her analyses and presented a report for League members outlining the status of bills in which the organization was interested and suggesting strategies by which it could achieve its legislative goals. Moreover, ER also spoke out at these monthly assemblies on such pressing nonlegislative issues as primary-election reform, voter registration, and party identification. Recognizing the extensive contributions she made, the League elected her its vice chair eighteen months later, after ER skillfully arbitrated a hostile internal organizational dispute.[11]

Ruby Black, Roosevelt's friend and early biographer, saw this time as the period when "Eleanor Roosevelt was traveling, not drifting, away from the conventional life expected of women in her social class." ER agreed, later labelling the last part of 1920 as the beginning of "the intensive education of Eleanor Roosevelt." Polio would not strike FDR until the following summer; consequently, ER was already in a position to keep her husband's name active in Democratic circles before illness sidelined him.[12]

This does not mean that after FDR was stricken she eagerly became his surrogate or that she did so solely for him or for herself. As James Roosevelt astutely recognized, his mother's motivations were much more complex. "When she put aside her fears and agreed to try the role that had been created for her as her husband's ambassador to public life, she did so to prevent his mother from making him a complete invalid, to help him as she felt he should be helped, to take part in his life and to assume a role in life for herself." Furthermore, the more ER stood in, the more at ease she became and the more she wanted to contribute. She became "filled with a passion for politics through which she saw the chance to right wrongs, to be of use." The more accepted she felt, the less shy she became. The more she succeeded, the more aggressive she became.[13]

In spring of 1922, ER agreed to a request from Nancy Cook, the secretary of the newly formed Women's Division of the New York State Democratic Committee, to give a fund-raising speech at a committee luncheon. That September, she joined Cook, Marion Dickerman, and future New York Congresswoman Caroline O'Day in a statewide tour to encourage the formation of Democratic women's clubs. Their organizational efforts created such strong support among the Democratic rank and file that at the state convention in Syracuse the women attendees demanded that ER, Dickerman, and O'Day each be considered the party's nominee for secretary of state. The following month, as Democratic Women's Committee vice president and finance chairman, ER edited and wrote articles discussing campaign strategies and the fall election for the *Women's Democratic News*. And throughout the following year, she participated in all

year election activities from stuffing envelopes and driving
ls to courting recalcitrant county chairmen.[14]

oined the board of the bipartisan Women's City Club, a
ivic center for women interested in municipal affairs"
...ᴏꜱᴇ major objectives were to inform women about pressing political and
social issues, introduce them in a pragmatic way to governmental operations, and "orchestrate publicity and lobbying campaigns for the issues the
club wished to advocate." During her four-year tenure as a Club board
member ER chaired its City Planning Department, coordinated its
responses on housing and transportation issues, chaired its legislation committee, pushed through a reorganization plan, arbitrated disputes over child
labor laws, promoted workmen's compensation and, in a move that made
banner headlines across New York State, strongly urged adoption of an
amendment to the Penal Law legalizing the distribution of birth control
information among married couples.[15]

Not all of the Roosevelts' friends supported her activism. Indeed, ER's
political prominence created some in-house sarcasm among FDR's advisers.
That May, Josephus Daniels taunted his former assistant secretary that he
was glad that "I am not the only 'squaw' man in the country." Jokingly referring to the picture of Eleanor Roosevelt *The New York World* had published
in an article announcing FDR's leadership role in Al Smith's presidential
campaign, Daniels mused "I have had the experience on similar occasions
and have always wondered how the newspapermen knew so well who was
at the head of the family."[16]

Such inside joking did not limit ER's political exposure nor did her
involvement in bipartisan civic groups curtail her commitment to the state
Democratic party or its Women's Division. She attended the 1924
Democratic National Convention as chair of the women's delegation to the
platform committee and as Al Smith's liaison to women voters. When the
committee rejected her requests and the convention rejected Smith, choosing John W. Davis as its standard bearer, ER returned to New York
undaunted. "I took my politics so seriously" she recalled in *This Is My Story*,
"that in the early autumn I came down to the state headquarters and went
seriously to work in the state campaign."

Assiduously ER courted voters throughout the state. New Yorkers living
in the rural areas often neglected by the party heard her personalized
appeals for support. She told the farm belt that the Democratic party was
more than just an urban machine. It also recognized the needs of those who
live in small towns and farm communities. Because "I live in both city and
country," she was in a unique position to see both sides of the state's needs.

She acknowledged that rural and urban problems often seemed to compete for the party's attention, but she also "realize[d] that the best interests of both are to be promoted by better understanding of each other's situation and cooperation rather than conflict." She pledged to keep their interests in front of the party leadership, if the farmers would continue to make their demands known and to vote Democratic.

But she also appealed to voters' more basic instincts. Despite her aversion to Tammanyesque political practices, ER occasionally participated in her own version of dirty politics, even if the candidate was a member of her own family. When the Republicans nominated her cousin Theodore Roosevelt, Jr., for governor in 1924, ER, without a second thought, tailed her cousin around the state in a roadster topped with a giant steaming teapot in a flagrant attempt to associate him with Teapot Dome corruption.[17]

The next election cycle prompted comparable action while providing new arenas of operation. A staunch supporter of Robert Wagner's 1926 campaign for the U.S. Senate, ER traveled New York as one of his leading speakers and debaters, accusing Wagner's opponent, James Wadsworth, of aloof and aristocratic behavior. He was so selfish that he had "the Marie Antoinette type of mind" and promoted a "'Let them eat cake'" political agenda.

ER then took to print to promote her candidates with the same level of energy she displayed in her speeches. Within the next twelve months, she continued her regular articles for the League's *Weekly News* and *Women's Democratic News*, and published four substantive political articles in publications ranging from the popular women's magazine *Redbook* to the more scholarly journals *Current History* and *North American Review*. She expanded her audience, broadened her themes, and carefully tailored her remarks. Women reading *Redbook* were urged to "learn to play the game as men do," while those more versed in political history were told that "Jeffersonian principles [were] the major issue in 1928."[18]

So strong an impression did her organizational and administrative campaign skills make on the state's professional politicians that both Al Smith and his political adviser Belle Moskowitz recruited her energies for Smith's 1928 presidential campaign. A longtime supporter of Smith, ER agreed to coordinate preconvention activities for the Democratic Women's Committee. The *New York Times Magazine* recognized ER's increasing political clout and featured a lead article on her influence in its April 8 issue. As a result of this continuous activity, by the time her husband received the party's nomination for governor, Eleanor Roosevelt was better known among the faithful party activists than was FDR.[19]

Learning To Be Independent

The 1928 election presented a new challenge to both Roosevelts. New York law prevented Al Smith, the Democratic presidential nominee, from seeking reelection as governor and Smith wanted FDR to succeed him. This decision placed ER squarely in opposition to her husband's most trusted aide, Louis Howe.

Howe vigorously opposed FDR's candidacy and FDR, heeding his adviser, refused to take Smith's phone calls. Smith, whose chief political aide was a woman, appreciated the scope of ER's expertise and the influence she held in her husband's innermost political circle. Consequently, Smith turned to ER, who had enthusiastically endorsed his candidacy and who was the only individual who might counteract Howe's opposition, to intercede with FDR. ER agreed, phoned her husband, told him that "she knew he had to do what he felt was expected of him," handed the phone to Smith, and left to address a Smith campaign rally.[20]

However, Eleanor Roosevelt did not endorse her husband's electoral aspirations unequivocally. She feared that FDR's victory would undermine all her automony. "It became clear," one of her sons later wrote, "that she felt if father won, she would lose" the autonomy she had worked so painstakingly to develop. Indeed, she recoiled at the prospect of returning to a life modeled after her early years at Hyde Park.

By the mid-1920s, the Franklin Roosevelt-Eleanor Roosevelt relationship had begun to move away from a traditional marriage and more toward a professional collaboration between peers. Her discovery in 1918 of his affair with Mercer destroyed marital intimacy and encouraged her to look elsewhere for closeness. Anna Roosevelt later recalled that her mother's discovery of the affair "spurred on" her activism and that her parents' "different priorities" became more apparent. Thus, while both treasured their friendship with Louis Howe and FDR enjoyed most of ER's associates, the separate strong attachments ER and FDR formed with different coworkers and companions were the rule rather than the exception in the Roosevelt households.[21]

"Partnership," ER declared in 1930, "is the major requirement for modern marriage." The few old friends and Democratic party commitments the Roosevelts shared were enough to sustain a friendship, but not an intimate one. Competing pursuits and divergent communities encouraged the Roosevelts to follow different paths and to develop separate lifestyles. "It is essential," ER responded when *Good Housekeeping* asked her to define a modern wife's job, for the woman "to develop her own interests, to carry on a stimulating life of her own. . . ." As a result, by the time FDR was elected governor, each Roosevelt had developed his and her own personal and political support system.[22]

"Having dropped out of society entirely," Eleanor Roosevelt saw "very little" of her old acquaintances, preferring instead the company of those who were most interested "in real work and not being a dilettante." With her ties to reform movements and women's political associations expanding, ER carefully and deliberately developed her own network. Caroline O'Day and Elinor Morgenthau became her life-long trusted friends. With Democratic Women's Committee (DWC) colleague Nancy Cook and her partner Marion Dickerman, with whom ER taught and who later administered the Todhunter School for Girls in New York City, Eleanor Roosevelt built Val-Kill, her home away from the Roosevelt house. Writing Dickerman in 1926 that it was a "new" experience for her to have someone respond to her mood-swings, she thanked her companions, housemates, and partners for introducing her to a new level of openness and support. "My friends," ER believed, "are responsible for much that I have become and without them there are many things which would have remained closed to me." Cook and Dickerman reciprocated ER's devotion. Indeed, the bond between the three Val-Kill residents was so strong that the cottage linens bore the collective monogram "EMN."[23]

While ER and FDR both expanded their levels of commitment to the state Democratic party and promoted the same candidates, they began to form different views of the political process. Although both Roosevelts realized that politics was part ego, part drive, and part conviction, they differed as to which component they valued the most. If politics was part game and part crusade, ER tolerated the game for the sake of the crusade. To her dismay, FDR enjoyed all aspects equally. Acknowledging that while it was "hard to disassociate" her husband's ambition and love of political contest "from his desire to achieve . . . real gains for the people," ER believed that the satisfaction FDR took "in the purely political side of the struggle" and "the play of his own personality on [others]" increasingly outweighed his interest in reform. To the extent that FDR failed to reverse this trend, he could no longer depend upon ER's unqualified support. ER's bond with him weakened. Consequently, by 1932 ER responded to a friend who confessed to having voted for Norman Thomas, that "if I had not been married to Franklin," she too would have voted for the Socialist candidate.[24]

FDR's victory did not change ER's priorities. She did not begin to play politics more than she struggled for reform. The dilemma the return to Albany presented ER was one of maintaining her independence: one involving time management more than political fidelity. Her bid for personal freedom was a more strenuous and longlasting campaign than her husband's 1928 run for office. The stakes were far higher.

Thus, Eleanor Roosevelt was not thrilled with the prospect of returning to Albany, a goldfish bowl in which all her movements would be both confined by and interpreted through her husband's political successes and failures. She told her son James that "she knew that [FDR] had wanted her to become active in politics primarily to keep his case in the public eye" and that he "would expect her to move into the shadows if he moved into the limelight." This depressed her immensely. As Marion Dickerman later told FDR biographer Kenneth S. Davis, ER's "dread" was so strong that it fostered a rebellion that "strained at the leash of her self-control."[25]

Yet ER also realized that her political expertise and her new support system was both an outgrowth and a byproduct of her relationship with FDR. Never did she fully expect FDR to withdraw from public life or expect that she would be immune from its scrutiny. Instead, once her "Griselda" moodiness subsided, Eleanor Roosevelt concentrated on how to find the most appropriate manner to promote two careers at once—how best to pursue her separate interests and not undermine her husband's public standing.

The three keys to her freedom, the DWC, the Todhunter School for Girls, and Val-Kill, lay outside Albany. Therefore, the extent to which ER could maximize her independence ran directly parallel to her efficient division of her life between the Governor's mansion and the family's East 65th Street residence in New York City. She understood how some pundits would be tempted to lampoon such a nontraditional schedule for the state's first lady. So, immediately after the election ER launched her own media campaign to encourage the press to treat her various activities in the most positive light possible.

When a *New York Times* reporter asked her the day she became New York's first lady what her new schedule would be, ER tried to balance her more acceptable occupations with her deep desire for independence. She announced her resignation from the Democratic Women's Committee, but refused to distance herself from her apolitical obligations. She would still support the furniture factory at Val-Kill and commute to New York City three days a week to teach her government and English literature classes and to fulfill her administrative responsibilities at Todhunter. Yet as deliberate as she was in this statement, she could not keep the desperation out of her voice. In a rare display of public emotion, she revealed her commitment and her desperate desire for autonomy. "I teach because I love it. I cannot give it up."[26]

If teaching was her public love, her private loyalty was the Democratic Women's Committee whose newsletter she continued to edit and contribute to covertly. ER was so dedicated to the DWC that one historian considered her "lasting contribution to New York" during her second tenure in Albany "her continuous work" with the committee. Nor did she restrict these clandestine efforts to editorials. She also continued surreptiously to direct DWC policy. ER successfully argued within the committee that women's political efforts must be year-round actions. And, although she refrained from delivering "political speeches," she continued to travel the remote upstate regions with DWC organizer Molly Dewson to foster Democratic organizational support among farm women. So fine-tuned was ER's ear to the political sentiments of the upstate region that after she and Dewson returned and she convinced FDR campaign chair Jim Farley to distribute a flyer she designed to upstate women voters, the Democrats carried the region for the first time in history. When postelection polls showed a twenty percent increase in the upstate Democratic vote, Farley credited the victory to ER. Her efforts showed, in the words of the chairman, a "genuine gift for organization work," the ability to handle difficult people with tact, and "above all a real 'sense of politics.'"[27]

Nor did her duties in New York City preclude political contributions to FDR's administration. She successfully lobbied Democratic National Chairman John Raskob for increased allocations to the Democratic State Committee and raised seed money for the Women's Activities Committee. Perhaps most important, ER began to apply the political finesse she demonstrated earlier in arbitrating League of Women Voters disputes to resolve disagreements within FDR's inner circle. With her friend Henry Morgenthau, ER pressured FDR to invite both Republican and Democratic mayors, rather than just the officials who supported FDR's goals, to the State Mayor's Conference. She regularly facilitated conflicts between FDR intimates Louis Howe and Jim Farley and acted as a political stand-in when FDR could not or chose not to participate in the discussion. Certainly there is no clearer indication of ER's prominence within the Howe-FDR-Farley triangle than its decision to send her to issue the administration's personal rebuke of Tammany Mayor Jimmy Walker's conduct.[28]

ER did not limit her contributions to political crisis management. Aware of how difficult it was for a politician and his staff to face unpopular decisions, Eleanor Roosevelt urged the appointment of individuals who had the nerve to disagree openly with FDR. She lobbied successfully for Frances Perkins's nomination as secretary of labor and for Nell Schwartz to fill the vacancy Perkins's appointment left on the State Industrial Commission. Believing that she knew Smith better than did her husband, ER strongly objected to FDR retaining any of Smith's cabinet. In particular, she opposed Belle Moskowitz's reappointment as personal secretary to the governor and Robert Moses' reappointment as secretary of state, writing her husband in Warm Springs that "by all signs Belle and Bob Moses mean to cling to you." If he was not careful, she continued, "you will wake up to find R.M. Secretary of State and B.M. running Democratic publicity at the old stand unless you take a firm stand."

ER understood just how effective a politician Belle Moskowitz was, warning FDR "don't let Mrs. M. get draped around you for she means to be . . . [and] it will always be one for you and two for Al." When FDR hesitated, she reasserted her concern, describing in detail just how easily he could be manipulated. "Mrs. Moskowitz is a very fine woman," she began a memo to her husband dated a week after his election. "I have worked with her in every campaign. I have never worked with anybody that I like to work with better. She's extremely competent, far-sighted, reliable. What she says she'll do, she does. I think a great deal of her, and I think we are friends."

Yet she warned FDR of the clandestine political rivalry that Moscowitz's appointment would create. "You have to decide, and decide now, whether you or Mrs. Moskowitz is going to be the governor of this state." If he insisted on naming her his assistant, "she will run you. . . . and will do it in such a way that you don't know it a good deal of the time." She will arrange everything "so subtly that when the matter comes to you it will be natural to decide to do the thing that she has already decided should be done."[29]

Perhaps ER's description of Smith's aide stuck a chord that was too familiar. Perhaps FDR did not want to be confined by two such strong women. Perhaps he truly trusted ER's judgment. But whatever his reasons, this time FDR listened to his wife. Moskowitz did not join his staff and Smith never forgave him.

Eleanor Roosevelt never disclosed in interviews or her memoirs the full range of her party activities or her influence on FDR. She applied such strict restraint in discussing her independence to defend her hard-won mobility, deflect the criticism of real and imagined detractors, and protect her husband's political image. Nevertheless, her testimony before state committees on protective labor legislation and her opposition to her husband's position on state unemployment insurance are matters of public record.

Sympathetic journalists appreciated how ER's independence made her prone to attack and tried to help her put the best face possible on her unique position. Interviews and articles by and about Eleanor Roosevelt published during the "governorship years" depict a woman committed to action who, in Ida Tarbell's opinion, was "a genuinely new woman . . . [who] develops unrealized possibilities." However, ER took care not to come across as a strident self-absorbed career woman, telling the *New York Times* that "work is a living for me. The point is whether we *live* in our work."[30]

Despite the care with which ER tried to balance her own career with FDR's aspirations, relations between the Roosevelts were often strained. Both had strong egos and both wanted to operate within the same arena. Competition was inevitable, yet their relationship survived. Joseph Lash rationalized this unique partnership, especially ER's "highly unorthodox actions," by creating a portrait of a pliable ER who let her husband control the agenda. "If she had been less tactful, less sensitive, if she had not always been careful to stay within limits set by Franklin and to check with him to be sure that her activities were consistent with what he wanted done," her actions would have backfired and "could have degenerated into a scandal of meddlesomeness."[31]

Such analyses miss the point. What Franklin controlled were the actions Eleanor Roosevelt took in his behalf, not the endeavors she undertook to pursue her own interests. Just as she recognized her own need for a distinct network, ER acknowledged that to maintain what separateness the social and political culture would tolerate she had to couch such activities in terms acceptable to both her private standards and the demands of FDR's public. "The lessons [I] learned," she wrote recapping these years, "were those of adaptability and adjustment and finally of self-reliance and the developing into an individual . . . ."[32]

The 1932 presidential campaign assaulted Eleanor Roosevelt's adaptability with increasing frequency. Although she supported her husband's political ambitions out of loyalty both to him and the Democratic party, ER astutely recognized the attacks she would encounter if she continued to pursue her individual projects with the same vigor she applied in the past. For his part, FDR continued to promote the image of "his Missus" as part of the Roosevelt team. Yet, ER recognized that this was a political screen designed to enhance her symbolic value to the campaign. Her future role remained uncertain.[33]

After the election, ER inadvertently turned to the national press to test her public standing. Whereas during the race she continued to declare to interviewers that she "would be very much at home in Washington" if FDR was elected, she confided her dread to reporters she trusted. Riding in a day coach to Albany a week after the election with Lorena Hickok, the Associated Press reporter assigned to cover her during the campaign, Eleanor Roosevelt unburdened her thoughts for the record. "I never wanted it even though some people have said that my ambition for myself drove him on. . . . I never wanted to be a President's wife." Fearful that her qualified support for her husband be misunderstood, she clarified her stance: "For him, of course, I'm glad—sincerely. I could not have wanted it any other way. After all I'm a Democrat, too. Now I shall have to work out my own salvation. I'm afraid it may be a little difficult. I know what Washington is like. I've lived there."[34]

The press quickly discerned what effective copy Eleanor Roosevelt's unique attitude toward her new position would be. On July 4, 1932, the Associated Press ran a two-column article under the headline "Eleanor Roosevelt Would Scrap Outworn Social Traditions: Can't Imagine Being Absorbed by Drawing Room Duties, Wife of Nominee Declares." *The Washington Star* followed suit, proclaiming that "Mrs. Roosevelt Would Scrap Outworn Social Traditions." By October, the image of "Eleanor Roosevelt: Tireless Worker" spilled across seven columns of a North American News Alliance wire release.[35]

Yet like the American public, the American press divided on the issue of how professionally active a first lady should be. Despite ER's courtship of the press, criticism of her commercial radio and journalism contracts increased. The attacks began after she suggested during a commercial radio broadcast that part of a young woman's responsibilities included learning "how to handle gin and whiskey in moderation." The prohibitionists were outraged. And bowing to pressure, ER refused to renew her contract. Caught off guard by their furor, she hoped that her resignation would calm her critics. But when she announced that she would edit the MacFadden publication *Babies—Just Babies* the negative articles reached new limits.

Suddenly, ER found herself ridiculed in such diverse publications as *The Harvard Lampoon*, *The Hartford Courant*, and *The Baltimore Sun*. To the Cambridge students, she was "tutor, just a tutor." The Connecticut newspaper took a more serious approach, arguing that while a woman should pursue her interests, "the fact remains that being the First Lady of the land is a full-time job in itself and that the dignity of the President and the country cannot but suffer when his name is used for commercial purposes." In an article discussing "Eleanor Roosevelt's Activities," *The Springfield Evening Union* snidely endorsed "the suggestion . . . that Eleanor Roosevelt's withdrawal from some or all of her professional or commercial activities might afford an opening for some of her needy sisters without imposing any hardship on the Roosevelt fortune." Anti-FDR publications, as well as conservative pro-Democratic editors, concurred with a Baltimore editorial that concluded "as a matter of propriety and in keeping with the dignity of the exalted position her husband is about to hold she ought to abandon some of her present occupations." By February, the press increasingly interpreted ER's professionalism as ER's commercialism.[36]

This was a difficult position for her politically and personally. While FDR often effectively used humor as a political foil during the campaign, the public did not easily accept political humor from a candidate's spouse. As a private person who often disdained idle chitchat, political frivolity did not come easily to her. Although Eleanor Roosevelt admitted to Hickok that she would "curtail somewhat her activities" because she "suppose[d] [she] had made some mistakes," ER adamantly refused to abandon the expertise she had worked so diligently to achieve. Aware of the criticism her position would provoke, she declared that she had no choice but to continue. "I'll just have to go on being myself, as much as I can. I'm just not the sort of person who would be any good at [any] job. I dare say I shall be criticized, whatever I do."

Publicly, ER tried once again to reason with her critics, telling an interviewer that she "really [was] not doing anything that I haven't done for a long time. It's only Franklin's position that has brought them to the attention of the people." She pleaded for a few more weeks of freedom. "I shall drop a good many things when we get to Washington. But . . . we aren't in Washington yet. . . . Until March 4, I hope to be permitted to enjoy the privileges accorded a private citizen." But, as Hickok recorded, that did not happen. When ER entered the new year doing "the things she had always done. The papers continued to carry stories about her. And some people continued to criticize her. They just could not get used to the idea of her being 'plain, ordinary Eleanor Roosevelt.'"[37]

Eleanor Roosevelt's aversion to any other role was so strong that in the week before the inauguration, she impetuously wrote Dickerman and Cook that she was contemplating divorcing FDR. She told Hickok, in a quote for the record, that she "hated" having to resign her teaching position at Todhunter, saying "I wonder if you have any idea how I hate to do it."[38]

Seventeen years later ER candidly recalled her election night "dread" of becoming first lady. She admitted to readers of *This I Remember* that while she "was happy for my husband" that evening, she felt "more deeply troubled" than her close friends knew. She thought her husband's victory "meant the end of any personal life of my own." She knew what would be expected of her. "I had watched Mrs. Theodore Roosevelt and had seen what it meant to be the wife of a president, and I cannot say that I was pleased at the prospect." Her career had given her a "certain amount of financial independence," which she "enjoyed" because she "had been able to do things in which I was personally interested." She ended the day not only with great "turmoil in my heart and mind" but also with the clear understanding that "the next few months were not to make any clearer what the road ahead would be."[39]

Clearly, when Eleanor Roosevelt entered the White House in March 1933, she did so reluctantly. Although she supported her husband's aims and believed in his leadership abilities, she feared that his political agenda would restrict her movements, curtail her personal independence, and force her to minimize the political issues she held nearest and dearest to her heart. Indeed, once FDR won the election, he asked her to resign her positions with the Democratic National Committee, the Todhunter School, the League of Women Voters, the Non-Partisan Legislative Committee, and the Women's Trade Union League. She then announced that she would no longer take part in commercial radio events and that she would refrain from discussing politics in her magazine articles. Though she tried to avoid it, public expectation was redefining her career and it hurt. "If I wanted to be selfish," she confessed earlier to Hickok, "I could wish that he had not been elected."[40]

Chapter Two

COMING INTO HER OWN
ER as First Lady

Questions "seethed" in ER's mind about what she should do after March 4, 1933. Realizing that FDR would not allow her the same mobility she had when he was governor, ER worried that she would be confined to a schedule of teas and receptions and tried to create a less restrictive place for herself within the White House. She volunteered to "do a real job" for FDR. During the campaign, she had worked to keep the "channels of communication" between FDR's advisers open, frequently mediating disputes between Howe and Farley. Moreover, she knew that Ettie Rheiner Garner served as an administrative assistant to her husband, Vice President John Nance Garner, and ER tried to convince FDR to let her provide the same service. The president rebuffed the first lady's offer. Trapped by convention, she begrudgingly recognized that "the work [was FDR's] work and the pattern his pattern." Frustrated and disappointed, she acknowledged that she "was one of those who served his purposes."[1]

Nevertheless, ER refused to accept a superficial and sedentary role. She wanted "to do things on my own, to use my own mind and abilities for my own aims" and struggled to carve out an active contributory place for herself in the New Deal. This was not to be a challenge easily met. Dejected, she found it "hard to remember that I was not just 'Eleanor Roosevelt,' but the 'wife of the President.'" Yet within her first two years in the White House, she had turned her "joblessness" into the freedom to investigate a variety of issues and the power to advance specific programs which she hoped would ease the problems she detected.[2]

Eleanor Roosevelt entered the First Hundred Days of her husband's administration with no clearly defined responsibility. Her offers to sort FDR's mail and to act as his "listening post" had been rejected summarily. Bowing to her husband's new prestige, she refused to renew her commercial radio contract and resigned as editor of *Babies—Just Babies* when its publisher wanted the magazine to discuss controversial issues in education and child care. And even though ER started to pay more attention to her wardrobe, society columnists were shocked that her clothes were so "simple" and "unchic." Others lamented that "she had no pride in her physical appearance at all."[3]

She was lonely. Her dear friend and bodyguard Earl Miller married the previous fall and did not make the move to Washington. Nancy Cook and Marion Dickerman, her partners in Val-Kill and Democratic politics, did not understand her reticence about returning to Washington nor did they empathize with her misgivings about the first lady's role. And while close friend Elinor Morgenthau did move from Hyde Park to the White House, ER missed others of her circle. "First Friend" Hickok, who continued to travel as an investigative reporter for the Federal Emergency Relief Administration after she resigned her position with the Associated Press, tried to fill the gap. By May, ER's frustration had given way to immense depression. "My zest in life is rather gone for the time being," ER confessed to Hickok. "If anyone looks at me, I want to weep . . . my mind goes round and round like a squirrel in a cage. I want to run and I can't, and I despise myself."[4]

However, ER had developed a few close friendships with some of the women who covered her campaign activities and, with Hickok's and their advice and support, eventually turned this media attention to her own advantage. Eager to advance their own careers and keenly aware of the interest articles on ER generated, many reporters, especially Ruby Black, Bess Furman, Martha Strayer, and Genevieve Herrick, hitched their wagon to ER's notoriety. Indeed Furman, a reporter for a Republican news syndicate who stayed in Washington to cover ER, later described 1933 and 1934 as the one time in her career when she was "swinging from a star."

This relationship was reciprocal. Just as ER helped advance their careers, reporters helped ER become more adept at fielding their questions and subtly inserting her opinions. It was a time, according to media historian Maurine Beasley, of "headlines and friendships."[5]

ER's relations with the press during the spring and summer of 1933 did nothing to curtail their interest. On March 6, two days after her husband became president, Eleanor Roosevelt held her own press conference to announce that she would "get together" with women reporters once a week. She asked for the reporters' cooperation. ER hoped that together they not only could discuss her duties as first lady but also explain "what goes on politically in the legislative national life" and encourage women to become active in the New Deal programs in their community. "The idea," she said, "largely is to make an understanding between the White House and the general public."

Initially ER tried to weight the discussion more in favor of her traditional social duties and away from her views of the problems the nation confronted. However, as she expanded her role, the topics covered during the press conferences also expanded. Her statements to the press notwithstanding, political issues soon became a central part of the weekly briefings.

FDR, at Howe's urging, had asked his wife to travel the nation as his "ambassador." Within three months, ER had logged 40,000 miles. Her observations during these tours only reinforced the impressions she had formed during the final days of the campaign. She returned to Washington convinced that relief programs alone could not counteract the Depression and that basic economic reforms were essential. She began to share these views with the women assigned to cover her.

By May she discussed the White House protocol for serving 3.2 percent beer, her opposition to sweat shops and child labor, the problems confronting those living in the Bonus Army encampment and poverty-stricken Appalachia, and her support for the Veterans National Liaison Committee and higher salaries for teachers. By early June she proclaimed that "very few women know how to read the newspapers," argued that they should pay close attention to international economic news, and delivered a tutorial on how "a busy woman" could keep track of the news "at a time when every one of us ought to be on [our] toes."

These pronouncements, when coupled with the image she made when she visited those the depression affected most, encouraged political reporters to cover her. This fostered an in-house rivalry between reporters assigned to cover hard news and those assigned to the women's pages. Society reporters complained that her meetings with the press did not cover enough social news and many eventually stopped attending her weekly briefings.[6]

Some political journalists, worried that such unorthodox comments would encourage criticism, urged ER to go off the record when she discussed political issues. Grateful for their concern, she nevertheless rejected their advice and argued that she knew that some of her statements would "cause unfavorable comment in some quarters," but, she told Emma Bugbee, "I am making these statements on purpose to arouse controversy and thereby get the topics talked about."[7]

By 1934 ER's press conferences had become one of the major ways she defended her own activity and the programs she championed. Although she never issued a formal statement to the reporters and met with the press only to answer their questions, she soon learned to use these conferences as a way to appeal directly to the people. As Bess Furman later recalled, "at the President's press conference, all the world's a stage, at Mrs. Roosevelt's, all the world's a school. . . . Give Mrs. Roosevelt a roomful of newspaper women, and she conducts classes on scores of subjects, always seeing beyond her immediate hearers to the 'women of the country.'"[8]

ER, not satisfied with just disseminating information, also wanted to know how the public responded to the positions she advocated and those positions promoted by FDR's major critics, Huey Long and Father Charles Coughlin. Consequently, when *Women's Home Companion* asked her to write a monthly column, she gladly accepted. Announcing that she would donate her monthly thousand dollar fee to charity, ER then proceeded to ask her readers to help her establish "a clearinghouse, a discussion room" for "the particular problems which puzzle you or sadden you" and to share "how you are adjusting yourself to new conditions in this amazing changing world." Entitling the article "I Want You to Write to Me," ER reinforced the request throughout the piece. "Do not hesitate," she wrote in August 1933, "to write to me even if your views clash with what you believe to be my views." Only a free exchange of ideas and discussion of problems would help her "learn of experiences which may be helpful to others." By January 1934, 300,000 Americans had responded to this solicitation, more than the total number of letters received by Abraham Lincoln and Woodrow Wilson in their first year in office and equal to the weekly circulation of Long's *American Progress*.[9]

This was not a token offer. ER had personal and political reasons for appealing for public input. Worried that Long and Coughlin supporters felt neglected by the New Deal, she wanted to make herself available to them. Also concerned that the Federal Emergency Relief Administration programs did meet enough of people's needs, she pressured FERA administrator Harry Hopkins to hire Hickok to tour different parts of the nation, observe

FERA programs, and report to him on their effectiveness. Hickok sent copies of these honest, harsh field reports to ER, daily confirming the many obstacles those seeking relief encountered. Plus, she was bored. "Your job is much more interesting than mine," she complained to Hickok that winter. She desperately wanted an assignment that was hers alone, an arena in which she could judge for herself the effectiveness of her husband's programs.[10]

Yet her appeal to the public was not motivated solely by her dissatisfaction. Her commitment to free and unrestricted public discussion was heartfelt and intense. She considered the free exchange of information and ideas central to democracy's success. The more informed the public about the issues it confronted, the more educated the society would become, and the more opportunities democracy would have to be realized.

"Men have dreamed of Utopias since the world began," she had written the previous April. But "as I see it we can have no new deal [for the human race] until great groups of people, particularly the women, are willing to have a revolution in thought." America, she believed, was so obsessed with material wealth that greed stunted its vision and constrained its policies. To overcome these limitations, the nation must develop a new attitude which redefined success in a way that deemphasized material possession and rewarded "outstanding service to mankind." Only then could society "look . . . for the dawn of a new day."[11]

The cornerstone of ER's emerging political philosophy was as simple as it was powerful: if the nation was to flourish, Americans must accept the responsibility of living in a democracy. They must study the issues and develop informed opinions about the best ways to solve the nation's problems because "knowledge will forever govern ignorance." Americans "must arm themselves with the power that knowledge gives" because government could only be as good as its people. Democracy was a two-way street. It not only "must have leaders who have the power to see farther, to imagine a better life but it must also have a vast army of men and women capable of understanding these leaders."[12]

When she entered the White House, ER believed that recovery could not happen unless all America took responsibility for correcting the economic problems that had pushed America into the Depression. In a 1932 speech to the Chautauqua Institute, an upscale summer resort in upstate New York with a long history of catering to those who wanted to mix public affairs with recreation, she argued that since people "made" the economy, people could make it "possible for those willing to work to receive adequate compensation." Yet she was no "believer in paternalism," she told the *New York Times* six months later. Legislation alone could not solve the problems facing America. What the country needed desperately was "some new changes in our rather settled ideas." Moreover, those who avoided personal commitment by claiming that no one would listen to their demands, she told "My Day" readers in 1935, were promoting a civic "inferiority complex" to provide themselves with "a comfortable alibi to side step responsibility."[13]

Yet after visiting many regions of the nation and observing the various responses Americans had to the Depression, ER shed some of the noblesse oblige that characterized this idealistic commitment to popular political participation. Her travels during the campaign had convinced her that the country was as much in need of structural economic reform as temporary relief programs. As first lady, ER came face to face with many Americans who had suffered as much from discrimination as from poverty. Moreover, the rise of fascism in Europe scared her and when many Americans refused to see the hypocrisy inherent in their own racism, she started to reevaluate her earlier more simplistic conviction that a restored economy would restore democratic values. These experiences helped mature her political perspective and forced her to realize that there was more wrong with America than a weak economy. The nation also needed a refresher course in democratic values.

By 1940, ER fervently believed that democracy's survival hinged upon people's acceptance of different political views and social customs. She chided those who were foolish enough to think that there was one "thing in this country which may be called society." America was so diverse that it could be best described as a "group of different societies" searching for common ground and common rights.

In *The Moral Basis of Democracy*, she pleaded with the nation to understand that community is an inclusive term and that difference was not a threat to, but a springboard for, democracy. Difference forced people to speak out to control their environment and speaking out would force a democratic government to be accountable. In short, civic awareness not only empowered individuals but also made the government keenly aware that its actions were being closely monitored and that voters expected decisive and effective action.

While she still believed that an informed public inspired the best government, by 1940 she had a more panoramic understanding of public opinion and the irrational passion an uninformed public could generate in its quest for knowledge; and while she readily acknowledged that Americans harbored many deep prejudices, she refused to accept that their biases were so ingrained that they could not be discarded. Americans, she believed, were basically optimistic in spite of themselves.

Throughout her tenure as first lady, ER strove to exploit this optimism. She hoped that with time it could become the key to widespread economic and social reform. She pleaded with Americans to realize that the nation had survived the economic and moral crises of the Depression because, despite the intensity and variety of the hardships it inflicted, they still had hope, they still believed that the future would be better than the past. Again and again she tried to create a vision of the future where "as individuals we will live cooperatively, and to the best of our ability, serve the community in which we live." Then the nation ultimately would have not only "a new deal in material things . . . but [an outlook] which will set new values and give a new social justice."[14]

From her first days in the White House, this conviction propelled ER's New Deal agenda. While FDR shared some of these beliefs, he did not actively promote them until late 1935 with the legislation most commonly associated with what historians have labeled the Second New Deal. Consequently, Eleanor Roosevelt's first policy task as first lady was to prod her husband to incorporate as generous a definition of minimum economic security and social welfare as politically possible.

Although most historians focus on ER's enthusiastic support for the model subsistence homestead community in Arthurdale, West Virginia, as the clearest example of ER's pressuring FDR toward a more encompassing relief effort, other New Deal programs, when examined as a group, offer a more thorough illustration of ER's democratic principles. While she doggedly advocated programs which would ensure "that a family shall have sufficient means of livelihood and the assurance of an ability to pay their expenses covering a stand which we hope to establish as something to shoot at," in her vision, the responsibilities of a democratic state were not to be confined to improving the lot of only one socioeconomic group.[15]

Continuously she urged that relief should be as diverse as the constituency that needed it. "The unemployed are not a strange race. They are like we would be if we had not had a fortunate chance at life." Whether the unemployed were young, blue or white collar, male or female, or minorities, the aid they received should not be subject to qualification. The distress they encountered, not their socioeconomic status, should be the focus of relief. Consequently, ER promoted programs designed to alleviate the problems of unemployed youth via the National Youth Administration and of artists and writers through the Federal One Programs of the Federal

Emergency Relief Administration while she consistently lobbied the administration, the Congress, and the American public for equitable economic and political recognition for African Americans.[16]

■ "One of the ideas I agreed to present to Franklin." The National Youth Administration

The huge numbers of unemployed youth of the 1930s underscored several fears adults had about society. Conservatives saw disgruntled young people as a fertile ground for revolutionary politics while progressives mourned the disillusionment and apathy spreading among American youth. Indeed, concern over the political susceptibility of youth concerned some within the administration so much that they wondered "whether the New Deal ought to establish a democratic alternative to the Hitler Youth." Educators feared that without some type of financial aid, colleges would suffer irreversible damage. Eleanor Roosevelt agreed with the progressives, telling the *New York Times* that "I live in real terror when I think we may be losing this generation. We have got to bring these young people into the active life of the community and make them feel that they are necessary."[17]

ER insisted that government had the responsibility to keep these young people from becoming even more "stranded." Although many in the White House agreed with her, New Deal officials differed over the means to reduce joblessness among high school and college-age youth and debated whether or not student aid should be provided as part of the relief package. Public opinion, fearful that students would take jobs that might otherwise help adult workers, was ambivalent over which course the government should pursue. Moreover, understanding the sensitivity of this issue, FDR proved reluctant to institute a program which might backfire. Although he wanted to put young people to work and believed that action must be taken to shore up youth's commitment to democracy, the president "never approved of ideological training for American youth." Furthermore, he did not want to be accused of favoritism or despotism. While everyone agreed there was a major problem, there was no consensus on how to address it.[18]

FDR signed the executive order creating the National Youth Administration (NYA) in the summer of 1935, two years after telling the press that he objected to "channeling direct federal aid to high school graduates or their teachers." He insisted that he had "pretty serious" disagreements with a program that would "do anything in the way of sending boys and girls to college." And lastly, he categorically rejected any proposal which would provide widespread vocational training. Instead he championed a more traditional approach that emphasized physical labor, strict supervision, and limited job training. In short, FDR promoted the Civilian Conservation Corps (CCC) as the model agency for youth relief.

ER, who could not have disagreed more strongly with her husband, emphatically rejected the CCC model. Although it certainly helped adults, she argued that it failed youth. Its camps were too militaristic to encourage independence and its instruction was limited to forestry. This was no way to bring disgruntled and disillusioned youth back into society. The specific problems facing youth needed to be recognized, but in a way that not only fostered self-worth but also encouraged faith in democratic capitalism. The government must show American youth that they had more options than the military and the dole.

By 1934, ER decided that the government had to develop a program tailored to the special economic, educational, and vocational needs of youth, and she dedicated herself to seeing a comprehensive program implemented. She lobbied the press and administration officials, appealed to the public to recognize the social and political benefits the program could offer, and coaxed student leaders into setting realistic goals. Having met regularly with student leaders and relief officials, she understood both sides of the argument. And she strove to form a consensus that could satisfy most needs of both groups.

"I think we could start out," ER wrote *Forum* publisher Henry Goddard Leach in January, "and make them the producers of the necessities of life during the first two or three years and in return give them their living and a training of some kind which they can use later in earning a living." In March, she pressured Harry Hopkins to "develop some kind of program for this group" which would provide a social, rather than a militaristic, focus. In April, she held long discussions with her friend Charles Taussig on what needs a program should address first. And in May, she devoted her *Woman's Home Companion* column to endorsing a "volunteer service . . . open to both boys and girls" as "a plan for the future." By providing job skills and education, she hoped that the program would foster a sense of civic awareness which in turn would promote a commitment to social justice and a resurgent faith in democracy. Then young Americans would be empowered to articulate their own needs and aspirations, to express "what they think would be a fair deal all around as well as a new deal."[19]

Although not the legislative architect of the NYA, ER nevertheless helped establish its priorities, and in so doing left an indelible imprint upon the agency's development. When FDR issued the executive order June 26, 1935, he authorized the NYA to administer programs in five areas: work projects, vocational guidance, apprenticeship training, educational and nutritional guidance camps for unemployed women, and student aid. Clearly ER's preference for vocational guidance and education triumphed over his earlier support of the CCC relief model. Even historian James Kearney, who believed that the first lady's sole contribution to political thought was her "goodness," acknowledged that over time, "the NYA moved toward [her] preferences." As the agency progressed from its initial emphasis on relief to placing more emphasis on recreation and clerical training to providing educational loans, this shift in emphasis was "more than coincidental."[20]

From the start ER's unofficial position within the agency was unchallenged for four reasons. First, with two of ER's close friends, Harry Hopkins and Aubrey Williams, supervising the agency and with another friend, thirty-six-year-old corporate executive Charles Taussig, chairing its advisory board, her influence within the agency was assured. Second, she already had begun to solidify her ties with the Mobilization for Human Needs and other youth organizations dedicated to forcing government action. She offered her New York home as a central location for their meetings, encouraged discussion of all points of view (including a lone but enthusiastic communist presence), urged administration officials to attend these sessions to see firsthand the problems confronting youth, and tried to attend as many of those sessions as she possibly could. Third, when the group had settled on a list of demands, she treated their concerns seriously and acted as their most public advocate, explaining their concerns in "My Day," magazine articles, and public statements. Finally, as she well understood FDR's concerns, she worked to frame her arguments supporting the NYA in ways that would answer his questions and prod him to action. When he seemed hesitant or other events competed for his attention, ER did not hesitate to push him. "You are going to make an appointment to see Charles Taussig and you are going to ask Myron Taylor to serve on the NYA Advisory Board," ER telegraphed her husband in 1936. FDR responded by asking his aide "Pa" Watson to "arrange an appointment with Taussig this week."[21]

With such strong ties to the parties involved, ER became both the agency's and youth's natural choice for confessor, planner, lobbyist, and promoter. She reviewed NYA policy with Williams and Taussig, arranged for NYA officials and youth leaders to meet with FDR in and out of the White House, served as NYA's intermediary with the president, critiqued and suggested projects, defended it against its critics in and out of government, and attended as many NYA state administrators conferences as her schedule allowed. Moreover, when Mary McLeod Bethune joined the NYA as director of the Office of Minority Affairs, the agency not only employed a woman ER greatly respected but also gave prominent voice to the other issue ER thought critical—the plight of black Americans. Finally, she visited at least 112 NYA sites and reported her observations in her daily column, telling readers that one such visit to a NYA exhibit "was heartening for the point of view of [its] real accomplishments."

Indeed, ER took such satisfaction in the NYA that when she briefly acknowledged her role in forming the agency, she did so with an uncharacteristic candor. "One of the ideas I agreed to present to Franklin," she wrote in *This I Remember*, "was that of setting up a national youth administration. . . . It was one of the occasions on which I was very proud that the right thing was done regardless of political consequences."[22]

■ **"The power to make people hear and understand."**
The Federal One Programs

On May 16, 1934, Eleanor Roosevelt addressed the Twenty-Fifth Annual Convention of the American Federation of Artists. Her speech, entitled "The New Governmental Interest in Art," succinctly summarized both her views of art's value to society and government's responsibility to promote American culture and protect freedom of expression. Art "expresses what many of us felt in the last few years but could not possibly have either told or shown to anyone else." It vividly depicted the strengths and weaknesses of society in ways that were both liberating and educational. It helped us recognize our triumphs and failures and encouraged us to address our vulnerabilities. Consequently, ER declared, free, unrestricted expression is vital to society.

ER, however, took great care to discuss the obligations that accompanied this talent. "The power to make people hear and understand . . . or to paint something which we ordinary people feel but can't reveal" is not just a gift, but a duty to help society find images and emotions for problems it cannot describe. Just as art has the power to paint portraits of images average citizens cannot envision, art has the power to influence the way society sees that image.

Government must respect that talent and encourage artistic expression just as it encouraged political participation. Moreover, government had a responsibility to listen to this voice just as it had a responsibility to address the needs of its citizens. "If we gain nothing but acceptance of the fact that Government has an interest in the development of artistic expression—no matter how that expression comes," she told the artists assembled before her, "and if we have been able to widen the interest of the people as a whole in art, we have reaped a really golden harvest out of what many of us feel have been barren years."[23]

This address publicly formalized the commitment to state-supported art that ER had made to a group of museum directors and Civil Works Administration (cwa) officials at the December 8, 1933, preliminary planning meeting for the Public Works Act Project (pwap). Sitting at the head table next to the planning session's organizer, Edward Bruce, an international financier turned professional painter, Eleanor Roosevelt knitted while she listened to Bruce propose a program to pay artists for creating public art. Advocating a program in which artists could control both form and content, Bruce recruited supporters for a cwa-funded relief project for unemployed artists that would produce artwork "appropriate in design and quality for the adornment of public buildings." Sitting quietly through most of the discussion, ER interrupted only to question procedure and to emphasize her support of the project. She found it "unbelievable," she told the group, "that a great nation could fail to utilize . . . its creative talents to the fullest."[24]

Once this group agreed to support the pwap concept, ER became its ardent public and private advocate. When pwap artists were sent to Civil Conservation Corps camps in mid-1934 and produced more than two hundred watercolors, oil paintings, and chalk drawings portraying camp life, she enthusiastically opened their "Life in the ccc" exhibit at the National Museum. When five hundred pwap artworks were displayed at Washington's Corcoran Gallery, she dedicated the exhibit, declared that in addition to its artistic merit the works liberated society by publicly expressing many private concerns, and pronounced the art "swell" in her column. Moreover, ER did not limit her support to major shows at prestigious galleries. She visited pwap artist Edward Lansing's studio in an abandoned New York City warehouse, corresponded with some minor pwap artists, and displayed in the White House south foyer five of the murals James Michael Newell designed for the New York University Reading Room.[25]

Bruce, who had been appointed director of the pwap, worried that the cwa funds would not be renewed and proposed that artists be eligible for wpa programs. Immediately he solicited ER's support, arguing "cultural projects enrich the lives of all our people by making things of the spirit . . . part of their daily lives." She agreed that artists needed government aid and supported the pwap proposal, in the process entering the internal dispute over whether fera should fund white collar programs. With the support of fera administrator Harry Hopkins, ER lobbied FDR to endorse Bruce's concept.

The president agreed, issuing an executive order on June 25, 1935, which created the Federal One Programs of the Works Progress Administration: the Federal Writers Project (FWP), the Federal Theater Project (FTP), and the Federal Art Project (FAP formerly PWAP). Pursuant to this order, these programs required both presidential approval and a presidential allocation of WPA funds for operations to begin. This structure allowed program designers to bypass the WPA Project Control Division and submit proposals directly to the president through the division of Professional and Service Projects. The combined efforts of Bruce, ER, and the PWAP staff thus created a routing system that avoided most administration censors.[26]

In 1936 Jean Baker, director of the WPA Professional and Service Products Division, tried to placate those regional WPA administrators resentful of Federal One's "national jurisdiction" by returning program control to state administrators. ER objected to this concession to censorship and supported Federal Theater Director Hallie Flanagan and Federal Art Director Holger Cahill's argument that the programs' "professional quality" could be assured only if the programs were administered by a professional staff based in Washington. ER then met with Baker, and after Baker refused to reverse her stand, ER convinced Hopkins that Baker should be replaced. Hopkins agreed and filled the post with ER's close friend, former director of the CWA Women's Division, Ellen Woodward, who supported the national jurisdiction procedure.[27]

Eleanor Roosevelt continued to run administrative interference after the programs were in operation and threatened by local censors and interagency turf battles. When Flanagan requested her assistance convincing Martin Dies, chairman of the House Committee on Un-American Activities, that the FTP was not a heretical attack on American culture, ER gave her unqualified, active support by attending as many productions as her schedule allowed and praising them in columns and speeches. When conservatives attacked *One Third of a Nation*, a dramatic indictment of life in a New York City slum which *The New York Times* called "a caustic and vibrant piece of theatrical muckraking," ER countered their objections and said that she thought the play would be "a great contribution to the education of Americans." When congressional moderates were offended by *Ethiopia's* parody of diplomacy and appealed to Baker to order the play closed, ER ran interference for Flanagan with FDR, who agreed not to interfere. Furthermore, when the House Subcommittee on Appropriations threatened to hold hearings on the FTP, ER told Flanagan that she would gladly go to the Hill because "the time had come when America might consider the theater as part of its education." The FTP director left ER "feeling that a great new social plan was underway [and that ER was] eager to help work it out." Although ER was invited to testify, she made her support for the project abundantly clear by praising the FTP in her column three days before the subcommittee report was to be released.[28]

When the Harlem Artists Guild rejected a grant from the Harmon Foundation and announced its opposition to the Foundation's planned Negro Art Exhibition at the Texas centennial, a volatile dispute erupted within both the endowment community and the artistic press. Declaring that the "Harmon Foundation does not serve the best interests of Negro artists . . . [because its] past efforts to advance Negro art have done the opposite by virtue of their [unprofessional] attitude," the black artists chastised the white philanthropists for presenting "Negro art from a sociological rather than an aesthetic standpoint." After meeting with members of the Guild, ER endorsed the Harlem artists' position and announced that she would attend the opening ceremonies of the Harlem Community Art Center.[29]

ER also believed that a limited number of FWP artists should be relieved of their primary assignments, preparing travel manuals, and allowed to create their own masterworks while on the FWP payroll. Indicative of this conviction is the encouragement she provided Richard Wright. When Wright completed *Uncle Tom's Children,* she endorsed the work as "beautifully written and so vivid that I had a most unhappy time reading it." Nor did her support for his work flag when he left the WPA. When Wright thanked her for her personal support and promotion of *Uncle Tom's Children,* he briefly outlined the plot of *Native Son,* concluding "this book will deal with the problems of youth among an unassimilated portion of our population from a Negro point of view." "Knowing your deep interest in the importance of this subject and problem," Wright requested her aid in securing a Guggenheim Fellowship. She would "be very glad to help him," ER responded and she hoped very much "that your new book will be a success." Society must understand the traumas of prejudice.[30]

No one within the New Deal endorsed the FAP, FTP, and FWP as consistently as ER. She supported both the right and the need for government sponsorship of the arts when many of its public and administrative supporters wavered. So diligent was her support for Federal One that William McDonald, a historian who has studied Federal One programs in detail, concluded that although FDR's active resolve was necessary to create the division, "it is equally true that the arts program in its entirety—not only in the beginning but throughout its duration—depended even more upon the active support of Eleanor Roosevelt."[31]

■ "People say I become 'too excited' about conditions." Segregation and Racial Violence

Despite the fervor with which ER campaigned for a more democratic administration of relief through the NYA and the three Federal One programs, these efforts paled in comparison to the unceasing pressure she placed upon the president and the nation to confront the economic and political discrimination facing Black America. In seeking to educate the public on the evils of racial discrimination, she underscored the moral imperative of the civil rights agenda. Although the first lady did not become an ardent proponent of integration until the 1950s, throughout the thirties and forties she nevertheless persistently labeled racial prejudice as undemocratic and immoral. Black Americans recognized the depth of her commitment and consequently kept faith with FDR because his wife kept faith with them.[32]

Whereas most of ER's successful efforts on behalf of the NYA and the Federal One programs involved program content, procedural suggestions, and administrative lobbying, with civil rights ER the journalist and public symbol overshadowed ER the closet administrator. This does not mean, however, that she refused to plead the civil rights legislative agenda within the White House or that she was reluctant to work with black leaders. On the contrary, as New Deal civil rights historians repeatedly illustrate, there was no more ardent champion of the civil rights agenda within both the administration and the Black Cabinet itself, nor a member of the administration who had a closer working relationship with civil rights leaders than Eleanor Roosevelt.[33]

ER's racial policies attracted notice almost immediately. Less than a week after becoming first lady, she shocked conservative Washington society by announcing she would have an entirely black White House domestic staff. And even though the staff would be supervised by the "bigoted" Henrietta Nesbit, White House maid Lillian Rogers Parks recalled that "it was the first time it was great to be black. It meant you could hang on to your job at the White House."[34]

By late summer 1933, photographs appeared showing ER discussing living conditions with black miners in West Virginia and the press treated her involvement in the anti-lynching campaign as front page news. Rumors of ER's "race-baiting" actions sped across the South with hurricane force. In August 1934, Barry Bingham, son of the publisher of the *Louisville Courier-Journal*, wrote FDR aide Marvin McIntyre that ER "has made herself offensive to Southerners by a too great affection for Negroes." Although

Bingham claimed not to believe the rumor, he needed reassurance. The first lady refused to comply completely, responding that while she was "very much interested in the Negroes and their betterment," the story that she "drove through the streets of a town with a negro woman beside me happens to be untrue." Yet she warned Bingham that while she "probably would not do it in North Carolina," she "would, however, not have a single objection to doing so if I found myself in a position where it had to be done."[35]

ER refused to be intimidated by rumor. In 1935, she visited Howard University's Freedman Hospital, attended the University's fundraising banquet, lobbied Congress for increased appropriations, and praised the institution in her press conferences. After intensive briefing by Walter White ER toured the Virgin Islands with Lorena Hickok investigating conditions for herself only to return agreeing with White's initial assessments. When White asked her to address the 1934 and 1935 national NAACP conventions, FDR vetoed her appearance, fearing political backlash from southern Democrats. ER acceded to his wishes; however, FDR's cautiousness did not affect her support of the organization. "I deeply regret that I was obliged to refuse to attend the conference," she telegraphed the delegates. Her commitment had not waned. She continued, "I am deeply interested . . . [and] I hope that ways can be found to accomplish some of the things that you and I both desire." She then joined the local chapter of the NAACP and the National Urban League, becoming the first white District of Columbia resident to respond to the membership drives.[36]

She mobilized cabinet and congressional wives for a walking tour of the slum alleys of Southeast Washington to increase support for housing legislation then before Congress. Lady Bird Johnson accompanied ER on this tour and recalled that as accustomed as she was to rural poverty, she "hadn't seen anything like this." The first lady strode "along streets . . . [which] you usually kept off" and shamed her companions into following her example, hoping that if they saw such deprivation, they would be spurred to action. And, in a truly unique outreach, enlisted her mother-in-law's assistance in pressuring FDR to speak out in favor of the Costigan-Wagner anti-lynching bill. FDR's refusal to make anti-lynching legislation a priority did not dissuade her from actively seeking its passage. Indeed, when the bill finally came to the floor for a vote in 1937, ER's presence in the Senate gallery throughout the entire seven-day filibuster stood in stark contrast to FDR's cautious endorsement of the bill.[37]

Unlike his wife, the president saw civil rights as more a political than a moral issue. Therefore, as the 1936 election approached and Eleanor

Roosevelt continued her very public inspections, she finally convinced FDR to let her address the NAACP and National Urban League annual conventions by arguing that he needed the black vote. When *The New Yorker* published the famous cartoon of miners awaiting her visit, ER aggressively defended her outreach to minorities and the poor in a lengthy article for *The Saturday Evening Post.* Directly she attacked those who mocked her interest. "In strange and subtle ways," she began, "it was indicated to me that I should feel ashamed of that cartoon and that there was certainly something the matter with a woman who wanted to see so much and know so much." She refused to be so limited, she responded to those "blind" critics who refused to be interested in anything outside their own four walls. In a more subdued tone, she argued the same point when questioned by high school students about her "excitement" over discrimination. "People say I become 'too excited' about conditions," she replied. "Not at all. It is simply that I prefer to have my excitement in advance when it may do some good."[38]

The liberal and conservative press gave such action prominent coverage. When ER warned the National Urban League against interpreting the progress the races have achieved "in understanding each other" to mean that "our situation and our relationship are so perfect that we need not concern ourselves about making them better," NBC radio broadcast the address nationally. When she visited Howard University and was escorted around campus by its Honor Guard, *The Georgia Woman's World* printed a picture of ER surrounded by the students on its front page while it castigated her for conduct unbecoming a president's wife. Mainstream media such as the *New York Times* and *Christian Science Monitor* questioned the extent to which ER would be "a campaign issue."

Yet for all the negative and speculative coverage she received, there were articles, such as the following editorial from the May 23 *Baltimore Afro-American*, praising the stances ER assumed on behalf of anti-lynching legislation and the inequities African Americans faced in the American education system. "Instead of dodging an issue, Mrs. Roosevelt gave her opponents something else to talk about." Once she has made up her mind, "the President's wife knows no such word as retreat." And when her opponents try to capitalize on her boldness, "she repeats it so often that she proves it commonplace and routine."[39]

By 1938, as FDR grew "too excited" about political conditions and decided to purge the party of those southern conservatives—such as Carter Glass, "Cotton" Ed Smith, and Walter George—whom he blamed for the demise of his wage and hour legislation, ER worked to capitalize on his anger. While the president caucused with aides to plan a primary challenge to nine of the twenty-nine Democrats up for reelection, the first lady met with southern organizers concerned with attacks on labor and civil rights advocates. When Clark Foreman, the Georgia native who had helped find the men who would challenge the targeted incumbents, suggested that the president's slate argue that the South's economic plight would worsen if the "feudal oligarchy that was killing New Deal reforms" won reelection, an intrigued FDR accepted his offer to prepare a report supporting the claim.[40]

In June 1938, as Foreman met with the Committee on Economic Conditions in the South to prepare this statement, ER corresponded with Lucy Randolph Mason, whom ER knew from the National Consumers League and who now worked as a southern organizer for the CIO. Mason had conveyed Joe Gelder's plan of a southern conference on civil liberties to ER and the first lady invited her friend to bring Gelders to Hyde Park to discuss this idea. The president quickly recognized the political advantages a gathering of southern progressives would bring but wanted it to focus on economic issues rather than civil liberties. ER argued that an economic theme need not exclude civil liberties problems; suggested that women, blacks, union representatives, and tenant farmers join elite whites as delegates; and recommended that the agenda "include such topics as the poll tax, lynching, equal justice, and the rights of laboring people." If they could convene such a gathering, the first lady volunteered not only to endorse their efforts but to address the group as well.[41]

By November Gelders and Mason organized the first meeting of the Southern Conference on Human Welfare (SCHW). It would be held in Birmingham; ER, Frank Porter Graham, and Hugo Black would give keynote addresses; and the delegates would be divided into subcommittees charged with addressing each issue discussed in the *Report on Economic Conditions in the South*. Not all southern liberals supported the event, however. Some opposed its reluctance to confront segregation directly. Others thought the event just another example of FDR's "machiavellian" politics. Tension and expectation ran high.

ER's train pulled into the Birmingham depot as dawn broke November 22. Aubrey Williams greeted her and the two began a whirlwind series of meetings throughout the city, including lunch with Governor Bibs Grave at which, as she later confided to a friend, she "had to argue at length" about the poll tax and black voting rights. Running behind schedule, the first lady and Williams hurriedly entered the First Methodist Church in the midst of a tense exchange over whether or not those assembled would obey the city's segregation ordinance. ER, unaware of the discussion around her, walked to the front row and sat down, as she later recalled, "on the colored side." When police informed her of the segregation policy, she refused to comply. She "felt rather uncomfortable," she wrote Hickok the next day, "and longed to answer [the questions] not as a visitor should." However, "rather than give in," she asked that her chair be placed between the two sections.[42]

The press treated ER's simple gesture of solidarity as an act of dramatic defiance of segregation policy. Rumors flew throughout the SCHW and the nation describing the event. Through these subsequent retellings, the story took on mythic proportions and an image emerged of an ER who would have never complied with the ordinance, who challenged the conference participants to follow her example, and who deftly faced down the county police commissioner, Eugene "Bull" Connor.

Ironically, ER's most outspoken attack on Birmingham politics received little coverage. After resolving the seating issue, the group began discussing the lynching of a young Mississippi black man the day before. Many delegates expressed outrage that their congressmen refused to support a federal anti-lynching law. When Representative Luther Patrick rose to argue that such a law would scapegoat southern mobs and ignore northern gang violence, ER rose and challenged him. Rather than blame the Congress, she asked "why the solution doesn't lie in the hands of the people of the South?" Urging him to take the initiative to develop legislation, she scoffed, "why isn't it at your door to frame a law that you think meets the needs and is satisfactory to the needs of the South?" Turning to face the congressman, she asked, "has there ever been a real effort by Southern lawmakers to pass an anti-lynching law that would apply everywhere?" Applause erupted, and a chagrined Patrick conceded that "as far as [he knew], there has not been." When Hickok learned of the day's events, she quickly dashed off a note asking "how did you finally get away with the trip to B'Ham? Have they torn you limb from limb yet?"[43]

■ **"The question is . . . shall you resign."**
The Marian Anderson Concert

By 1939, ER's support of civil rights was so well known that she could have dodged the controversy surrounding Marian Anderson's performance and have few question her commitment to racial justice. But she did not sidestep the affair. Indeed, her bold actions on the diva's behalf not only "gave her opponents something [more] to talk about" but also provided her with unquestionable proof of her own political power.

Marian Anderson, the world's greatest contralto, was black. She had entertained all the crowned heads and elected officials of Europe, had won the highest awards her profession could bestow, and entertained the Roosevelts in the White House. Her previous performances in the District of Columbia before sold-out racially mixed audiences had received rave reviews. In January, Howard University had asked Anderson to perform a benefit concert for its School of Music on Easter weekend 1939. Anderson gladly accepted.

The problem surfaced when the Daughters of the American Revolution (DAR) refused to rent its auditorium, Constitution Hall, to Anderson because she was black. While at first the DAR denied that race was the reason preventing her leasing the hall, the truth soon emerged; and the University and the NAACP launched an immense lobbying campaign to force the DAR to change its policy. The DAR refused. Prominent black and white Washingtonians then formed the Marian Anderson Citizens Committee and petitioned the District of Columbia School Board for permission to use the Armstrong High School Auditorium for the concert. Following the DAR's lead, the school board denied the request.[44]

ER debated what action to take on Anderson's behalf. By early January, she already had agreed to present the Spingarn Medal to the artist at the National NAACP convention, met with NAACP Secretary Walter White and conference chair Dr. Elizabeth Yates Webb to discuss the broadcast of the awards ceremony, invited Anderson to perform for the British King and Queen at the White House in June, and telegraphed her support to Howard University. Although initially she thought she should not attack the DAR's decision, she changed her mind and resigned from the organization in late February. Still angry and embarrassed at the treatment Anderson received, ER worked behind the scenes to arrange for the concert to be held at the Lincoln Memorial.[45]

As important as ER's interventions on Anderson's behalf were they pale in comparison to the pivotal role she played in highlighting the discriminatory conduct of such a prestigious organization as the DAR. The power of understatement displayed in her "My Day" column of February 28, 1939, revealed ER's hand on the pulse of the nation. Carefully portraying the situation in impersonal, nonthreatening terms with which the majority of her readers would identify, she refrained from naming the issue or the organization that had caused her distress.

She introduced the dilemma simply: "I have been debating in my mind for some time a question which I have had to debate with myself once or twice before in my life. Usually I have decided differently from the way in which I am deciding now." She then outlined the problem and her response to it. "The question is, if you belong to an organization and disapprove of an action which is typical of a policy, shall you resign or is it better to work for a changed point of view within the organization?" Telling her readers that she preferred to work for change, she "usually stayed in until I had at least made a fight and been defeated." When she lost, she "accepted my defeat and decided either that I was wrong or that I was perhaps a little too far ahead of the thinking of the majority of that time." Indeed, she "often found that the thing in which I was interested was done some years later." But this case did not fit that pattern because this organization is one "in which I do no active work." Moreover, "they have taken an action which has been widely talked of in the press. To remain as a member implies approval of that action, I am resigning."[46]

The next day, the column splashed across the front pages of American newspapers from San Francisco to New York City. Although others had resigned from the DAR over this issue, although other major public figures had publicly lamented the DAR's policy, Eleanor Roosevelt put Marian Anderson, the DAR, and racial discrimination on a national stage. By placing her political clout and personal popularity squarely behind Anderson and in front of the DAR, she moved the conflict into another arena.

After the concert was over, ER worked to keep the issue before the public. She invited Anderson to the White House to perform for the visiting British royalty and presented the Spingarn Medal to Marian Anderson at the NAACP national convention in Richmond. The inherent symbolism of the first lady of American civil rights agreeing to present an award to an African-American woman in the birthplace of the Confederacy on Independence Day weekend could hardly be overlooked. The demand for seats was so overwhelming that tickets for the event were unavailable a week after the announcement was made. Such potent response enabled Walter White to convince NBC and other radio affiliates to create a temporary nationwide hook-up to broadcast the first lady's remarks live. On the day of the ceremony, the crowd overflowed the Richmond Mosque's 5300-seat capacity and spilled out into the streets to hear her. She minced no words in this address. People not only must confront the discrimination they encounter in an assertive manner, she argued, but also be ready to delay, or if necessary sacrifice, an individual desire so that "improvement in the opportunities for people" society passed over can be obtained.[47]

Eleanor Roosevelt understood the political implications of Anderson's talent and success and risked herself while she strove to remind the public what the controversy represented. By associating herself as the motivating force behind the concert, by allowing herself to be photographed sitting next to black political and social leaders on stage at the NAACP national convention in a stronghold of southern conservatism, ER made the event overtly political two months after Anderson's final encore.

The Marian Anderson venture taught ER a valuable lesson. She clearly saw the impact she had when she used her column for political persuasion. In 1939, ER was just beginning to use "My Day" as her own political forum. The controversy and the response it generated from her readers showed Eleanor Roosevelt the direct impact she had when she spoke out on a political event. She received more mail supporting her resignation from the DAR than she did on any other issue she associated herself with in 1939. Gallup and other public opinion polls revealed that her backing of Anderson increased her popularity in all areas of the country, except the deep South, and even there, the decrease was minuscule.[48]

The political and organizational lessons this event taught her about coalition building and the power of her column would not be overlooked. Although "My Day" continued to be primarily an insight into the first lady's personal schedule, by mid-July 1939, ER recognized the political power she could muster in her own right for an issue she chose to highlight. In April 1940, United Feature Syndicate acknowledged the first lady's appeal by awarding her a five-year renewal for "My Day" at a time when President Roosevelt's reelection plans were not known.[49]

The Anderson experience reinforced Eleanor Roosevelt's venture into the politics of confrontation and helped steel her for the 1940 campaign. Although the first lady was no stranger to criticism by April 1939, the strong and widespread reaction her endorsement of Anderson generated was a new experience for her. By fall she had become the Republicans' most popular target and attacks she discounted in public as "mudslinging" became so intense, she wrote her aunt, that "the campaign is as bad in personal bitterness as any I have ever been in."[50]

But ER's influence within the party held fast. When FDR's choice for vice president, Henry Wallace, unquestionably the most liberal member of FDR's cabinet, was in jeopardy, the president called his wife and asked her to fly to the convention and salvage Wallace's candidacy. Earlier that day, Ickes frantically telegraphed FDR that the "convention is bleeding to death." Delegates needed more direction from him. They were "milling around like worried sheep." FDR had alienated delegates by insisting that he would only respond to a draft (thereby refusing to ask for their support directly); and after they had swallowed their pride and renominated him, the convention fractured over the issue of his running mate. Furthermore, the candidate FDR wanted to replace the retiring Garner, had just left the Republican party. Chaos reigned in the Chicago convention hall when ER arrived. She later recalled that when Wallace's name was placed in nomination, the noise generated by the various floor fights was so "deafening" that "you could hardly hear yourself or speak to your next door neighbor."[51]

No first lady had ever addressed a national political convention and Malvina ("Tommy") Thompson, ER's secretary and valued confidant, adamantly opposed her boss's appearance. Thompson was not ER's only friend who worried that she "would be sacrificed on the altar of hysteria." Even Frances Perkins and Lorena Hickok, the two who had convinced ER to come to Chicago, panicked at the disorder reigning beneath the speaker's podium and urged the chair to delay her address. ER discounted their concern and strode across the dias. Although taken aback by the delegates' frenzied conduct, she hoped that when they saw her, tempers would calm. She read their mood correctly. Her sudden appearance not only stopped the floor fights but also ignited a passionate, spontaneous demonstration in her honor which even surpassed the sustained applause Jim Farley had received the night before when he had used his nomination speech to ask the delegates to unite behind Roosevelt.

Briefly pausing to acknowledge their praise, ER then began to speak, without notes, to the Democratic crowd below her. Without mentioning Wallace by name, she appealed to the delegates to give the president the help he asked of them. Reminding them that "no man who is a candidate or who is President can carry this situation alone," she asked them to remember that "this is no ordinary time" and that we have "no time for weighing anything except what we can best do for the country as a whole."[52]

Wallace received the necessary votes on the first ballot. ER's skillful, dramatic rebuttal of the delegates' challenge to Wallace's nomination for vice president in 1940 received banner headlines across the land. Party regulars considered her speech to the Democratic National Convention a masterstroke. Her performance, the quintessential progressive George Norris wrote, made her "the Sherman of that convention [who] caused men of sense and honor to stop and think before they plunged." Only ER's deft handling of the delegates, the senator concluded, "turned a rout into a victory." Sam Rosenman, FDR's adviser who usually disapproved of ER's politics and who sat with the president in his White House study listening to the address over the radio, agreed. She had managed to lift the convention "above the petty political trading that was going on and place it on a different level."[53]

Coming into Her Own

As Eleanor Roosevelt struggled to carve out a role as first lady which would fulfill her political and individual expectations, she learned that to be an effective politician one must have a strong offense and a solid defense. To the extent that she was able to implement her desires for a more comprehensive education-centered relief program for youth and a multidimensional relief program for unemployed artists, ER asserted a strong legislative and administrative influence within the administration. However, when her recommendations for civil rights action were rejected, she attacked the status quo with an increasing sense of social justice and defended her stance with a righteous indignation that underscored existing inequities. And when her husband's coalition appeared to be unraveling, she rarely hesitated before entering the fray. This position was not easy to protect. Such conviction and the press coverage it generated bred passionate responses from critics both outside and inside the administration. To them, she was more than a thorn in their side; she was a symbol of all that was wrong with the country. In 1933, when she tried to justify theft by a man whose family was starving—telling those attending her civics course at the New York Junior League that "she wouldn't blame him [because] you would be a poor wishy-washy sort of person if you didn't take anything you could when your family was starving"—she was accused of condoning looting and disrespect for the law. When the American Liberty League called a meeting in Macon, Georgia, in support of Governor Eugene Talmadge's 1936 presidential campaign, its members distributed to each attendant a photograph which showed, in the words of the convener of the gathering, Vance Muse: "a picture of Eleanor Roosevelt going to some Nigger meeting, with two escorts. Niggers on each arm." Even Republican Alice Roosevelt Longworth could not resist needling her cousin in an article discussing "the ideal qualifications of a president's wife." "We didn't elect her," the sharp-tongued daughter of Theodore Roosevelt wrote, "what is she horning in for?" By 1940, some lapels sprouted campaign buttons that read "We don't want Eleanor either" and Malcolm Bingay, editorial director of the *Detroit Free Press*, pleaded to a "Merciful God" to have her "light somewhere and keep quiet."[54]

Nor were these rebukes solely from those outside her own circle. Frequently, FDR's immediate concerns dictated not only the topics she examined but also the extent of the action she could undertake. Often his friends objected to her influence. Doc O'Connor and Sam Rosenman, FDR's legal advisers, told Rexford Tugwell when he joined the 1932 campaign team that their first task was "to get the pants off Eleanor and onto Frank." Many New Deal officials, like Secretary of Labor Frances Perkins, disapproved of her civil rights employment policies and feared the response they would provoke from southern congressional leaders. Secretary of the Interior Harold L. Ickes resented ER's participation in the development of the subsistence homestead in Arthurdale, West Virginia, and feared being upstaged within the civil rights community. Others, like the secretary of agriculture, feared her power within the administration. "Now, Will, I want to give you some advice," Henry Wallace told his newly appointed Farm Security administrator, Will Alexander, "You want to let that woman alone. She's a very dangerous person. You don't want to get mixed up with her." And as numerous historians have reported, when FDR became preoccupied with winning the war, ER's insistent focus on domestic issues irritated the president, angered his advisers, and provoked outrage from conservative members of Congress. By the time FDR sought a fourth term in 1944, the Roosevelts' divergent politics were blatantly apparent.[55]

Thus, even within the confines of the White House family quarters, politics was not always compromise, but was often confrontation. Advocates of each opposing view joined ranks and justified their positions by arguing that their individual packages for more broad-based reform were more important than any single policy. No stranger to political arbitration, ER sometimes won these contests. However, when she lost, Eleanor Roosevelt did not concede defeat easily. A skilled and committed player, she studied the rules and continued playing. As Rexford Tugwell, one of the original members of FDR's Brain Trust, described her powerful attempts to modify FDR's agenda, "No one who ever saw Eleanor Roosevelt sit down facing her husband, and, holding his eye firmly, say to him, 'Franklin, I think you should . . .' or, 'Franklin, surely you will not . . .' will ever forget the experience." With the vigilance of a wrangler riding herd, she spurred the administration's side "even though the spurring was not always wanted or welcome." "It would be impossible," Tugwell concluded, "to say how often and to what extent American governmental processes have been turned in new directions because of her determination."[56]

No first lady took her commitment as seriously as did Eleanor Roosevelt. "She had this sense of having to do whatever was humanly possible in a difficult time," Trude Lash recalled. Her energy was so intense that a standard joke of the day was "Please, Lord, make Eleanor tired." Author, columnist, politician, and educator, this woman appeared indefatigable. From 1933 to 1945, she wrote, without a ghost writer, more than 2,500 columns, and 200 articles, published 6 books, and delivered at least 70 speeches a year. She lobbied for legislation, advised politicians and reformers, met with Democratic party leaders, and traveled the country as her husband's representative.[57]

Although the history of Eleanor Roosevelt's actions as first lady is far from complete, all studies of both her life and the Roosevelt Administration agree that she redefined the role of president's wife and set the standard by which all future presidential spouses would be judged. So strong an imprint on contemporary American culture did this woman's struggle for self-reliance and independent action leave that when Katharine Hepburn was struggling to find the appropriate demeanor with which to approach her most famous character, the prim, but feisty missionary Rose Sayer who rode the rapids on *The African Queen*, her director John Houston simply instructed, "Play her like Eleanor Roosevelt."[58]

That Eleanor Roosevelt could achieve such status and have such a profound impact on American political and cultural institutions is a testament both to her tenacity and strength of character. Rather than succumbing to the sorrows and disappointments of her past, as those historians who accept "the woman of sorrow" interpretation suppose, ER transcended them to find other ways of professional and personal fulfillment.

No longer reluctant in her position, Eleanor Roosevelt expanded the image of first lady from ceremonial spouse to political leader. By 1940, columnists labeled her "a political force" in her own right and "one of the ten most powerful people in Washington." As speculation of a possible third term for FDR increased, speculation about ER's future increased as well. In its New Year's Day issue, *Time* reported that certain "prominent Bryn Mawr alumnae" were diligently lobbying ER to become the college's new president while *Harper's* reported Republican complaints about "the team of Roosevelt and Roosevelt." "It isn't fair," unnamed Republicans are quoted as saying, "for the President to cash in on his own popularity and his wife's too. It's a Fascist trend."

Although Eleanor Roosevelt could not be more different than Signora Mussolini, she did have an extensive following. "My Day" was reprinted in forty-eight newspapers with a combined circulation of four and a half million, putting her on a par with pundits Westbrook Pegler, Dorothy Thompson, and Raymond Clapper. Furthermore, more than 350 Americans wrote to her each day. By mid-year the Gallup poll reported she had the approval of sixty-seven percent of the people while a *Fortune* survey determined that she was more popular among all groups of Americans than was FDR. Such widespread respect lead *New York Times* columnist Arthur Krock to speculate that "because [many people] look upon her as a great leader. . . . [they] have uttered the hope that she will prove to be her husband's choice for nomination as his successor." "Stranger things have not happened," Krock concluded, "but they could." Louis Howe agreed and talked privately of making her president after her husband's terms expired.[59]

■

Chapter Three

HOLDING TRUMAN ACCOUNTABLE
Full and Fair Employment at Just Wages

Despite the frustration she experienced during World War II as the lone voice for domestic reform within a "pussyfooting" White House, Eleanor Roosevelt still believed that politics was a virtuous calling with noble goals, just as she realized that it was also a struggle for the power necessary to achieve those goals. She learned that presidential protocol, congressional alignments, and the media were tools to be used to advance one's causes, not restrict one's behavior. Consequently, by the time of her husband's death on April 12, 1945, ER was a veteran politician with a history of not conforming to conventional expectations. She knew that the years ahead would be different; "a period in history" had ended. Yet she knew that once the details of FDR's estate were settled, she could start again. She was as prepared as she could be for the future. The challenge she faced leaving the White House was the one she faced when she moved in: how not to give in to others' expectations, how to set her own priorities.

"I never did like to be where I no longer belonged," she confided to Joe Lash a few days after FDR's death. The emptiness of the White House made her feel "desolate" and "without purpose" and, although she was "weary," she could not "rest." Now that she was no longer first lady, ER was anxious to leave.[1]

Within a week of FDR's death, she coordinated his funeral, responded to friends' condolences, oversaw the boxing of possessions acquired and documents generated during her twelve years in Washington, said goodbye to colleagues and staff, and pondered her future. Despite the intensity of this schedule, ER made time on April 19 to host a farewell White House tea for the women's press corps. Although the reception was a private affair, ER did answer some questions for the record. After scotching various rumors of her own political ambitions, ER declared that her only aspirations were journalistic. She wished to be their colleague, she told the group, not their subject. Yet, the next evening after arriving in Manhattan, she faced those questions for a second time. Confronted by a small group of photographers and reporters outside her Washington Square apartment, ER refused to comment on their speculations. "The story," she said, "is over."[2]

Despite her denials, politicians, pundits, and the public speculated on what actions Eleanor Roosevelt should take next. Speaker of the House Sam Rayburn and New Jersey Congresswoman Mary Norton urged ER to join the American delegation to the conference charged with planning the United Nations. Secretary of the Interior Harold Ickes, who had grown to see ER as more a colleague than a meddlesome rival, pleaded with her to run for the United States Senate while New York Democratic party leader Ed Flynn argued that she should be the Empire State's next governor. Others proposed that she be the new secretary of labor. Even the syndicated columnists Joseph and Stewart Alsop belatedly joined the conjecture, satirically suggesting that their cousin become Truman's new political "medium."[3]

Close friends and the media reinforced this expectation of a political career. As they rode the train from Hyde Park back to Washington, Henry Morgenthau, Jr., recommended that FDR's estate be settled as soon as possible so "she could speak out to the world as Eleanor Roosevelt." "It [is] most important that [your] voice be heard," the secretary asserted. Taking a different approach, Lorena Hickok consoled and prodded simultaneously. After encouraging her friend to "take a few days off this Spring and Summer to rest," she then reminded her that "you are going to be more your own agent, freer than you've ever been before." ER must be prepared, Hickok concluded, for the "very active and important place" awaiting her. The Associated Press agreed, succinctly summarizing the pressures confronting ER with this front page headline: "Mrs. Roosevelt Will Continue Column; Seeks No Office *Now*."[4]

Eleanor Roosevelt had her own expectations about the future; but, unlike her friends and the media, she was undecided about what actions she should take to achieve them. Fearing that her public life had died along with FDR, she struggled to set her own course. Although she declared her determination not to be seen forever as a former first lady, ER feared that without the "ear of the president" she would lose the influence she had struggled so diligently to attain. At times she succumbed to these anxieties only to encounter jocular criticism from those closest to her. When ER lapsed into a moment of despondence and informed young friends that she merely wanted to write, visit her family, and live "a peaceful life," Trude Lash teasingly suggested that they all go buy ER a lace cap as a retirement gift.[5]

Recalling the anxiety of these transition months, ER noted in *On My Own* that she was sure of only three things when she returned to Hyde Park: she wanted to continue her columns, simplify her lifestyle, and "not feel old . . . [or] useless." She knew her keen interest in the world around her, her eagerness to confront "every challenge and opportunity to learn more," and her "great energy and self-discipline" were tremendous assets. She astutely understood how much weight her support carried but she worried that her influence might tip the political scales in ways that she could not control. Consequently, while she was now free of the "certain restrictions FDR demanded," ER faced 1945 impatient with slow-paced domestic reform and uncomfortable with her undefined future. "Of one thing I am sure," she wrote in early May, "in order to be useful we must stand for the things we feel are right, and we must work for those things wherever we find ourselves. It does very little good to believe something unless you tell your friends and associates of your beliefs." Vowing that she would not become "a workless worker in a world of work," she struggled to define the parameters of a new life in politics.[6]

Yet these new boundaries did not mean new politics. Eleanor Roosevelt had no plans to forsake the goals and ideals of the New Deal. In fact, she planned to do the exact opposite. If FDR had abandoned Dr. New Deal to become Dr. Win the War and resented her wartime insistence on domestic reform, ER anticipated that his successor would be even less likely to pursue the controversial programs FDR had abandoned when conservatives seized control of Congress. She recognized that if the New Deal was to regain the political arena, she would have to assist in orchestrating its return. Whether she did this by promoting candidates or policy was up to her. The path she selected was not the pivotal point in her strategy. What was important was that she select a mode of operation that allowed her the greatest leeway in pursuing her own goals while she protected her husband's legacy.[7]

Although she took a few deliberate acts to rebuild her life after FDR—relinquishing ties to Hyde Park, making Val-Kill her home base, and actively pursuing a career as a political columnist—most of Eleanor Roosevelt's plans for the future remained vague. She did believe that "the story is over." After all, FDR had died; and although their relationship had been more professional than personal for the past several years, ER did grieve. What took time for her to recognize was that FDR's death expanded, rather than limited, her sphere of influence. No longer just FDR's "Missus," she could now choose to speak out and act as either his widow or as herself. The challenge facing ER in mid-1945 was how to balance these two identities.

Eleanor Roosevelt was not the only person freed by the events of April 12. FDR's death also lifted the "certain restrictions" FDR placed on Harry Truman and Henry Wallace's actions. However, unlike ER, these leaders were not prepared for such sudden independence. To Truman, who had a recurring dream depicting Roosevelt's death in office, 1945 seemed like a nightmare come true. To Wallace, still recovering from a bruising confirmation hearing and an in-house battle with Jesse Jones for control of the Reconstruction Finance Corporation, life without public anointment as FDR's successor was time spent in political purgatory. While these two men, who had been rivals for the vice presidential nomination the summer before, deliberated which policies to pursue and which route they should take to promote their individual political careers, ER acted to ensure that whichever man won the contest the liberal approach to reconversion and social reform would not suffer.

As the war drew to a close and Americans focused once again on domestic issues, liberals feared a recession-induced financial panic, widespread unemployment, and a resurrection of American nativism. Consequently, the liberal plan for postwar economic reconversion emphasized the maintenance of wage and price controls, firm government commitment to economic planning, affordable housing, and the institutionalization of the Fair Employment Practices Commission (FEPC). As National Farmers Union President James Patton declared the day before the 1944 election, "nearly all our problems start with the possibility of mass unemployment; [therefore] nearly all our solutions must start with full employment." ER could not have agreed with Patton more.

From April 12, 1945 until November 2, 1948, Eleanor Roosevelt, Harry Truman, and Henry Wallace struggled to define and implement Democratic economic and social policy. This battle was not a contest to see who could fill the void FDR's death left in the liberal ranks, but was rather a fierce rivalry over which direction postwar America would take in balancing its traditional republican economic principles with the demands for a more inclusive democracy. Each Democrat had different priorities and different strengths. Truman was a politician, not a liberal. Wallace was a liberal idealist who disdained and often bungled political games. As both the foremost symbol of liberalism and a master of hidden-hand politics, Eleanor Roosevelt juggled these two men's egos, dreams, and policies in an attempt to promote a new direction for American liberalism that would adhere to the values she believed intrinsic to democracy: participation, inclusion, dissent, and security.[8]

The campaign to implement the "Economic Bill of Rights" was the first policy question in which this triumvirate competed. Although all favored government economic intervention, they disagreed as to what form government stabilization should take, how much action was necessary, and who the primary beneficiaries of the policy should be. Their differences came to a head over full employment proposals, price and wage control policies, and the call for a permanent Fair Employment Practices Commission.

■ **"You are the one in trouble now."**
Truman and Presidential Leadership

Eleanor Roosevelt had been outspoken in her belief that FDR should have kept Wallace as his running mate. Thus Truman was well aware that he had not been ER's choice for vice president in 1944, and his brief tenure in that office did nothing to assuage her doubts that he possessed either the political expertise or the moral commitment necessary to implement FDR's polices. ER subtly reminded him of these differences as well as of the difficulties facing him when she told Truman of FDR's death. With her arm draped over his shoulders, she deflected the new president's stunned condolences to offer instead her political aid. "What can we do for you?" she asked, "for you are the one in trouble now."[9]

The wariness with which Harry Truman and Eleanor Roosevelt regarded each other did not imply that their political aims were at complete cross-purposes. Rather it reflected the tension within the Democratic party over what course liberalism should pursue and what methods should be used to implement liberal reform. In contrast to the progressive billing Vice President Truman received in such liberal journals as *The Nation, The New Republic,* and *PM,* President Truman saw himself as a practical politician dedicated to perpetuating only as much of FDR's wartime domestic policies as was politically possible. However, those liberals who demanded a return to the more encompassing New Deal agenda soon came to interpret Truman's support as campaign rhetoric. "Let us not fool ourselves," Freda Kirchwey warned *The Nation's* readers, Truman's election year promises did not equal Wallace's commitment. *The New Republic* agreed, rhetorically asking its readers, "Will Truman go conservative? Just look at the election returns."[10]

Like Kirchwey, Eleanor Roosevelt doubted Truman's devotion to liberalism. Not only did she object to his strong ties to political bosses and the conservative wing of his party, especially its southern members of Congress, but she also doubted that he had the political magnetism and administrative finesse necessary to lead the public through the uncertainty the postwar world would face. Like Margaret Marshall, she believed that Truman would not fight for reform but would settle for whatever "he could get without creating enemies." Like I. F. Stone, ER saw Truman's replacement of Henry Morgenthau with John Snyder as secretary of the treasury as a shift away from Wallace's "century of the common man" toward a Truman era of "new mediocracy." Adding insult to injury, Truman did not even attempt to conceal his disdain for the liberal intellegensia close to ER, labelling them "crackpots and the lunatic fringe."[11]

Truman's actions during the first week of his presidency did little to alter ER's initial misgivings. The day after FDR's death, Truman invited FDR's assistant James F. Byrnes, a former senator from South Carolina whom ER despised both personally and politically, for an afternoon conference in which they discussed foreign policy "from Tehran to Yalta" and "everything else under the [domestic] sun." As Truman began to assemble his own Cabinet, ER's concerns mounted. At FDR's funeral, stalwart New Dealers Morgenthau and Perkins reported to her that they would be replaced and that party bosses Robert Hannegan and Edwin Pauley would receive Cabinet appointments or high-level agency directorships. Compounding these reports, rumors spread by Truman supporters promoted Byrnes for secretary of state. Thus, rather than open his administration up to include all aspects of the Democratic coalition, Truman appeared to rely increasingly on what one historian has labeled "government by proxy."[12]

After the funeral, tensions escalated. Byrnes's conduct at the Hyde Park ceremony further outraged ER and those close to her. The South Carolinian had already objected to some of the funeral arrangements and now tried to force ER to ride in Truman's train car so that Byrnes might use her car to caucus with congressional leaders. When she refused, Byrnes "protested vigorously." "He made it obvious," Trude Lash wrote that evening in her diary, "that he wanted it understood that he belongs to the new era." Harry Hopkins, furious over Truman's reluctance to rebuke Byrnes, was still steaming when he discussed with ER a conversation he had with the president earlier that day. Truman "would not know where to begin," FDR's special assistant told her. Nor did he see "much hope for cooperation" between the two administrations. This briefing did little to ease ER's discomfort.[13]

Truman realized that his support of Byrnes must not undermine his new status with New Deal loyalists. Therefore, as the train approached Washington, Truman invited ER to his car to discuss the speech he was to deliver to Congress the following night. There is no record of that conversation or of what ER thought of the draft presented her. What is clear, however, is that this invitation illustrated the corner in which the new president found himself. As a pragmatic politician, Truman knew that to build his own following he must do two things: wrap himself in the mantle of FDR's popularity and carve out a plan of his own.

Eleanor Roosevelt was both the key to and the biggest obstacle to his success. As the symbol of New Deal social and economic reform, she was more closely identified with FDR than was Truman and her vision of the postwar world differed substantially from Truman's. To the extent that each of these leaders would succeed in implementing their respective goals, they either had to defeat one another's policies or unite in opposition to common political foes. The outcome of this contest shaped the future of liberalism and the Democratic party.[14]

As FDR debated whether to seek a third term, the liberal consensus that characterized the legislative base of the Second New Deal rapidly evaporated. His decision to balance the budget in 1937 and his attempt to "pack" the Supreme Court backfired among his supporters. Congressional conservatives and newly elected Republicans formally began to dismantle some of the New Deal's most progressive legislation. Furthermore, the political crisis in Europe so concerned FDR that the president had entered his third term more concerned about stopping fascist aggression than furthering economic reform.

ER disagreed with her husband's priorities. She saw the New Deal not as a dream to be deferred but as an approach with which to spur economic development and fight fascism. Indeed, the only way to mobilize the nation to fight foreign aggression was to make sure the nation understood how this threat not only violated democratic principles but also jeopardized Americans' basic interests. The New Deal's commitment to small business and economic reform must not fade into the preferential treatment to the corporate giants FDR thought essential to rapid mobilization or the nation would once again find itself "taking from the bottom and adding to the top." The more Wallace represented her view, the more ER supported him.[15]

After the 1940 Democratic convention, Eleanor Roosevelt's support of Henry Wallace became well known throughout the party and the nation. Ironically, ER's greatest victory for Wallace occurred before she became his stalwart. Wallace did not secure her unconditional support until he delivered his evangelical speech, "The Price of Free World Victory," in May 1942. With a passion and eloquence that galvanized liberal America, Wallace interpreted the war as a life and death struggle against the satanic trappings of unlimited wealth and privilege. Reviving the image of the Social Gospel, he promoted a democracy firmly rooted in the Christianity that had spurred the great democratic revolutions of the nineteenth century. Firmly convinced that want threatened American democracy more than war, the vice president promoted a people's revolution and challenged America to strive for unlimited production and a "just and charitable peace." Arguing that "no half measures" could be allowed, Wallace proclaimed that Americans had "a supreme duty" to place "the greater interest of the general welfare" before their own "lesser individual demands."[16]

Such conviction and oratorical passion convinced ER, just as it did *The New Republic*, that Wallace was the liberal envoy capable of presenting the global vision the war-torn world desperately needed. Moreover, the more she considered his arguments, the more sure she became of his vision. "I am reading . . . Wallace's 'Democracy Reborn'," she wrote Joe Lash the spring of 1944. "It is just a collection of his speeches but as I reread them carefully I find them impressive and I think that the man has grown to be a statesman" in spite of his political naivete.[17]

Wallace's call for a "century of the common man" was not the only reason ER supported him. She also continued to favor Wallace as FDR's heir apparent because Wallace presented his vision forcefully and eloquently. America, she believed, needed a strong president to unify a divided Congress. Truman, friendly with those conservatives who opposed bold presidential initiative, appeared initially to succumb to, rather than inspire, congressional approval.

Although ER recognized that Wallace was not "a very good politician," she nonetheless thought his ability to rally the people crucial to both an Allied victory and postwar liberal reform. FDR's sudden death had stunned the American people and she feared that his most severe critics would capitalize immediately upon the void his death had left. Moreover, with the end to the war clearly in sight, many people worried not only about a new depression but also whether the man charged with negotiating peace and reconversion might not be up to the tasks.

When America had entered the war, ER had argued that one of the president's major responsibilities when the nation faced a crisis was to lead the people to discuss the critical issues associated with that event in ways that promote thought, deliberation, and commitment. As the war drew to a close, she saw Americans "economize" in their willingness to see issues in a bold perspective, and she worried that their resolve would weaken, liberalism would fracture, reconversion sputter, and disorder triumph. The president must fight this tendency because "government has to assure not only political democracy to its people, but economic democracy as well." Hence, when ER left the White House she left convinced that if liberal reform was to survive FDR's death, the president must take control of an unravelling consensus and skillfully move it to the left.

Compared to Truman's disdain for the bully pulpit, Wallace's dedication to public education and political ingenuity no longer seemed such a glaring deficiency. Indeed, ER worried that Truman would fail to provide the inspiration liberalism needed to prevail. Consequently, while Truman delivered the speech he had reviewed with ER aboard FDR's funeral train and sought the support of a special session of Congress, Eleanor Roosevelt implored his once and future rival to pick up liberalism's fallen mantle. Wallace, she asserted, must continue the fight for reform because he was the leader most "peculiarly fitted to carry on the ideals close to my husband's heart."[18]

If ER adhered to the liberal line in her desire for a forceful, articulate president, she nevertheless planned to remain faithful to her party's leader once he was in office. She understood that Truman would need all the support the party could provide to implement his vision. Yet this political allegiance had its price. If ER the widow was the model of party fidelity, ER the journalist planned to be the paragon of the loyal opposition. Subtly tacked within a column designed to rebut rumors of her political aspirations, ER served notice to the Truman administration and her public that she would continue to speak out. Yet she would speak with a different voice, a freer "My Day." "Because I was the wife of the president, certain restrictions were imposed upon me," she announced in her April 19 column, but "now I am on my own."[19]

■ "Are Congress and the capital having a sit-down strike?" Wallace, Truman, and Full Employment

The fear of massive unemployment dominated all discussion of reconversion economics. By December 1944, economists were predicting a postwar high of twelve to sixteen million unemployed. In an attempt to calm this fear, the president, congressional liberals, unions, and progressive organizations such as the Union for Democratic Action (UDA)and the National Farmers Union reviewed plans designed to ensure a stable reconversion to a peacetime economy. Despite their shared focus, though, the groups differed as to what steps the government should take and how strong a role, if any, deficit spending should play in guaranteeing employment.[20]

FDR still appeared reluctant to embrace full employment, but his 1944 battle against Thomas Dewey forced him to reconsider. In January 1944, he flirted with the proposal, calling for the "economic bill of rights." By midsummer the phrase "full employment" appeared in his speeches, and by fall he issued a call for sixty million jobs. After the election, however, FDR had not yet endorsed a specific jobs proposal. By late December, as he met with Wallace to discuss employment forecasts, FDR rebuffed both Bowles's plea for legislative action on the "economic bill of rights" and Wallace's efforts to enlist his support for James Patton's full employment proposals, and he continued to oppose legislation that mandated deficit spending as a way to maximize employment.[21]

FDR's evasion prompted an orchestrated response from ER. She had kept close watch on the National Resources Planning Board (NRBP) through her friendship with Frank Porter Graham, its chairman, and by corresponding and meeting with Dr. Alvin Hansen, the economist who most pressured the NRBP to adopt a full employment policy. She resolutely shared their concern that if postwar economic planning was not an integral part of the war effort, American could win the battle only to lose the peace.

Indeed, the more she tried to discuss these issues with FDR, the more disgusted she became with his wartime priorities and the advisers who encouraged him to set them. FDR "was only interested in ambassadors and admirals and generals," she complained to an administration official who shared her frustrations. "I bring the American people to the President and

I represent them with the President. I'm constantly reminding him of the American consumer and the people of this country [with] whom he's gotten out of touch." As she later confided to her friend Chester Bowles, director of the Office of Price Administration, FDR's reluctance to implement his call for the creation of sixty million jobs so frustrated her that she, regardless of her or the president's schedules, had phoned FDR daily throughout the winter of 1944 to push for "an immediate beginning of postwar planning" and full employment. Moreover, she carefully devised a strategy that always gave her the last word. "I have learned by experience," ER admitted to Bowles with barely disguised satisfaction, "to recognize the point at which the President's patience is about to give out and he will begin to scold me. At that moment, I shall hurriedly say, 'Franklin, my car is waiting. I must be on my way. I will call you tomorrow.'"[22]

FDR's reluctance did not dishearten congressional liberals as strongly as it did ER. They, like members of such liberal interest groups as the Union for Democratic Action and NCPAC, optimistically believed that with the war close to an end, "Dr. New Deal" would return. After all, they argued, FDR had commissioned a 1944 White House paper on full employment and in January 1945 he had removed the conservative Jesse Jones from the Cabinet and nominated Henry Wallace, the administration's most articulate defender of full employment, to replace him as secretary of commerce. If Congress prepared the legislation and the interest groups and supportive administration officials assiduously gathered public support, liberals rationalized, the president would have the political stimulus he needed to refocus on domestic issues.[23]

By early 1945, all three players had taken steps to prod FDR into reconversion. In Congress, while the Senate debated Wallace's appointment as secretary of commerce, liberal and conservative factions mobilized in response to the Wallace nomination. Conservative Democrats and Republicans on the Senate Commerce Committee, realizing Wallace's inevitable confirmation, united behind Chairman Walter George and removed the Reconstruction Finance Corporation from the Department of Commerce and, thereby, from Wallace's jurisdiction. Liberal Democrats not only vigorously supported Wallace but also, led by James Murray, Robert Wagner, Elbert Thomas, and Joseph O'Mahoney, introduced S. 380, the Full Employment Bill. The federal government, Murray and his colleagues argued, should encourage private investment to increase public works programs and thus provide job opportunities for all people "able to work and seeking work." One hundred fifteen representatives agreed with Murray and signed on to introduce the bill into the House.[24]

Once again congressional liberals placed more faith in FDR's intentions than did ER. When an embittered Jesse Jones released his letter of dismissal from FDR to the press and FDR appeared to back away from keeping the agency within commerce, an angry ER strongly urged the president to keep the promises he had made to Wallace when Wallace left the vice presidency. Moreover, as Wallace's confirmation hearings became more belligerent, ER aggressively defended Wallace and, when Hopkins and other presidential aides refused to ask FDR to intercede, ER pressured FDR, who was en route to Yalta, to speak out more forcefully on Wallace's behalf. Nor did she keep her support private. She sat next to Wallace at the testimonial banquet the Union for Democratic Action held for him and used her column to reaffirm her strong support for his call for sixty million jobs and her opposition to the removal of the RFC from the Department of Commerce.

Liberal public interest groups quickly capitalized on the attention this new controversy generated. The UDA and the National Farmer's Union initiated a media campaign to recruit support for Wallace's confirmation, the Murray-Wagner bill, and their respective organizations. Finally, in a joint manifesto published in *The New Republic*, their executive directors chastised readers who wrung their hands and mourned liberalism, challenged them to develop their own progressive initiatives, and urged them to rally in support of full employment legislation. The CIO-PAC, its political arm NCPAC, and the Independent Citizens Committee of the Arts, Sciences and Professions followed suit.[25]

Although Truman supported full employment in the 1944 campaign, Wallace became the proposal's champion within the administration. Throughout his futile attempt to keep the vice presidential nomination and throughout the Roosevelt-Truman campaign, Wallace never veered from the Keynesian path. He steadfastly argued that "management could adjust production to demand . . . to sustain prices and profits" and that judicial application of science to management was the way to end poverty and hunger. "Modern science," he proclaimed, "when devoted wholeheartedly to the general welfare, has in it potentialities of which we do not yet dream." In his March 1944 "Broadcast to Little Businessmen," Wallace demanded "full use of our resources in all-out production for peace" to ensure that all Americans who "have ambition and a willingness to work hard . . . have the opportunity" to do so once the war ended. Indeed, his strident support of this principle provoked conservatives to strip the RFC from commerce once FDR appointed him secretary.[26]

Because Wallace remained convinced that the true test of public policy must be "whether it contributes to the full use of our resources or whether it tends toward the destruction of full production," he dedicated his short tenure as secretary of commerce to an attempt to prove the humanity of scientific planning. As Norman Markowitz asserts, Wallace was irrevocably committed to "transforming the department into a clearing house for economic planning and for the creation of a balanced full-employment economy and expanded world trade." The key to this policy was Murray's Full Employment Bill, S. 380. As Wallace argued in *Sixty Million Jobs*, only a national budget could provide federal officials with both the information and tools necessary to implement a full-employment economy.[27]

Despite Truman's dutiful endorsement of full employment and his opposition to removing the RFC from the Department of Commerce, Wallace quickly recognized that Truman's interpretation of full employment principles differed substantially from his. Wallace wanted to implement programs that would expand the principles FDR introduced while Truman's stated objective was merely "to carry out, during the reconversion period" the economic bill of rights FDR had advocated. Where Wallace believed that government had a responsibility to provide both conditions favorable to employment and the economic stimuli necessary to create jobs in the public and private sectors, Truman did not. "Making jobs or making people work was in no sense a part of the full employment program," Truman later declared in his memoirs. The government's primary task was to assure employers and employees that the economy was sound. The government only had the responsibility "to inspire private enterprise with confidence" by providing them "all the facts about full employment and opportunity and consistency in public policy so that enterprise could plan better by knowing what the government intended to do."[28]

Truman's planning was a reactive sharing of information, while Wallace's planning was a proactive attempt to formulate policy. Thus, although Truman placed S. 380 on his must list of legislation, Wallace did not "glory" in Truman's action as he had in FDR's initial proposals. Although the new president seemed "exceedingly eager to agree" with Wallace's positions, the secretary of commerce doubted his chief's commitment. Recalling a discussion with Truman on employment proposals, Wallace bitingly recorded in his diary that the president "seemed as though he was eager to decide in advance of thinking."[29]

Eleanor Roosevelt certainly detected these differences and worried that the philosophical gap between the two leaders' versions of full employment legislation would in fact undermine the proposal's ultimate political impact. Yet she hesitated to criticize Truman. ER had not yet carved out a place for herself within the new administration and she was reluctant to lobby the new president as intensely as she had pressured FDR. ER understood that her position in the White House had changed. As she confided to a friend, she felt like a stranger when she "visited" her old residence, and her actions on behalf of S. 380 reflect this new status and give a unique insight into the development of ER's new lobbying strategy.

She wrote Joseph Lash that she would tell Truman what she thought, "but she would tell him only once—after that the responsibility would be his." This caveat notwithstanding, ER did not shy away from offering political advice. She merely planned to act in ways that not only held Truman accountable for his policy but also apprised him, and other leaders in the party, of how she rated his performance. If Truman needed her aid, she would offer it gladly and unsparingly. Having presented her case, she would then lobby other key players to second her arguments and pressure the president to act.[30]

Rather than question Truman's commitment to full employment, she decided to encourage him to be more assertive with Congress and with the Democratic leadership to achieve the goals he publicly proclaimed. When Truman rejected her advice, an undaunted ER took a different approach and appealed directly to Democratic party chairman Robert Hannegan. The president must assert his leadership immediately, she wrote the DNC chief in early June. Carefully couching her words in tones that would imply support for Truman, ER nevertheless presented a case against what she saw as his cautious, reactive leadership. The honeymoon period was ending and liberals wanted to see the president control the agenda rather than yield to congressional moderates and party hacks. If he was seen as being controlled by the party rather than in control of its agenda, ER thought, liberals would lose faith in him.[31]

Although Truman did issue a liberal call to arms in his address to Congress on September 6 and included the Murray-Wagner bill as a major point in his twenty-one point legislative program, by then many liberals, including ER, feared that this advocacy came too little too late. An unamended version of S. 380 had passed the Senate but the House objected to the concept of a national budget and preferred to discuss government's responsibility to "maximum" rather than "full" employment. The immense frustration ER felt over Truman's response reflected the widespread sentiment within the liberal community that the president had waited until the bill was bogged down in congressional posturing before he tried to implement FDR's initiatives or to protect the liberal agenda.

ER worried that Truman was not prepared to be president. After lunching with him, she wrote Hickok that he seemed overwhelmed by the job. The White House seemed "bare & stiff" and Truman acted like "the loneliest man I ever saw." "He's not accustomed to night work or reading and contemplation and he doesn't like it." Dwarfed by his responsibilities, "he's not at ease & no one else is." "I am sorry for him & he tries so hard."[32]

But, with her dissatisfaction with his performance growing daily, ER replaced this sympathy with impatience. She developed a new, more dramatic strategy. Rather than only confront a novice president, she turned instead to her column to try to prod Congress into action. In an angry "My Day" addressed to a Capital Hill audience, ER declared that the House of Representatives' inability to release full employment and unemployment compensation bills out of committee are making people begin to wonder why we fought the war. However, try as she might to remove the president from the center of her criticism, she still could not exempt Truman completely from her scorn. "Are Congress *and* the capital having a sitdown strike?" she satirically asked her readers.[33]

Yet once summoned to confront the president, she responded swiftly and decisively. When Truman's October 30 radio address failed to convince Congress to free the full employment and unemployment proposals from their committees, ER discarded deference and boldly instructed the president to revise his lobbying strategy. On November 1, she confessed that she was "very anxious" about the administration's full employment efforts. She thought that George Allen, coordinator of White House legislative affairs, needed help. Yet she distrusted the commitment of John Snyder, the fiscal conservative who directed the Office of War Mobilization and Reconversion, to the original proposal and wanted to ensure that he alone did not fill the void in Allen's office. "It seems to me that if a group of people, such as those who worked on special legislation in the past, might be formed within Snyder's office," they "might do some very good work."[34]

Truman's reply reflected his inability to take a firm stand on this issue. After defending the actions he had already taken to promote the bill, especially his two speeches, he assured her on November 6 that "I am doing all I can privately to get the bill out of committee." Continuing to plead his case, he argued that he did have a group working under Snyder, but "it is not easy to get the right kind of people with the correct social point of view who have influence with those Congressmen who are blocking the program." Could she recommend someone with such skill, he asked?[35]

ER recognized that this was an evasive tactic and she was displeased. Truman was pleading one case to her while he was presenting a different interpretation to the congressional leadership and instructing his staff to pursue yet another version with Congress. The day after the president delivered his wage and policy address in support of the Murray bill, he wrote John McCormack to clarify his position. "I do not refer to any specific bill," he told the House majority leader. "I refer only to the general purposes . . . of full employment legislation." When House liberals threatened to revolt and demand passage of the initial version, Truman instructed Wallace to stop their efforts. Wallace, trying to support the administration in hopes of having the differences resolved in conference committee, reluctantly agreed to press his supporters in Congress to refrain from challenging Carter Manasco, the Alabama conservative Democrat who chaired the House Committee on Expenditures.[36]

By early 1946, the Truman-Wallace-Roosevelt alliance for full employment split. What began as joint efforts to pursue an economic bill of rights had degenerated into recalcitrant efforts by Truman and Wallace to avoid a public commitment to long-term Keynesian planning. Of all the questions this dilemma prompted, three stand out. If Truman revealed his true intentions to Wallace, why did he try so diligently to avoid sharing his plans with Eleanor Roosevelt? If Wallace was so principled a champion of a planned economy and full employment principles why did he agree to support Truman's minimal initiative? And finally, why did Eleanor Roosevelt wait until the Manasco Committee began gutting the bill to confront Truman's actions?

In the midst of these machinations, Truman confided to Byrnes that there were only two leaders whose support he had to keep: ER and Wallace. As the president told his secretary of state, both liberals were valuable because of the special esteem in which they were held by two major groups of the Democratic coalition: blacks and labor. By mid-fall, both groups were increasingly displeased by Truman's performance. Walter Reuther and other labor leaders had rebuked Truman for his procrastination on defense plant reconversion plans and wage and price control policies. Charles Houston, NAACP national board member and former legal director, meanwhile, resigned his FEPC position to protest Truman's refusal to desegregate the capital's transit system. Consequently by November 1945, the president's symbolic association with ER and Wallace was even more important to his public image than when he assumed the office in April.[37]

Eleanor Roosevelt had close ties to both blacks and labor. Although the president referred only to her strong ties to minority communities in his instructions to Byrnes, by fall 1945 he could not be unaware of her strong affiliation with labor's political committees. Throughout the war her respect for Walter Reuther increased and she became his most outspoken advocate, his "secret weapon," within FDR's White House. Her keynote address to the 1944 CIO national convention resulted in a raucous sustained ovation that was widely publicized in both liberal and conservative campaign material. Moreover, Sidney Hillman, director of the CIO's Political Action Committee (CIO-PAC), was so convinced of ER's commitment to labor that he pleaded with her to assume the directorship of National Citizens Political Action Committee (NCPAC), a political coalition designed to mobilize the support labor had in other interest groups. After serious consideration she declined the offer, because, as she wrote Hillman, "I have decided that if I became chairman instead of being helpful with the Democratic party it would alienate the Democratic party and I think it important to keep the Democratic party close to both the CIO and NCPAC." She threw her support behind the PAC both by endorsing its activities in her column and by addressing NCPAC banquets across the nation. Furthermore, when the UAW and CIO workers struck the Ford plant, ER, despite the allegations of communist influence among the CIO and UAW leadership, publicly defended their actions and served as honorary co-chair of a committee to raise funds for the striking workers. In short, Eleanor Roosevelt posed a triple threat to Truman's proposed employment program—as one of a few with strong ties to rival union leaders, as one of NCPAC's major fund-raisers and political advisers, and as the author of a nationally syndicated political column.[38]

If Truman seemed inhibited by the three hats that ER wore as a defender of labor, why did ER wait until November to capitalize on this and confront him on the full employment issue? Was it her "customary deference" and politeness that tempered her conduct as some historians argue or was it her stubborn pride? Did she initially refrain from challenging Truman because she knew she could not get the response she wanted? In a word, no.

ER waited until the last minute to lecture Truman on his political obligations because she wished to see what kind of leader he would become once he adjusted to his new responsibilities. And, sensitive to her new, as yet undefined status, and fearful of undermining her own influence within his administration, she struggled to keep both her impatience and her condescension in check. Only when it became clear to her that the damage the party was suffering might persist through the 1946 and 1948 elections did ER treat Truman like she had FDR. This does not mean, however, that the Democratic party as a political institution was more important to ER than the political principles for which it stood. Rather, it implies that she inextricably linked party politics and political change. If the party suffered, ER believed that reform would die; and she had vowed not to let that happen.

Since the summer of 1944, ER worried that the coalition of minority groups, labor, farmers, urban workers, and women, which both she and FDR had struggled to assemble throughout the 1930s, would unravel as Democratic leadership moved toward an "unholy coalition of Southern Democrats and Northern Republicans." As FDR's intermediary, she experienced the frustration labor and blacks felt when FDR had refused to make domestic issues a priority. This experience also enabled her to recognize how much labor and black support for the party was tied to their personal devotion to FDR. She knew that Truman commanded no such loyalty and ER feared that without swift action to enhance his standing within these constituencies the coalition would succumb to infighting, eventually dissolve, and weaken the party.[39]

To offset this, ER reminded DNC chair Robert Hannegan that labor and people of color would not automatically vote Democratic and that their votes were vital to Democratic victories. Although she carefully couched her analysis as her understanding of the problems confronting New York State, by the end of this three-page letter she argued that the principles necessary for a victory in her home state were also essential to a national victory. She had "been thinking a good deal about the political situation" and had come to a few conclusions about actions the party must take to win in 1948. First, Dewey must be defeated in his 1946 bid for reelection as governor of New York. Second, to win in 1948, Democrats must win the 1946 elections so that conservatives within Congress would not be allowed to dictate reconversion policy. Finally, Democrats should do all they could to prevent a third party from forming by "build[ing] up the Democratic party organization throughout the country."[40]

This goal could not be reached, ER wrote, unless minority groups, labor, veterans, and women actively supported the party's efforts. Otherwise, she worried, disgruntled Democrats would either vote Republican or form a third party. "We may lose a certain number of people to that party who would ordinarily be Democrats," she warned Hannegan, "but who want to serve notice that there is one issue on which they will vote with the party which they consider is doing the right thing on that issue." While she knew "of course" that a third party "will not win," she also recognized that "it will defeat the Democratic party because we know that the Democratic party can not win unless it has the liberal vote *and* some liberal Republican elements voting with it." ER sent a copy of the letter to Truman. Three days later, the president met with her to discuss it.[41]

Despite his denials, ER realized Truman had wavered from the position he had shared with her on full employment. She hoped, however, that she could force his cooperation by appealing both to his position as party leader and his heritage as a machine politician. She delayed her rebuke because she first tried to mobilize other "professional politicians" to guide the president. When this did not work, she took her case to the people directly through "My Day." Only when it appeared that all other avenues to Truman were closed, only when she saw direct intervention as a last resort, did she revert to tactics she had relied on when she had been first lady. As she told the president earlier that year when she first gave him advice, she did so "out of genuine interest in the Administration and in the party, and above everything else, out of interest in the country."[42]

If full employment was the major item promoted by liberal organizations and politicians, then the passage of the Employment Act of 1946 was not a major liberal accomplishment, as some historians argue, but, rather, the first step in liberalism's interminable decline. This does not imply that compromise legislation is automatically anti-liberal, but rather that the actions of both congressional and administration leaders reflected their decision that there were other more pressing economic issues that they must confront. Eleanor Roosevelt was the exception to this rule. Although she recognized that compromise was a political necessity, she also recognized the political value of a good fight. Full employment was central to her vision of the government's economic responsibility. However, her study of Reuther's plan for a Peace Production Board and her meetings with wartime consumer groups opposed to Office of Production Management policies convinced her that it was not the panacea for all the reconversion woes the nation faced. Rather, full employment was a vehicle through which the government could enact the other economic proposals she championed: wage and price controls and fair employment practices.[43]

■ **"I wonder whether our greed makes it impossible for us."**
Truman, Bowles, and Wage and Price Controls

If liberals pinned a great deal of their hope on the passage of the Murray-Wagner Full Employment bill, conservatives mounted an all-out effort to overturn price control policies. To most Republicans, the National Association of Manufacturers, and the American Farm Bureau Federation, price controls represented "creeping socialism." Just as anti-liberal members of the Manasco Committee united to purge the Reconstruction Finance Corporation from the Department of Commerce, Senator Robert Taft and his supporters on the Senate Banking and Currency Committee vowed, first, to end price controls and limit wage increases or if that proved impossible, second, to undercut the OPA and the Office of Economic Stabilization's power to determine and enforce these controls. American workers, union and nonunion, agricultural and industrial, were caught in the middle of this political fray.[44]

Chester Bowles, whom Truman promoted to director of the Office of Economic Stabilization, was the point man on wage and price control policy for administration liberals. The initial architect of FDR's "Second Bill of Rights" speech, Bowles had looked to ER for career guidance and political advice throughout the late thirties and early forties. Their collaboration continued once Bowles joined Roosevelt's Office of Price Administration in mid-1943. Consequently, when Truman assumed the presidency and seemed to vacillate on wage and price control policy, Bowles naturally continued to seek ER's counsel.[45]

While the Truman administration struggled to devise a compromise employment bill, it also tried to control inflation by holding the line on prices. Implementing this economic measure proved even more irritating to the administration than the full employment bill because the issue of price and wage controls genuinely provoked both labor and industrial leaders. From the fall of 1945 until he abolished controls after the November 1946 election, Truman's actions on price and wage control policy proved to be even more inconsistent than his full employment stance. Yet on this matter, unlike the situation concerning employment legislation, he made no efforts to conceal his intent. Here he was simply torn between following Chester Bowles's economic recommendations or John Snyder's political advice. When the winter of 1945–1946 brought a rush of industrial strikes and a meat shortage, tensions reached new heights and the battle between what John Morton Blum labeled "the politics of comfort" and "the politics of resentment" became more intense.[46]

Like those of his colleague Wallace, Bowles's policies stemmed from his belief that increases in consumer spending were vital to a full employment economy. With overtime pay eliminated as the war drew to a close, and with veterans returning to claim jobs the war had opened to women, minorities, and other replacement workers, salaries must be increased to spur consumer spending. Bowles believed that price inflation was the major domestic crisis facing the nation and that the reduction in spending that the Committee on Economic Development proposed would increase infla-

tion, not control it. The economy could grow if it were managed scientifi-
cally and the government continued to expend the "radical energy and
investment that had been necessary to open up the West and the South and
to build mushrooming new cities."[47]

The economy had neither "matured" nor leveled off. Although the war
had guaranteed buyers for defense goods, the postwar world—if properly
managed—could provide the same market assurance. Bowles argued that
if price controls remained in place on specific goods, the policy would
increase consumer spending, which would prompt increased production
which, in turn, would begin "to free most families from economic want."
If the government, at all levels, "assumed a new, dynamic role, even those
most fearful of change would begin to see that the problems of racism,
poverty, housing, and ill-health could now be solved on a scale never
before imagined." Consequently, tomorrow must be faced "without
fear."[48]

If Wallace was the thinker ER most admired, Bowles was the administrator with the practical and political expertise necessary to draft policy and
guide its implementation. As moved as she was by Wallace's vision of "the
century of the common man," ER recognized that exceptional political
finesse would be needed to move the country and the Congress to endorse
the programs she deemed necessary to enter the new era. As far back as 1938,
ER had seen Bowles as a young man destined for politics. His actions in the
OPA and Office of Economic Stabilization only reaffirmed her initial assessment. Thus, although once again Eleanor Roosevelt waited to intervene
until she was asked to do so, by the winter of 1945 she was in the thick of
the battle to mobilize public support for Bowles's policies.

By mid-November, the administration lifted price controls from the
construction industry and failed to arbitrate the UAW-General Motors dispute. The White House summit on labor-industrial relations ended in a
stalemate. Industry, represented by automobile manufacturers, refused to
raise wages unless prices could be raised as well. Republicans seized the
political initiative in Congress and argued that price controls were intended
not to benefit the consumer, but to control profits and thereby redistribute
income. Succumbing to criticism from labor, industry, and anti-control
advocates within his own party, the president asserted in his October wage
and price message that "we must get away from controls." Yet fearing the
damage to the Democratic coalition that a disgruntled union movement
could induce, Truman tried to appease both sides by issuing an executive
order authorizing "three classes of cases in which wage increases may be
granted even though price increases may result." Unable to decide between

John Snyder's political advice and Bowles's policy recommendations, Truman tried to play both ends against the middle.[49]

As ER worked closely with Reuther on full employment, FEPC, and UDA issues, it is logical to assume that their discussion included wage and price control topics as well. In addition to the direct communications between them, Joseph Lash, then director of the UDA's New York Office, often acted as Reuther's intermediary. Consequently, when the administration failed to broker its first labor-management dispute over wage increases, ER not only had the labor contacts to determine what would be acceptable to the union but she also had the contacts within the administration to whom some settlement advice should be offered. "The suggestion that was made the other day that a survey of our natural resources be made," she wrote the president November 20 (the day before Reuther called for a strike against General Motors), " . . . would seem to me sound, if the person making the investigation had sufficient standing to be accepted by management and labor as well." Deftly steering Truman away from appointing a "crony," ER invoked FDR's legacy and promoted Bernard Baruch as survey administrator. The millionaire's standing with industry was impeccable and, in addition, she believed "that even the young labor leaders, like Walter Reuther and James Carey, believe in his integrity." If handled immediately and sensitively, such an appointment would delay a strike in Detroit and give "both management and labor something so they would at least agree to work until, let us say, next October."[50]

Trying a different approach from the one she used with the full employment proposals, she spoke to the president before she approached the media. As ER once again reminded Truman, "I have a deep sense that we have an obligation first of all to solve our problems at home." However, when he rejected her advice, she took her case to the people. The day after Truman went to Congress to request permission to appoint an arbitration panel, ER devoted the entire "My Day" column to warn against such precedent-setting practices. "The unions offered to arbitrate but the management apparently did not object to the strike," she told her readers. Why should management object when it is the workers who suffer most? In a ringing defense of labor and a not too subtle rebuke of the administration, she argued that "we had better remember that the gains of organized labor have been eventually the gains of all workers." This was a clear case of workers standing up against "the very great powers in the hand of industrial associations and organizations." The administration should only impose an agreement with which the "two parties in the present struggle" agree. Any attempt "to impose" a solution without "that agreement," she concluded, was not only an act of "tyranny" but also "an abrogation of fundamental rights which eventually would do harm to every citizen."[51]

Three days later ER directly linked the UAW strike and the proposed steel strike to the issue of price controls. Chastising management for viewing a "strike" as a way to avoid discussing the issue, she argued that most "management seems to be trying to bring about less strong workers' organizations and a lower labor cost." However, not all industrial leaders suffered from such tunnel vision. If the Ford Motor Company were indeed to adopt a fair annual, rather than hourly, wage for its employees, this would link higher profits to higher production and "might lead to some really revolutionary thinking" within management.[52]

Chester Bowles shared ER's opposition to Truman's wage and price efforts. Like ER, he objected to Truman's plan to amend the Railway Labor Act and decided to confront the president directly over his inability to follow a consistent policy. In exchange for his remaining in the Office of Economic Stabilization until the following summer when the Price Controls Act was scheduled to expire, Bowles asked Truman for action on several internal fronts. The administration had to decide who determined price control policy, himself or Snyder; Truman had to pressure more members of the administration to speak out on this issue so that the public could see a "team effort" supporting price controls; and the president must issue an "emphatic statement" on extending price and rent controls after the June 30, 1946, deadline. In sum, Bowles no longer wanted to be Truman's "lone wolf" on this issue.[53]

By January 20, 1946, the 320,000 striking UAW members were joined by 750,000 steelworkers, almost 200,000 meatpackers, and more than 200,000 electrical workers. The country seemed susceptible to an epidemic of strikes unless a manageable wage-price policy could be instituted. When Truman proved unable to present a consistent policy either to the steelworkers or to their employers, Bowles's frustration reached new heights. "The fact that we are dealing with vast industries and powerful unions is no reason for a retreat or a surrender," he told his superior in late January. Echoing ER's stance, Bowles exhorted Truman to display leadership on this issue. Congress and the public realize that the "government's stabilization policy is not what you stated it to be" and that the president's true policy is "instead one of improvising on a day-to-day, case-by-case basis, as one crisis leads to another." "In short," Bowles concluded, everyone recognized "that there really is no policy at all." He encouraged the president to act quickly because, although "it is not too late to stamp out this belief," time "is rapidly running out."[54]

Truman responded to Bowles's plea by issuing his third directive on wage and price controls, which did nothing more than end the six-month trial period he previously had imposed on manufacturers who wanted to raise prices. Yet even though political expediency and Snyder emerged as victors, Bowles and ER remained undaunted in their pursuits for a coherent policy that would promote economic growth and protect labor without harming industry. When their direct suggestions to the president were ignored, both liberals appealed to the public to pressure Truman to comply with their suggestions. These appeals took different forms. Bowles waited until April when the House, according to one historian, "went on a rampage and mutilated the price-control bill" to launch his public offensive against the National Association of Manufacturers and their congressional supporters. Even then his attack was very specifically focused: the issue, he asserted, was not the concept of price controls but rather what kind of controls would be imposed.[55]

Eleanor Roosevelt responded earlier and with a different approach. Rather than just focusing on the family budget, as Bowles had done, now that she had been appointed to the United States delegation to the United Nations, she linked American economic policies to international perceptions of democracy in general and the United States in particular. "When you are on the continent of Europe," ER wrote that February, "facing the needs of human beings, the dispute over rights and wrongs between American management and labor suddenly falls into perspective." America won the war, not only because of its skill and conviction, but because God wanted it to "give spiritual, moral, and physical leadership to the world." If America buckled under to internal divisiveness and did not provide this guidance, ER feared its selfishness "will boomerang on our own heads." "This is no time for men and women of narrow vision." The world was watching America to see if democracy was a viable alternative to the "trend in the world toward socialism." Consequently, labor, management, and the government needed to look at their actions from "the world point of view" and provide economic leadership that would expand faith in democratic capitalism.[56]

ER's UN position did not always dictate the tone of her column. She continued to cite those "men and women of narrow vision" who undermined reform at home and American prestige abroad. If narrowness persisted, ER warned her readers a month later, fewer goods would be produced, unemployment would increase, and the economy would contract. Although she hoped that both her readers and their leaders had learned the lessons of the Great Depression, she feared that the avarice of powerful trade associations would pressure the government to forget what it had learned from its past mistakes. "[W]hen I see the National Association of Manufacturers demanding that we remove price controls before we are in full production," she fumed, "I wonder whether our greed makes it impossible for us to profit by the lessons of the past." She reiterated this theme a month later in her support of Bowles's April appeal. Certain members of Congress were buckling "under the influence of powerful lobbies" and were "rapidly trying to return control to big business." Such a policy would steer "us straight for inflation." Bowles was doing everything he could "but without the support of the people . . . [he] will be defeated by the people's representatives." Exhorting her readers to more effective action, ER concluded, "write your Representative . . . . Writing to me is of very little use."[57]

As the statutory limitation on price controls neared, her support for the policy increased and, despite her disappointment in Truman's efforts, she tried to balance commitment to her policies against loyalty to the president. When Congress tried to limit Truman's authority to set controls, she attacked "the majority in the House of Representatives . . . [who] thought only of the immediate future." Elected officials have an "obligation to go back to their constituents and tell them how they see a situation whenever they feel that their constituents are not seeing it as they themselves are able to see it Washington." Just as she rebuked Truman for reacting to criticism rather than setting policy, she attacked Congress for following the polls to determine their votes. Politicians should not only reflect public sentiment but also lead their constituents to reconsider policy when they believe strongly that the policy is necessary. Consequently, when Truman vetoed the Price Control Act (HR 6042) because it did not do enough to stabilize the economy, ER finally had reason to praise the president's price control efforts.[58]

By taking such actions, by mid-summer 1946 the Truman administration entered its most perilous period, a time that historian Herbert Parmet has labeled the "Crisis of the New Order." When the obstreperous president of the United Mine Workers, John L. Lewis, called his union out on strike because the mine owners refused to establish a health and welfare fund, Truman requested congressional approval to seize the mines and place them under government operation. When the Railroad Trainmen and Locomotive Engineers brotherhood strike paralyzed the rails, Truman went to Congress a second time and asked for power to draft the strikers into the army. Such actions increased skepticism among the president's liberal critics. By the end of July, they no longer viewed the president as inactive and indecisive, but as an activist for the opposition.[59]

Once again Eleanor Roosevelt searched for a way to support both labor and the administration. The day after the railway strike began, she wrote "I do not blame labor itself, but the leadership in industry and, to some extent, in labor [unions] . . . ." However, as the administration assumed an increasingly hostile position toward labor, ER's allegiance waned. When Truman threatened railway workers rather than brotherhood leaders, she could no longer support him. While she privately cautioned the president against "slip[ping] into a military way of thinking," she still worried that he would act impulsively. "I hope that now you will not insist upon a peace-time draft . . . of the strikers. That seems to me a dangerous precedent." Nor could she keep the bitterness completely out of her column. "Dictators of all varieties must chuckle these days," she ruefully wrote on the day of Truman's draft request, "for certainly the great self-governing democracy is not functioning very smoothly."[60]

■ "We cannot out conserve the Republicans." Truman, Wallace, and the Election of 1948

By late summer 1946, tensions between Truman and ER had reached their zenith. Although the president had appointed her to the American delegation to the United Nations and struggled to keep her as one of the focal points of his administration, her support was far from certain. She held his two most controversial administrators, Chester Bowles and Henry Wallace, in higher esteem than she held him and she had not refrained from criticizing the president in private or questioning his policies in public. However, by the time Truman needed her endorsement for his reelection in October 1948, ER reluctantly complied with his request and in the process rejected Wallace, the man she once urged to lead the progressives into action.

Why ER reached such a decision is another issue that historians treat superficially. Some argue, with James MacGregor Burns, that she supported Truman merely because he was the party's nominee and Wallace had come too much under the control of left liberal factions to be an effective leader. Others agree with Joseph Lash that ER supported Truman as part of a general Americans for Democratic Action (ADA) "get-out-the-vote" drive to protect the congressional liberals facing reelection. Regardless of their interpretations, all analysts of ER's role in the 1948 election point to a single motivation as prompting her response rather than interpreting her endorsement as an outgrowth of the frustration she experienced both with the Democratic party leadership and with the liberal interest groups.[61]

Eleanor Roosevelt supported Truman's reelection efforts belatedly and without enthusiasm—not because Wallace appeared to be led by forces he could not control, but because there was no other way she could continue to support the policies she had promoted throughout Truman's first term. ER was not blind to his weaknesses nor did she think that he was the best candidate to promote the policies she advocated. Certainly she did not value her seat in the United Nations more than the outcome of the presidential election. Indeed, earlier than other political liberals within and without the Democratic party, she recognized "a crisis of the New Order" and worked to offset the damage it would inflict on liberalism in general and the Democratic party in particular.

As younger progressives aligned themselves against communism and promoted the consensus of "the vital center," Eleanor Roosevelt struggled to reconcile her belief in political diversity and cultural freedom with her commitment to achieving liberal reform in the Cold War climate. Rather than succumb to a fear of internal communist encroachment or embrace a policy of blanket American-Soviet cooperation, she struggled to achieve as much reform as possible within an anti-reform climate. When Lash decried "the reversion to type" by the Democratic party and implied that a new party might be necessary to challenge the backsliding Democrats, she agreed that new alignments were necessary. "I would still be opposed to a third party, but in the end you are right and I think we must have a *new* party, not necessarily a 3rd party." When Fiorello La Guardia tried to recruit her support for an alternative party, her refusal was even more blunt. "It takes so long before a third party wields any power," she told New York's mayor, a Republican who had won election on an anti-Tammany Hall "Fusion" ticket. "I can not see much point in trying to build up one at the present time when things need to be done quickly."[62]

She applied the same standards to those who demanded that she participate in the system in a more direct way. Weighing her options, she rejected calls for her own candidacy and instead issued challenges to party officials, members of Congress, and liberal activists to view reform as both morally necessary and politically expedient. This could not be achieved unless the American public and political leaders tolerated dissent and promoted free discussion. For example, if Wallace wanted to defend his Communist party supporters, that was his right; but it was not politically or morally acceptable for him to be heckled, interrupted, and threatened for this position. Furthermore, unlike other liberals active in the late 1940s, Eleanor Roosevelt did not view the economic and international issues confronting America as an "either/or" proposition. Although she endorsed full employment and price control legislation as solutions to the major economic problem facing postwar America, she did not believe that there was one specific approach to democratic reform. Nor did she think one issue should serve as an economic litmus test for liberals. Rather the question was the framework in which the problems confronting America were examined.[63]

Three events in 1946 pushed ER further into the Truman camp. The first occurred when the American voters defeated liberal Democrats and sent increasing numbers of conservatives to Congress, both houses of which would now be controlled by the Republicans. The second occurred when the voters of New York reelected Thomas Dewey governor by a wide margin and thereby made him once again the likely Republican presidential nominee in 1948. Finally, when Wallace refused to moderate the pressure he placed on Truman to develop a more cooperative relationship with the Soviet Union, liberals who had escaped these first two electoral challenges became more susceptible to defeat.[64]

While Eleanor Roosevelt did not support the brashness with which Truman addressed Soviet policy, neither did she support Wallace's pleas for unquestioning cooperation. As Wallace increasingly made his foreign policy criticisms in public forums, his relationship with his former mentor deteriorated. Whereas only months before she had pleaded with the secretary of commerce to leave the administration and develop a liberal policy group that would help chart the future direction of the Democratic party, by September 1946, ER saw Wallace caught in political whirlwinds he could not control. Although she initially tried to defend his Madison Square Garden "spheres of influence speech" in her column, by the end of the week, as Wallace continued to speak out forcefully rather than try to argue his case privately within the administration, ER reluctantly tried to limit the damage this public battle was inflicting on the secretary, the president, and American foreign policy. "The basic thing to be held in mind," she argued, "is that we want peace and that it cannot exist if the United States and Russia do not find a way to live together." Searching for a way to promote common ground within the administration, she concluded, "that is the basis of Secretary Wallace's whole thesis and also the basis of the President's and of Secretary of State Byrnes's policy."[65]

When Wallace refused to curb his pronouncements even though Truman had requested his resignation, and continued to act in ways that ER viewed as politically naive and damaging to the liberal agenda, ER's respect for him diminished. Thus, by January 1947, while she denied that she and Wallace "were at odds" she nonetheless admitted her disappointment. "I have always believed in Mr. Wallace's integrity and admired his ability, but that does not mean that you agree in the way in which you wish to work for your objectives."[66]

Eleanor Roosevelt entered 1947 fearing for the future of the liberal wing of the Democratic party and worrying that vital center Democrats had confused liberalism with anti-communism. Chester Bowles left the administration when Congress abolished his department. Henry Wallace resigned in conflict with the president over his foreign policy, refused to moderate his stance and join the ADA, and formed his own political action organization, the Progressive Citizens of America. With the moderating presence of Wallace and Bowles removed from his Cabinet meetings, the president increasingly appeared to devote most of his energy to promoting a remarkably harsh Cold War foreign policy. Furthermore, throughout 1946, domestic reform seemed to attract the president's attention only when events reached a crisis, and Truman's actions in 1947 reflected this earlier pattern.

Spring and summer of 1947 saw the president introduce the Truman Doctrine, a stringent loyalty program, and an ineffective campaign to prevent the adoption of the Taft-Hartley anti-union legislation. Once again, Eleanor Roosevelt was compelled to warn him that the Democrats cannot "out conserve the Republicans." When Truman recommended the conservative former Secretary of Agriculture Clinton Anderson, an ardent foe of Wallace and Bowles's efforts to promote full employment and price control policy, to replace Hannegan as chair of the Democratic National Committee, ER launched a one-woman campaign to block Anderson's appointment. Once again, she bluntly informed the chief executive, "we cannot be more conservative than the Republicans so we cannot succeed as conservatives." Predicting losses in the 1948 election as a result of the nomination, ER finally seized Truman's attention. Concerned, Truman dropped Anderson from consideration and appointed Rhode Island Senator J. Howard McGrath to the DNC leadership position. Still solicitous of ER's support, the president cautiously wrote her before he announced the appointment, "I hope you approve of Senator McGrath."[67]

With such tension evident between the president and his ambassador to the United Nations, Truman's hopes for ER's active participation in his reelection campaign were slight. Yet not all the actions Truman undertook between mid-1947 and his reelection displeased ER. She praised his promotion of the Marshall Plan and diligently lobbied for its support within the UN. And when Truman finally recognized the need for a Jewish home-

land and endorsed the UN resolution calling for an Israeli state, she strongly
endorsed his decision and refrained from acknowledging that it had taken
her very biting letter threatening resignation to force the president to act.
Despite these concessions in foreign affairs, however, Truman ultimately
earned ER's endorsement by his boldness on the domestic issues she had so
persistently promoted throughout her days in the Roosevelt and Truman
administrations: fair employment and civil rights.[68]

While ER praised Truman's efforts in 1945 to promote the Fair Deal and
his summoning Congress into special session in mid-1948, she reserved her
highest praise for his civil rights initiatives. When Truman vetoed the measure placing the U.S. Employment Service under state supervision, she
declared that this "impressed [her] not only as a courageous action but as
showing a real understanding of the procedure which should govern legislation." Procedures and methods by which a program was administered
controlled the program's policy and the president's actions, ER continued,
"demonstrated his . . . grasp of the human situation involved." She had also
studied the report issued by his Commission on Civil Rights and "thought
it very good."[69]

When, reversing previous decisions, Truman accepted the invitation of
the NAACP to address its 1947 annual convention, ER not only extolled the
moral courage of his action but also predicted realistic political gains from
his appearance. She suggested to her "My Day" readership that his appearance at the Lincoln Memorial could be the most constructive, as well as the
most symbolic, civil rights act of his presidency. As she listened to his
speech, she "looked out over the sea of faces below us and thought how significant this meeting before the Lincoln Memorial must be to most of the
people there."Although Lincoln had abolished slavery eighty years earlier,
he had not been able to remove "the bitterness of inferiority" that accompanied emancipation. "Now," she declared, "we were gathered here to try
to really accomplish the ends which he envisioned but could not accomplish." Truman's "fearlessly spoken" speech "should give hope that tangible
strides towards the fulfillment of" this vision of equality "can now be
taken." She felt "very proud" of Truman and believed his courage made
"our country . . . stronger."[70]

When the president introduced his civil rights package to Congress in a
special address the following February, ER's faith in his commitment
appeared justified. Although less than a month earlier she had worried that
the issues introduced in his State of the Union Address might not be aggressively pursued, this special message eased her doubts. Asserting that "there
is a serious gap between our ideals and some of our practices . . . [which]

must be closed," Truman informed Congress that "the federal government has a clear duty to see that constitutional guarantees of individual liberties and of equal protection under the law are not denied or are abridged anywhere in America." He then presented a ten-point civil rights program, which not only clarified his intentions, but also adhered strongly to the programs that ER had championed throughout the thirties and forties: a permanent FEPC, anti-lynching legislation, the establishment of a Civil Rights Division within the Department of Justice, and an increasingly vigilant protection of the vote.[71]

Just as she praised the president for his stance, she rebuked his critics for theirs. She did not hesitate to criticize those Democratic politicians who boycotted the Washington, D.C., Jefferson-Jackson Day dinner to express their displeasure at the supportive reception Truman gave to the report of his Civil Rights Commission, *To Secure These Rights.* Although she acknowledged that "some things must be done more slowly in some places than in others," ER chastised those Democrats who feared political repercussions and lamented that those who opposed racial reform were "beyond [her] understanding." Consequently when the party adopted a strong civil rights plank at its 1948 presidential convention, she hailed it as a "step toward greatness."[72]

The Democratic party finally seemed to be moving away from Republican conservatism. However, ER still worried that the major influences on party policy were the moderate stances of Republican candidates Thomas Dewey and Earl Warren rather than liberal political ideals and pragmatic Democratic politics. When her sons Franklin, Jr., and Elliott promoted Dwight Eisenhower as the possible Democratic nominee in 1948, she refused to support them. The general was a political unknown, she reasoned, and the party needed a leader who would stick to the principles its liberal membership had struggled so to introduce into public debate. When Americans for Democratic Action circulated a thirty-four-page harangue against Wallace in April 1948 and quoted Roosevelt family and associates to refute Wallace's claim that he was FDR's only true heir, ER, while supportive of ADA's general principles, declined to endorse the diatribe. By the convention, Eleanor Roosevelt begrudgingly acknowledged that the chances for a liberal victory were, at best, remote. "The Republican ticket is a strong one and I feel Eisenhower will not be drafted," she wrote David Gurewitsch that summer. Dejectedly, she concluded, that although the president would be renominated, "I don't think Truman can win against it." Plus, she expected an orchestrated "reaction as far as they dare" to the reforms she most supported.[73]

Although ER had confided to journalist May Craig earlier in the spring that she had not yet "made up [her] mind" as to which presidential candidate she would support, by late October, ER clearly placed her support behind Truman. Yet this was a very belated endorsement and one which was shrouded in innuendo. Her previous references to the election referred primarily to the need to prevent another conservative conclave on Capitol Hill. "What seems to [me] far more important," she told her readers in August, "[is] the record of the Congress." Party affiliation was not just electing a leader, but promoting policy. By endorsing a Democratic president, a voter is also casting a ballot against "a new party with a very old and assured record of conservatism." Although the candidate's individual record as a liberal is important, a record alone cannot set policy. The candidate "deserves to be able to carry out the things he believes in." Consequently, the voter "must elect Democrats all the way up and down the board." Yet despite her repeated and impassioned references to party leadership and political fidelity, she never mentioned the president by name. Nor did ER name Truman in subsequent columns in which she announced her support for gubernatorial and mayoral candidates.[74]

Such omission caused the political rumor mills to work overtime. When the nationally syndicated columnist Drew Pearson speculated that ER was silent because she was really for Dewey, public curiosity about ER's intentions peaked. Recalling Clark Clifford's admonition that "the 'right' may have the money, but the 'left' has always had the pen," Truman requested that she refute Pearson's claim. When Frances Perkins heard the Pearson allegation, she immediately telephoned ER in Paris to request that she specifically endorse Truman. ER complied with her friend's request, yet felt compelled to explain her position once again.

She had not endorsed Truman earlier "because he has been such a weak and vacillating person and made such poor appointments in Congress." Furthermore, "unless we are successful in electing a very strong group of liberals in Congress, in spite of my feelings for the Republican party and Governor Dewey, I cannot have much enthusiasm for Mr. Truman." She needed "good reasons" for an endorsement and she found those "very difficult" to discover. However, she agreed with Perkins's assessment of the situation. "I am [endorsing Truman] because . . . if we go down to defeat, we probably should go down having done what we could for the candidate and we should try for a good vote."[75]

Consequently, with the press debating an ER defection, and with her unyielding commitment to liberal reform, she had no choice but to state her position in a clear and forthright manner. "I am unqualifiedly for you as the Democratic candidate for the Presidency," she telegraphed the president. Continuing on the themes she had introduced earlier, she repeated her conviction that "a Democratic administration, backed by a liberal Democratic Congress, could really achieve the policies for which you have stood." Once Truman had her endorsement and her permission to release it, he had no choice but to promote it as widely as possible, so, as soon as he received her statement, the president wired her requesting permission to circulate it, even though he was angry that "she had to be dragged kicking and screaming into the campaign."[76]

Eleanor Roosevelt did not expect her endorsement to sway the election. She fully believed that she had done all she could to mobilize support for the party and to keep disgruntled liberals in line. She had criticized Wallace's platform and endorsed liberal Democratic state and local officials in "My Day" columns, and while acknowledging Truman's shortcomings promoted his reelection. These actions did stop the damage her silence might have caused among undecided voters. As TRB editorialized in *The New Republic* the week after the election, "Harry Truman won the election because FDR had worked so well." Clearly, Eleanor Roosevelt was an instrumental part of the public's association of Truman with FDR. Yet this does not mean that ER saw Truman in the same light. She still yearned for a "realignment of all the liberals in the Democratic party," but she was astute enough to appreciate that "at present they are hopelessly scrambled." To ER, Truman was the best possible candidate under the existing circumstances. Therefore, while she criticized his performance on economic issues, she could praise his efforts to promote fair employment practices. While she objected to the Truman Doctrine and the president's enthusiastic endorsement of Churchill's 1946 "Iron Curtain" speech, which the former prime minister delivered in Truman's home state, she could ardently support the Marshall Plan. Finally, while she could question his ability to inspire bold congressional initiatives, she trusted his commitment to legislation designed to promote racial justice.[77]

In short, Eleanor Roosevelt supported the Democratic party in spite of its leaders' half-hearted efforts in behalf of liberal reform because after careful deliberation she concluded that it was the best vehicle through which to achieve the domestic reforms she most earnestly advocated. While the personal convictions of its leaders were important to her, she struggled against replacing political realism with political ideology. Full employment, price controls, fair employment practices, and civil rights programs were the means to implement ideology. What ER understood better than most liberals was that this program needed a strong element of political pragmatism, party loyalty, and moral vision. While she did not always act immediately to direct party action, she nevertheless acted tirelessly as an unflinching observer and articulate reporter of party conduct.

Perhaps most important, when she entered the fray, Eleanor Roosevelt strove to do so in ways that would promote political agendas rather than political personages. Ironically, those leaders who courted her endorsement most assiduously often failed to understand either her motivations or her connections. Often the Democratic leadership failed to appreciate the degree of her political expertise, her ability to mobilize public support, and her network among various political factions. They were content to rely on her devotion to FDR's legacy rather than examine the positions and influence she had achieved in her own right. Consequently, as they struggled to create their agenda and, later, to implement their program, both Harry Truman and Henry Wallace recognized that they had underestimated their need for Eleanor Roosevelt's public and private support and liberals found themselves cornered in the vital center.

■

Chapter Four

CHAMPIONING CIVIL RIGHTS
From Patience to Protest

If Democratic leadership recruited Eleanor Roosevelt's endorsements and political advice half-heartedly, the leadership of the civil rights community did so enthusiastically. From the earliest days of the New Deal through the tumultuous events of the Freedom Rides and Freedom Schools of the early 1960s, civil rights advocates, demonstrators, and lobbyists constantly solicited her support for their respective agendas. In fact, ER's commitment to racial justice was both so public and so routine that her name became synonymous with early demands for civil rights.

Yet Eleanor Roosevelt was not always a champion of civil rights. For most of her life, she counseled moderation to those activists who attacked the system instead of the mentality behind it. However, once aroused to the racial abuses blacks suffered at the hands of American democracy, ER increasingly confronted this undemocratic behavior and called it by its rightful name. As she continued to grow as an individual, her insight into this "American dilemma" increased. No other noted white American of her stature spoke out so consistently, so eloquently, and so brazenly on this issue or encountered such vicious public ridicule for this stand than Eleanor Roosevelt. Consequently, by the time of her death in late 1962, Martin

Luther King, Jr., could write, "The courage she displayed in taking sides of matters considered controversial, gave strength to those who risked only pedestrian loyalty and commitment to the great issues of our times."[1]

ER did not always agree with civil rights activists or endorse their tactics. However, throughout the thirties, forties, fifties, and early sixties, black activists trusted her commitment to racial equality, her financial support to civil rights organizations, and her outspoken and honest responses to their questions and tactics. Whether campaigning against the poll tax; helping to found the Southern Conference for Human Welfare (SCHW); championing integrated housing; serving on the NAACP national board of directors; chairing the National Committee for Justice in Columbia, Tennessee; endorsing the Southern Conference Education Fund (SCEF); facilitating Democratic party platform disputes; lobbying for federal civil rights statutes; supporting the black students of Little Rock's Central High School; or decrying the violence Freedom Riders encountered in Alabama and Mississippi, ER steadily acted out her convictions and challenged others to do the same.

To reach this position, Eleanor Roosevelt took a course fraught with limitations, personal struggles, and political constraints. Yet once she reached a decision, she acted despite the consequences. Sometimes a public injustice prompted a response. At other times, appeals from unknown individuals spurred her into action behind the scenes. At still other times, she responded to a request from black leaders to investigate a specific situation or intervene on behalf of an individual unjustly treated. Consequently, some historians view ER's civil rights legacy as a melange of highly emotional, uncoordinated responses to public injustice rather than as an integral part of a multifaceted approach to political action.[2]

Such cursory assessment misses the point. ER's overt commitment to racial justice bespoke not a sporadic response of conscience but an unwavering allegiance to democratic principles. She believed wholeheartedly that a democracy must be inclusive and protect minority rights and insure safe, peaceful protest or it ceased to be democratic. Moreover, as she aged, she came to see democracy in broader terms. Consequently, she could learn to transcend to a remarkable degree most of the limits of her old progressive heritage, ultimately placing less emphasis on working patiently within the system and more on forcing the system to be accountable. Repeatedly she urged minorities, especially black Americans, to be "dynamic" in their drive for freedom. Passive acceptance of unjust social norms was amoral. "Staying aloof is not a solution," she declared in *Tomorrow Is Now*. "[I]t is a cowardly evasion."[3]

ER's consistent response in the face of constant extraordinary criticism indicates the depth of her commitment. Of all the controversial people and policies Eleanor Roosevelt promoted throughout her life, none generated a response equal to that provoked by her support of civil rights policies at home and abroad. In fact, she was so closely associated with the movement for racial justice that the almost 4,000-page dossier the FBI kept on her is filled with references to her civil rights activities and the outrage it generated among her detractors. Rumors spread throughout the thirties and forties reflected this connection. J. Edgar Hoover, director of the FBI, even speculated that "Negro blood" inspired ER's perverse behavior. Other Americans suspected this as well. "I don't mean to be rude," a woman wrote to ER as part of her monthly "If You Ask Me" column, "but do you have colored blood in your family, as you seem to derive so much pleasure from associating with colored folks?"[4]

Nor were the insinuations limited to ER's racial heritage. Just as frequently she was accused of aggressively inciting blacks to challenge southern customs. Rumors that she actively encouraged southern black domestics to form Eleanor Clubs to counteract their exploitative working conditions were so widespread that the news media treated them as fact. When this rumor refused to subside, ER ultimately asked the FBI if any such associations existed. Despite bureau affidavits denying the existence of the clubs, many Americans continued to believe in them and refused to view her civil rights actions more dispassionately.[5]

All this suspicion failed to moderate ER's positions. On the contrary, her unwavering resolution underscored the depth of her commitment to economic and political equality for black Americans. As she wrote Missouri Governor Lloyd C. Stark, when he complained about the "severe" treatment he had received for his inclusive sharecropper policies, "I am sorry you are being attacked, but the negro sharecroppers have such a big stake in this problem that they have to be included. All of us have to take this kind of criticism." Moreover, she held private citizens to the same standards she set for public leaders. When Evans C. Johnson, of Langdale, Alabama, wrote her criticizing "her extremism on the race question" and declaring that "the extremity of her position was embarrassing to Southern liberals," he received a "paragraph by paragraph answer [that] pretty well cut me down to size."[6]

"I am not letting my ideals . . . blind me to the facts," her two-paged, single-spaced response began, but "I am afraid that many people are letting their prejudice blind them to the real facts." Americans must face "certain fundamentals" if the nation is to continue as a world power. The nation must recognize that the "unrest among the colored people is part of the world revolution of all colored peoples against the domination of white people." Southern blacks, especially "those who have had an opportunity to obtain an education, know that they have never been given their rights as citizens of the United States." Moreover, they "are drafted into the Army and expected to fight for a country which denies them the rights guaranteed to every citizen in our Constitution." This is democracy in its most shameful form.

Furthermore, Johnson's fear that democracy would promote racial violence could not have been further from the truth. Riots will happen "*unless* we refuse to grant four fundamental rights: the right to an education according to ability; the right to earn a living according to ability; the right to equal justice before the law and the right to participate in Government through the ballot." As for his claim that she was too far ahead of southern liberals, ER tersely replied that the liberals should realize how condescending their benevolent stand was. "No one, certainly not I, is trying to reform any one either over night or in any way." And while she knew that "the majority of white people in the South have been kind and benevolent to the colored people," these whites also need to recognize that chivalry was no substitute for equality. Blacks were "human beings brought to this country against their will, and as such, entitled to the same rights as we accord aliens who become citizens."[7]

■ "No one can claim that the Negroes of this country are free." Black Americans and the Home Front

ER's convictions led Swedish sociologist Gunnar Myrdal to place her among the first Americans he wanted to interview for his study of American race relations, *An American Dilemma.* The responses she gave to Ralph Bunche, the political scientist assisting Myrdal, clearly indicate that by the outbreak of World War II, ER still believed that solving the nation's economic troubles was essential to easing its racial tensions. If America could defeat the Depression and Hitler, racism would no longer be as pervasive or as vicious. Class, she told Bunche, was a dangerous distinction because it gave Americans an avenue through which to accentuate racial differences. When people no longer competed for scarce resources and the government assumed its responsibility to assure a basic quality of life for its citizens, ER, in true progressive fashion, initially assumed that such a calm environment would promote tranquil race relations.

Throughout the 1940s ER emphasized economic opportunity as a key component of racial justice. Yet she also recognized that personal beliefs increasingly played an important role in directing American racism and argued that American hypocrisy must be confronted boldly. The country was extremely "guilty of writing and speaking about democracy and the American way without consideration of the imperfections within our system with regard to its treatment . . . of the Negro." Americans, she informed Bunche, wanted to talk "only about the good features of American life and to hide our problems like skeletons in the closet." Such denial only fueled violent response; Americans must therefore recognize "the real intensity of feeling" and "the amount of intimidation and terrorization" racism promotes and act against such "ridiculous" behavior. This conviction led Ralph Bunche to report to Gunnar Myrdal, "I do not believe I have interviewed anyone about whose sincerity I am more impressed."[8]

As World War II approached Eleanor Roosevelt firmly believed the civil rights issue to be the real litmus test for American democracy. Thus she declared over and over again throughout the war that there could be no democracy in the United States that did not include democracy for blacks. In *The Moral Basis of Democracy* she asserted that people of all races have inviolate rights to "some property." "We have never been willing to face this problem, to line it up with the basic, underlying beliefs in Democracy." Racial prejudice enslaved blacks; consequently, "no one can claim that . . . the Negroes of this country are free." She continued this theme in a 1942 article in *The New Republic*, declaring that both the private and the public sector must acknowledge that "one of the main destroyers of freedom is our attitude toward the colored race." "What Kipling called 'The White Man's Burden,'" she proclaimed in *The American Magazine*, is "one of the things we can not have any longer." Furthermore, she told those listening to the radio broadcast of the 1945 National Democratic forum, "democracy may grow or fade as we face [this] problem."[9]

ER also realized that such continuous demands for democratic conduct did little to ease the pain black Americans encountered on a daily basis and she tried very hard to understand the depths of their anger. "If I were a Negro today, I think I would have moments of great bitterness," she confessed to readers of *Negro Digest*. "It would be hard for me to sustain my faith in democracy and to build up a sense of goodwill toward men of other races." She certainly could appreciate black rage because she knew that if she were black, her anger would surface. Nevertheless, she hoped she could channel her fury constructively because "there now remains much work to be done to see that freedom becomes a fact and not just a promise for my people."[10]

However, just as blacks should be wary of promises, ER cautioned all Americans to be suspicious of those who preach tolerance. She believed that "we must . . . take the word 'tolerance' out of our vocabulary and substitute for it the precept live and let live, cooperate in work and play and like our neighbors." "The problem is not to learn tolerance of your neighbors," she lectured to those who promoted such complacency, "but to see that all alike have hope and opportunity and that the community as a whole moves forward." Moreover, America cannot neglect its conscience where race is concerned because to do so would be denying its heritage, tainting its future, and succumbing to the law of the jungle.[11]

Despite the mild language she used in discussing black frustration, when during World War II Eleanor Roosevelt dared to equate American racism with fascism and argued that to ignore the evils of segregation would be capitulating to Aryanism, hostility toward her reached an all-time high. Newspapers from Chicago to Louisiana covered the dispute and numerous citizens pleaded with J. Edgar Hoover to silence her. Typical of such outrage is the argument presented by one irate American who accused ER of "deliberately aiding and abetting the enemy abroad by fermenting racial troubles at home."

Trying to turn the allegations of fascist behavior back onto the first lady, the author labeled the *Negro Digest* a publication dedicated to promoting communist-inspired racial propaganda and proclaimed ER guilty by association. The vast majority of the "*loyal* American population . . . are not afraid to express . . . their honest opinion that the wife of our nation's President and Commander-in-Chief heads the list [of enemies]." Although she professes "to speak as a private citizen," if any other private citizen expressed such opinions "all loyal Americans would name her a traitor." Moreover, ER's statements on behalf of black Americans "are calculated to arouse distrust and suspicion between the white and negro race here in the United States." Outraged that "white citizens of the United States have sacrificed their careers" to advance the stature of blacks, he predicted that if ER were not silenced veterans would come home "only to return to find the Roosevelts and the negroes in complete charge of our so-called 'democracy' they fought to save." Furthermore, she not only damaged American morale but also encouraged the Axis powers to think the nation weak. "Can you wonder that the Germans and Reds are laughing up their sleeves at us?," he concluded.[12]

Even those Americans professing to support economic equality for blacks objected to ER's positions. For example, Frank McAllister, a socialist who sat on the SCHW board with her, was so jealous of ER's influence within the Conference that he spread rumors that she was having an affair with Paul Robeson (and therefore was nothing more than a closet communist) as part of his efforts to undermine her stature.[13]

Nothing could have prepared the administration, however, for the venomous attacks ER received throughout 1943 after she continued to argue that black defense workers should be allowed to occupy federally constructed housing units in Detroit. ER argued unsuccessfully within the administration that the critical housing shortage could be used as a cover for slum clearance, that the housing constructed should last longer than the war, and that proper planning could produce integrated neighborhoods. Opposed by Charles Palmer, who coordinated the federal housing program, ER watched as Congress stripped slum clearance from its housing appropriations bill. Then she encouraged Clark Foreman's plan to divert some funds to the Sojourner Truth Project in Detroit. Outraged that their neighborhood could be integrated against their will, Polish neighbors of Sojourner Truth appealed to their congressman to stop the plan. Representative Rudolph Tenerowicz labeled the black tenants communist pawns and then had a rider attached to the appropriations bill declaring that "no money would be released unless that 'nigger lover' [Foreman] was fired and the project returned to white occupancy." The Federal Works Agency capitulated, forced Foreman out, and stopped recruiting black tenants.[14]

ER then appealed to the president on behalf of the civil rights leaders who requested her intercession. Arguing that the black tenants had support from a variety of leading white politicians, such as Mayor Edward Jeffries, Walter Reuther, and other UAW officials, she convinced FDR to reverse the white-only policy. By the end of February 1942, two dozen black families, accompanied by 300 black supporters, prepared to move into the project only to be met by cross burnings and a crowd of 700 armed white resisters. The families turned back, the police arrested 104 rioters and, after a series of compromises failed, the city delayed occupancy for more than a year.

In April 1943, the city, supported by 800 state police, moved the black families into their new homes. Within two months, tensions boiled over as fights broke out between the blacks and whites seeking refuge from the summer heat at Belle Isle, an amusement park located on an island in the Detroit River. As rumors flooded the housing districts adjacent to Sojourner Truth, sporadic outbreaks of violence coalesced into a sustained, brutal riot on June 21. Twenty-five blacks and nine whites died. ER had just returned to Washington from Chicago the week before where she had met with an over-flowing, predominantly black, crowd distraught over the race riot which had closed the Addsco shipyard in Mobile, Alabama, three weeks earlier. She used her speech as a plea for racial cooperation. When White House aides told her of the Detroit uprising, she mourned the deaths but was not sur-prised. As she later wrote Trude Lash, "Detroit never should have happened, but when Congress behaves as it does why should others be calmer?"[15]

The country was stunned and many held ER responsible. One Detroit resident told the FBI the first lady has "done more to agitate the whites and over-encourage the negroes . . . than any other single group outside of the Communists in the United States." Another wrote FDR that ER and the mayor had encouraged the outbreak by "their coddling of the negroes." The southern press abandoned all decorum. "It is blood on your hands, Mrs. Roosevelt," the *Jackson Daily News* pronounced the day after the riot. "You have been personally proclaiming and practicing social equality at the White House. . . . What followed is now history." By August, the White House, concerned that her positions were too damaging to the president, began its own counteroffensive. As Henry Wallace and Gardner Jackson later recalled, "Mrs. R . . . was ordered to go" to New Zealand "because the Negro situation was too hot." Although she had long wanted to visit the troops, ER understood why the administration suddenly honored her request. "I suppose when one is being forced to realize that an unwelcome change is coming, one must blame it on someone or something."[16]

Although her tour of the South Pacific got ER out of the country, it did nothing to deter her commitment to racial justice at home. Haunted by her visits with soldiers on bases, in hospitals, and in battle zones, she obsessed over how to honor their sacrifices. More and more she referred to the prayer she had carried with her. "Dear Lord, Lest I continue my complacent way, help me to remember, somewhere out there a man died for me today. As long as there be war, I must ask and answer am I worth dying for?" As she confessed to a friend, her visit with the troops filled her with "a sense of obligation which I can never discharge."[17]

Thus, she accepted the CIO's invitation to host the opening of their inte-grated canteen in Washington in February 1944. When the wire services carried photographs of a smiling ER serving refreshments to a crowd of black soldiers and white hostesses, the furor over her racial policies resur-faced. Typical of this reaction is the caption *The Greensboro Watchman* placed under the photo: "This is Mrs. Roosevelt at the CIO canteen party in

Washington as she served negroes along with whites, and joined in singing love songs as negro men danced with white girls." Letters poured into the White House objecting to her participation and newspapers from Tampa to Houston to Memphis editorialized against her conduct.[18]

With such criticism escalating as the war drew to a close, ER's warnings about the future increased. Worried that an uncertain postwar economy would exacerbate white racism and that a refusal to recognize the contributions of black veterans would encourage black distrust of whites, she repeatedly challenged America to recognize that racial injustice was the biggest threat to American democracy. The United States must "stop generalizing about people" and recognize stereotypes as racist propaganda. "If we really believe in Democracy," Eleanor Roosevelt said to black and white audiences throughout 1945, "we must face the fact that equality of opportunity is basic" and that grievances expressed by black Americans were "legitimate." "We have expected [the Negroes] to be good citizens and . . . we haven't given them an opportunity to take part in our government." Refusing to concede to her opponents, she asserted that if the nation continued to honor Jim Crow, America would have defeated fascism abroad only to defend racism at home.[19]

Eleanor Roosevelt said the same things in private that she did in public. She pressed to keep civil rights issues on the top of the domestic political agenda, whether interceding with the president for Walter White, Mary McLeod Bethune, A. Philip Randolph, or W. E. B. DuBois; raising money for Howard University or Bethune-Cookman College; investigating discrimination black women encountered while stationed at the Women's Auxiliary Army Corps base in Des Moines, Iowa; pressing the FEPC to investigate complaints; or supporting anti-segregation campaigns and anti-lynching legislation. This was not a popular position to take and led FDR's aide Jonathan Daniels to admit that while she "did a lot of good," she really was a "hair shirt" to the administration who was always complicating policy by "bringing a hell of a lot of cats and dogs" into the discussion. Consequently, throughout the war years, her standing with civil rights leaders increased while her standing with some key White House aides decreased.[20]

Nor did she limit her energy to confronting national problems. Frequently an individual who had been unjustly treated prompted effort equal to that she expended on a more widespread problem. Throughout the New Deal and war years, ER acted as both a spokesperson and lobbyist for tenant farmers and black sharecroppers. Whether working within the administration with Will Alexander on Farm Security issues or Harry

Hopkins or Aubrey Williams on WPA, NYA, and Subsistence Homestead projects, Eleanor Roosevelt strove to force the administration to recognize that Jim Crow and the Depression often combined to give a knockout punch to southern black farmers. Outside the White House, ER tried to mobilize support for sharecroppers by discussing their problems in her speeches, columns, and articles; actively supporting the Southern Tenant Farmer's Union; meeting with small groups of individual sharecroppers to discuss their plight and review their suggestions for reform; and sponsoring National Sharecroppers Week.[21]

When Randolph, Bethune, and Pauli Murray, a young black woman with whom ER developed a friendship grounded in "confrontation by typewriter," informed her that sharecropper Odell Waller had been sentenced to death by a jury from which blacks had deliberately been excluded, Eleanor Roosevelt's efforts reached new heights. She launched a one-woman campaign within the White House to commute Waller's sentence. She wrote and telephoned Virginia Governor Clement Darden to plead Waller's case, and forced FDR to follow-up on her request with his own call to Darden. At the same time, she met with Waller's supporters, discussed his plight in her column, contributed to his defense fund, and advised his defense committee. When readers challenged her stance, she minced no words in her reply. "Times without number Negro men have been lynched or gone to their death without due process of law. No one questions Waller's guilt, but they question the system which led to it."[22]

After all other efforts on Waller's behalf failed, ER still refused to concede defeat and on the day of his scheduled electrocution, repeatedly interrupted FDR's war planning meeting with Harry Hopkins until the president took her call and refused her plea for further intervention. Two hours before the sharecropper was to die in the electric chair, a dejected ER phoned A. Philip Randolph at NAACP headquarters. As Waller's supporters listened to her over five extensions, in a trembling voice she told Randolph: "I have done everything I can possibly do. I have interrupted the President . . . I am so sorry, Mr. Randolph, I can't do any more."[23]

Although Waller was executed, the intensity of her efforts on his behalf solidified ER's ties with civil rights leaders. Thus, despite Randolph's increasing frustration with FDR's reluctance to enforce fair employment policies, he could urge a national conference of black leaders to pursue a dual strategy of nonviolent direct action and working with Eleanor Roosevelt. The NAACP agreed. Walter White knew that when he phoned ER before the 1944 Democratic Convention to warn that blacks might vote Republican if a strong civil rights plank were not adopted, she would not discount his analysis. In fact, she repeatedly tried to obtain an audience for White with either the president or DNC chair Robert Hannegan. Consequently, despite FDR's thinly disguised disregard for the association and the unwillingness he showed in responding to its requests, White encountered no opposition when he recommended that ER join the NAACP Board of Directors.[24]

Despite the close working relationship she had with black leaders and her outspoken championing of racial equality, there was one issue Eleanor Roosevelt was reluctant to address directly: social equality. The reasons for her reluctance were more political than personal. As she confided to Walter White, she had to choose her words carefully when discussing racial discrimination with administration officials because some senior members immediately assumed that desegregation implied support for racially mixed marriages. Even Edith Wilson, the only other twentieth-century first lady subjected to intense media scrutiny, could not resist deriding ER's actions.[25] Furthermore, throughout the 1944 campaign, Republicans capitalized on this fear and spread allegations that ER "advocated intermarriage of the negro with the whites." To one columnist, her "innocent, wholehearted, humane enthusiasms" were "only a disguise" for "some scheme containing the most binding elements of Communism and Hitlerism." And *The Alabama Sun* devoted an entire issue to "Eleanor Demands Equality for Negroes in Address" and featured numerous photographs under the caption "Eleanor and Some More Niggers."[26]

Eleanor Roosevelt feared that this backlash would undermine what little progress had been made to date. Therefore, when she did discuss social issues relating to civil rights, such as education and housing and employment, she tried to define clearly the parameters of the discussion. She frequently made the opposition define their terms rather than immediately assuming a defensive posture. "I do not know what you call equality," she used in rebuttal to Eufala, Alabama, Mayor M. M. Moulthrop's objections to her position. "We are fighting a war today which is going to require of us this type of respect for other races. This does not mean you have to sit at [a] table or meet in a social way anyone whom you do not wish to meet." Moreover, "no one can tell me I've got to ask someone to dinner if I don't want to," she told reporters who challenged her views. "Neither can they tell me not to ask people I want to ask."[27]

Eleanor Roosevelt answered questions from her supporters with the same care she gave to those who opposed her views. When Pauli Murray questioned her statement that she "had never advocated social equality," she responded in a two-page, single-spaced letter that the term "does not mean at all what it seems to mean to certain people." "I think it is important," she told her young friend, "that every citizen in the United States have an equal opportunity and that is why I have emphasized the four basic things we should fight for," education, employment, housing, and voting rights. Practicing democracy is the key, not social egalitarianism. Thus, when Atlanta attorney Pearl Burnette wrote praising ER's courage, ER responded that they had different interpretations of social equality. "I take it as meaning the association of people who are friends, who want to be together and who enjoy the companionship of one another." This did not necessarily mean intermarriage; however, she continued, "I do not think this is something that we can legislate. Laws will not prevent anything so personal." Yet those who watched her closely saw through her disclaimers. She might have argued "don't push too fast," Murray recalled in her autobiography, but she always "took the next step."[28]

In short, when ER joined the NAACP board in 1945 she brought with her an increased awareness of the complex problems black Americans confronted at the end of the war. Like Myrdal, she agreed that the war would stimulate black protest in a way that would promote "a redefinition of the Negro's status in America." Like DuBois, she saw the war as "a way to take democracy off of parchment and give it life." Like White, she feared an increase in lynchings and racial violence as black veterans returned home to compete for wages and housing. Finally, like Bethune, she feared that the Veteran's Administration would neglect the needs specific to black soldiers, sailors, and air force personnel, and blacks who had served the country would again be deprived of their rightful share of its benefits. Consequently, when Eleanor Roosevelt formalized her ties to the NAACP she shared both its projections of and its aspirations for the future.[29]

■ **"The Negro is always the first to lose out." The NAACP from Columbia, Tennessee, to Brown v. Topeka Board of Education**

The immediate events of postwar America justified ER's fears. As the FEPC struggled vainly to pressure veterans and defense agencies not to discriminate, reconversion plans more often than not placed minority defense workers on the unemployment line. The employment future for both black veterans and defense workers looked increasingly dim. As reconversion plans and wage programs continued to overlook discriminatory practices, civil rights advocates within the administration aggressively challenged existing customs.

When the administration failed to respond, some black leaders opted to dramatize the plight of black workers. For example, FEPC member Charles Houston, former special counsel to the NAACP and an acquaintance of ER's since the 1939 Marian Anderson "Freedom Concert," resigned from the committee to protest Truman's reluctance to enforce anti-discrimination statutes in Washington. Yet fears of a national chain of black-initiated, economic-based race riots similar to the disturbances that had rocked the nation in 1943 failed to materialize. Instead, postwar racial violence was spurred by whites who feared an onslaught of black protest. This climate of racial suspicion coupled with a backdrop of returning black veterans in Columbia, Tennessee, provided the stage for Eleanor Roosevelt's debut as an NAACP board member.[30]

Early on the morning of February 26, 1946, Gladys Stephenson and her nineteen-year-old son James, who had just returned from a three-year naval tour of the Pacific, entered the Caster-Knot Electric Appliance store to pick up her radio from the repair department. The radio had not been repaired to Mrs. Stephenson's satisfaction and she told the repairman, William Fleming, that the unit needed additional work. When the repairman refused to repair the radio further, she stated that the price for the repair work should be reduced. Fleming refused and slapped and kicked her. James Stephenson then hit Fleming, who fell through the store's front plate-glass window. Although Stephenson did not seriously injure Fleming, several whites who observed the incident attacked Mrs. Stephenson while a white police officer clubbed her son. When Mrs. Stephenson tried to restrain the officer and urged him to investigate Fleming, the officer struck her in the face with his fist. He then arrested the Stephensons without talking to Fleming. The Stephensons pled guilty, paid a fifty dollar fine, and were released. Fleming's father, irate over the affront to his son, then charged both Stephensons with attempted murder and demanded that a second warrant for their arrest be issued. Columbia officials complied with Fleming's request and the Stephensons were rearrested and remained in jail until a leading black businessman posted bond.[31]

As news of both the confrontation and the Stephensons' rearrest spread throughout the town, a crowd of whites gathered at the town square to plan a raid on the jail. When word of the impending lynching reached the black community's business district, located only one block away from the jail, both black residents and the Columbia police feared a repeat of the riots that had occurred in 1944 and 1945. Trying to prevent retaliation, black businesses put out the street lights lining their major thoroughfare and closed for the day. Meanwhile the entire six-man Columbia police force left the jail and entered the darkened area without announcing themselves. An unidentified voice shouted "here they come" and shots were fired. No one could determine where the shots came from or who fired them. A riot ensued and eventually the State Police and the National Guard were called in to reinforce the Columbia police force.[32]

The next day the national press treated the riot as major news. However, like the officer who initially arrested the Stephensons, the media also neglected to investigate the complaints and who initiated the attack. Rather, the press blamed the black community for the violence. When a Columbia sheriff shot and killed two of the 100 blacks arrested on attempted murder charges as they allegedly tried to escape, the "Columbia pogrom" became front page news. Among the white press, only *The New Republic* and *New South* questioned whether the black community had started the violence. Responding to this biased coverage, representatives of sixty organizations concerned with civil rights and civil liberties met in Washington and decided to form a commission to investigate and publicize the true causes of the riot. Mary McLeod Bethune and Clark Foreman agreed to chair the committee and raise money to finance the investigation.[33]

While the Washington coalition, organized as the United Committee against Police Terror in Columbia, Tennessee, planned its investigation, the NAACP met in New York to determine how best to represent those blacks arrested during the riot. By mid-March an all-white grand jury in Columbia indicted thirty-one blacks, twenty-eight of whom were arraigned on charges of attempted murder in the first degree. Only four whites were indicted, two of whom had not yet been arrested. The NAACP Legal Committee, fearing a speedy conviction and a national outburst of racial violence, held an emergency session to revise its defense strategy. After the committee agreed on the action the defense team should take next, Walter White called Eleanor Roosevelt and asked her to meet with Channing Tobias, Mary McLeod Bethune, Arthur Spingarn, and Clark Foreman to plan the NAACP's political response. She agreed immediately.[34]

Three days later the five met with representatives from the CIO-PAC, the National Lawyers Guild, the American Veterans Committee, and the Federal Council of Churches to plan the political strategy necessary to ensure a coordinated and comprehensive campaign. Worried that two national committees concerned with the Columbia situation would undermine one another's efforts, ER entered the meeting determined not to let that happen. As chair, she moderated the meeting so adroitly that a compromise was reached that pushed the NAACP to the left and the more radical representatives to the right and that merged the two groups into the National Committee for Justice in Columbia, Tennesee (NCJCT).[35]

As a result, the NAACP agreed to launch a national publicity campaign and to begin legal and educational actions "to prevent the recurrence of such violence." For their parts, the National Lawyers Guild, the CIO-PAC, and the American Veterans Committee representatives dropped their demand for financial restitution for the destruction of black property and agreed to let the NAACP coordinate defense strategy. Committee members were so impressed by the skill with which ER arbitrated the dispute over the committee's immediate and long-range goals that they not only named her chair of the steering committee but also empowered her to appoint all its members.[36]

In addition to mediating tactical differences within the civil rights legal community, ER continued to support the black victims of Columbia violence by endorsing the NAACP legal strategy when she met with state and federal officials. Throughout the summer and fall of 1946, she served as the NAACP's intermediary with the U.S. Justice Department, frequently appealing directly to Attorney General Tom Clark. Often these discussions surpassed the compromises reached on April 4 and reflected ER's interest in pursuing white restitution for damage to black property and in counteracting the deliberate exclusion of blacks from the Columbia grand jury process.

Nor were these exchanges limited to correspondence. For example, ER did not accept Clark's explanation of why the grand jury "could not fix responsibility for damage on any identifiable officer of the law." Concerned that NAACP counsel Thurgood Marshall's opinion carried more weight with her than his, the attorney general thought that if she came to see him, he could make a stronger case for his position. This strategy did not work. Eleanor Roosevelt did visit Clark, but she still believed Marshall's assessment and continued to endorse the SCHW's and the NCJCT reports of the Columbia riot in the face of stiff government opposition.[37]

This strong allegiance to the NAACP did not necessarily imply ER's unquestioned support of its other demands. In the midst of the national campaign for justice in Columbia, *Crisis* Editor and Director of Special Research W. E. B. DuBois completed his assessment of the status of black America and submitted it to the NAACP board for review. At a meeting—which ER's United Nations responsibilities prevented her from attending—the board recommended that the 155-page "Statement on the Denial of Human Rights to Minorities in the Case of the Citizens of Negro

Descent in the USA" be submitted as part of a petition of grievances to the
UN's Human Rights Commission's Subcommission on Minorities and
Discrimination. As a member of both the NAACP national board and UN
Human Rights Commission, Eleanor Roosevelt was the logical choice to
introduce the NAACP's "appeal for redress."[38]

Yet despite requests from her close friend Walter White, ER refused
either to introduce the petition or to represent the Human Rights
Commission when White and DuBois presented the document to the secretary general. Her schedule precluded her appearance, she informed the
activist. Undaunted by these refusals, White tried a different tactic in his
final appeal for her endorsement. "Would it be possible," he telegraphed
the day before the presentation ceremony, "for you to be present as a
demonstration of deep concern of responsible American opinion with this
problem . . . ." Once again, she rejected his plea. Responding immediately
upon receipt of the wire, she told her friend that she was "very sorry" but
protocol prevented her appearance.[39]

Undoubtedly Eleanor Roosevelt understood the status her appearance
would lend to the petition. The document already had created a furor
within both the United Nations and the U.S. State Department as representatives of Third World and communist delegations requested copies and
debated its contents while American diplomats struggled to defuse the criticism of U.S. internal policies. Moreover, the decision of the National
Negro Congress, the NAACP's chief rival, to hold regional hearings across
America to supplement the petition's findings compounded the international interest in the petition. Such immediate publicity intimidated UN
officials. As White confided to ER, despite the cordiality, both the
Secretariat and the Human Rights Division representatives were "apparently afraid of the document."[40]

ER wanted to lend her support to the issues the petition raised, but
feared endorsement would prevent her from taking action on its behalf in
the future. "I should like to be present," she cabled White, "but as a member of the delegation I feel that until this subject comes before us in the
proper way, in a report of the Human Rights Commission . . . , I should
not seem to be lining myself up in any particular way." Yet she still wanted
to help and did not stand aside without internal struggles. "It isn't as though
everyone did not know where I stand," she rationalized. "It is just a matter
of proper procedure."[41]

Although White accepted this argument, DuBois did not and the tension between the *Crisis* editor and ER increased. DuBois held her partially
responsible for the UN's delay in investigating the petition's grievances.

While White made a distinction between ER's official stance as a representative of the Department of State and her personal politics, DuBois did not. Consequently, when Senator Warren Austin, head of the American delegation to the United Nations, requested that ER represent him in a meeting with DuBois, DuBois interpreted her arguments on Warren's behalf as her own.

Patiently, she tried to explain the difference. The State Department did not want the petition debated because "no good would come of it." However, the Declaration of Human Rights would be introduced and had a strong chance of passage. Unmoved by this argument, DuBois replied that although he knew that no international action could change American custom, he "thought that the world ought to know just exactly what the situation was in the United States so that they would not be depending upon vague references concerning our race problem."

This point, ER retorted, was extraneous to the issue. Such a stance would embarrass the U.S. in ways which would undercut its push for human rights and would be used by the Soviets as "an excuse for attacking the United States." Fully aware of the allegations of communist influence within the NAACP, ER tried to lead DuBois to see how such allegations within the UN Human Rights Commission would impede the General Assembly's adoption of the Declaration and delay action on civil rights in general. This would be an untenable situation for her because if the Soviets attacked U.S. policies, then she would find herself in the abhorrent position of having to defend American racism.[42]

Finally, to underscore the depth of her feeling on this issue she told DuBois that if he pursued this line of attack the "situation then might be so unpleasant that she would feel it necessary to resign from the . . . delegation." The activist, refusing to be cowed by this threat, argued that an admission of imperfection by the U.S. would not necessarily equal embarrassment. Undaunted by his persistence, ER rebuffed him and requested simply that if he took any action toward introducing the petition that "she be notified as soon as possible so that she could prepare to act accordingly."[43]

Ambivalence played no part in this decision. This threat was not a bluff. Both the United Nations and the National Association for the Advancement of Colored People were organizations to which ER had unquestioned devotion. Nevertheless, she would not allow one of these groups to play her off against the other. Although black civil rights was an issue to which ER was passionately committed, her passion did not dictate the terms of her commitment. In fact, she was forced to choose between ideology and pragmatic politics, and doing so, she strove for balance. When this was not possible, power politics triumphed. ER knew that she would never abandon the issue, but that if she did not play the political game strategically she could lose the arena in which she could implement this conviction most effectively.

Eleanor Roosevelt understood the dissension within the NAACP staff and refused to let the rift with DuBois sour her relationship with White, Marshall, Spingarn, and other association officials. Ironically, as DuBois became more and more intransigent, NAACP leadership increasingly sided with ER rather than with their own staff member. The battle climaxed early in the fall of 1948 when, after he refused to drop his demand for the petition and continued publicly to deride her and to criticize White for supporting the positions she advocated, the association dismissed him for "basic policy differences." At the time the NAACP began to implement its judicial drive to complete school integration, DuBois left and ER remained.[44]

Throughout the petition dispute, ER continued to work outside the UN for other NAACP campaigns. She served as honorary chair of the life membership campaign, opened Val-Kill to summer training institutes for NAACP youth, addressed the NAACP's National Youth Conference, spoke from the steps of the Lincoln Memorial to a crowd of 100,000 attending the 1947 annual NAACP convention, and defended the legal strategy introduced in *Sweatt v. Painter*—that "if *Plessy* applied to education, it should be overruled because the framers of the Fourteenth Amendment rejected separate-but-equal and because segregation inevitably resulted in inequality." As she wrote in her cover letter supporting the NAACP membership campaign, "the NAACP stands in the forefront for the struggle to make democracy extend to all American minorities."[45]

Furthermore, as she prepared to deliver an address at the Sorbonne discussing the United Nations' "struggle for human rights," ER battled Secretary of State George Marshall and his aide Dean Rusk when they requested she delete from her prepared remarks any references to "the urgent need to eliminate racial discrimination in the United States." While she did agree to state that "steady progress [is] being made in the solution to these problems," she cast aside the compliance that characterized her role as an instructed delegate, and this time rejected State Department demands that she avoid the topic. Instead, she issued her own call for action. After praising recent Supreme Court decisions, she concluded, "no one race and no one people can claim to have done all the work to achieve greater dignity for human beings and to develop human personality. In each generation there must be a continuation of the struggle and new steps forward must be taken since this is preeminently a field in which to stand still is to retreat." Clearly, while she did avoid the specifics the DuBois report contained, she could not sidestep the issue.[46]

Indeed, civil rights became the domestic issue to which she paid most attention during summer breaks from her General Assembly duties. This was especially clear in her unceasing efforts to promote affordable housing for black America. Although she struggled to provide desegregated housing in the model community of Arthurdale and championed fair housing practices throughout the war years, the housing shortage precipitated by the lack of wartime construction made the housing available to black Americans even more scarce. By July 1945, she reported to "My Day" readers that "in practically every place the most important questions seems to be housing and unemployment."[47]

When both the Roosevelt and Truman administrations yielded to conservative congressional pressure to modify their public housing proposals, ER pushed officials to resist the onslaught and to meet with community leaders. In the spring of 1945, she lobbied the Budget Bureau and New Deal housing advisors to ensure that the criticisms of the McCarran housing bill presented by D.C. Citizens Council for Community Planning Representative Pauline Redmond Coggs would be given a fair hearing. A year later, she strongly endorsed the slum clearance and low-income housing aspects of the proposed Wagner-Ellender-Taft Housing Bill. When the Truman administration acquiesced in congressional opposition, she criticized both its initial shortsightedness and its reluctance to oppose the House amendments to the housing bill.[48]

Repeatedly she asserted that low- and middle-income housing and slum clearance plans should take priority. The emergency housing bill "was one of the most important things for us to be concerned about," she declared. Although she recognized that the price tag was steep, she also knew that this was the cost the nation had to pay for its failure to plan adequately for the postwar period. "We should have foreseen many of the needs which now face us," she lamented in "My Day." "Having failed in preparation, however, we can at least do the right thing now and provide low-cost housing quickly."[49]

Her lectures reflected this commitment. In fact, the first address she agreed to deliver after FDR's death linked housing and community planning to the plight of black America. In a speech to the Downtown Community School entitled "Housing and Community Planning—One Approach to Intercultural Relations," ER asserted that segregated residential patterns, poor management, and racial stereotyping perpetuated racial animosity and promoted distrust of public housing. In the question and answer period following the lecture, she interpreted the 1943 Detroit race riot as a white response to fears that black neighbors would decrease their property values. Nor were politicians exempt from ER's rebuke. As she told those attending the opening dinner for the school's fall term, "the failures in this country" also can be attributed "to leaders who were not able to have confidence in the people here or peoples of different races . . . because of fear of them."[50]

ER continued this stance throughout the forties and early fifties. Two months before her housing speech, she endorsed *The War Worker*, a publication for black enlisted personnel, which, according to the FBI, devoted "much of its space to local housing problems, and to pictures of Negroes and white employees working together." To an overflow black crowd at the Andrew Rankin Memorial Chapel in Baltimore, ER declared that democracy in the United States "falls short of what it ought to be" and cited available housing as a key example. People of color comprised most of the world's population and they continuously observed American race relations as the lens through which to view democracy. "There is no surer way to kill democracy," she told an international symposium at Columbia University, "than for a country to be so self-satisfied as to believe there is no reason for a chance in that country."[51]

Black Americans appreciated ER's unflinching connection of housing rights to civil rights. Frequently they appealed to her for assistance in finding safe and affordable living quarters as well as direct intervention in local housing disputes. When white mobs prevented Clarence Wilson from moving into the home he purchased in Amityville, Long Island, ER addressed an NAACP-sponsored mass meeting called to discuss the discrimination Wilson encountered. When Herbert Hill appealed for the NAACP to establish a "Fighting Fund for Freedom" to cover Wilson's legal expenses, she supported the motion. After Caroline Shirley repeatedly encountered unnecessary roadblocks to her efforts to move out of a Lexington, Kentucky, slum, she turned in desperation to Eleanor Roosevelt. Shirley's account of local racist practices and bureaucratic inefficiency, coupled with the description of her tin shack on a mudslide, seized ER's attention. ER forwarded Shirley's letter to *Louisville Courier* publisher Barry Bingham and asked him to investigate the Lexington woman's complaint and to promote construction of low-income housing in the Lexington area. A few months later Bingham responded that "the conditions which Mrs. Shirley described in her letter were absolutely in accordance with the facts." The neighborhood "is quite as bad as Mrs. Shirley described." Fortunately, however, ER's interest in this family's plight had started an investigation and real estate agents and loan company officials had made it clear that a better type of affordable housing would be available. "The essential difficulty seems to be settled," Bingham reported. Although ER had concealed her actions on the family's behalf, when the Shirleys' situation improved they knew whose hand was operating behind the scenes and gave her all the credit for their future quarters, enclosing a family photograph painstakingly autographed by their six-year-old son.[52]

Black civic associations followed suit by recruiting her sponsorship of their campaigns and publicizing her efforts on their behalf. When the SCHW defiantly resisted congressional allegations of communist influence and continued to pursue its housing program aggressively, ER the member of the board encouraged this stance while ER the journalist publicized SCHW's actions. In response, the SCHW seized on her endorsement and used her prestige as the cornerstone of its public refutation of the charges. "I think the lessons we have learned from such dissolute fearless souls," Emcee Roscoe Dunjee said in praise of ER at a SCHW testimonial dinner held in her honor, "is that progress [comes] through facing—not dodging—evil."[53]

As opponents of civil rights became more shrill in their resistance, and black demands for redress became more assertive, Eleanor Roosevelt increased her support of demonstrations and public protests. While she continued to prefer to act in support of rather than in opposition to an issue, she now refused to back away from endorsing confrontational demands for racial equality. Consequently, when the National Committee on Segregation in the Nation's Capital launched its sit-in campaign to integrate Washington National Airport, ER not only joined the Committee but also praised its activism in her column. When the Civil Aeronautics Administration responded to the protests by integrating airport facilities, she cheered the decision. "This is a substantial step forward in the fight that must be waged to bring our National Capital into line with what must be government policy."[54]

Housing inequities must also be brought in line because the housing situation was getting worse, not better. As she wrote RCA Chairman David Sarnoff to solicit his support for radio spots highlighting the inequalities New York City blacks suffered in housing and employment, when times are uncertain "the Negro is always the first to lose out." Manhattan housing was scarce but nowhere were the conditions more deplorable than the nation's capital, where the flood of new wartime federal employees drastically intensified the prewar housing shortage. ER had toured Washington's alleys in 1933 and the situation had not improved since that visit. Blacks who lived in the District were "always being crowded into houses which have been condemned and should be torn down." The Senate needed to open its eyes and recognize this rather than just making a congressional pilgrimage through poverty every ten years.[55]

While Eleanor Roosevelt acknowledged that the question "whether a human being acquires more characteristics through heredity or environment" was still open for discussion, she felt "quite sure" that those "who live in the Washington slums are conditioned to a great extent by their environment." She remained resolute in her conviction that adequate housing and the nurturing environment it provided were crucial to an individual's development as a citizen. Assessing the correlation between slums and racism, ER asserted that poverty and the misery it produced encouraged racial violence and suspicion to such a widespread extent that many Americans are "beset by fear and unnatural hate." Recognizing that most Americans professed a desire to eliminate this prejudice, she nevertheless lamented that she was "not sure that we try hard enough or move fast enough."[56]

Yet she also realized that blacks in the North and the South had different needs, so that if reforms were to succeed, priorities must be set and clear plans of action implemented. Community reform organizations must play an integral role in determining this agenda and should decide for themselves how and when the problems in the community should be addressed. In her keynote address to the National Council of Negro Women's Interracial Conference, she cautioned the women to set their own priorities and be united in working for these goals. "If you are doing too many things at once you will lose the drive that is necessary." One group cannot do the "same thing everywhere and everything at once in the fight for racial equality." Groups must pick their battles and organize in ways that will advance their issue the most. Consequently the South may focus on voting rights and the North on housing rights.[57]

The Supreme Court may have initiated the elimination of Jim Crow school systems with *Brown v. Board of Education* in 1954, but as ER told audiences and readers throughout the fifties, as long as housing remained segregated and substandard, school systems would remain substandard as well. In addition, she admonished those northerners who believed that discrimination was only a southern phenomenon to recognize that until housing was not divided along racial lines, the North was as Jim Crow as the South. "I have repeatedly said that the North has one essential step to take in complying with the Supreme Court decision," she wrote a southerner who questioned the regional scapegoating the South received for American racism. "It will, of course, take time but discrimination in housing must be wiped out and such communities as are completely segregated . . . must disappear or we cannot possibly have integrated schools." When segregationists questioned her commitment to desegregation and implied that she did not practice what she preached, she replied simply that she had "lived in a neighborhood . . . with colored people and have never found it any different from any other neighborhood."[58]

To ER, education was central to black advancement. As both a longtime proponent of public education and a former history teacher, she strove as a cornerstone of her activities to promote educational reforms and ranked quality education for black Americans as one of her top priorities. Her close friendship with Mary McLeod Bethune had already emboldened the National Youth Administration to include black Americans in their proposals. As a member of a Board of Directors for both Bethune-Cookman College and Howard University, she actively solicited funds for these institutions, frequently hosting fundraising events in her home and keynoting a myriad of campus events. In addition, whenever she came in contact with integrated school systems, such as the Fieldston School and the Wiltwyck Academy, or education programs that included a racially diverse enrollment like the Highlander Folk School, she praised their courage. But it was her position as a member of the NAACP's Legal Affairs Committee, reorganized as the NAACP Legal Defense and Education Fund in 1950, and her unquestioned championing of the Association's school desegregation legal strategy that most clearly reflects ER's commitment to integration. In recognition of this commitment and the actions she took on its behalf, the Fund named ER its vice president in 1951.[59]

Eleanor Roosevelt did not wait until the Supreme Court ruled in favor of school desegregation to begin her campaign to mobilize public support for decisions favoring integration. Just as the Association became more assertive in its legal campaign to abolish Jim Crow graduate and secondary programs, ER's role as its most noted white advocate grew as well. Initially, her role in promoting equal education for black Americans was to act as a leading spokesperson for the NAACP's education strategy. As the Association increasingly appreciated the influence public opinion exerted upon controversial court decisions, however, her role as NAACP board member expanded from merely representing the Association's positions to the public to becoming a key planner and advocate of its strategy.

Members of both the Legal Affairs Committee and the Public Relations Committee recruited her support for their efforts. As early as May 1947, when Thurgood Marshall prepared to argue *Sweatt v. Painter*, the director of public relations for the NAACP, Oliver Harrington, asked ER to "mercilessly expose" the facts Marshall would present in the suit. She agreed and devoted the same attention in her column to the discriminatory practices of the University of Texas Law School that she accorded the bigots of Columbia, Tennessee. When the Association decided to reorganize its operations, the board asked ER to serve on the committee charged with reviewing various organizational proposals. She agreed and, despite her inability to attend the committee meetings, she diligently scrutinized the various reorganization plans.[60]

Moreover, as *Gaines* v. *Canada, Sweatt* v. *Painter,* and *McLaurin* v. *Oklahoma State Regents* drained the Legal Defense and Education Fund coffers, Walter White turned to Eleanor Roosevelt for help. These victories have given [us] "an unprecedented opportunity . . . to carry our battle successfully into the fields of undergraduate college training, secondary and elementary education." Would she, White asked, write testimonials supporting this work to foundations with whom she had contact? She responded the day she received his request and drafted an unabashed letter of support for the Fund.

Declaring that "the NAACP is doing as urgent and constructive a work as any organization in the nation," ER urged those who read her words to recognize how much the group "has made our country a better democracy." Because she had "been close to this work," she "had the highest regard for those who plan and direct" its program of dismantling segregated schools, and she wanted "to add [her] plea" for its support. Furthermore, as subsequent challenges to *Brown* continued to deplete the Association's finances, ER, though in financial difficulty herself, agreed to give one thousand dollars toward this effort and to encourage twenty-five other individuals to do the same.[61]

Eleanor Roosevelt contributed more than her money and her prestige to the drive for equal education. She contributed her political and organizational expertise as well. When the NAACP stumbled in its efforts to define specific long-range goals and reach consensus on the best way in which to achieve these goals, ER played an integral role in steering the Association through its evaluation process. Walter White initially refused to schedule a NAACP policy summit at his Breakneck Hill home unless ER could attend. When Breakneck policy statements were circulated among those who attended the conference, White carefully included her recommendations even though she had not been part of the discussion and even though they conflicted with those proposed by other members at the meeting.[62]

After Roy Wilkins criticized White in the spring of 1950 for marrying Poppy Cannon, a white woman, and ER attacked Wilkins with the tenacity she had displayed previously with DuBois, the White-Roosevelt alliance strengthened. For example, when White considered a fact-finding expedition to South Africa, ER not only encouraged the trip but also suggested that the UAW and the CIO finance the endeavor. Furthermore, she advised him on ways to expose the connection between British colonialism and apartheid. In fact, her influence on the Association's executive secretary was so strong that White sometimes refused to propose specific solutions to a problem until he had first discussed the issue and his response with ER. Before the NAACP launched its "all-out fight" against the Wherry compromise requiring a two-thirds majority of all senators rather than just those present in the chamber for the Senate to invoke cloture, an issue crucial for civil rights legislation, White asked to review his strategy with ER. "I'd like to talk this over and a number of other matters," he wrote the day the resolution was introduced. Two days later, he drove to Hyde Park and spent the night.[63]

Consequently, when the Supreme Court handed down the *Brown* decision in the fall of 1954, Eleanor Roosevelt was at the height of her influence within the NAACP. If the Association did not always embrace the position she advocated, what is clear is that on the issues of housing, education, and justice before the law, the Association and Eleanor Roosevelt never doubted each other's commitment despite the different routes each may have taken to reach their goals.

∎ **"We are on trial to show what democracy means."**
The Democratic Party and the Struggle to Implement 'Brown'

Nowhere was this mutual respect clearer than in the different approaches the NAACP and Eleanor Roosevelt took to ensure that *Brown v. Topeka Board of Education* was implemented with more than, as the Supreme Court had written, "all deliberate speed." Civil rights was one of the most controversial domestic issues in the 1956 presidential campaign and during the presidential primary months the NAACP centered its efforts on promoting policies that would force recalcitrant school districts to comply with the Court's decision. With Democrats needing to carry the segregated South as well as northern urban centers and the black vote, both Republican and Democratic presidential candidates approached the *Brown* decision with caution. The Association and Eleanor Roosevelt recognized this and mobilized their respective troops behind the candidate they believed most supported the civil rights agenda.[64]

Yet the NAACP and ER endorsed different candidates and strove to promote different campaign images for civil rights. Although Adlai Stevenson was running again for the Democratic nomination, his selection by the party was far from assured. He faced challenges from Averell Harriman, a stalwart cold warrior who had the unabashed support of Harry Truman and the endorsement of the NAACP, and from Estes Kefauver, whose televised crusade against organized crime and coonskin cap flair for publicity threatened Stevenson's image as the witty, intellectual candidate.

Both Harriman and Kefauver unequivocally endorsed both the *Brown* decision and the Powell amendment, which would deny federal education funds to school districts that refused to integrate. When his civil rights statements were compared to those of his two rivals, Stevenson appeared to deviate from his 1952 image as the icon of liberalism to become yet another candidate whose honor was corrupted by his political ambition. Despite his meeting with NAACP leaders and his reiterated support for *Brown* and voting rights legislation, throughout the 1956 campaign he never shook his image as an equivocating moderate on civil rights. His intellectual support never translated into readily observable moral conviction and compassion. In addition, when he refused to speak out repeatedly against the Emmett Till lynching and argued before a black crowd in Los Angeles's Hotel Watkins that America "must proceed gradually" with school desegregation, he irrevocably damaged his image as a strong supporter of civil rights and left himself open to attacks from Kefauver, Harriman, and Eisenhower.[65]

Stevenson's Watkins remarks also provoked a furor within the civil rights community. When he implied that school desegregation would not be completed until January 1963, the 100th anniversary of the Emancipation Proclamation, even the more patient members of NAACP leadership questioned his commitment to racial justice. Recognizing the potential damage to both the campaign and the candidate's psyche, ER initiated her own damage control operation. First she tried to reassure the candidate that his faux pas was not as devastating to his election as some of his staff feared. Then she tried to close the gap his comments had created among his black supporters.[66]

ER wrote to Pauli Murray that Roy Wilkins, who had assumed the leadership of the NAACP in 1955, was too "hot-headed" in his response to Stevenson's statement. Indeed, she thought Wilkins's response was as intemperate as that of the national press corps. Conceding Stevenson's use of "gradualism" was "unwitting," she nevertheless rationalized, gradualism "means one thing to the Negroes" but something "entirely different" to him. She then phoned Ralph Bunche to assess the extent to which Stevenson's remarks undermined his support in the civil rights community. Although she acknowledged to Bunche and Murray that she and Stevenson did not agree on all civil rights issues, ER minimized their differences with Stevenson and worked to tone down the rhetoric on both sides. Thus, even though she supported Powell's amendment and Stevenson did not, she continued to assert that he was as committed to equal education and civil rights as she. "Fundamentally," she wrote her young friend Murray, "there is [not] any cleavage between my point of view and that of Mr. Stevenson and the really wise Negro leaders."[67]

However, despite her irritation with Wilkins's criticism of Stevenson, the NAACP's increasingly acerbic attacks on moderate Democrats, and Stevenson's pleas for support within the civil rights community, ER refused to compromise her position on Powell or her endorsement of Stevenson. While most historians emphasize ER's loyalty to Stevenson above her loyalty to civil rights, they overlook the finesse with which Eleanor Roosevelt played these camps against one another to promote school desegregation and the extent to which she believed she could make Stevenson do the right thing.

Indeed, her unceasing support of the Powell amendment reveals her ultimate strategy. When faced with either forsaking *Brown* or undermining Stevenson, ER did neither. Rather, she skillfully defined the issue in ways that could satisfy most of the parties involved in this dispute without betraying her own conscience in the process. At first, she tried to keep the Association from endorsing the Powell amendment, she wrote Congressman Richard Bolling. However, when the Association refused to accept her position and voted to stand behind the rider, she followed their lead. While she appreciated his argument that the amendment would provoke a filibuster, destroy the bill's chances for passage, and provide ammunition for Republicans, ER argued that she was not an elected official but a spokesperson for civil rights. She had the responsibility, therefore, to endorse the proposal. To do otherwise would be shirking her responsibility.

While ER conceded to Bolling that members of Congress might have valid reasons for opposing the amendment, she did not. On the contrary, because she was not an elected official, ER believed she had a strong "obligation" not to compromise and "to live up to the principles in which I believe." Ending segregation, especially in education, "is essential to our leadership in the world and to the development of true democracy." Moreover, because she remained convinced that racial barriers would fall only when "the situation becomes so bad that the people are worried about all education," she "feared nothing will be done in the area of discrimination." The Powell amendment compelled the nation to act.[68]

As Eleanor Roosevelt struggled to reconcile ideology and political pragmatism, Stevenson increasingly turned to her to clear his path. Although she continued to support his election effort, she did not comply with his requests for intercession with civil rights leaders. Nor did she sit by when Roy Wilkins and Channing Tobias questioned Stevenson and the Democratic party's commitment to civil rights. When Wilkins suggested that black America should consider "swapping the known devil for the suspected witch," ER trumped his proposal with a declaration of her own. If he did not control his tongue and think through his positions, she would resign from the NAACP Board and release her letter of resignation.[69]

ER argued tersely that now was the time for power politics, not passionate outbursts. While she remained a loyal supporter of both Stevenson and the NAACP, she would make her own decisions. Thus, by convention, she still had enough clout among the Democratic leadership and the civil rights community as an independent figure in her own right to arbitrate the Democratic platform hearings on civil rights.

As the primary battle between Harriman and Stevenson intensified, civil rights received even more attention when Harriman tried to use his support of federal force to implement *Brown* to undercut his rival's support among the black community. To some extent, this tactic succeeded. The NAACP endorsed him, but Eleanor Roosevelt did not. She saw Harriman's move as less a genuine policy difference than a political ploy, she told Stevenson. But when her appeals to his moral indignation failed, she once again cautioned her candidate to recognize the political importance on his civil rights stance. While she fully appreciated the need to mobilize the "understanding and sympathy of the white people in the South" as well as the "understanding and sympathy and support for the colored people," she admonished Stevenson against doing anything that would undermine the black vote. "So you can't take away the feeling that you want to live up to the Supreme Court decision and go forward." That situation would do nothing but play into the hands of the Republicans and increase the chances for a divided convention as well as a bolt of southern conservatives. Finally, she suggested that there were two keys to a united convention: a more astute handling of *Brown* and a carefully worded platform supporting the decision's principles.[70]

Paul Butler, chair of the Democratic National Committee, agreed and recognized the unique status ER would bring to the platform dispute. As

Working with the Women's Division of the Democratic Party, ER actively campaigned for Al Smith in 1924, traveling to every county to organize his supporters, and often hosting a meeting of party leaders in her New York City home. Louis Howe is seated to her right. *(FDR Library)*

ER, believing the problems youth confronted during the Depression needed special attention, pressured FDR to create the National Youth Administration to address their concerns. ER lent her public support by visiting NYA programs, where photographers captured her enthusiasm for the controversial programs. *(FDR Library)*

MRS. ROOSEVELT CARRIES A PISTOL!

'Packs' a Weapon on Lone Auto Journeys---And Knows How to Use It

NEW ORLEANS, March 6 (U.P.).—Mrs. Eleanor Roosevelt modestly revealed today that she is somewhat of a marksman with a pistol.

She was trained, she said, by New York State prison guards as a matter of protection when she drives about the country alone.

In a press conference here preceding the first of a series of lectures on a six-State tour, the President's wife casually told of her adeptness with a gun. She said: "Only when I travel by automobile—that is, when I drive alone, have I any protection. And then I carry a pistol."

"Can you use a pistol?" asked astonished reporters. She replied: "Oh, yes, I was trained by the prison guards of New York and I'm a fairly good shot."

At her lecture, Mrs. Roosevelt re-emphasized that she had no desire to become President of the United States. The time is not yet ripe, she said, for women in that field. "Not that many of them are not worthy, but at this time no woman can obtain and hold the support necessary for election."

Mrs. Roosevelt was to speak in Baton Rouge tonight.

MRS. FRANKLIN D. ROOSEVELT AT WHEEL OF HER AUTOMOBILE
First Lady was Starting for a Drive Through Rock Creek Park

When ER became first lady, she refused Secret Service protection, insisting that she be able to travel as freely as possible. The agents complied with her wishes only after they discovered she knew how to shoot. and convincing her to carry a pistol when she drove alone. Intrigued by yet another example of ER's independence, the press treated ER's "packing" as front page news— especially after she nonchalantly remarked: "I carry a pistol,and I'm a fairly good shot."

(Earl Miller, Washington Herald)

Aboard the presidential yacht the *USS Sequoia*, ER works on her correspondence. Working with secretary Malvina Thompson, she would either forward letters to relevant government agencies or begin her own investigation, often answering many individual queries in detail. By 1935, she would answer approximately 150 letters a day. *(FDR Library)*

The Howard University Honor Guard escorts ER to the University Faculty Club in May 1936. The publication of this picture enraged southern segregationists and became the opening salvo in Georgia Governor Eugene Talmadge's presidential challenge to FDR. *(Library of Congress)*

ER addresses the founding meeting of the Southern Conference for Human Welfare in Birmingham, Alabama, November 1938. Only moments before, she had defied local segregation ordinances by placing her chair in the aisle between sections designated for black and white conferees. *(Wide World)*

ER presents the NAACP's highest award, the Spingarn Medal, to Marian Anderson at the association's 1939 annual convention. In a nationally broadcast address, she praised the contralto's courage, dignity, and talent. With ER's help, Anderson had given an open air concert at the Lincoln Memorial three months before, after being denied use of the DAR's Constitution Hall. *(Wide World)*

When the Dies Committee implied that the American Youth Congress was riddled with communists, ER invited AYC leadership to the White House to help them prepare their testimony. Here, surrounded by the press, she accompanies William Hinckley, former AYC chair, to the hearings.　　*(FDR Library)*

When delegates to the 1940 Democratic convention refused to nominate Henry Wallace, FDR's choice for vice president, Harold Ickes wired FDR, "the convention is bleeding to death." FDR sent ER to stop the revolt. James Farley, who had challenged FDR for the nomination, met ER at the plane, where the press besieged them.　　*(UPI/FDR Library)*

The convention floor was so chaotic when ER entered the hall that Frances Perkins and Lorena Hickok urged ER not to speak. Conceding the scene was "deafening," she nevertheless strode to the podium and spoke without notes, leading one senator to label her speech a ``masterstroke.'' The convention nominated Wallace on the first ballot. *(UPI/FDR Library)*

ER highlighted contributions made by black Americans to the war by visiting black defense workers and praising their contributions in "My Day." During a May 1943 visit to Lucy Stows Hall, a dormitory for black women defense workers, she warmly greets Mary McCleod Bethune, whom ER later called "my dearest friend in my own age group."

(OWI/Library of Congress)

As attacks on black Americans increased during World War II, ER became more convinced that racial justice was the litmus test for democracy. She asked the nation why it could support Jim Crow while it cursed Adolph Hitler and appealed to those listening to a broadcast of "My People" to hold democracy accountable.   *(Office of War Information/Library of Congress)*

Disturbed by riots in two internment camps, FDR agreed to let ER meet with interned Japanese Americans. After visiting the Gila River, Arizona, camp, ER posed with interned children and WRA Director Dillon Meyer. She left the camp caught between FDR's demand for internment and her guilt over her public deferment to his wishes.   *(FDR Library)*

The
ALABAMA SUN
VOL. I—NO. 6   BIRMINGHAM, ALA., APRIL 28, 1944   PRICE TEN CENTS

ELEANOR DEMANDS EQUALITY FOR NEGROES IN ADDRESS

Sun Gets Commended For 'Exposure' Of Vic Hanson's Press

'There Is A Race Problem' And It Must Be Solved By Honest To Goodness Southerners

From comments of the people, the SUN is rapidly rising in estimation and prestige for the fearless manner in which the double-dealing of the Victor Hanson press, the News-Age-Herald, were exposed in last week's issue. It will be recalled that the SUN printed the comments of the columnist of those papers in which he loudly and truthfully proclaimed, "THERE IS A RACE QUESTION IN ALABAMA." This statement was in defiance of the statements published in the so-called news columns and the

CLAIM SOUTH IS APT TO SWITCH IN ITS VOTING

editorial page of the Hanson papers who have repeatedly agreed with some brain-crippling politicians in the statement that there is no such problem existing in our state.

Of course, anybody with common sense, who is a REAL Southerner and loves the traditions of Dixie, knows "THERE IS A RACE PROBLEM." But some people, and that are absent in their beliefs, can't

Eleanor and Some More Niggers

Stops From Travels To Tell Communists Of Her Convictions

Seems To Enjoy Talking To Negroes And Making Them Think They Are As Good Or Better Than White Women And Men

Every time Eleanor opens her big mouth, it's big news for the Negro newspapers, who boast of a circulation of over 2,000,000 in the South. The past week, Eleanor was journeying as usual but stopped at Newark, N. J., where a bunch of Negroes were having a jamboree, and naturally Eleanor had to stop there and have her picture taken again with a nigger.

The Urban League, mentioned in this article, is a Communistic-type organization, advocating equality for negroes principally. So it will probably be easy to figure out the reason for Eleanor being the guest of honor.

It may make you sick but go ahead and read of Eleanor's doings with the negroes in New Jersey. Here it is:

NEWARK, N. J.—Over 700

Look Out, Big Shot Coons!!

The ALABAMA SUN sent one of its representatives out of the city this week to check on a matter

Her public support of civil rights enraged many southerners. *The Alabama Sun,* a segregationist newspaper with statewide circulation, devoted an entire issue to ER's views, declared her a threat to America, and called for her arrest and deportation.   *(Alabama Sun/FDR Library)*

Although FDR replaced Hebry Wallace with Harry Truman in the 1944 campaign, ER continued to favor Wallace. She had the former vice president seated next to her at the 1945 inaugural dinner. Truman is seated on the far right.

(FDR Library)

By October 1945, ER resumed her schedule of speeches and public appearances. Large, attentive crowds, such as this gathering at Times Square to hear her open the Victory War Bond drive, typified the response ER received when she reentered politics after FDR's death. *(UPI)*

When A. Philip Randolph threatened FDR with a march on Washington if the president did not act to prevent employment discrimination in defense work, ER served as their interm diary. She later joined Randolph and New York's mayor LaGuardia at this February 1946 Madison Square Garden Rally to Save the FEPC when Congress threatened to abolish it. *(UPI)*

ER joined the NAACP board of directors in 1945. Although her UN appointment prevented her from attending some meetings, she frequently changed her schedule to meet the NAACP's needs. Appointed along with Walter Reuther and Roy Wilkins to the Legal Defense and Education Fund, she became its co-chair in 1950. *(Library of Congress)*

ER accompanies President Truman and her close friend Walter White, executive secretary of the NAACP, to the steps of the Lincoln Memorial where all would address its annual convention. Truman's speech, the first presidential appearance before the NAACP, helped revise ER's initial impression of the new president. *(Wide World)*

ER and UAW President Walter Reuther, photographed at a 1949 Workers Defense League award banquet, had great respect and affection for one another. From the late 1940s until her death in 1962, they would meet once a year to read their most vitriolic hate mail aloud to one another. *(FDR Library)*

an unrivaled advocate of civil rights who also had negotiated the Declaration of Human Rights, she brought both unquestioned credibility and experience to the controversy and rancor the platform hearings would certainly provoke. As the convention drew nearer, three distinct camps within the Democratic party promoted three different civil rights planks. The NAACP and Americans for Democratic Action (ADA) demanded a plank that strongly endorsed federal action supporting *Brown*. Stevenson supported the decision but opposed using federal force to implement it. Finally, many southern constituents who signed the Southern Manifesto supported former Virginia Governor John Battle who threatened a repeat of the 1948 Dixiecrat walkout.[71]

If not handled adroitly, the civil rights plank might explode at the convention. As the person charged with preventing such a melee, Paul Butler tried to keep this from happening. ER had strong ties to the first two groups and the forbearance necessary to work with the latter discontents. Consequently, as the primary season drew to a close, Butler phoned ER and asked her not only to begin drafting a model platform statement on civil rights and *Brown* but to consider chairing the session as well.[72]

Most historians of the 1956 Democratic campaign agree that "none of the convention's work had been arrived at under greater pressure than the platform committee's work on civil rights." Preconvention media coverage predicted a platform fight over civil rights which would fracture the party and destroy its chances for victory in the fall. When party officials turned to Eleanor Roosevelt to prevent this anticipated dispute, they recognized both the unique power she commanded in moderate and liberal Democratic camps, as well as her unparalled influence within the civil rights community. If ER clearly understood the dangers in accepting this assignment, she also saw it as an opportunity to commit the party to civil rights more strongly than it had been in the past. She shouldered this responsibility not only because she wanted to help Stevenson, but also because of the opportunity to define the civil rights issue in a way that both expanded party support and strengthened its commitment to racial justice.[73]

Because the platform she drafted did not mention *Brown* by name, Lash believed that ER compromised when she should have fought for explicit endorsement. By drafting a plank that was acceptable to Stevenson and that failed to give carte blanche support to the desegregation decision, he argued that ER did not have her "finest hour." Although this clearly was not ER's most shining moment, it was not for the reasons Lash promoted. She did not abandon her principles, she merely lost a major battle.[74]

The specific language that Eleanor Roosevelt chose to use reflected her continuing struggle to balance ideology with political reality. While unquestionably ER might have drafted a more ringing endorsement of *Brown*, her reluctance to cite it by name is not a reflection of her loyalty to Stevenson or her lack of devotion to civil rights. ER sagaciously tried every political maneuver she knew to achieve a plank that would keep the segregationists in line and not undermine the liberals' commitment to civil rights. As committee chair, she presented her arguments to the public prior to convening the platform subcommittee on civil rights. When tempers flared, she calmly sought to reconcile differing points of view. She postponed votes and held caucus meetings until three o'clock in the morning. She cajoled delegates and debated with state officials and civil rights and party leaders. She was determined not to let any extreme position determine the terms of the debate and often used her power as chair to schedule testimony that would make zealous segregationists look desperate. For example, when Circuit Judge George Wallace, who would become Governor of Alabama in 1962 after campaigning on an "anti-Nigger" platform, harangued subcommittee members about the evils of integration, he presented a stark contrast to Martin Luther King, Jr., who at ER's request, had preceded the judge and opened that day's session with a prayer.[75]

This finesse kept the committee focused. As a result, the plank Eleanor Roosevelt promoted was the one adopted by the convention. While it opposed both federal force and southern resistance, the plank committed the party to racial justice; "emphatically" reaffirmed the party's "support of the historic principle that ours is a government of laws and not of men;" and recognized the Supreme Court as "superior to and separate from any political party, [whose] decisions of which are the law of the land."[76]

Even with the specific omission of *Brown*, the vote on the plank was close. Of the seventeen-member subcommittee, all five southerners voted against the plank. ADA National Chairman Joe Rauh was outraged and Wilkins threatened to send black voters to the Eisenhower ticket. No one group was the clear winner and eventually Rauh realized what ER had tried to do—conceding that when ER played political hardball she had the ideals to which she was committed foremost in her mind.[77]

The final wording of the platform reveals two things: first, the extent to which ER was unable to negotiate a compromise more acceptable to liberals than moderate and conservative Democrats, and second, her desire to keep the party together so that Vice President Nixon, who she thought would be running the country behind the scenes because of Eisenhower's poor health, would not be reelected with a large mandate.[78]

Eleanor Roosevelt did regret avoiding specific mention of the decision. But she spent the entire fall campaigning for the Democratic ticket because she believed that the only chance *Brown* and the other components of the civil rights agenda had was with a Democratic administration. ER did play politics with the civil rights plank, but she played it with the principles of civil rights foremost in her mind. Although she enjoyed the contest, she did not play politics as though it were a game for personal glory. She well understood the tensions inherent in a tenuous coalition trying to unseat an incumbent president. Consequently, in her view, the 1956 civil rights plank was not a step backward to 1952 but a step forward in the spirit of 1948.[79]

Clearly, there were limits to ER's power. First, while she could sway moderates and liberals, she could not convince Democratic conservatives that a compromise on *Brown* was justified. Moreover, she could not completely convince the civil rights community that her candidate was the most qualified to be their candidate. Yet in spite of these defeats, she could apply a great deal of pressure on those Democrats who only gave lip service to civil rights to practice what they preached. "We must have a united party," she told the delegates in a fifteen-minute extemporaneous address to the convention. "It is true we have differences. . . . [but] We are on trial today to show what democracy means . . . and democracy means freedom." She recognized that implementing democracy was not easy and she urged the delegates to understand that society must constantly review its mores and practices. "Our Democracy may be the oldest," she continued, "but it must be a young party with young leadership. . . . It must have the courage to look ahead."[80]

If power is defined as "the production of intended results," then ER proved herself a key power broker of the convention. She entered the convention with three goals: to prevent a divided convention, to promote the civil rights agenda, and to ensure Stevenson's nomination. Her skillful leadership during the platform hearings kept the party together while simultaneously advocating civil rights demands. Moreover, her close relationship with the candidate ensured that he would not only be apprised of civil rights proposals but also be expected to respond more directly to black requests than he had in the past. As one *Washington Evening Star* columnist commented, "probably the best politician in the Democratic party is Eleanor Roosevelt."[81]

ER understood that there were two components of political action: process and result. While her platform work during the convention emphasized the process she deemed necessary to achieve civil rights, her work during the campaign underscored the need for strong civil rights action and highlighted the products that would result from a Democratic victory. Throughout her whistle-stop campaign tour for Stevenson, she repeatedly praised the courage and dedication of black and white Americans who confronted racial discrimination boldly, assailed the Eisenhower administration's record on civil rights, and asserted that the Democratic party and Stevenson were the only chances the nation had for immediate implementation of racial reform.

"Being a war leader," she told rallies across the nation, "does not necessarily mean you know how to fight civilian battles." The president has a responsibility to lead the nation. "We haven't seen him lead the fight." Eisenhower could have defused the tension the *Brown* decision promoted. "It could have been a simple thing," she told reporters in Columbus, Ohio. "He could have called the white southern leaders and the colored leaders together to see at what point they could agree." Furthermore, the president has used the Powell amendment as an excuse to keep from supporting federal aid for education. This was inexcusable politics. The federal government must support education, ER told audiences in as diverse communities as Detroit, Michigan, and Beckley, West Virginia, "because we want to see our schools integrated and all our young people have equal opportunities."

Yet the people also had the responsibility to promote civil rights. Consequently, when she appeared with Martin Luther King, Jr., Harlem Congressman Adam Clayton Powell, and Autherine Lucy at a sold-out rally in Madison Square Garden, ER could tell the crowd that while she knew they were there to honor Lucy's courage in confronting the University of Alabama, where she had been the first black to seek admission, northerners must have the courage to recognize that prejudice was as much a problem in the North as in the South, and she exhorted the audience to confront their own racism, organize around their issues, and vote their convictions.[82]

Behavior such as this led Pauli Murray to write "one of the reasons we 'firebrands' (your own term) love you so is that when you're 'riled up,' you're a bit of a firebrand yourself." The civil rights activist praised ER for her conduct during the campaign. "I gloried in you," because she had "labored a lifetime to build values of peaceful solutions . . . , and could see it slipping away because of stupidity, dishonesty and downright apparent lack of integrity."[83]

Although Eisenhower was reelected, Eleanor Roosevelt did not ease up on the allegations she had leveled toward him during the campaign. She continued to assail his avoidance in implementing *Brown* and his reluctance to submit civil rights legislation. When the Civil Rights Act of 1957 was finally introduced, ER carefully avoided referring to the president, opting

instead to discuss the attorney general as the primary force behind the legislation. "It is a relief to know Attorney General Herbert Brownell, Jr., actually and finally has asked Congress to pass the civil rights bill," she wrote
the last day of April 1957. Perhaps, she continued, the Justice Department
will finally begin to live up to its responsibilities.[84]

Nor did she exempt conservative members of her own party from
scathing criticism. When Lyndon Johnson, then Senate majority leader,
joined forces with Georgia Senator Richard Russell to defeat the jury trial
amendment to the 1957 Civil Rights Act, ER castigated his concession to
consensus, labelling it a parliamentary attempt "to fool the people." And
she used her review of Carl Rowan's *Go South for Sorrow* not only to renew
her commitment to speedy implementation of *Brown* but also to attack its
major opponent in bold, disgusted language. It had been three years since
Brown, and all that had happened was that Misissippi Senator James
Eastland, chair of the Senate Judiciary Committee, had defined the terms
of the debate. She mourned how easily parts of the South and some "in the
Senate . . . have accepted the leadership of a man like Senator Eastland."[85]

When she learned that the first White Citizens Council met in the
Senator's Mississippi home five days after the court decision, she could not
restrain her disgust. "I could hardly believe that our country would allow
such a man to lead and that our people would allow themselves to be guided
by such ideas and such untruths." By acquiescing to Eastland, the country
not only abandoned its conscience but also promoted its own hypocrisy
throughout the world. "We say," she continued, "that democracy is inspired
by Christianity" yet the nation allows Eastland to use the Bible to justify
"doctrines entirely opposed to the whole spirit of Christianity, or ethics, of
human brotherhood." Such behavior depressed her immensely. "I do not
have to go South for sorrow. I sorrow here for the shame of our past three
years."[86]

Such outspoken bitterness had its personal costs. ER well understood
the political and financial repercussions of unrestrained support of civil
rights. The Republican editorial board of the Scripps-Howard chain
instructed all affiliates to drop "My Day." Every paper in the chain except
The Washington News complied with the order. The death threats and
harassment ER received increased during the *Brown* controversy. When she
spoke in favor of integration in 1955 in Guilford, North Carolina, her critics dynamited a 200-year-old-tree not 300 yards away from the church in
which she spoke. Upon learning of ER's scheduled appearance in Houston
in 1957, the Texas White Citizens Council telegraphed her demanding that
she leave Texas "immediately." When ER refused and kept her speaking

engagement in Houston, they picketed her address at the Hotel Watkins, hurled racial epithets at those attending the event, and threatened to run her out of town on a rail. Furthermore, when the Monteagle chapter of the Ku Klux Klan planned to raid the Highlander School the day ER was scheduled to address an integration workshop, support for their plan was so widespread that the county sheriff agreed to turn his back and disavow any foreknowledge of the raid. ER, despite warnings from the FBI to stay away, not only attended the workshop, but drove unescorted through country roads to reach the school.[87]

Consequently, when the Mothers League of Little Rock decided to incite white segregationists to rise up against the integration of Central High School in the summer 1957, Eleanor Roosevelt's own personal experiences and ideological commitment to civil rights placed her squarely behind Daisy Bates and the black students Bates championed. After praising the courage of those involved in the struggle to integrate Central High School in "My Day," she then assailed the moral cowardice of the Faubus and Eisenhower administrations. Governor Orval Faubus lacked the scruples necessary for true leadership because he was "interested only in his own future" and promoted a selfish and "dangerous game" of blatant disregard for the law that "called out all the worst side of other prejudiced individuals." As leader of his party and the nation, Eisenhower could counteract this by exerting "greater leadership" than he had shown on integration and education.

When the president hesitated, ER mourned the lack of executive leadership with a resurgent bitterness. "No one [in elected office] . . . tried to control and draw out the best in the people instead of the worst." America, she castigated, has not yet learned "the lesson that where there is prejudice and oppression in one area it invariably spreads to many other areas." Through the absence of presidential and congressional leadership, national politicians encouraged irresponsible opposition and allowed citizens to turn their backs to the nation's founding principles.[88]

■ **"We must be prepared . . . to hazard all we have."**
Nonviolent Resistance from SCEF to the Freedom Riders

By the late 1950s, as white supremacists increasingly attacked black and white civil rights workers, ER allied more and more with those who argued that court challenges and legislative proposals were no longer the only effective way to implement reform. While she had supported orderly demonstrations protesting segregation throughout the late thirties and forties, with the notable exception of her defiance of Birmingham's segregation ordinance at the founding meeting of the Southern Conference of Human Welfare in 1938, her endorsements were selective and usually couched in restrained language. By the early fifties, infuriated by the red-baiting of civil rights organizations, her reticence vanished and she became more bold in her support for dramatic demonstrations. "Like the scream of 'red,' the scream of race has become a political symbol and each man thinks he has to outscream the other to prove his purity," she angrily wrote in early 1956. "Pious hopes and inaction cannot change this behavior." Change can only come by "cool heads . . . soft speech and firm action within the law."[89]

Eleanor Roosevelt's endorsement of civil disobedience was an endorsement of nonviolent resistance, not a blanket approval of law-breaking and black nationalism. Separatism was as much of an anathema to her as segregation and she chastised those Black Muslims who preached that social division was the only avenue to equality. Just as she admired the discipline and self-sacrifice Gandhi personified in his struggle to free India from British rule, the discipline exercised by those involved in the Freedom Struggle personified to ER the continuing evolution of American democracy. ER supported nonviolent resistance because she believed that pressure applied within the confines of the law to force those who disregarded the law to obey the Constitution was both intrinsicly moral and American. Thus in the early postwar years, when Bayard Rustin coordinated civil rights workshops across the nation to "help blacks understand the principles of Ghandian techniques," he asked ER to help get "whites to face their responsibility" and recognize "the need to be in alliance with blacks when they moved." She lent support to this project not only by attending the workshops but by "encouraging blacks and whites [to] divide up into teams" and by trying peacefully to integrate restaurants. Dorothy Height recalled often being part of a small group of young black women whom ER would join for a Saturday night dinner in a downtown southern white restaurant and how serene ER was in her challenge to segregation.[90]

Although this endorsement of peaceful protest and civil disobedience did not please many of her closest associates, ER nevertheless supported civil rights organizers and activists with the intensity she had previously devoted to policy analysts and politicians. Therefore, by the end of the fifties ER believed that the Southern Conference Education Fund (SCEF), Southern Christian Leadership Conference (SCLC) activists, and the Freedom Riders sponsored by the Congress on Racial Equality (CORE) were as central to the success of the civil rights agenda as the NAACP, Americans for Democratic Action, liberal politicians, and the Southern Regional Council.

ER's ties to SCEF were strong from its inception. Initially begun as a committee of SCHW, on whose board of directors ER sat, SCEF separated from SCHW in 1948 and elected as its first president Aubrey Williams, the New Dealer whose social and economic politics most closely resembled ER's. Moreover, as the only biracial group in the South committed to dismantling segregation, SCEF reflected ER's longstanding commitment to integrated housing, education, and voting rights. Anxious to keep her support, Williams asked ER to sit on the SCEF board. She agreed, lent her name to SCEF organizational efforts, and rapidly began raising funds and promoting SCEF's agenda in her columns and speeches.

ER knew that this was a risky political endorsement. SCEF's attack on segregation and its social underpinnings quickly drew national attention and in 1950 ER found herself squarely amidst the controversy surrounding sexuality and segregation. When seven black men were sentenced to death for raping a white woman, SCEF editorialized against their execution in *The Southern Patriot*, arguing that a "study of the death penalties in rape cases showed that execution for rape was a penalty directed against the Negro." When Virginia Governor John S. Battle refused to commute the sentences, SCEF bitterly criticized his cowardice, by comparing Battle's conduct to that of the U.S. high commissioner for Germany who had granted a stay of execution to seven Nazi officials convicted of killing eighty American prisoners during the Battle of the Bulge.[91]

This stance and the fact that some of the defense attorneys had been members of the Communist party and the Civil Rights Congress served as a lightning rod for SCEF's critics. Ardent supporters of the House Committee on Un-American Activities (HUAC) now joined forces with the outspoken segregationists in attacking SCEF. Criticism increased in 1951 when SCEF launched a well-publicized campaign to integrate southern hospitals and professional schools. Undaunted by the ferocity of the Fund's critics, ER lent her very public support to SCEF not only by hosting a fundraiser in the midst of the public outcry over SCEF's position but also by insuring widespread press coverage by bringing Madame Pandit, the sister of Prime Minister Nehru, and Mary McLeod Bethune to the reception as guests of honor.[92]

In 1955, the lynching of Emmett Till and the murders of Lamar Smith and The Reverend George Lee, two black men who had resisted pressure to remove their names from the voter registration list, compelled SCEF and ER to become more assertive in their drive for civil rights laws that would give federal protection to civil rights workers. SCEF decided to circulate a petition nationwide demanding that the Senate Subcommittee on Human Rights hold hearings to determine whether federal intervention was needed to protect the civil rights of black Mississippians and their white supporters and to assemble a biracial delegation that would present the petition to Subcommittee Chairman Senator William Langer.[93] Even though ER was embroiled in the 1956 primaries, she was happy that SCEF took action and did not moderate her support to the Fund. She sent letters to Langer endorsing the Fund's request for congressional inquiry and praised their plan in "My Day." And when their petition was denied, she publicly expressed disappointment in her column.

Nor did her support wane when, in spring 1956, SCEF began to pressure the New Orleans School Board to hold public hearings on school desegregation. When the board agreed, the Senate Internal Security Subcommittee, chaired by Senator Eastland, counterstruck and released its report declaring that SCEF had, among other things, concealed the names of its communist members and was committed to dismantling American "social traditions." Inspired by the press coverage the Eastland report received and aware of Eastland's own commitment to resistance, White Citizens Councils formed in New Orleans and circulated copies of the Senate report, a reprint from *Firing Line* charging SCEF with treason, and a petition demanding that the school board rescind its decision allowing SCEF to hold hearings. Although the NAACP opposed SCEF's efforts and must have cautioned ER against supporting them, after consulting with Williams and SCEF Executive Director Jim Dombrowski, ER once again endorsed their efforts and clearly stated her support for public hearings. Her concern with presidential posturings did not temper her support of local initiatives or compromise her interpretation of *Brown*.[94]

ER's most crucial support for the Fund occurred in 1957 when it hired Anne and Carl Braden, two Kentucky journalists who had been blacklisted for challenging Louisville's restrictive housing covenant and for possessing "subversive" literature. In 1954, Andrew Wade, a friend of the Bradens who was trying to move his family "outside the ghetto," asked them to help him find a house. The Bradens then bought a home in an all white-suburb and resold it to Wade. After the Wades moved in, neighborhood hysteria quickly escalated into vigilante violence. Despite shootings, cross burnings, and numerous other assaults, the Bradens and the Wades remained in the house until Klansmen destroyed it with dynamite. A politically ambitious district attorney, emboldened by the silence of the cowed black community, argued that Carl Braden had incited the violence and arrested him for sedition against the state. A search of the Braden home produced political literature the prosecutors immediately labeled "seditious" and an all-white jury quickly convicted Braden and sentenced him to fifteen years in prison. Eight months into his sentence, the Supreme Court declared in the *Nelson* decision that state sedition statutes were unconstitutional and Braden was released.[95]

SCEF then hired the Bradens as field secretaries in 1957 to help make the "Fund become a nerve center of inter and intra-racial communication in the South." Though leery of the damage that charges that Carl Braden was a communist might do, ER expressed pleasure with the programs the Bradens had developed to promote compliance with *Brown*, endorsed the sympathy boycotts they planned in the North against branches of national chains whose southern branches complied with Jim Crow policy, and, despite increased pressure from ADA and NAACP leadership, continued publicly to support SCEF until her death. Moreover, when Anne Braden's *The Wall Between*, a strong assault on segregation, racial customs, and the bias of the southern judicial system, appeared in spring 1958, four ringing endorsements were prominently displayed on its book jacket: Aubrey Williams, Martin Luther King, Jr., A. Philip Randolph, and Eleanor Roosevelt.[96]

ER's support of SCEF placed her in stark opposition to the NAACP, the ADA, and many of her Democratic allies who argued that the Bradens' suspiciously "red" credentials damaged the cause of civil rights. Weary and fearful of FBI and HUAC allegations, moderate civil rights organizations, which concentrated on legal redress, feared that their efforts would be tainted by Carl Braden's refusal to answer questions before HUAC in the fall of 1958. The NAACP began an "all out" lobbying effort to persuade ER to disavow SCEF. Although ER did resign from the SCEF board in 1960, after the Fund hired William Howard Melish, an Episcopal priest with long ties to the American Labor party and the Council on Soviet-American Friendship, leading some within the Fund to argue that she had succumbed to the NAACP's arguments, she continued to endorse and raise funds for their work while she shifted most of her active public support to CORE and SNCC.[97]

SCEF was not the only rift that developed between Eleanor Roosevelt and the NAACP in 1958. The Association refused to take cases that could be seen as assaults on social practice rather than legal custom. Its staff already had more cases than it could handle and the legal division worried that extraneous cases might derail its master plan for challenging the legality of segregation. While sympathetic, ER now disagreed; consequently, when Conrad Lynn (a black attorney who had defended the Bradens in Kentucky) asked for her support in "the kissing case," a case that the NAACP refused to take, she cooperated without hesitation.

Hanover Thompson, age nine, and Fuzzy Simpson, age seven, rode their bicycles home Halloween week and passed a group of children who asked them to stop and play. The boys eagerly joined the group and soon began to play house. Sissy Marcus then recognized Hanover as the young boy whose mother used to work for her mother and with whom she had played as a toddler. Marcus, excited to see her old playmate, kissed him on the cheek and ran home to tell her mother. Thompson sat on the curb, stomping spiders. Bernice Marcus, enraged by her daughter's delight, washed Sissy's mouth out with lye, and called the police to report that a black youth had sexually assaulted her white daughter. The police arrived while the children were still playing.

Thompson and Simpson were charged with rape and held incommunicado for a week in an underground cell in the Union County, North Carolina, jail. No NAACP attorney would defend them, opting instead to refer the case to Lynn. After accepting the case, Lynn learned that Juvenile Judge Hampton Price had already held a "separate but equal trial," declared the boys guilty, and sentenced Simpson to twelve and Thompson to fourteen years in prison. Price had summoned Bernice and Sissy Marcus to his chambers, heard Mrs. Marcus describe the assault, and then separately summoned the boys and their mothers to hear their response. As Price later told Lynn, "since they just stood silent and didn't say nothin', I knew that was a confession of guilt." Despite Lynn's argument that this procedure violated the defendants' constitutional right to confront their accusers, Price stood firm in his ruling. Lynn's subsequent appeals failed; no North Carolina judge would overrule Price.

Lynn then telephoned Eleanor Roosevelt, whom the attorney knew from his investigation of the Till lynching and his work on NAACP and SCEF events. When he finished relaying the case, a very angry ER wondered aloud "whether this country would ever learn" and lectured the attorney for not calling her sooner. She did not know what she could do now, other than pressure other attorneys to help. Lynn suggested that she emphasize the international repercussions such an event might have and then told her that he had arranged for a petition signed by several thousand students of the Roosevelt High School in Rotterdam to be delivered to her on Lincoln's Birthday. ER volunteered to take the petition to Eisenhower and use it as a lever to demand the boys' release. The day the petition arrived ER phoned the president and Justice Department officials, argued that the case was an ethical and international disgrace, and demanded that he "put a stop to this persecution." Eisenhower, who had known of the case prior to his conversation with ER but had refused to take action, then phoned North Carolina Governor Luther Hodges and ordered the children released and their records destroyed.[98]

Lynn's call for aid came as ER prepared to help the NAACP and the ADA mobilize congressional support for a new civil rights bill. Southern segregationists, displaying the hyperbolic intransigence that would soon surface in Little Rock, so dominated both the House and Senate Judiciary Committees' hearings on the Civil Rights Act of 1957 that they depicted Section III, the provision allowing the Justice Department to use injunctions and other legal maneuvers on behalf of individuals who alleged violation of their civil rights, as a resurrection of Reconstruction power politics in which the North would once again invade the South and demanded that any suit alleging violation of civil rights must be tried in front of a jury.

Angered by the "extremely inflammatory speech" of southern opponents, ER took the unusual step of devoting almost half of July and August "My Day" columns to the debate over the 1957 bill. In clear, impassioned language, she appealed for support for Part III and for opposition to the jury trial amendment, arguing that if the two amendments were passed she could understand why "many people would feel that perhaps there had never been any real intention of passing a civil rights bill at all." She also scathingly attacked Georgia Senator Richard Russell, whom she depicted as sounding "a little like old General Toombs, who walked out of Congress on much the same note to finally fight in the Civil War."[99]

The Senate voted overwhelmingly to strike Part III from the bill and, after southern and western Democrats joined forces, passed the jury trial amendment by a 51–42 vote. ER struggled not to succumb to sarcasm and despair. "Little as this civil rights bill seems to do," she was hopeful that Congress would pass the weakened act, writing that she "would prefer to have even the little that will come with this bill than to have nothing." Yet all restraint vanished when she warned segregationist Democrats of the consequences of their actions.

"I think the Southern Senators, led by Senator Johnson and Senator Richard Russell, have won a costly victory—because this fight for civil rights is not going to stop." The world is changing and reactionaries cannot stop it. "If the people of Africa are on the move, the people of the United States are also on the move." Furthermore, "our people are not going to be satisfied with crumbs such as this civil rights bill gives them. It will bring us no peace."[100]

The behavior of Judge Price and the inability of Monroe Country blacks to unseat him only compounded the frustration that ER felt during the debate over the 1957 legislation and underscored the urgent need for federal protection of civil rights for southern blacks. In a blatant appeal for votes as a presidential election approached, both parties in 1959 introduced civil rights bills, two of which included the provisions for federal intervention deleted from the 1957 act. Sectional and political rivalries prevented consensus and Congress adjourned without having taken action. An embittered, dispirited ER worried that once again animosity would triumph over principle.

She began 1960 by taking her case directly to Senate leadership and attacking the critics of federal protection in her column. In late January, she wrote Lyndon Johnson to serve notice that "there are three things I think absolutely essential in any civil rights bill": *Brown* must be complied with immediately, the "Attorney General must have the power to move in all cases of civil rights violation," and federal registrars should be sent to districts that have denied blacks the vote. Sending a clear message that she intended to play a much more assertive role than she had in 1957, she offered to change her schedule and meet with Johnson when she returned from the West Coast on February 11. Appealing to his party position, she concluded "I think it is absolutely necessary that we make a Democratic record on this bill. The Negroes are going more and more to the Republicans, and those that we can count on as Democrats need a real achievement on the part of the Democrats to point to as a reason for backing the Democratic Party."[101]

The challenge that she presented to the public, liberals, and the party through her columns was just as uncompromising. "It seems a pity that there has to be argument about the best way to assure part of our citizenry the rights that it should automatically enjoy," she wrote in mid-February. "In looking back over the many years since Lincoln's Emancipation Proclamation . . . how little we have to be proud of." When Clarence Mitchell informed her that Democratic whips were being outmaneuvered on roll calls because Republicans were calling for votes in the evening when the liberals had left the floor, ER scathingly reproached those Democrats who seemed to be more interested in watching the clock than passing legislation. "No liberal should be more than five minutes away from where he can be reached in case of a vote until the continuous session is over," she wrote in a "My Day" column which appeared in the midst of the filibuster.

"A liberal cannot give lip service to civil rights. He must be on hand if a vote is going to be obtained on the civil rights bill in this session."[102]

When the Senate bowed to southern pressure and refused to approve the sections of the bill that would have given the Justice Department the power to prosecute civil rights cases, ER sarcastically criticized the Senate's cowardice. She asked readers to envision "long lines of colored people waiting to register in Alabama, Mississippi or some of the other southern states and someone walking quietly up and down in a low voice saying: 'Wait till you come out of that registration booth then we will get you.'" Would whites have that courage? Could they "brave the immediate threat and go in to register and meet what difficulties had to be met at that time," only to "get home to find that [their jobs were] gone or that some [other] threat would be made?" This legislation "will be of no practical value unless the Negro is protected by Federal authority and it is given from the first move to the last."[103]

Clearly by 1960, Eleanor Roosevelt was losing patience with those who counseled moderation. The convention fights over civil rights, the violent intensity of the white backlash, the lack of leadership in both the Democratic party and the Republican White House, the strong egos of liberal leaders and the timidity of their responses, and the extreme reluctance of many Americans to confront their own prejudice became increasingly more difficult for her to tolerate. Furthermore, ER knew that her influence was waning and that she no longer commanded the power she once did. Yet, rather than wallow in bitter frustration, she increasingly turned to youth as well as older mainstream activists for both information and inspiration. In the course of her career, she had always maintained strong contact with students and activists. But now, in the throes of Little Rock, Louisville, Monroe, and Freedom Summer, she increasingly identified with these younger and bolder agents of social change.

Justine Wise, the daughter of ER's close friend Rabbi Samuel Wise, worked in a Macomb, Mississippi, school run by civil rights activists and regularly wrote ER about her activities. The author and civil rights activist Lillian Smith also regularly sent ER information regarding racial violence in Georgia. Myles Horton and other Highlander alumnae also kept her informed of racial justice and civil disobedience training programs the school offered. But perhaps the most revealing assessment of ER's increasing support of civil disobedience was made by Joe Rauh to Joe Lash. Resentfully, Rauh complained that ER was paying more attention to Anne Braden than she was to ADA, concluding, "I suppose it's hopeless" to continue arguing against the Fund.[104]

It became increasingly more difficult for ER to discuss civil rights without discussing racist violence and to discuss segregation without comparing it to apartheid. With each speech she gave on civil rights, her support of the freedom workers became more clear. As she was fond of telling college audiences, "we must be prepared . . . to give and hazard all we have" in the pursuit of democracy. Weldon Rougeau, the nineteen-year-old chair of Baton Rouge CORE, was the perfect example of ER's new passion for protest. The Southern University student spent fifty-seven days in an isolated seven-foot-square cell until bond was posted for his 90-second picket of a downtown department store that refused to integrate its retail staff at lunch counters. When released, he resumed his distribution of "don't buy" leaflets, was rearrested, and resentenced to seventy-eight days in solitary confinement. As she told the organizers and politicians she solicited for CORE, his "conviction and willingness to sacrifice himself" impressed her greatly. "The only way we can change human behavior," ER wrote in 1962, "is by human behavior, and behavior is modified and changed and developed and transformed by training and surroundings, by social custom and economic pressure."

Those who practiced what she preached held a special place in ER's conscience. As she confided to her secretary Maureen Corr after Corr asked ER why she was humming at breakfast, "I had the most wonderful dream last night, Maureen. I dreamt I was marching and singing and sitting in with students in the South." Consequently, protecting the civil rights of civil rights activists became one of Eleanor Roosevelt's top priorities.[105]

Marvin Rich, community relations director for CORE, who recognized the depth of ER's commitment to civil disobedience, requested that she write the introduction to "Cracking the Color Line." Designed to "describe techniques [CORE] has found effective in eliminating racial discrimination" in public recreational, educational, and employment facilities as well as confronting barriers to voting and housing, the twenty-six-page pamphlet presented a "how-to-do-it approach" by examining successful "action projects." ER gladly accepted the assignment. "Advocating civil rights," she wrote, did not "constitute criminal anarchy."[106]

While much of ER's support for student civil rights activism was firmly grounded in her idealistic concept of democracy, when the students' lives were threatened the hard-nosed political realist in ER took over. ER was outraged when white citizens groups attacked the Freedom Riders in Mississippi and Alabama; she immediately responded to requests for aid from the Congress of Racial Equality. She took CORE attorney Carl Rachin's complaints against Mississippi Judge Ellis directly to the president and when John Kennedy failed to give the response she wanted, she continued to press his brother the attorney general for a reprimand.[107]

While the Kennedy administration deliberated over what course to take to protect the Freedom Riders, Eleanor Roosevelt and CORE pressured the media to pay more attention to the violence the activists encountered. Although suffering from the illness that would kill her six months later, ER became so incensed by the violence that she left her sick bed that spring to serve as convener of the Committee of Inquiry into the Administration of Justice in the Freedom Struggle. "We cannot allow such sacrifices to be made without raising our voices in protest," she argued when she asked prominent civil libertarians to join the Committee. If the administration and the Congress refused to act to protect the civil rights and civil liberties of the activists, then public pressure had to be exerted to force the government to live up to its responsibilities.[108]

Convened by CORE in May 1962, the Committee held two days of hearings to educate the public about, and pressure the media to devote more attention to, the "legal roadblocks" used throughout the South to deprive black citizens of their civil rights. With ER chairing, the seven-member panel heard testimony from such civil rights activists as Bob Moses, Weldon Rougeau, and Albert Bigelow. Throughout the weekend, the Committee heard witnesses recount: the lack of police protection for nonviolent demonstrators; police violence against peaceful demonstrators; police use of dogs, tear gas, water hoses, and billy clubs; the fact that violent white racists were almost never arrested and that courts and police took almost no actions against them; the high bail and bond assigned civil rights cases; the obstruction of the ordinary channels of raising bond and bail; the excessive sentences imposed for civil rights actions; and the brutality of jail officials.[109]

As chair of the Committee, ER engaged in her last public fight for civil rights. At the age of seventy-seven, ill with tuberculous and aplastic anemia, she entered the Community Room of the *Washington Post* Building determined to assemble the testimony necessary to force reluctant members of Congress to press their local officials to comply with federal statutes. As the day progressed and witness after witness described in great detail the physical and emotional violence they had encountered during their work for civil rights, ER's patience wore thin. After the lunch break, she displayed a rare burst of temper. When Committee counsel Joe Rauh objected to citing the names of corrupt judges for the record, she banged her gavel and abruptly discounted his pleas to enter executive session. These officials should be accountable for their conduct, she retorted. The public should know how unjust some justices were. As chair, ER won the dispute. The offending officials' names were entered into the public record.[110]

Just as the violence in Columbia, Tennessee, framed the beginning of ER's postwar civil rights activism, so holding the perpetrators of violence accountable in the Committee of Inquiry into the Administration of Justice in the Freedom Struggle completed her commitment. Her experience on the Committee was "one of the most difficult experiences [she had] ever been through." Although all the presidents of the three national television news divisions and the publishers of twenty major newspapers responded defensively to her criticisms and promised more prominent coverage of the attacks on civil rights advocates, she could detect no discernible difference in their coverage. And while the Kennedys ultimately took steps to protect the Freedom Riders, she believed that this action was too little, too late. She "found it terribly painful," she wrote two months later in *Tomorrow Is Now*, "to accept the fact that things such as I have described could happen here. . . . This was the kind of thing the Nazis had done to the Jews in Germany." How little the nation had progressed in its "practical application of democratic principles."[111]

During the last twenty-seven years of her life, Eleanor Roosevelt worked to bring racially inclusive democratic principles to practical politics. As she aged, she became more assertive in supporting a multifaceted approach to combating racial injustice. In this struggle, she became convinced that for democracy to succeed, America must address its racism. While she often succumbed to moments of bitter frustration, she nevertheless strove to trust "the future of essential democracy." It was a delicate, often disheartening balance.

Such heartfelt and consistent commitment to civil rights placed her in a unique position among party officials and civil rights activists. While they might disagree with her positions, they could never question her dedication. Therefore, Martin Luther King, Jr., could write her after a conference they had in 1961 discussing the best way to pressure Kennedy into issuing executive orders on civil rights issues, "I am always inspired by your words and your presence." Bayard Rustin could argue that Coretta Scott King should stop presenting herself as Martin Luther King's widow and should begin modeling herself after ER. And Conrad Lynn, when asked to assess ER's understanding of racism and civil rights, could reflect thirty years after her death that "she was to the left of the NAACP. She was the only one there who saw the big picture—the social and the political."[112]

■

Chapter Five

CONFRONTING THE VITAL CENTER
Civil Liberties in War and Peace

For most of her life, Eleanor Roosevelt defended civil liberties with the same zeal with which she tackled racial discrimination. Yet, unlike her unceasing public defense of civil rights, her support of civil liberties was sometimes modified and curtailed by her husband's foreign policy. Consequently, her record as a defender of dissent and protector of the suspect is marred by her sporadic and reluctant compliance with FDR's wartime security priorities.

These compromises do not alter ER's fundamental identity as a civil libertarian. Indeed, from her earliest years at Marie Souvestre's Allenswood Academy, she believed that the rights to speak one's mind, to dissent, and to associate with whomever one wanted were inviolate. Her compromises suggest that although she did not share FDR's belief that the emergencies of wartime should override the Bill of Rights, after America entered the war, ER nevertheless conformed to her husband's demands. In short, she did not challenge programs that FDR believed necessary to sustain his foreign policy with the abandon with which she challenged his delaying of domestic reform. The historical record does not fully reveal why ER complied with FDR's wishes. What is clear, however, is that as soon as her husband died, she returned to defending her own civil libertarian principles with fervor.[1]

A review of Eleanor Roosevelt's position on civil liberties from 1940 until 1962 amply demonstrates three aspects of this phase of her career. First, the curtailment of wartime civil liberties caused ER great pain. Second, she strove whenever possible to defend the liberties of Americans whose actions were questioned by the administration. And third, once the war was over, she spoke out forcefully and consistently in defense of civil liberties as if to make up for lost time and missed opportunities. Such strident defense of postwar civil liberties often placed her in the center of the debate over free speech and created yet another reason for both the right and the communist left to criticize her. Consequently, throughout the New Deal and the Second World War, ER increasingly had to defend her positions on free speech and dissent to both her critics and her supporters. Conservative and communist activists assailed her commitment to "moderation"; liberal politicians questioned her political savvy; and intellectuals ridiculed her columns for their simplistic, unanalytical approach. This created a new dilemma for her. ER intended to defend civil liberties the same way she defended civil rights. She planned to show the nation through her own actions that there was nothing to be afraid of but the paralysis unreasonable fear inspired. However, when her activism failed to allay public concern and the assault on political nonconformity intensified, she often assumed an unaccustomed role of lay political philosopher.[2]

By the beginning of the Cold War, when the vast majority of New Deal liberals either followed Arthur Schlesinger, Jr., and Reinhold Niebuhr's lead and denounced popular front alliances or enthusiastically endorsed Henry Wallace's progressive crusade, ER had already carved out a different path. While her observations of FDR's relationship with Stalin led her to view American-Soviet cooperation as unrealistic, she refused to capitulate completely to a policy characterized by "iron curtain" and consensus politics. She would not follow her husband's lead and temporize civil liberties. Although she believed that American communists did not keep their word, allowed the Soviet Union to set their agenda, and promoted a public duplicity she labeled "the philosophy of the lie," she repeatedly refused to endorse the public demand to outlaw membership in the Communist party. Moreover, she insisted that fear must not dominate American domestic and foreign policy and agonized over the rift this issue caused among the liberal rank and file. Such positions placed her outside the vital center and exposed her to criticism from the moderate and liberal left and the conservative right.[3]

Eleanor Roosevelt's dual stature as FDR's widow and as a political leader in her own right made her the major symbol for both protecting FDR's legacy and expanding domestic reform. Her insistent wartime demand for civil rights and widespread social and economic reform underscored her deviance from mainstream American politics. Consequently by 1945, many conservatives and most members of the far right believed she represented all that threatened America, all the dangers they associated with liberalism and feared from communism.

To these critics ER's danger lay in her ability to dissuade average Americans from unconditionally accepting what they saw as the heart and soul of the American heritage: repudiation of communism, unbridled patriotism, and the politics of segregation and social conformity. As the right's chief target from the 1930s on, ER, more than any other noted liberal, encountered both its fury and its scorn. Her detractors were so vitriolic that one prominent columnist asserted "never before in American history has a respectable woman been subjected to such reckless and relentless attack."[4]

Indeed, as the editors of the ever-vigilant, anti-communist newsletter *Counterattack* asserted, the positions ER promoted "aroused more temperature than temperateness." One had only to look briefly at her obsession with reform to recognize that she was the "honorary head of the Communist front." To other correspondents, her speeches were nothing more than "Russian propaganda [designed] to stir up trouble at a time when we can least afford it." They pleaded with J. Edgar Hoover to recognize that she was "a Traitor and no longer worthy to remain a citizen." Not to be outdone by his supporters, the arch segregationist Theodore Bilbo agreed and even proposed his own solution to ER's treachery. She should be deported to Liberia, he told his Senate colleagues, where she could rule over as many American blacks who could be deported along with her.[5]

As irate as the rabid anti-communists were in their condemnation of Eleanor Roosevelt, their rebukes paled in comparison to the hyperbole of Protestant fundamentalists. The Reverend Dan Gilbert, director of the Christian Press Association, argued that ER's support of Planned Parenthood proved that she was really a communist at heart because she deliberately "invaded the sanctity of the white family." Others saw her as nothing more than "a pro-Stalin politician [and] an alien-minded traitor" who insisted on forcing "Negro rule." Anti-ER sentiment even dominated the debate when an unidentified southern clergyman tried to defend FDR's war policies. When the pastor claimed that the congregation should be

Confronting the Vital Center

patient with FDR because the president "depended upon a higher power for guidance," a stalwart member of his congregation jumped up and shouted, "I don't like her either." Consequently, most revivalists would agree with Gerald L. K. Smith's assessment. "The only good thing I can say about Eleanor Roosevelt," he told a 1946 Tulsa, Oklahoma, gathering of the Christian Nationalist Crusade, "is that she gave her old gold teeth to the Elk Lodge."[6]

Such attacks spurred her efforts for two reasons. First, she experienced the personal and political damage that unwarranted attacks caused. As she acknowledged in a rare disclosure, by 1944 she was "getting a little weary of the criticism heaped on me" when she acted as a foil for other leaders. Second, she realized that she, unlike many of the victims of the right's anti-communist propaganda, was in a unique position to combat it. Opinion polls repeatedly proved that whatever issue she tackled, more of the public approved of her conduct than disapproved. With the platform this reservoir of support afforded her, ER throughout her long career strove to educate America about the dangers of labeling anything unconventional "Communist." Formerly the White House activist, after leaving Washington she assumed the role of the nation's civics instructor. Using both her column and her lecture tours as forums, ER urged her readers to understand three major points: that difference promotes democracy; that it is essential for citizens to honor their civic responsibilities; and that if the first two conditions were not met, the nation's future would be in jeopardy.[7]

As the suspicion of Soviet espionage began to dominate postwar American political rhetoric, Eleanor Roosevelt expanded the focus of her writings and speeches to counter the political backlash this anxiety provoked. In a style that often bordered on oversimplification, she strove to educate the average American about the inherent danger of stereotyping difference and of unquestioned acceptance of unsubstantiated accusations. Often using "My Day" and magazine articles as a one-woman teach-in, ER never strayed from her commitment to dramatizing complex issues for ordinary readers. Sometimes these portrayals galvanized her readers to take the stand she supported. More often, her readers admired her integrity while they questioned her position. Yet whatever the response her words provoked, her commitment to political speech and freedom of association served as an omnipresent reminder that politics need not be dictated by bullies and demagogues.

This staunch commitment to the democratic ideal did not cloud Eleanor Roosevelt's astute and hard-headed assessment of the political arena. First and foremost a political realist, ER struggled to keep political ideals in front of an apolitical public. Moreover, she recognized the diffi-culties inherent in this effort. As the Cold War deepened and the public rejected the arguments she presented, she found herself in the unusual posi-tion of trying to explain the liberal philosophy to a public more concerned with immediate results than with long-term analysis.

This role was not always comfortable for her. While she always had been an educator, she never claimed to a philosopher. However, she always had believed in study, deliberation, and action. The more she spoke out, the more of a lightening rod she became. Conservatives pounced on her will-ingness to take the postwar lead on civil liberties and civil rights and depicted her simplistic statements as the quintessential example of liberal-ism's theoretical weakness. By 1954, she began to worry that Americans were so afraid of criticism that many saw any admission of American shortcom-ings as a declaration of communist sympathy. As she told readers of the *New York World Telegram,* "I am beginning to think . . . that if you have been a liberal, if you believe that those who are strong must sometimes consider the weak, and that with strength and power goes the responsibility, auto-matically some people will consider you a Communist." She continually worried that this deep-seated fear of difference would deter the next gener-ation from speaking their minds and advocating new policies. As she acknowledged a few months before she died, it was becoming "increasingly difficult" for a person to appreciate "himself [as] a unique human being." The constant pressure for conformity undermined individual character and demanded vigilant opposition. She urged Americans to resist, to think for themselves. Unless a person "keeps the sharp edges of his personality and the hard core of this integrity intact, he will have lost not only all that makes him valuable to himself but all that makes him of value to anyone or any-thing else."[8]

When the public preferred unquestioning compliance to her thoughtful dissent, ER refused either to wallow in martyrdom or mount a pedestal. Instead, she tried to concentrate on the long-range goals she promoted. This was not an easy process. While she often criticized herself for her weaknesses, she nevertheless recognized that public ridicule was part of the price she must pay for a public career. As ER noted often, she took great comfort from the example of Thomas Paine, who endured slander and still kept the faith. Frequently she responded to queries about her perseverance with a favorite quote from *Common Sense.* "Those who expect to reap the blessings of freedom, like me, must under go [sic] the fatigues of support-ing it." In short, she knew that she must lead by example and not just gen-erate liberal rhetoric.[9]

Eleanor Roosevelt tried to pass these hard-won lessons on to the rising generation of activists. When Myles Horton and Rosa Parks came to tea in 1955, one of the first questions she asked was "have you been called a Communist yet, Mrs. Parks?" When Parks replied that much to her surprise she had been, ER then criticized Horton for not preparing the Montgomery woman for the venom she would encounter. Clearly, earlier than other major leaders in America, ER not only understood how demands for social and political change promoted what historian Robert Griffith would later label "the politics of fear" but also strove to support those brave enough to risk these attacks.[10]

■ "We do not move forward by curtailing people's liberty." Conscientious Objectors and Japanese Americans during World War II

Unlike his wife, FDR did not accept criticism graciously. Less than fifteen months into his administration he instructed the FBI and military intelligence to investigate "the subversive activities" of American communists and fascists. When opposition to his policies increased, the president ordered his staff to monitor the actions of the nativist, fascist, and fundamentalist organizations leading the right's attack on the New Deal. Labeling these zealots "Trojan Horses" who undermined the national security, FDR prodded the FBI to take up the slack when Attorney General Francis Biddle failed to act quickly enough to satisfy him. As the attorney general later reminisced, FDR was "not much interested . . . in the constitutional right to criticize the government in wartime."[11]

Eleanor Roosevelt took a different approach. Throughout the forties and fifties, she insisted that the "real value" of any democratic relationship is that people's differences are respected. While her husband hid behind the vaguely worded rhetoric of freedom of thought, ER challenged her audiences to understand exactly what freedom meant. Repeatedly, she asserted that the nation would reach its full potential only when it was not afraid of dissent. She warned: "when fear enters the hearts of people, they are apt to be moved to hasty action" and accept self-destructive policies. Thus, to succumb to suspicion was not only poor government but imprudent politics as well. As she told readers of *The Nation* in 1940, "We do not move forward by curtailing people's liberty because we are afraid of what they may do or say. We move forward by assuring to all people protection in the basic liberties under a democratic form of government, and then making sure that our government serves the real needs of the people."[12]

As the fear of fascism swept America in the thirties and early forties, ER continued to insist that democracy demands that the individual's right to self-expression be upheld. "The tendency that you find today in our country only to think that these are rights for the people who think as we think" distressed her a great deal. While ER recognized that consensus was essential for political stability, she also argued that the majority should not determine the scope of the discussion. As she told a 1940 gathering of the Chicago Civil Liberties Committee, "I believe that you must apply to all groups the right to all forms of thought, to all forms of expression."[13]

In direct opposition to her husband, who professed allegiance to free speech while he monitored his antagonists, Eleanor Roosevelt argued that one's critics must have the same rights as one's supporters. As first lady, she continued to defend her belief that the United States must "be willing to listen or to allow people to state any point of view they may have, to say anything they may believe." To do otherwise is to believe that people are not capable of choosing "for themselves what is wise and what is right." The nation confronted a challenge: "to decide whether we believe in the Bill of Rights, in the Constitution of the United States, or whether we are going to modify it because of the fears that we may have at the moment." She knew that this choice would not always be an easy decision or popular position. Nevertheless, she argued that it was crucial to the nation's survival. "That is the only way we are going to keep this country a law-abiding country, where law is looked upon with respect and where it is not considered necessary to take the law in your own hands."[14]

As the war with Germany neared, Eleanor Roosevelt struggled to reconcile her own anti-war sympathies with the information FDR presented on German conduct. She detested Franco and Hitler, but she had a long-standing commitment to anti-war activism. Throughout the twenties, she campaigned tirelessly for America's entry into the League of Nations and the World Court, strongly endorsed the Women's International League of Peace and Freedom (WILPF), co-chaired the Edward Bok Peace Prize Committee, lobbied in support of the Kellogg-Briand Treaty, and circulated memoranda discussing economic reform as a deterrent to war to all her New York State Democratic Women colleagues. In the 1930s, she had supported the efforts of the National Conference on the Cause and Cure of War, helped finance the Quaker-run Emergency Peace Committee, joined the advisory board of the American Friends Service Committee, keynoted the 1937 No-Foreign War Crusade, and praised those Loyalists who resisted Franco. She so admired Carrie Chapman Catt's work for WILPF that she told FDR that Catt was the greatest woman she would ever know. In 1938, she published *This Troubled World,* in which she argued that negotiation and economic boycott, rather than military conflict, were the best ways to curtail aggression and that the nation could "profit" from a careful review of the mistakes made by the League of Nations.[15]

But, as Blanche Wiesen Cook demonstrates, this passionate commitment to peace did not mean an unswerving allegiance to fascism or isolationism. Indeed, as fascist aggression increased, ER became more outspoken in her opposition to isolationist policies. She described her stance to Lewis Chamberlain in 1934 as that of a "very realistic pacifist." When he objected to her support of the president's plan to increase naval appropriations, she replied that while she wanted peace, military preparedness was both expedient and necessary. "We can only disarm with other nations; we cannot disarm alone." In 1936, she seconded recommendations made by a senatorial investigation of the munitions industry chaired by George P. Nye that characterized the relationship between weapons manufacturers and the military as "shameless profiteering." The government, she declared, either should nationalize or tightly control the munitions industry. By 1938, she used "My Day" to denounce the Japanese attack on China and announce support for the Abraham Lincoln Brigade's fight against Franco. When pacifists questioned these positions, she replied, "I have never believed that war settled anything satisfactorily, but I am not entirely sure that some times there are certain situations in the world such as we have in actuality when a country is worse off when it does not go to war for its principles than if it went to war."[16]

When FDR phoned her at 5 A.M September 1, 1939, to tell her that Germany had invaded Poland, ER knew that the United States would eventually enter the war and began to assess the role she would have to play. "I . . . could not help feeling that it was the New Deal social objectives that had fostered the spirit that would make it possible of us to fight this war," she later admitted. Well aware of the role she played in fostering these objectives, ER could not easily avoid recognizing that she would have a major part in defining the domestic conduct of the administration's war effort. She recognized that "to win the war" America would "have to fight with our minds, for this is as much a war for the control of ideas as for control of material resources." Her challenge was to highlight the ideas she thought essential to winning both the international war against fascism and the domestic war against intolerance and prejudice.[17]

Her letters to close friends throughout 1939 and 1940 are filled with references to reconciling this conflict. She pleaded with Carola von Schaeffer-

Bernstein, an Allenswood classmate who now lived in Berlin, to explain why Germans supported Hitler's policies. She repeatedly turned to Pearl Buck for advice on Asian politics and began to question FDR's policies restricting Japanese importation of American products. When students with whom she worked in the American Youth Congress passed a resolution declaring that they would not participate in any war, she angrily challenged them to help her solve her own dilemma. "What if you are pushed into war? . . . What if you are pushed into a fight you do not seek but which you are obliged to accept?"[18]

When friends could not help answer her questions satisfactorily, she turned to literature for advice. But, the works of Thomas Mann, Bertold Brecht, Pearl Buck, Lillian Hellman, Adolph Hitler, Carrie Chapman Catt, and Leo Tolstoy produced more questions than answers. "It is very difficult for me to think this situation through," she confessed in September 1938. "If we decide again that force must be met with force, then is it the moral right for any group of people who believe that certain ideas must triumph to hold back from the conflict?" Consequently, when Harry Hopkins returned from a secret visit with Prime Minister Winston Churchill in 1940, he faced a barrage of questions from her about England's ability to meet those domestic crises, such as food and housing shortages and acerbic political criticism, which were exacerbated by the incessant bombing of London.[19]

Furthermore, having watched the Wilson administration promote the First Red Scare and knowing very well how intransigent FDR could be toward his critics, ER immediately intuited that he would make anti-fascist and rabid pro-Allied propaganda a major part of the American war effort. Although she ruefully concluded that America must fight, ER worried that the war against fascism could easily inspire an ever-escalating domestic propaganda campaign to promote unquestioning compliance with American policy. She recoiled at the arguments made by America Firsters. And while she conceded that propaganda was essential to keeping American hearts and minds behind the war effort—and indeed made her own contribution by making the first Radio Free Europe broadcast—she feared the damage that another Creel Committee (the World War I Committee on Public Information, which promoted American support for the Allies by attacking anything German) would inflict.[20]

ER's ability to see the complex relationships between war and peace, propaganda and education, and consensus and dissent placed her in an uncomfortable position politically and personally. The peace movement wanted her to be its voice within the administration and the administration expected her to defend its position with its anti-war critics. But rather than let these expectations confine her, ER worked to find a position she could advocate with conviction.

Just as she refused to believe that the emergencies of wartime justified postponing domestic reform, ER also refused to believe that the war warranted total suspension of political criticism. Consequently, she worked to restrain the zeal with which the administration reprimanded its critics. She knew her position would not be popular with either her husband or the public. Perhaps better than anyone else, she recognized that her husband would not tolerate critics of American war policy. Yet rather than downplaying the president's vindictiveness, ER tried to counteract FDR's obsession with silencing his opposition. Thus, despite the contempt in which she held their beliefs, ER defended the rights of the German American Bund, the America First Committee, Westbrook Pegler, and Father Charles E. Coughlin to state their opinion of American war policy. Moreover, she repeatedly refused to moderate her staunch opposition to censorship of any sort. For example, not only did ER refuse to rebuke Pegler, the quintessential FDR-hater, for disparaging her children, she also attacked those within the administration who argued that the novels of Howard Fast and Lillian Smith were too controversial, and therefore obscene, to be handled by the post office.[21]

Still, the lists of those she defended had important and significant gaps. In fact, there were times when her silence was so notable that she could reasonably be accused of turning her back on her principles. She did not speak out when eight alleged Nazi spies were tried in a military rather than a civilian court. Furthermore, when Walter White asked her aid in promoting a 1944 civil rights campaign that linked the racist treatment of the Japanese Americans to the segregationist policies of Jim Crow, ER, after consulting with FDR, balked and advised White to abandon this strategy. Focus more on individual cases, she pleaded, rather than across-the-board indictments.[22]

World War II not only tested the limits of Eleanor Roosevelt's power within the administration, but also presented her with a more personal crisis of her own. She had already strained her relationship with FDR and his advisers by publicly rebuking his decision to put the New Deal "away in lavender." When the administration's energies increasingly focused on war planning, FDR's staff increasingly resented her interruptions on issues they considered extraneous. In the face of such mounting opposition, ER prioritized her causes.

Despite her suspicion that some Americans would experience sudden religious conversions to avoid military service, Eleanor Roosevelt supported

Americans who, out of a genuine commitment to a "higher calling," refused to take up arms but who agreed to serve their nation as noncombatants. Indeed, from early 1940 until V-J Day, she admonished those who attacked conscientious objectors. In a nationally broadcast radio address on October 14, 1941, ER not only praised the service the objectors were providing in medical facilities, but also reproached her audience for condoning those who impugned the objectors' convictions and harassed their families. Make no mistake about it, she insisted, "the test of democracy and civilization is to treat with fairness the individual's right to self-expression, even when you can neither understand nor approve of it."[23]

ER did not qualify her support once the American fleet at Pearl Harbor had been attacked. In fact, her commitment to this issue proved so unwavering that she refused to drop the subject when the German and Japanese press interpreted her activism as a reflection of FDR's weak leadership. Nor did ER limit her support of conscientious objectors to public pleas for tolerance. She actively campaigned within the White House and on Capitol Hill for a new program that would provide these men with "college-level training" for special noncombatant positions in "foreign relief work." However, much to ER's dismay and to the Selective Service and War Department's delight, Congress killed the four-month-old program when the American Legion protested. And when she learned that the Civilian Public Service camps, the noncombatant details to which the objectors who agreed to serve were assigned, often abused their workers, she sided with the objectors against their supervisors.[24]

ER understood that congressional retaliation against conscientious objectors echoed the sentiments of many enlisted personnel. She knew firsthand how intense reaction could be when people believed their lives and patriotism threatened. When she published her response to an outraged mother who asked her why ER could defend those who stayed at home while her son faced death daily, Americans responded by the hundreds, incensed that she could be so faint-hearted in her support of American military personnel.

Beleaguered, but unrepentant, ER continued to urge that both sides, if they could not respect one another, should at least agree to acknowledge each other's sacrifices. "I can not help feeling very sorry for honest conscientious objectors," ER wrote in a June 1944 "My Day" column completely devoted to this issue, "for I am quite sure many a young man must find it bitter to let other young men of his own age die and fight and give up time . . . ." Yet soldiers had a right to bitterness too. "It is only because of these young men, however, who are willing to fight that anyone can indulge himself in a personal viewpoint."[25]

Ultimately ER sided with those who decided to serve in non-military capacities rather than with those who refused to support the war in any way. While praising the ethics of those men who chose prison over compromising their conscience, she nevertheless conceded that she could not in good conscience follow their lead. "Some men go to prison and will not do anything during the period of war." That not only is their choice but also "is the price of doing what [they] believe in." She tried to understand their point of view—that "when the day arrives when war is no more, these men may feel they have hastened it"—but could not. She was more concerned with the immediate crisis. The Axis powers must be stopped because they threatened world civilization. While these young men of conscience had the right to dissent, she hoped that they would recognize that "they might not be alive or they might be slaves to other more warlike people if their brothers were not willing to defend them against other warlike peoples."[26]

Her contact with war had modified her views. She still valued pacifism, but she detested fascism more. Although she worked to state her positions clearly, continued to meet with peace groups, and supported the rights of those who refused to serve for reasons of conscience, the peace movement felt betrayed. But ER had no regrets.

Eleanor Roosevelt was not as true to her convictions when the civil liberties of Japanese Americans were at stake. Indeed, her actions on this issue reflect how conflicted she felt when her husband authorized policies that treated all members of the same race as potential enemy aliens. At first, she responded in her usual fashion—press conferences, speeches, and photo opportunities. Yet, after such an immediate endorsement of the loyalty of the Japanese American population, a strange silence overtook her. In glaring contrast to the numerous other controversial issues that she attacked during the war, there is no clear paper trail to follow to reconstruct ER's changing actions on internment. In fact the dearth of evidence indicates the extent to which she felt constrained. Perhaps ER and FDR never found common ground, and frustrated by his decision to defer reform, she resented the restrictions his war policies placed on her actions.[27]

What is clear is that at the beginning of the war, ER and FDR held opposite views of the rights of Japanese Americans. Less than a week after Pearl Harbor was bombed, ER toured the West Coast; praised a plea for racial tolerance by Mayor Harry Cain of Tacoma, Washington; posed with Japanese Americans for photographs that would be distributed over the Associated Press wire service; and editorialized against retribution. Respecting the rights of Japanese Americans, she told readers of "My Day"

December 16, "is perhaps the greatest test this country has ever met." "If we cannot meet the challenge of fairness to our citizens of every nationality," America will "have removed from the world the real hope for the future." FDR, on the other hand, determined to capitalize on the procedures he had utilized to monitor his critics throughout the 1930s, immediately summoned aides to discuss the wholesale detention of Japanese and German Americans.[28]

Eleanor Roosevelt never considered internment anything but "absurd" and "vicious" policy. She thought the treatment Japanese Americans received in 1941 "pathetic" and the attack on Pearl Harbor did not change her mind. These people "are good Americans," she told FDR, "and have the right to live as anyone else." Moreover, the policy would be countereffective. "Being bitter against an American, because of the actions of the country of his predecessors, does not make for unity and the winning of the war." Thus, when Yaemitsu Sugimachi offered a less dramatic proposal "for dealing with alien Japanese in wartime," she forwarded his plan to Attorney General Francis Biddle; and when Sam Hohri, press agent for the Japanese American Citizens League, told her that the San Francisco chapter of the Red Cross refused offers of aid from Japanese Americans "on the grounds that we might poison the medicines or bandages, treat knitted goods to injure the wearer, and deliberately sabotage its work," she appealed to the organization's national president to overturn the chapter's policy.

ER wanted to prevent the evacuation. She worked closely with the attorney general to ensure, first, that she understood how the Constitution applied to internment and, second, that the Justice Department presented a strong case against the policy to FDR. Furthermore, since ER was a faithful supporter of the American Civil Liberties Union as well as a close friend of Roger Baldwin, she probably participated in at least a few off-the-record conversations with him on the issue the ACLU called "the worst single wholesale violation of civil rights of American citizens in our history."[29]

However, once FDR signed Executive Order 9066 and internment began, ER fell silent. Although neither ER nor the president left any record of their conversations on internment, it is safe to assume that FDR presented the same case supporting internment to his wife that he presented to her ally, the attorney general. Convinced that internment was a military necessity, which superseded constitutional protections, FDR made it painstakingly clear to Biddle and other Justice Department officials that he would tolerate no opposition to this policy. Uncomfortable with the policy, ER nevertheless refused to continue to challenge it. She replaced the righteous indignation that characterized earlier "My Day" discussions of intern-

ment with oblique references to Japanese American patience and patriotism. By late March, she ruefully conceded that "unfortunately in a time of
war many innocent people must suffer hardships to safeguard the nation."
The president won the first round.[30]

Yet, once the relocation of Japanese Americans began, ER tried to ease
her conscience in many quiet ways. She told the *Washington Star*, "the
biggest obligation we have today is to prove that in a time of stress we can
still live up to our beliefs and maintain the civil liberties we have established
as the rights of human beings everywhere." Her refusal to White still fresh
in her mind, ER increasingly linked the civil rights of black Americans to
Asian Americans in her speeches and columns. She contributed to Japanese
American cultural associations and patriotic organizations and praised
their contributors in "My Day." And she corresponded with Japanese
American soldiers and an interned "pen pal." Unable to remain aloof, she
decided to act behind the scenes by monitoring evacuation procedures,
intervening to keep families together, helping to secure early releases, and
interceding with War Relocation Authority (WRA) personnel on behalf of
those few noninterned Japanese Americans who protested the treatment
their relatives were receiving in the camps. When she learned that the former assistant director of the Oriental Section of the Library of Congress,
Dr. Shio Sakanishi, had been detained without having charges brought
against her, ER asked the attorney general "to tell her whether the Naval
Intelligence had anything on" the librarian. When internees of the
Harmony Camp center wrote her decrying their accommodations, she
pushed the WRA to investigate its housing. And when a young Californian
suggested that consumer cooperatives be established within the resettlement areas, an intrigued ER encouraged WRA official Milton Eisenhower to
give the proposal serious consideration.[31]

The WRA was not the only department to encounter ER's pressure.
She prodded the Justice Department to oppose efforts to disenfranchise
Japanese Americans living in California and to investigate claims of
employment discrimination and retributive violence against Japanese
American fishermen. When interned women who had cleared FBI background checks wrote asking her assistance in enlisting in the Women's
Army Auxiliary Corps, ER quickly wrote Colonel Oveta Hobby, interceding on their behalf. Moreover, when Hungwai Ching told her during a
White House meeting of the attack against Japanese American soldiers stationed in Shelby, Mississippi, ER not only pushed FDR to act, but also
encouraged General George Marshall to investigate the assault, transfer the
soldiers to a safer base, and to send her "a report on this situation."[32]

ER waited until late 1943 to address internment publicly. By then the vast majority of the Japanese American population had been removed from the West Coast and those interned in the Poston, Arizona, and Manzanar, California, camps had either struck or rioted in protest of their incarceration. A concerned Ickes wrote FDR that the situation demanded attention and argued that the president must no longer "disregard the unnecessary creation of a hostile group right in our own territory."Although ER had wanted to visit the camps in the fall of 1942, it was not until FDR—worried that his interior secretary might be right—asked her to visit the Gila River camp on her way home from her Phoenix vacation that she actually agreed to make the journey. She announced that she would inspect the camps and report her findings to the nation.[33]

Yet instead of discussing the psychological and political climate of the camps, she wrote glowing accounts of the internees' attempts to beautify their small plots of land. She also avoided discussing the concerns about racism and resettlement the internees raised during her meeting with them. She tempered her discussion of the efforts the internees made to "take part in the war effort" with the reassurance that their "loyalty" must be authenticated by both the FBI and the War Relocation Authority before they could begin work. Given her previous statements, this deliberate evasion of racial and civil liberties stands out as a glaring omission.[34]

Despite this momentary lapse into public acquiescence, a decidedly anguished tone resonates through her other depictions of internment life. The night she left the camp, she confided to a friend that she had "just asked FDR if I could take in an American-Japanese family" only to have him evade her request by rationalizing that "the Secret Service wouldn't allow it." This evasiveness hurt and haunted her. No matter how loyal she tried to be in her defense of the administration's internment policy, no matter how many times she stated that "the whole job of handling our Japanese has, on the whole, been done well," she could not temper her belief that security was not the sole motivation. Suspicion of Japanese in America increased because one region "feared [them] as competitors" while the rest of the nation "knew so little and cared so little about them that they did not even think about the principle that we in the country believe in: that of equal rights for all human beings."[35]

Moreover, when ER tried to present the administration's case that loyal Japanese Americans were interned for their own protection, as hard as she tried she could not completely suppress her own doubts about this argument. For example, when she tried to justify the administration's demands for immediate relocation and the "unexpected [economic] problems" this caused Japanese property owners by arguing that "an effort was made to deal with [their financial holdings] fairly," she introduced as many arguments questioning this statement as she did endorsing it. Finally, she lambasted those West Coast xenophobes who believed that "a Japanese is always a Japanese" by declaring that such "unreasonable" bigotry "leads nowhere and solves nothing." Consequently, despite her endorsement of the policy, she could never completely convince herself that internment was either morally or strategically justifiable. As she confessed to a wounded Japanese American soldier who asked her to help expedite his parents' request for citizenship, "war makes far too much bitterness for people to be reasonable."[36]

Why ER acquiesced in FDR's probable demand that she be silent on such issues as internment of the Japanese Americans will never be known. Perhaps she kept quiet in public so that she could be more effective in modifying the policy within the administration. Or maybe she knew that this was one time in which FDR would not tolerate any deviance from his position. Or possibly she temporarily convinced herself that the suspension of Japanese American civil liberties actually protected them from zealous xenophobic violence. Or maybe she combined the best aspects of each of the above reasons to rationalize her behavior. Or perhaps she chose to give other critical domestic issues—racial violence, labor unrest, and postwar economic planning—higher priority.[37]

Unquestionably, Eleanor Roosevelt equivocated on the civil rights and civil liberties of Japanese Americans during the war. But it is also very apparent that she could not completely abandon her conscience and deny her convictions. Stark images reflecting her guilt occasionally surfaced in her public and private writings. She confessed to the nation that she could "not bear to think of children behind barbed wire looking out at the free world," and she confided to her friend Flora Rose that "this is just one more reason for hating war—innocent people suffer for the few guilty ones." Tormented by the policy, she conceded that "we must build up their loyalty, not tear it down." Thus, she promoted dissent and criticism as diligently as she dared. For example, when Secretary of War Stimson refused quick response to a November 1943 request by Dillon Meyer, director of the War Relocation Authority, to relax enlistment standards against interned Isseis, ER joined ranks with Meyer and Ickes to advocate closing the camps and proposed "a massive public education campaign to reiterate American commitment to democracy." Refusing to change course, FDR rejected her plan summarily, saying simply "it would be a mistake to do anything so drastic." Yet by this time, ER no longer deferred to his priorities. She corresponded with her "dear" friend Judge William Dennan of the U.S. Circuit Court of Appeals regarding his dissents in the *Hirabayashi* and *Korematsu* cases and carefully read the briefs he sent her, noting in the margins, "thanks. I get it."[38]

What is striking about ER's decision to support those whom the administration considered suspect patriots is, first, that in assuming such a position she deliberately contradicted her husband during the most crisis-ridden period of his administration and, second, that she refused to discount the hypocrisy inherent in her complicity with FDR's racist restrictions. ER chastised herself when she chided Americans who divorced the rights of the Japanese from their own rights and liberties. Reminding readers that a principle was only as effective as it was practiced, she subtly asked her fellow Americans to recognize that their rights would be protected only when they defended the rights of others. "We retain the right to lead our individual lives as we please, but we can only do so if we wish to grant to others the freedoms that we wish for ourselves." Many interned Japanese Americans intuited the anxiety ER felt and continued, like their black American compatriots, to keep faith with the first lady, even though she had not completely kept her pledge to them. Nowhere is this respect more clearly demonstrated than when Togo Tanaka, the organizer of the protest which rocked the Manzanar Camp, named his first born child after ER.[39]

Clearly ER did not speak out as forcefully and as continuously in behalf of wartime civil rights and civil liberties for all races and nationalities as she would in the postwar era. But it is also clear that her decision to challenge FDR during the war set the precedent for the more outspoken defense of civil rights and civil liberties stances she took during the Cold War. In an early draft of an article FDR eventually overruled, she blatantly conceded that "to undo our mistakes is always harder than not to create them originally—but we seldom have the foresight and therefore we have no choice but to correct our past mistakes."[40]

■ **"There is no such thing as a bystander on these questions." The House Committee on Un-American Activities and the Federal Bureau of Investigation**

During the late 1940s Eleanor Roosevelt continued to reiterate this theme, insisting repeatedly that "we must preserve the individual's right to be different." In a 1948 lecture tour, she urged her listeners to insist that the country "very carefully guard against" laws that would punish those who held beliefs to which the majority objected. If these rights were not guaranteed, the American citizen would be "as much an obedient servant as any individual living under a totalitarian form of government."[41]

The onset of the Cold War did not cause ER to moderate her position. She continued to proclaim that communism would succeed only in areas where democracy failed. When the vocal majority of the country increasingly began to detect communism in all aspects of American social and political life, her frustration finally overcame her usual restraint. "My Day" columns reflected this anger. In 1949, she minced no words in attacking those citizens who saw the red menace in any activity that differed from their own practices. "One thing I deplore in this country is the fact that we occasionally find people here and there who allow themselves to be carried away by hysteria and fear." Such constant and easy acquiescence was a pervasive threat to civil liberties. Whether people agree or not was not the point. "We must not reach a state of fear and hysteria which will make us all cowards! Either we are strong enough to live as a free people or we will become a police state. There is no such thing as a bystander on these questions."[42]

ER did not adopt this position solely in response to Cold War rhetoric. Rather, she had a long history of defending the civil liberties of liberals accused of communist sympathies and of communists themselves prior to the formation of the Popular Front in 1935 and the birth of the Cold War. In 1934, when the FBI tried to deport the anarchist Emma Goldman for a second time, ER interceded on Goldman's behalf. Moreover, she engaged in spirited debate with journalist Anna Louise Strong throughout the thirties and early forties as well as reading communist publications sent to her by Eleanor Levenson, manager of the Rand School Bookstore.[43]

As early as 1939, the year before Congress passed the Alien Registration Act, later known as the Smith Act, to restrict communist activism, she confronted Representative Martin Dies and the House Un-American Activities Committee. When Chairman Dies summoned leaders of the American Youth Congress and American Student Union before his committee in November 1939 to investigate allegations that the AYC was nothing more than a front for young communists, ER lent immediate public and political support to the student leaders. She met their train at Union Station, helped them prepare their testimony, and invited them to dine at the White House.[44]

The action that attracted the most attention, however, was also the act that most clearly revealed her opinion of HUAC investigative techniques. When the press treated her support of the activists as major news, the committee's two chief accusers, Representative Dies and committee member J.

B. Matthews, decided not to attend the hearing and left Joseph Starnes, a junior member, to chair. An hour into the hearings, ER entered the caucus room. Her sudden appearance at the committee was especially dramatic because only a week before the committee had rejected her offer to testify about her own AYC involvement.[45]

Trying to defuse the situation, Representative Starnes stopped the questioning and recognized "the first lady of the Land and invite[d] her to come up here and sit with us." ER understood the implications of this offer and refused to sit with those investigating her young associates. Deftly, she thanked the chair for his offer, responding instead that "I just came to listen." Yet when Starnes's questioning of Joseph Lash became more of an inquisition than an examination, ER moved from her seat in the visitor's section and took a seat at the press table and began to take notes. Immediately, Starnes adopted a less combative tone and the tenor of the hearings changed. Clearly, the first lady had outflanked HUAC. While she fervently believed that free association may be a constitutional right, she also astutely recognized that it was good politics.[46]

Although she had previously questioned the validity of HUAC investigations, with such a public defense of young political activists ER now became a major symbol of anti-HUAC action. Once again, her actions inflamed her critics and worried some of her close advisers. Even Barnard Baruch, one of her most intimate confidants, tried to convince her to moderate her position. For once, she did not take his advice. The FBI should be doing HUAC's job, she retorted. The charges made by the bureau must "be proved in court and they have to have real evidence. They cannot just make statements about people and take any amount of time to prove them." She thought that "if we allow ourselves to be so conditioned that we cannot believe in people whom we see and meet and work with for fear that somewhere in the background there may be a sinister influence," those who worked for reform "are never going to be able to do anything again." True liberals had no choice. "[A]s long as the work done is credible work, I think we must go ahead and help."[47]

This did not mean that ER, who knew from firsthand experience how zealous its director could be in persuing false allegations, thought the FBI should investigate all the allegations HUAC could present to it. Hoover's distrust of ER bordered on obsessive hatred. To Hoover, ER was nothing but an "old hoot owl" whose conduct approached treachery. He even presented FDR with tape recorded "evidence" proving that ER and Joseph Lash were lovers. Yet Hoover, in his rush to prove her disloyalty to FDR, apparently failed to detect the difference between ER's high-pitched, unmodulated voice and Trude Lash's throaty German accent. FDR, outraged at this intrusive assumption, ordered Hoover to disband the team that gathered this information. Yet the presidential rebuke only increased the director's determination to undermine ER's credibility. He not only refused invitations to appear on her radio program, but also aided efforts to prove that her political conduct was undermining America. For example, when the FBI received one of the several hundred letters asking for proof that ER either was or was not a communist sympathizer, the director instructed the Bureau to respond with a classic "non-denial denial" statement which said in effect that the bureau had no evidence on her only because they had not investigated her. Moreover, he reviewed all FBI memos discussing her "suspicious conduct," frequently making sarcastic references in the margin. "I often wonder whether she is so naive as she professes or whether she is just blind to lull the unsuspecting," the director noted beside a memo he had received on her activities. He even refused to believe her when she praised the agency. Indeed by the mid-fifties, his extreme animosity toward ER took on an even more perverse character. When rumors of W. C. Fields's extensive pornography collection reached Hoover, who was notoriously self-righteous, the director requested a meeting. The comedian feared arrest. Nothing could have been further from Hoover's intent. Rather than confiscate the collection, the director wanted to know, first, if Fields had a copy of an obscene caricature of ER and then, after enjoying the grotesque parody immensely, if Fields would copy it for him. Relieved, Fields immediately complied with Hoover's request.[48]

Yet ER again proved that she could play hardball as well as Hoover could, slyly reporting in later columns that FBI agents questioned her "about the loyalty and competence of John Foster Dulles." An enraged and embarrassed Hoover responded by instructing his staff that "this character is never again to be contacted by FBI unless I personally authorize it."[49]

Such conduct made ER extremely wary of J. Edgar Hoover's biases and his ardent desire to suppress criticism and dissent. Although ER endorsed the legal guidelines to which the agency was supposed to adhere, she did not approve of Hoover's leadership or of the agency's actual practices. While she acknowledged that treason was possible and that the government should guard against it, she nevertheless believed that bureau investigations, like any other legal exercises, should be based on constitutional principles rather than political rivalries.[50]

ER accelerated her criticism in 1948 when HUAC announced that communists had infiltrated American industry and government. In a voice resounding with frustration and outrage, ER proclaimed that she could not object strongly enough to such blatant "Gestapo tactics." Continually, she argued that the key concern should not be whether an individual was a communist, but whether there was incontrovertible evidence, achieved through constitutional procedures, that an individual advocated violent overthrow of the government.[51]

"I have never liked the idea of an Un-American Activities Committee," ER wrote in late 1947. "I have always thought a strong democracy should stand by its fundamental beliefs and that a U.S. citizen should be considered innocent until he is proven guilty." That the committee did not behave in such a fashion alarmed her. "[L]ittle people have become frightened and we find ourselves living in the atmosphere of a police state, where people close doors before they state what they think or look over their shoulders apprehensively before they express an opinion." Americans must learn to hear both bad and good opinions about their actions. Since the fear generated by the committee continued to dominate political discussion, ER concluded "the Un-American Activities Committee seems to me to be better for a police state than for the U.S.A."[52]

As the committee expanded its focus from the entertainment industry to government employees and civil rights activists, Eleanor Roosevelt continued to question its legality and condemn its conduct. For example, when the committee accused Dr. Edward Condon, the theoritician who found the security procedures at Los Alamos so restrictive that he returned to Westinghouse Research Laboratories after three weeks on the Manhattan Project and who now headed the National Bureau of Standards, of spying for the Soviets, ER sprang to his defense. Condon's supporters had the "My Day" statement entered into the *Congressional Record* only to have ER's longtime foe, Representative John Rankin, demand that the column be stricken. Her comments, according to the Mississippi Democrat, were "the most vicious attack I have ever known to be made on the Un-American Activities Committee." He pleaded with Congress not to listen to her, declaring that "Mrs. Roosevelt has done more harm than any other woman since Cleopatra."[53]

The week following Rankin's outburst, an unintimidated ER co-sponsored a half-page ad in the *Chicago Sun* which asked readers "did you ever think you were un-American?" As she told the International Federation of Business and Professional Women, "the great fear of communism" encouraged people to "label anything they didn't like as Communist." "This is dangerous," ER argued, "because people begin to be afraid to think." In a tone that slipped from inspirational to impatience, ER tried to convince her audience that people, and their nation, only grew when they stood for principles that encouraged debate and constructive criticism.[54]

When the civil rights movement became HUAC's next special target, ER launched a vocal counterattack. In the early 1950s, the Southern Conference Education Fund aggressively pursued a two-pronged strategy of court battles and public education to desegregate southern hospitals and defend blacks accused of raping white women. This brash conduct piqued HUAC's interest and hearings were conducted in New Orleans. When witnesses implied that SCEF leaders Aubrey Williams, Myles Horton, and Jim Dombrowski were communists, ER became the group's most loyal public defender. Moreover, after the Senate followed HUAC's lead, she not only defended the Fund but also assailed its attackers in the Senate. The un-American behavior was not SCEF's, she argued, but the "smear tactics and witch hunts" the Subcommittee on Internal Security used in its investigation. Consequently, ER agreed to be the lead signer of a petition to Senate Judiciary Committee Chairman William Langer which praised Williams, Horton, and Dombrowski as "loyal, courageous, self-sacrificing men." [55]

■ "I am not afraid of the Communist Party." The Smith Act and American Communists

While ER assailed HUAC's conduct, most citizens took the opposite view. As the Cold War escalated, American sentiment gradually returned to the suspicious frenzy reminiscent of the first Red Scare. By early 1954, polls revealed that almost three out of four Americans believed that communists should be stripped of their citizenship. Furthermore, almost half of the country believed American communists should be jailed for expressing un-American convictions.[56]

Politicians of both parties, as well as the federal and state courts, played to this sentiment. Eleanor Roosevelt did not, even though she knew very well that it was not easy to work with communists. Her experience with the CPUSA's attempt to control the American Youth Congress in the 1930s, Josephine Truslow Adams's blatant distortion of their conversations, and the prolonged exasperation she had experienced working with Andrei Vishinsky, the head of the Soviet delegation to the United Nations, reinforced her suspicions. Angered by what she saw as their hypocrisy on American race relations and their duplicitous portrayal of both American goals and her own conduct, ER often charged that when communists could not win a point in debate fairly they often resorted to the politics of deception.[57]

However, when Truman, Eisenhower, the Supreme Court, and the U.S. Congress began to violate the civil liberties of American communists, Eleanor Roosevelt found herself in the ironic position of championing the rights of her opponents to practice a belief she thought irresponsible and deceptive. If her detractors thought she had communist sympathies because she questioned the legitimacy of the House Un-American Activities Committee and supported the Southern Conference Education Fund, when she opposed the Smith Act, criticized the *Dennis* decision, and steadfastly defended the rights of Americans to believe any nonviolent political ideology they wanted, the wrath she provoked among Cold War stalwarts reached an all-time high.

Introduced during the period of the Nazi-Soviet Pact, the Smith Act made it a federal crime to "knowingly or willfully" aid, encourage, teach, or promote "the duty, necessity, desirability or propriety" of using force to overthrow the federal government. It also outlawed any attempt to organize "any society, group or assembly of persons who teach, advocate, or encourage the overthrow or destruction of such government by force or violence; . . . or [any person who] becomes or is a member of, or affiliates with, any such [group], knowing the purposes thereof."[58]

ER opposed the Smith Act from the moment it was introduced in mid-1940 and argued against it until the Supreme Court overturned Smith Act convictions in 1957. She believed that the legislation not only was a clear violation of constitutional protections of speech and assembly but also a blatant attempt to control political thought. In mid-August 1940, less than a month after the legislation became law, critics organized the Northern California Conference for Protection of the Foreign Born and ER agreed to sponsor the planning meeting. She also denounced the act during her winter 1940 lecture tour and in her magazine articles.[59]

Once again ER found herself in an extremely uncomfortable position politically. Her immediate opposition to the legislation placed her in a coalition that every other major elected official would have avoided at any cost: the Communist party of the United States; Representative Vito Marcantonio, the American Labor party Representative from Harlem; and the American Civil Liberties Union.[60] Indeed, ER's firm conviction that this law was unconstitutional translated into her refusing to be moderate in her position even when the coalition dissolved. Her sustained and increasingly isolated opposition to the Smith Act fanned the diatribes her critics leveled against her and encouraged her foremost opponent, columnist Westbrook Pegler, to label her "the madam of the [communist] whorehouse" and "the chief prostitute of those who pretend to extol the First Amendment."[61]

In July 1948, while Mao Tse-tung was defeating Chiang Kai-shek, the Truman administration indicted twelve members of the Communist party's national board for conspiracy. Arguing that any attempt to reorganize or restructure the CPUSA was a clear violation of the Smith Act, the government based its case on the organization's long-range goals rather than immediate party activities. The prosecution produced no witnesses but relied completely on party publications as the basis of the indictment. Advocating revolution in the classroom, prosecutors reasoned, equaled engaging in revolutionary activity in the streets. In short, the prosecution's case rested on communist theory rather than on evidence of any overt attempt at either espionage or revolution.[62]

The defense vehemently objected to this strategy and repeatedly asserted that violence was not the only way to introduce socialism into American politics. The jury rejected their argument and the judge sentenced eleven of the defendants (charges against one had been dismissed earlier for health reasons), to three to five years in federal prison. The defendants appealed, but in 1951 the Supreme Court, in a six to two vote, ruled in *Dennis v. United States* that the First Amendment protections of speech and assembly did not extend to "conspirators or foreign agents seeking violent overthrow [of the government]." "The structure and purpose of the statute," Chief Justice Vinson wrote in the majority opinion, "demand the inclusion of intent as an element of the crime."[63]

Unlike the majority of American liberals, Eleanor Roosevelt mourned the decision. "We do not have to go totalitarian to protect ourselves," she told her readers in 1950. If the country "did not intend to tolerate some of the very things we are trying to prevent," neither could it "prevent the establishment of a Gestapo in our midst, . . . [or] . . . the curtailment of the right of free speech and free association." Steadfastly, she refused first, to "look for a Communist under every bed" and second, to believe that intent equaled action. Instead, she endorsed the position Justice William O. Douglas expressed in his dissent, namely, that freedom of speech means "all shades of advocacy from lukewarm endorsement to partisan promotion." As she wrote the day following the *Dennis* decision, "I am not sure our forefathers—so careful to guard our rights of freedom of speech, freedom of thought and freedom of assembly—would not feel that the Supreme Court had perhaps a higher obligation . . . ."[64]

Although most histories of the Smith Act lump ER together with liberals who opposed the act only in the mid-1950s when it became politically chic to do so, Eleanor Roosevelt stood outside the centrist liberal camp. Indeed, ER's opinions differed from those held by some of her closest associates.

Norman Thomas, Sidney Hook, and Arthur Schlesinger ultimately supported the law and embraced the court's ruling. Concerned that the vital center hold its own against "Stalinism," most liberals rationalized that communist ideology was covert espionage because Soviet ideologues controlled the CPUSA's agenda. "To repeal the Smith Act," Hook argued in a 1953 essay, "would probably lead many to conclude that either the Communist party had changed its character, or that it did not really advocate the overthrow of democratic institutions by force or violence." If American communists were able to establish cells within major American liberal reform organizations, leading liberals believed these secret agents could inflict irremediable damage on reform. Many did concede that Americans had a right "to hold loathsome ideas," but they disagreed as to how they could be practiced. [65]

Even ACLU Executive Director Roger Baldwin and *The New Republic* agreed that the communist ideology was a real threat. Mainline liberal support for Smith and *Dennis* was so widespread that even *New York Post* editor James Wechsler, who defied Senator McCarthy's demands to name names, gave in to it. "Rational men [must] use their minds in defending their liberties," Wechsler editorialized, or else know-nothing ideologues will dominate liberalism just as "Stalinists" dictate the CPUSA agenda. Liberals must be pragmatic and judiciously defend liberty, Weschler concluded, or liberalism and communism could be reduced to "rival absurdities in the age of suspicion." [66]

Such formidable opposition did not deter Eleanor Roosevelt from continuing to oppose the act. For the following two summers, ER joined Justice Douglas in forums to speak out against the *Dennis* decision and the "Black Silence of Fear" it promoted. Even when the furor her stance generated cut into her lecture tour and deprived her of income she needed, ER refused to moderate her stance. The banning of her appearance by all but one public auditorium in Los Angeles also failed to silence her. [67]

She was "quite willing to have Communists come in" she told a 1954 "Spotlight, New York" radio audience. Furthermore, she counseled her listeners to recognize the danger of their unquestioned acceptance of anticommunist paranoia. While ER recognized that some people would always fear what they could not understand, she nevertheless pleaded with her audience to recognize that fear of the unknown was much more threatening to society than dissent and economic hardship. "If we don't get to the point where we feel secure," she declared, "we're much worse off than we were after the depression." [68]

She continued the same themes the following year, telling readers of *McCall's* in 1955 and again in 1956 that outlawing communism was "very dangerous." Asking her readers to recall the freedom with which union organizers criticized both the government and industry, she pointed out: "Before the Smith Act . . . people who discussed their ideas but did not try to take action by force against our government were not subject to imprisonment." Now they were. This development must be reversed because "to curtail our right of discussion may be only a step from accusing people for what they think, rather than for what they do."[69]

Consequently, when A. J. Muste, director of the Fellowship of Reconciliation, asked her in 1955 to sign a petition urging Eisenhower to commute the sentences of those sixteen communists convicted under the Smith Act to time already served, ER gladly agreed to lend her support. She also endorsed the additional request that the more than 100 Smith Act cases pending in federal and state court be postponed.[70]

ER did not support the tepid argument advanced by the petitioners. In fact, only she opposed the act from the beginning. Most cosigners followed the lead of Norman Thomas and Reinhold Niebuhr and only pleaded for amnesty after the Supreme Court announced its intention to review convictions obtained under the California "little Smith Act." Even then signers were careful to assert that they were in "fundamental disagreement" with communist philosophy and only endorsed the petition because of their "deep attachment to the democratic way of life and the desire to maintain and strengthen it."[71]

When the Supreme Court overturned the sedition convictions in 1957, ER expressed pleasure with the decision and relief that the Court had finally recognized its duty. Once again, she painstakingly tried to explain this controversial decision to her readers in words that would elicit their support. The justices were correct in barring indictments for "organizing" because "the word 'organize' was being construed in its narrow sense, meaning that simply bringing a communist group into being was found to be a cause for indictment." The Court had finally decided what ER had been declaring all along: that political thought did not equal political action.[72]

In short, while the Supreme Court and some noted centrist liberals ultimately reached the conclusion that ER held from the onset of the Smith Act debate, they did so more than seventeen years after she voiced her initial objections. Of all the American leaders who joined the bandwagon urging clemency for Smith Act prisoners, Eleanor Roosevelt was the only liberal activist who had asserted in the years both before and after *Dennis*, "I am not afraid of the Communist party of the Soviet Union."[73]

∎ **"The big bully."**
Richard Nixon from Alger Hiss to Helen Gahagan Douglas

Such adamant support for civil liberties placed Eleanor Roosevelt squarely in opposition to stances adopted by two of the major political figures of the Cold War: Richard Nixon and Joseph McCarthy. While most ER biographers concentrate on her criticism of the senator from Wisconsin, she actually loathed Nixon more than she did McCarthy. McCarthy's skill as a demagogue contributed to the escalation of anti-communist rhetoric, but it was Nixon's skill as a crafter of legislation that made such persecution possible.

Nixon won his congressional seat in 1946 by implying that Jerry Voorhis, his Democratic opponent whom ER enthusiastically endorsed, had ties to numerous communist-front organizations, by advertising his rival's youthful flirtation with socialism, and by exaggerating his own war record. Rather than promoting his own accomplishments, Nixon made Voorhis's allegiance to principles Nixon labeled the "Moscow-[CIO]PAC-Henry Wallace line" the centerpiece of his campaign. To ensure that the voters understood this message, a clandestine Nixon telephone campaign declared that Voorhis, a member of the House Un-American Activities Committee, was indeed a communist. Such strident campaign rhetoric and public ridicule of liberal sentiments not only provided Nixon with the votes necessary to defeat Voorhis but also to capture his seat on the House Un-American Activities Committee. Consequently, even before he began his congressional career, Nixon personified both the issues and the tactics ER opposed.[74]

Nor did he show any signs of moderating his behavior after the election. As a new HUAC member, Nixon did not hesitate to advocate restrictions on the political activity ER strove to protect. He campaigned relentlessly for legislation to require communists to register as foreign agents and argued unceasingly that the scope of the Smith Act should be expanded. ER was incensed. To her, Nixon was just "the big bully" whose major contribution to the House was to incite "a bunch of amateurs [to] fuss around and smear . . . the reputations of so many people."[75]

Nixon's HUAC colleagues disagreed. Impressed by his cool justification for the indictment of the Hollywood Ten, members of the committee looked favorably on their new colleague. He quickly capitalized on this approbation and asked to be appointed chair of the special legislative subcommittee. The committee, relieved to relinquish this tedious function, agreed. Immediately, Nixon began to draft legislation that would assure his place both as HUAC's dominant member and as the politician ER distrusted most.[76]

On February 3, 1948, Nixon introduced the legislation he and fellow HUAC member Karl Mundt had drafted during the winter break. Arguing "freedom of speech is one thing and freedom of revolution is another," he asserted that the CPUSA was an agent of a foreign government because its members placed their allegiance to the Soviet Union before their allegiance to the United States. Therefore, the CPUSA was "not a party at all and has no resemblance to a political party. It is a revolutionary conspiracy" that demanded immediate attention. Outlawing the party was not enough. The party and its members must be exposed "for what they are—to get them and their front organizations out in the open, label them as Communists, and let the good sense of our people take care of them."[77]

But every care must be taken, Nixon argued, to expose these saboteurs democratically. The Mundt-Nixon bill was designed to do just that. The legislation would require all communist organizations to register with the Justice Department; establish a Subversive Activities Control Board to determine which organizations were communist fronts; deny members of such organizations federal employment and passports; deport members who were not citizens; and forbid the "use of the mails or mass media to designated organizations, except for material or programs clearly labeled as Communist propaganda."[78]

After deftly chairing hearings on the bill, Nixon coordinated the floor debate with such finesse that he accused anyone who implied that the bill would undermine the credibility of liberal reform of missing his point. "That is exactly the trouble in the country today. There is too much loose talk and confusion on the Communist issue. By passing this bill the Congress will go on record as to just what is subversive about communism in the United States." He had drafted this legislation with great care to ensure that it preserved, not curtailed, democratic institutions. He could assure his critics that the Mundt-Nixon bill was "far from being a police-state bill, [but rather] was a bill which will prevent the creation of a police state." Consequently, in a masterful rhetorical maneuver, he concluded that members should discount election-year politics and vote their consciences. The House, his assertions to the contrary, voted with the election foremost in their minds and voted 319 to 58 in favor of the bill.[79]

Eleanor Roosevelt rarely devoted a whole column to one particular issue until the early fifties, but she was so outraged by the Mundt-Nixon proposal that the entire June 1, 1948, "My Day" argued against its adoption. It was a "curious thing," ER conceded, that she found herself allied with the libertarian right and the communist left in opposing the bill. Yet she welcomed their support and declared such "repressive measures" were preludes to acts "which dictatorships—both fascist and Communist—use to stay in power." This legislation was a critical assault on the nation's democratic heritage, and must be rebuffed. "If Americans acquiesced in its passage," ER proclaimed with hyperbole, then "we are no better off" than if we lived under a totalitarian regime.[80]

Directly confronting Nixon's assertion that communist free speech is freedom to revolt, ER said that she knew several "theoretical Communists" and they "certainly were not going around with guns." The war against communism should not be waged against political thought but should be focused instead on the social conditions that made Americans susceptible to communist ideology. Indeed, suppressing criticism rather than correcting the conditions that caused the criticism was not only misguided policy, but "dangerous." Pleading with her readers to oppose the bill, ER concluded, that unless freedom from want is assured, people would continue to see more of democracy's flaws than its blessings.[81]

If the campaign for the Mundt-Nixon bill served as Nixon's launching pad into legislative notoriety in the House, his efforts to indict Alger Hiss served, in the words of one Nixon biographer, as his "springboard to both the Senate and the Vice Presidency." Nixon intuited that anti-communist activism did not have a long political future unless a substantial allegation of red infiltration into the federal government could be substantiated. Consequently, when Nixon learned that Hiss, a quintessential example of East Coast, New Deal liberalism, had been accused of being a communist, he pursued the allegations with bulldog tenacity. Indeed, his investigation into Hiss's loyalty was so steadfast, that he refused to abandon the inquiry after HUAC had rejected charges.[82]

In the Hiss case, Nixon and ER were once again polar opposites. This does not mean that ER remained convinced of Hiss's innocence, but rather, unlike most vital center liberals, she never inferred that a perjury conviction implied that Hiss was guilty of espionage. She needed stronger evidence than Whittaker Chambers's pumpkin papers, corroboration Chambers had produced belatedly to substantiate his allegations, to convince her that Hiss had passed secrets to the Soviets. While she later conceded that Hiss may have lied, she resolutely refused to believe that he was a spy. Thus, ER stood once again outside the vital center.[83]

When Whittaker Chambers named Alger Hiss, who not only had accompanied FDR to Yalta but also was now serving as president of the Carnegie Foundation for Peace, as part of a communist cell in 1948, Hiss demanded to appear before the committee to respond to the allegations. Hiss's resume and references from prominent New Deal officials were the cornerstone of his rebuttal. While ER did not know Hiss well enough to vouch for his character, she thought the allegations made against him were so patently outrageous that the case against him would collapse like a house of cards. However, after Nixon's zealous pursuit of Hiss ensured that the charges against him would not be dropped and Hiss's credibility became the central issue in the hearings, ER clearly entered the Hiss camp.

Eleanor Roosevelt supported Hiss for a variety of reasons, not the least of which was her adamant conviction that both HUAC and Nixon had deliberately misled the nation for political gain. She also believed Hiss. Both her professional and personal contact with him had always been productive and pleasant. Hiss helped brief her on the procedures and issues she encountered as a delegate to the United Nations. She trusted the work he did for John Foster Dulles. Her children spoke well of him. Finally, Chambers crystallized all the political and patrician objections she had to the HUAC process.[84]

How could she believe Chambers, a man whose major character trait she described as "a very unsavory personality" and whose veracity was only supported by a committee whose integrity she never believed in the first place? Consequently, when Chambers and Hiss were both summoned to testify before the committee, ER could not refrain from parodying HUAC. "It seems to me that the committee must begin to see how funny this whole situation is," she wrote the week before the hearing, "when they sit in secret sessions for several hours with each man and then have to admit that 'from the testimony, it is impossible to tell which one is telling the truth.'"[85]

HUAC's conduct throughout the Hiss affair reinforced ER's claim that the committee served no purpose. When the press asked her during Hiss's first appearance before the committee to clarify her position, she responded by first accusing HUAC of usurping FBI jurisdiction and second of also missing the point the allegations raised. Rather than exploiting a man of Hiss's reputation to get their names in the paper, committee members should first examine the credibility of their witnesses and then scrutinize the evidence those witnesses produced. Chambers's only "proof" was his memory. Since HUAC had not produced any evidence to support his allegations, ER assumed he had none and then tongue-lashed HUAC for its grandstanding behavior.[86]

Even after the Carnegie executive was convicted of perjury in 1950, ER continued to argue that Chambers's credibility, rather than Hiss's loyalty, was the key to the trial.[87] She told reporters in Ames, Iowa, that the case against him was not conclusive, that she remained unconvinced of Hiss's guilt, and that she felt "awfully, awfully troubled about the whole thing." No matter how much she tried to evaluate the case against Hiss, she conceded that when it came down to believing Chambers or Hiss, she could not believe the accuser. ER could never escape feeling that Chambers had accused Hiss primarily to salvage his own reputation. In her opinion, Chambers was as guilty as Iago.[88]

Thus, although ER did admit that Hiss "may have perjured himself," she adamantly refused to believe that "he ever sold any secret papers." Her inability to reconcile doubts about Chambers's credibility with Hiss's inability to refute Chambers's allegations depressed her. She struggled to understand why a man like Hiss, with his commitment to the United Nations and world peace, would lie. Yet unlike Adlai Stevenson and other liberals and moderates who grappled with the case and ultimately backed away from Hiss, ER stood out from the crowd because she refused to take this easier path. As opposed to Stevenson, who proclaimed that he "never doubted the verdict of a jury," ER worried that the jury had been unduly influenced by the media frenzy that surrounded the trial.[89]

Indeed, the hysteria that the press helped generate with its coverage of Chambers's accusations moved ER closer to Hiss. Convinced that Nixon and HUAC's obsession with trying Hiss in print was so effective that the jury could not avoid being influenced by it, she worried that the judicial system had failed Hiss. "Trial by your peers is supposed to be the last word in safeguarding the innocent," ER lamented. She regarded Hiss as much a victim of the politics of fear as a target of Chambers's self-interested allegations. And in moments of tremendous gloom, ER questioned whether rabid fear of communism might be skewing judicial process.[90]

She then kept a forlorn three-year silence on the case. Yet her silence also separated ER from most consensus liberals. While they ruefully conceded that Hiss had spied for the Soviets and tried to rationalize their earlier support, ER did neither. Perhaps she secretly agreed with those few liberals, like her friend Frank Porter Graham, who believed that Hiss was keeping silent to protect his wife. However, when columnists argued that her "strange silence" amounted to nothing more than a refusal to concede defeat and challenged her to reassess her defense of Hiss, she finally spoke out. Although she initially tried to dodge this question by professing her reluctance to criticize the court's decision and the likelihood that his jury had been influenced by the vast press coverage the allegations received, she ultimately admitted the real reasons behind her silence.[91]

"I have always been convinced that he did not tell the complete truth," but she had "never been able to make up [her] mind" about what the truth was or to understand why he lied. Bitterly disappointed in both Hiss and the system that so zealously exploited him to advance causes and politicians she detested, ER conceded that while Hiss might be a liar, she still was not convinced that he was a traitor. Americans who concluded that Hiss was a spy because he had lied had succumbed to the politics of fear and perverted the judicial process to convict a low-level bureaucrat who had no influence on U.S. policy.[92]

This distortion of justice distressed ER more than the possibility that Hiss could have been a communist after all. As she told the conservative columnist Burt Drummond, even if she was wrong and Hiss was guilty, the nation suffered more from Chambers than from Hiss. Hiss was a minor official who had no authority to make any decisions. He was merely a researcher, "but Whittaker Chambers as a Communist and now as an ex-Communist has done much harm" because he promoted a trial system in which the end justified the means.[93]

Nor did she back off from this statement after Drummond's readers barraged her with correspondence. "I have never questioned Alger Hiss' conviction for perjury," she replied to attorney Arthur C. Grafflin's indignant letter of condemnation, "but many people who really knew him, which I did not, have felt that he had not actually committed treason." Furthermore, "it is better for those of us who do not want to add to the present hysteria, not to go on accusing him." And she brusquely dismissed Grafflin's appeal for her silence. If the FBI had been allowed to "continue its work" without HUAC intervention, "we would not have reached the hysteria and discontented situation in which this country now finds itself." She found this attitude "far more dangerous than the feeling that the F.B.I. would not be able to protect us as it did between World War I and World War II." Indeed, she believed "this so deeply" that she felt compelled to speak out, concluding that "I would think I was doing the country a great injustice if I kept silent as you suggest."[94]

As the person most responsible for promoting Chambers's testimony, Nixon was the legislator most responsible for Hiss's conviction. Overnight Nixon achieved celebrity status in a country obsessed with ferreting out those whom President Truman dismissed as "red herrings." Eager to capitalize on his publicity, Nixon decided in early 1950 to run in the California GOP senatorial primary. Senator Sheridan Downey, the Democratic incumbent, was also being challenged by liberal members of his own party. As it turned out, once again, Nixon and Eleanor Roosevelt would go head to head in a bitter contest. Yet this fight would be much more personal because his opponent in the general election and the target of his allegations was one of ER's closest friends, Congresswoman Helen Gahagan Douglas.[95]

Less than three weeks after Nixon and Douglas won their respective primaries, the People's Republic of Korea invaded the Republic of Korea and Nixon had yet another example of communist aggression to exploit. While both candidates were among the most ardent defenders of the Marshall Plan, Douglas opposed aid to Greece and Turkey and the Internal Security Act, questioned the aims of the Truman Doctrine, and vehemently argued, as did her friend ER, that HUAC was an un-American institution. Nixon quickly latched onto Korea as the most dramatic way to exploit Douglas's opposition to staunch Cold War policies and to promote his image as a valiant defender of American security.[96]

Nixon then pounced on Douglas's liberal record by circulating half a million copies of a campaign flyer, printed on pink paper to emphasize the "pink lady's" politics, which highlighted the "Douglas-Marcantonio Voting Record." His campaign staff even implied that Douglas's support of civil rights proved that she was disloyal. Nixon volunteers mailed thousands of postcards from the fictitious "Communist League of Negro Women" that read "Vote for our Helen for Senator. We are with her 100% percent."[97]

When Nixon turned Douglas's friendship with Eleanor Roosevelt into a campaign issue, ER immediately came to her friend's aid. She toured California campaigning for Douglas and assailing Nixon's policies and integrity. Just as the congresswoman attacked Nixon's ethics as the electoral shenanigans of "Tricky Dick," ER constantly argued that Nixon flung allegations at his opponent as a way to deflect a close examination of his own proposals and conduct.[98] Nixon skillfully turned the Douglas-ER alliance to his favor, however, when the two candidates appeared before the San Francisco Press Club. Responding to questions from the press, Douglas admitted that her campaign funds were low and Nixon playfully tried to sympathize with her. He too was in desperate need of money. Times were hard and he was forced to rely on small donations. For example, he just happened to have received such a sum that morning on his way to the Press Club. Grinning, he then pulled a contributor's letter from his pocket to share with the audience. The letter read: "I am enclosing a small contribution to your campaign for the Senate. I only wish it could be ten times as much. Best wishes to you and Mrs. Nixon." Dramatically, Nixon paused and announced the source of such devoted support: "Eleanor Roosevelt." Douglas and the media gasped. Having made his point, Nixon waited for the crowd to calm down and continued, in the words of one biographer, "in a deadpan fashion" that he too "was amazed by this contribution" until he noticed that it was not postmarked from Hyde Park but from Oyster Bay, New York.[99]

Eleanor Roosevelt was not a sore loser, but when Richard Nixon defeated Helen Gahagan Douglas by implying that she was a communist, ER was livid. She encouraged Douglas to challenge the election and file charges of voter fraud against the Nixon campaign and sent Hickok to California to gather evidence against Nixon and his campaign staff. She then launched her own media attack against him. After rebuking Nixon in her column, on radio, and on television, she continued to scold America for listening to a candidate who was so desperate for victory that he would "do anything to get elected." She told anyone who asked that an elected official should not have so much of himself invested in an election. Politicians must uphold the Constitution first and then win elections. Nothing in Nixon's career indicated that he was capable of such public-interested behavior. With determined fervor, ER argued that Nixon's political career was filled with examples of his questionable character.[100]

When Nixon joined the Eisenhower ticket in 1952, ER was appalled. She had declared the previous year that only Joseph McCarthy was as big a threat to American democratic principles. Now Nixon, whom she considered to be one of the two most dangerous men in America, would share the White House with Eisenhower, whom she saw as a "glamorous, successful General" who had little political conviction, who was closer to the military than the public, and who was more administrator than leader.[101]

■ **"I despise the control they insist on."**
Joseph McCarthy and His Supporters

The year Richard Nixon left the Senate for the White House, Joseph McCarthy reached his peak as the senator most obsessed with disclosing subversive activities. To Eleanor Roosevelt, both men were despicable demagogues. If Nixon's attacks on Hiss, and on Douglas during their senatorial race, proved the electoral value of conviction by innuendo, then the attention the world community gave to McCarthy's efforts to win reelection by accusing ER's diplomatic associates of communist sympathies underscored how vulnerable the image of American democracy was abroad.

Although most vital center liberals overcame their internal rivalries and opposed McCarthy, few were as vocal or as persistent in their opposition as Eleanor Roosevelt. Even so, ER did not attack McCarthy with the same intensity with which she assailed Nixon. Like some liberals, she initially thought McCarthy such a ludicrous figure that there was no need to give him any additional press. Consequently, she waited until he attacked Judge Dorothy Kenyon in March 1950 before she spoke out against him.[102]

How could these allegations be taken seriously, she asked "My Day" readers, when they "were one of the funniest things ever suggested." A sagacious strategy lay underneath this lighthearted response. ER knew that Nixon had depended upon strong media coverage to bolster his career, and she did not want to add to McCarthy's prestige by expanding the coverage he received. Moreover, the Senate Committee on Foreign Relations, chaired by Maryland Senator Millard Tydings, was investigating McCarthy's conduct and the media was already treating the senator's attack on Kenyon as a joke. She hoped that these more formal, subdued responses would undermine his allegations and thereby undercut his popularity.[103]

However, by the fall of 1951, this had not happened and ER's tone had changed. She now saw McCarthy as both a threat to civil liberties and an international embarrassment. Consequently, less than two months after McCarthy delivered his speech in Wheeling, West Virginia, charging that the State Department was infested with communists, she chided Americans for Democratic Action for the role they played in fueling "the contamination by association" mentality. She urged those attending the ADA annual convention to work to "preserve our right to think and differ." And she scoffed at those who feared working with new organizations and new activists. "The day I'm afraid to sit down with people I do not know because five years from now someone will say five of those people were Communists and therefore you are a Communist—that will be a bad day." Americans must be able "to sit down with anyone who may have a new idea and not be afraid of contamination by association." Arguing "your point of view—[with] people you have not screened beforehand" is the cornerstone of free political debate and "must be a part of the freedom of people in the United States."[104]

She reassessed her position for several reasons. First, she realized that she had underestimated the attention the public paid to his allegations. Second, McCarthy had more speaking invitations than all of his colleagues combined and she recognized how that popularity would attract Republican support. Third, Senator William Jenner's "outrageous" slander of George

Marshall as "a living lie" who served as "a front man for traitors" convinced her that the Senate had capitulated to demagogues. Finally, she recognized that Nixon's victorious use of anti-communist hysteria and General Douglas MacArthur's continued opposition to Truman's Korean policy, which had led to the general's removal from his command, only encouraged McCarthy to escalate his attack on those "appeasers" whose actions he could interpret as encouraging communism.[105]

All these factors combined to reinforce ER's concerns that fear of difference would paralyze the nation. When students told her that they feared participating in politics because their involvement might be used as ammunition against them, she mourned their cowardice and worried that the backlash led by Nixon and McCarthy would stifle liberal political action. Moreover, when the Justice Department charged that Julius and Ethel Rosenberg had leaked secrets about the atomic bomb to the Soviets the same day the Tydings committee released its report criticizing McCarthy, ER's experience as a journalist and a politician told her that the coverage of the Rosenbergs would overshadow the rebuke of McCarthy. As she surveyed this spreading political paralysis, ER examined her own conduct to see if any of her actions abetted this behavior. She decided that perhaps they had and that she needed to clarify her position.[106]

When conservative Republicans used the taint of communism to justify their opposition to the United Nations, ER launched a one-woman campaign to rebut their allegations. Within an eighteen-month period, she argued that isolationism was a cowardly approach to world affairs, defended State Department officials who believed that the United States should work with Communist China, and campaigned day and night against the Bricker Amendment, which would have required Senate approval of all international agreements. Throughout, two basic points resounded: McCarthyism should not dictate the terms of American diplomacy, and an anti-communist foreign policy need not restrict American civil liberties.[107]

Capitulation to the right would be politically and intellectually self-defeating. Thus, ER chided members of the Senate Foreign Relations Committee who voted to oppose Philip Jessup's appointment to the United Nations General Assembly despite their belief in Jessup's integrity. When Senator Guy Gillette defended his vote against Jessup by arguing that McCarthy's allegations undermined Jessup's effectiveness, ER reprimanded the senator. "The net result" of his argument "is that you have told Senator . . . McCarthy that you don't agree with his accusations but you have let him obtain the result that he desired." As she told readers of "My Day," if the nation did not allow its career foreign service officials the right to examine policy from all viewpoints, "we might as well have robots in position[s] of trust."[108]

By late 1951, as McCarthy assumed the dominant position in the anti-communist debate, ER worried that most Americans would not hesitate to violate the First Amendment protection of free speech in their zeal to squelch communism. Accordingly, as the year progressed, she attacked McCarthy with increasing frequency and with unabashed disdain. Just as McCarthy utilized his media skills to promote a campaign characterized by "Multiple Untruths" and accusations by deadline, ER capitalized on her own press connections and public relations skills to provide the American public with the information she thought they needed to make informed decisions.[109]

ER's attacks were frequently launched in conjunction with the other issues she championed. Although ER used "My Day" primarily as a forum for her opinions on legislation, international affairs, and the Red Scare, by the late 1940s she would often turn to literature to augment her arguments. Initially the plays and novels to which she referred dealt primarily with American race relations. However, by the early 1950s, they increasingly emphasized the individual's struggle for personal autonomy and political independence. And she often connected the struggles the characters faced to the restrictions the Cold War zealously placed on American freedom. For example, "rarely" had a play "gripped [her] harder" than did Arthur Koestler's *Darkness at Noon.* She described her intense response for her readers: "You never want to hear the phrase 'the end justifies the means' again, or listen to the hollow excuses that the 'work' must go on regardless of the suffering of a few individuals or groups." McCarthy's tactics were just as vicious as those the communists in the play used to persecute their enemies. Heartily, ER endorsed Koestler's message: America's "only defense against Communism" was the preservation of civil liberties and the insurance that none of them would be sacrificed to the "hope of being saved from communism." Consequently, when McCarthy's aides Roy Cohn and David Schine confiscated and burned books in American libraries overseas, ER was incensed. Indeed, she never forgave Eisenhower for the cowardice he displayed when Eisenhower criticized "book burning" in a Dartmouth address and then called McCarthy the next day to assure him that he was not the target of the remarks.[110]

ER soon realized that no matter what topic she addressed, questions about McCarthy would dominate the question-and-answer period. After a student attending her September 1952 address to the F.D.R. Young Democrats of City College asked her to gauge McCarthy's conduct, she responded, "What I think of Senator McCarthy can hardly be put into words." She paused and then called him the "greatest menace to freedom we have in this country." She also scolded the Young Democrats for hesitating to condemn his actions. Nor were young people the only targets of her impatience. If Democrats and the nation continued to tolerate McCarthy, she told the Democratic National Convention in 1952, "we would condemn ourselves to endless struggle for survival in a jungle world."[111]

Eleanor Roosevelt opposed McCarthy as vigorously in private as she did in public. Her correspondence is filled with letters to average Americans, who wrote her either degrading or praising her stance, in which she repeatedly asserted that the true test of democracy is to create a political climate in which differences are debated intelligently. As she testily responded to one critic, "my devotion to my country and to democracy is quite as great as that of Senator McCarthy." She strongly disapproved of the methods he used, the effects they had on American politics, and the damage they inflicted on loyal citizens. "Perhaps better than most American citizens," she knew "the dangers of Communism" because for the last six years she "sat in meetings" with Soviet representatives to the UN. She had seen them work and she "despise[d] the control they insist on holding over men's minds." McCarthy was no different from the communists. "And that is why I despise" what he "has done, for he would use the same methods of fear to control all thought that is not according to his own pattern—in our free country." Furthermore, his tactics were as ineffective as they were immoral. "I think those of us who worked with young people in the thirties did more to save many of them from becoming Communists than Senator McCarthy has done for his fellow citizens with all his slurs and accusations."[112]

Clearly, McCarthy's ability to impair the nation's judgment pushed ER's outrage to the limit. She continued to speak forthrightly against the tactics that the senator represented. Yet ER was too much the political animal to believe that average Americans could topple McCarthy. She advised an "average housewife" who asked what she could do to oppose the demagogue to pressure her elected officials to act courageously because the senator would be stopped only when "some of the biggest people in America [decide] to serve as leaders" rather than politicians.[113]

Conservative intellectuals pounced upon ER's impassioned attacks on McCarthy as well as her consistent defense of free speech. To William Buckley, these "demonstrated Mrs. Roosevelt's lack of intellectual rigor." While the founder of the *National Review* was careful to acknowledge that ER was "one of history's truly remarkable women," he nevertheless declared that her sentimental attachment to liberalism proved that she was "also a fountain of confusion." Following ER "in search of irrationality was like following a burning fuse in search of an explosive; one never had to wait very long." Similarly, James Burnham bitingly satirized that ER's "furious energy [and] gigantic ego" made her as dangerous as a "great tank with a drunken driver loose in the crowded streets of a city."[114]

On the other hand, some liberals used her stature to defend their positions. When McCarthy assailed the anti-communist Americans for Democratic Action, leaders of the organization feared that they be would subpoenaed. Consequently, less than one week after McCarthy implied he would investigate the ADA, Joe Rauh, Joe Lash, and James Wechsler asked ER to serve as its honorary chairman. As Rauh recalled, the ADA needed ER because "she would give us the added strength in the fight against McCarthy because McCarthy would have to . . . attack Mrs. Roosevelt as a communist." Fully aware of the risks inherent in this offer, ER agreed without hesitation. In a front page article, the *New York Post*, edited by Weschler, reported that ER's affiliation with the ADA "suggests to the reactionaries and the timid alike that the time for the counter-offensive of decency is at hand. Perhaps better than anyone else, she is capable of communicating to millions the wise reminder that free men have 'nothing to fear but fear itself.'" Rauh and Schlesinger agreed and believed that when ER faced down McCarthy's implied investigation of the ADA, she "saved" the organization.[115]

Eleanor Roosevelt was not the lone liberal voice in the wilderness crying out against McCarthy, but she was the only one of her stature who took such an early and vocal stand. Senator Paul Douglas (Democrat, Illinois), for example, whose credentials for liberalism and integrity were heretofore impeccable, refrained from discussing McCarthy until it was politically safe to do so. McCarthy's attacks even moved the moderate Adlai Stevenson to the right. Some up and coming new senators, such as John Fitzgerald Kennedy, deliberately evaded the issue. Other liberals who would later make their name fighting corruption, such as Robert Fitzgerald Kennedy, began their congressional careers as researchers on his staff. Even the political cartoonist Herbert Block, who coined the term "McCarthyism," waited until 1952 to attack the senator.[116]

After the 1952 election, more political leaders and opinion shapers adopted ER's position. Even so, challenging the senator still proved perilous. Indeed, some leading liberals eagerly complied with the anti-communist frenzy. With dismay, ER watched Hubert Humphrey, who had galvanized liberal Democrats with his civil rights stance in 1948, now comply with McCarthyism by helping push the Communist Control Act of 1954 through the Senate. Eleanor Roosevelt was appalled. As she wrote an ADA colleague, "If the Democratic liberals do many more things like outlawing the Communist party, I'm not sure I'll consider them liberals."[117]

In short, unlike other liberals in the 1940s and early 1950s, Eleanor Roosevelt braved massive rebuke, financial loss, and criticism within her own circle for airing her civil libertarian views so consistently. Moreover, while she may have agreed with vital center liberals that American communists were a threat to American democracy, she remained convinced that harsh restriction of political dissent was the true danger facing the nation. Consequently, ER steadfastly defended the communists' right to speak out and to be protected by the Constitution. This daring placed her in a political class by herself and provided her with yet another standard by which to judge the men who would be president.

Chapter Six

CHALLENGING THE PARTY
John Kennedy and the Election of 1960

Throughout the 1950s Eleanor Roosevelt never wavered from her basic convictions that liberal political leaders must state their positions clearly and that they must work diligently to move the public to the liberal point of view—despite the backlash this might generate among zealous anti-communists. Yet, as the decade drew to a close, ER decried the absence of true risk-takers within the Democratic party hierarchy. A realpolitik politician, she well understood the vituperation that unpopular positions would generate. However, as one who had spent her whole public life in the center of controversy, ER had little respect for those politicians who were more concerned with promoting their own profiles than with implementing liberal policy.

John Kennedy's rise within the Democratic party presented Eleanor Roosevelt a dilemma that underscored her dissatisfaction with party leaders and her concern for civil rights and civil liberties. While throughout the 1950s ER had argued that the Democratic party must be more receptive to change and to young vigorous leadership, the new generation of leaders seemed to her to lack the courage she thought necessary to lead America into a future that must be defined by what opportunities democracy could offer rather than by what dangers it could defeat.

A few victories for civil liberties and civil rights had occurred: the Senate did vote to censure McCarthy, and the nation was not as completely obsessed with internal subversion as it had been in the early 1950s; Congress finally passed a civil rights bill; and the liberal wing of the Democratic party seemed to be reclaiming a few positions of power. But ER knew how easy it would be for the nation to slide back into the reactionary politics she fought so diligently.

While ER continued to believe that the Democratic party was liberalism's best hope, she nevertheless understood that working in tandem with party leaders did not ensure that the party would practice what it preached. With a mixture of increasing disappointment and frustration, ER grudgingly accepted two disheartening facts about the Democratic party: that party leadership and liberal Democrats frequently dropped the ball when the opposition was too imposing; and that working with reform groups outside the party was essential to keeping liberal demands for civil rights and civil liberties in front of both the public and their elected officials.

ER did not reach these conclusions easily nor did she accept them graciously. She was seventy-six when John F. Kennedy won the 1960 presidential election. Almost deaf in one ear and acutely anemic, she tired easily. She recognized the limits of her energy and started declining invitations she would have accepted in the past. Within a year she would be hospitalized with tuberculosis and aplastic anemia, misdiagnosed as leukemia.

Eleanor Roosevelt recognized that this would be the last time she would watch a Democrat control the White House. Ever the Democrat, she was happy that the party had recaptured the presidency. Nevertheless, she approached this administration warily, unable to shake the fear that McCarthyism had instilled in her. As she confided to a young colleague, the fact that Americans had given McCarthy a free reign "disturbed me as much as anything in my life."[1]

Kennedy's reluctance to acknowledge the damage the Wisconsin Republican had done to the nation deeply enraged her. Although the senator was in the hospital during the censure debate and vote, ER refused to believe that Kennedy's back surgery was the sole reason for his refusal to speak out and rebuke his colleague. Rather, she saw his illness as a convenient excuse to avoid a delicate political and family problem. The Kennedys had a decade-long friendship with McCarthy. Not only did Kennedy's younger brother, Robert, serve as an aide to McCarthy, but Joseph Kennedy, the senator's father, was such a close friend of McCarthy's that McCarthy refused to campaign in behalf of Massachusetts Republican Henry Cabot Lodge, a McCarthy supporter, when John Kennedy sought his Senate seat. To ER, these family ties, McCarthy's reluctance to cross Joseph Kennedy, and John Kennedy's continuing refusal to speak out against McCarthy spoke volumes about where Kennedy's true convictions lay. Consequently, she was extremely concerned that Kennedy would be unable to lead the country out of the climate of fear that had so dominated the politics of the previous decade.[2]

Furthermore, she knew that her influence was waning and saw no one of her stature who could continue her fight. More and more she worried that without bold executive leadership the American people were much too vulnerable to the politics of emotion, and grew even more resolute in her belief that the country desperately needed a vision articulated in strong, clear, and unquestionable terms. She feared that politicians would no longer provide this leadership and only hoped that organizations could overcome their traditional rivalries to meet this challenge. As she wrote that fall, "the search for community" was never more essential.[3]

Despite longstanding doubts about both his and his father's character, ER wanted to believe that Kennedy could lead the nation into a new liberal age defined by respect for individual rights and liberties and international sovereignty. She hoped that as president he could provide the leadership necessary to "fan the spark of conviction" she thought central to "building a new and peaceful world." Although she never doubted that ambition rather than vision motivated Kennedy's drive for power, ER also later acknowledged "he was not simply ambitious to be president." After carefully evaluating his conduct throughout the campaign, she concluded that, in spite of the weaknesses he had displayed in the Senate, Kennedy "wanted to be a truly great president." Yet a careful review of their ten-year association reveals that JFK failed to convince ER completely that he was capable of putting the nation's needs ahead of his own aspirations.[4]

For his part, Kennedy understood that ER had serious reservations not only about his character, but also about his political vision as well. Consequently, throughout both the 1960 campaign and the early months of his presidency, the young candidate ardently wooed the most senior icon of liberal values. From the moment he secured the Democratic nomination in July 1960 until spring 1962 when ER's illness finally impeded her activism, Kennedy pursued her with a careful tenacity that underscored the prestige and political value he believed her endorsement would contribute to his administration.

Eleanor Roosevelt recognized the game that Kennedy was playing and planned her strategy accordingly. Rather than quickly responding to his solicitations or implying that her support would come only if certain appointments were made, she directly challenged him. As a loyal Democrat, she would support the party's presidential candidate, but she would actively campaign for him only if he developed into the kind of leader she thought the nation deserved. If his presidential campaign displayed the ambivalence and the evasion he displayed as a senator, she would not work vigorously for his election. In short, even though he was running against Nixon, Kennedy had to prove himself worthy of ER's support.[5]

Whether or not Eleanor Roosevelt completely overcame her objections and joined those Democrats who believed that John Kennedy represented the best leadership the postwar generation had to offer is a matter most historians treat superficially. Most Kennedy biographers accent ER's belated campaign efforts on Kennedy's behalf, her enthusiastic endorsement of the Peace Corps, and her appointment as chair of the President's Commission on the Status of Women. If she supported him in these efforts, they argue, she must have joined, albeit belatedly, the Kennedy team.[6]

ER's biographers tend to agree. Even ER intimates Joseph Lash and Lawrence Fuchs argue that she eventually overcame her initial suspicions and became one of Kennedy's staunchest supporters. Yet instead of emphasizing the assignments the Kennedy administration delegated to ER, her associates, most of whom were Kennedy loyalists, focus on promoting the legend of "the Senator and the Lady." In this version, the recalcitrant, aging liberal succumbed to the young politician's campaign courtship, charismatic inaugural address, and proposals for a New Frontier to become one of the president's most loyal supporters. As if this depiction of a twentieth-century Elizabeth and Essex were not enough to convince the nation of ER's loyalty to the Camelot legacy, ER's defenders propose yet another reason for the change of heart: seduced by Kennedy's legendary charm and wit, ER saw Kennedy as the 1960s political incarnation of FDR.[7]

A closer examination of the record reveals a different scenario. Eleanor Roosevelt did change her mind about John Kennedy. But she did not reverse herself so completely that she overcame all her initial suspicions about his character. She saw both his strengths and his weaknesses and refused to allow one to cancel out the other. Instead she developed as confrontational a relationship with Kennedy as she had had with Harry Truman, the last Democrat to reside in the White House. Indeed, what an analysis of the Eleanor Roosevelt-John Kennedy relationship reveals is not the limits of ER's idealism or the boundless nature of Kennedy's charisma, but rather the extent to which ER knew which battle to fight and how diligently she should fight it. She might find the president charming, but she knew very well that charm was not leadership.

∎ "Where do you stand on McCarthyism, Senator?" Kennedy and the Election of 1956

Although ER supported Kennedy in his 1952 quest for the Senate, she did so only after he won the party's primary. Soon, however, even her traditional party loyalty could not offset her disenchantment with his conduct. Moreover, Kennedy's blatant ambition for the 1956 vice presidential slot on the Democratic ticket and his enthusiastic courtship throughout the 1960 presidential campaign of the political machines ER abhorred did little to give her confidence in him. While several historians argue that ER's distrust of Catholics, which intensified after her battle with New York City's Cardinal Spellman over federal aid to parochial schools in 1949, was the real reason she opposed Kennedy, a closer review of the evidence supports a different interpretation. Undoubtedly ER did suspect that conservative Catholic clergy would have a strong influence on him. However, Kennedy's religion was less important to her than his cowardice toward McCarthy, his lukewarm civil rights record, and what Democratic Advisory Council chair Robert Benjamin called her "great suspicion" of his father's "instincts." Another friend recalled, "the hurts with Kennedy were very, very deep." "She just didn't like" Joe Kennedy.[8]

John Kennedy was too closely affiliated with the zealous anti-communist congressional hearings held by the House Education and Labor Committee and McCarthy's investigative staff for ER not to question Kennedy's claim that recuperation from back surgery was the only reason he did not vote to censure the senator from Wisconsin. As historian Herbert Parmet noted, Kennedy's anti-communist activism predated Truman's loyalty program, Nixon's pursuit of Alger Hiss, and McCarthy's rise to power. In fact, the freshman congressman was so ardent in his desire to purge the United Electrical, Radio and Machine Workers of American of alleged communist leadership that Kennedy even attacked one of his own professors who appeared before his committee. Indeed, not only did Kennedy precede Nixon in the use of anti-communism as a vehicle to political stardom but he also supported all of the anti-communist legislation his future rival introduced. Even Nixon agreed that their endeavors were similar, comparing their camaraderie on the House Labor Committee to "a pair of unmatched bookends." Moreover, Kennedy's staunch support of the House Un-American Activities Committee compounded ER's suspicions of the young congressman's drive for recognition. Everything he had proposed could not be further removed from the positions ER strove to have Democratic members of Congress adopt.[9]

When Kennedy decided to challenge Humphrey, Estes Kefauver, and Stuart Symington to become Adlai Stevenson's running mate in 1956, he knew that the surest path would be securing Stevenson's blessing and that of his key supporters. Since Stevenson adamantly insisted that the convention choose his running mate, Kennedy's advisers argued that an endorsement from ER, Stevenson's most ardent supporter, would solidify the support he needed to win on the first ballot. The evening before the balloting began, the Kennedy campaign sent an emissary, Kennedy family attorney James Landis, whose law partner Abba Schwartz was a good friend of ER's, to her suite to gain her backing.[10]

The go-between failed. ER told Landis that she could not support his candidate because Kennedy "had avoided taking a position during the [McCarthy] controversy." Kennedy's illness may have precluded his participating in the formal vote, she argued, but he had numerous opportunities to state his position for the record, and his lack of directness angered her. When Landis tried to argue that McCarthyism was an out-dated issue, she dismissed this evasion, brusquely responding, "I think McCarthyism is a question on which public officials must stand up and be counted. I still have not heard Senator Kennedy express his convictions. And I cannot be sure of the political future of anyone who does not willingly state where he stands on that issue."[11]

As the vice presidential balloting drew nearer and the field of candidates narrowed, Kennedy decided to appeal to ER personally. However, the legendary Kennedy charm did not succeed. She met with him but refused to be swayed. Instead, she gave the candidate a lesson in political hardball. As they sat facing each other on twin beds in ER's suite in the Blackstone Hotel, Eleanor Roosevelt grilled John Kennedy for his evasiveness on this issue. As one eyewitness to the encounter recalled, as soon as the introductions concluded, ER confronted Kennedy. "Where do you stand on McCarthyism, Senator?" she asked. When he equivocated and tried to change the subject to two of her sons' support for his candidacy, she bluntly retorted that she could not possibly see how she could endorse him. Great senators did not sacrifice principles for politics. "McCarthyism is a question on which everyone must stand up and be counted. You avoid committing yourself, while your brother Robert was actually on the McCarthy staff." She was surprised, she concluded, that he sought *her* help. She ended the discussion, Kennedy left without her support, and Kefauver won the nomination on the second ballot.[12]

None of Kennedy's actions over the next four years did anything to reverse ER's assessment of his character. Party liberals joined with DNC chair

ER was a frequent guest on "Meet the Press." In this 1949 appearance, she discusses Harry Truman, civil rights, and the United Nations with Lawrence Spivak and Martha Roundtree.   *(FDR Library)*

ER flew to California September 1950 to campaign for the Democratic ticket. Her son James, the gubernatorial nominee, and her dear friend Helen Gahagan Douglas, the senatorial candidate, caucus with ER at her Beverly Hills press conference. Richard Nixon had just labeled Douglas "the pink lady," inferring she had communist affiliations.   *(Wide World/Associated Press)*

ER began her career as a political organizer in the early 1920s with the Democratic Women's Committee, an affiliation she enthusiastically kept throughout her life. When the New York branch opened its new headquarters in 1956, ER led a day-long workshop on effective campaign strategy and lobbying techniques. *(Wide World/Associated Press)*

When black citizens of Montgomery, Alabama, launched a bus boycott to protest segregated seating practices, ER described their courage in her "My Day" columns and helped raise money to support the protest. She appeared with Rosa Parks, who had tried to integrate the University of Alabama, and Autherine Lucy at a Madison Square Garden fundraising rally.

(Wide World/Associated Press)

The 1956 Democratic presidential primary once again found ER and Truman in a public disagreement. Truman and the NAACP endorsed Averill Harriman while ER, who had just finished chairing the platform hearings on civil rights, championed Adlai Stevenson. The two leaders pose before the convention convenes. *(Library of Congress)*

After Stevenson alienated many of his black supporters by endorsing a gradual approach to school integration, ER publicly defended his unwitting remarks while privately chastising him and pressuring him to reassess his position. The two conceal their differences as they enter a 1956 Stevenson rally in Harlem. *(Wide World/Associated Press)*

McCarthyism "scared me as much as anything in my life," ER confided to a friend. When Washington University students asked her to name the major danger facing the nation, she removed her glasses and replied the problem was not a specific issue but rather how "stupidly complacent" Americans had become.

(Wide World/ Associated Press)

Truman invited ER to the groundbreaking ceremony for the Truman Library. She greets the former president, Speaker of the House Sam Rayburn, Majority Leader Lyndon Johnson, and Chief Justice Earl Warren as they prepare to leave for the laying of the cornerstone.

(Library of Congress)

Lorena Hickok loved this picture of ER, which she kept on her beside table.   *(FDR Library)*

ER meets with students attending a 1958 workshop on integration and non-violent resistance at the Highlander Folk School. The Ku Klux Klan, with the cooperation of the county sheriff, had offered a $25,000 reward to any member who would kidnap her en route. Informed of this by the FBI, ER still kept the appointment. *(FDR Library)*

Although she had earlier refused to tell Stevenson whether or not he should seek the presidency in 1960, she reconsidered in July when Kennedy appeared to have the nomination in hand. Convinced the senator was not presidential material, she pressured Stevenson to declare his candidacy and addressed a Washington rally urging Democrats to draft Stevenson.

(Wide World/ Associated Press)

By October 1960, Kennedy promised to end discrimination in federal housing and became more clear in his support for civil rights. This led ER to put aside her reservations about the Kennedy-Johnson ticket and, fearful of a Nixon victory, to campaign on its behalf. She attended events such as this New York City fundraiser and endorsed the ticket. *(Library of Congress)*

ER also spent the weekend before the election canvassing New York City to get out the black, labor, and liberal vote. Sunday night ended with a massive rally in the Coliseum at which she worked the large crowd alongside the candidate and urged them to vote for Kennedy. *(Wide World/Associated Press)*

Although ER often criticized Kennedy's foreign policy, she enthusiastically supported the Peace Corps and invited the president to discuss the program on
"Prospects for Mankind," her television program.   *(FDR Library)*

Martin Luther King and ER admired one another very much, often citing each
other as examples of courage and conviction. Thus, when the ADA asked her to
present its award to King at its Roosevelt Day dinner, ER accepted with enthusiasm. New York Senator Herbert Lehman assisted in the presentation.

(Wide World/Associated Press)

ER's political views drew intense criticism from conservatives, such as these Racine, Wisconsin, pickets who accused her of communist sympathies. Undeterred, ER entered the auditorium through a side door, the pickets left, and she delivered her address undisturbed to 1,600 listeners.

(*Wide World/Associated Press*)

ER meets with reporters in Deerfield, Illinois, to support the Progress Development Corporation, an interracial housing project, which built the two homes in the background. After town leaders had the new homes declared condemned, ER flew to Illinois to help the project raise money for its suit against the city. *(Wide World/Associated Press)*

ER thought Walter Reuther and James Carey, president of the International Brotherhood of Electrical Workers, represented labor's interest with skill and integrity. In December 1961, despite her grave illness, she campaigned on their behalf at the AFL-CIO national convention.

(FDR Library)

Despite increasing ill health, ER continued to monitor Kennedy's civil rights leadership closely. The president's reluctance to issue his "one stroke of the pen" pledge to desegregate federal housing angered her. She appears impatient as she listens to his speech dedicating an ILGWU financed integrated housing project. New York State Governor Nelson Rockefeller is seated next to ER. *(FDR Library)*

ER died November 7, 1962 and was buried next to FDR in a plain pine casket on the grounds of the Roosevelt estate. Her name was inscribed beneath his on a simple marble rectangle. Three presidents, two first ladies, and one vice president were among those who attended her funeral. *(Wide World/Associated Press)*

ER traveled simply and without fanfare. Often this amazed those who found themselves in her company—as it did Lawrence Jordan, Jr., who in the fall of 1960 photographed a solitary, seventy-six year old ER deep in thought and carrying her own luggage.   *(FDR Library)*

Paul Butler to form the Democratic Advisory Council after Stevenson's defeat in 1956 and invited both ER and Kennedy to become members. The senator, reluctant to commit himself to something which might damage his chances in 1960, waited until spring 1959 to join, while ER, despite the risks such affiliation might have to her income and her stature as an independent political commentator, immediately agreed to serve as a consultant.[13]

As civil rights moved to the forefront of the domestic agenda, Kennedy tenaciously avoided allying himself with one side in the debate. His behavior amazed ER. When he refused to denounce the Southern Manifesto condemning school integration, ER was furious. When Congress grappled with the Civil Rights Act of 1957, Kennedy's moderation posed a sharp contrast to ER's increasing commitment to federal protection of voting rights, civil disobedience, and integration, and led her to include him in the group of Democrats who have not "intended to do much" for civil rights. Consequently, when readers wrote asking her to name the best new candidates for the 1960 campaign, John Kennedy did not make her list. Instead, in recognition of his stalwart sponsorship of civil rights legislation, she praised Humphrey as the only senator who demonstrated "the spark of greatness" necessary to be president.[14]

In her eyes, Kennedy not only refused to admit his past mistakes but also seemed more concerned with securing the broadest possible constituency than with inspiring bold political action. Nothing could be further from the type of leadership the nation needed. Fear must not dominate America's response to dissent, she declared; indeed, "one of the primary duties of the President" is "to be the educator of the public on national problems." If the chief executive shirked this responsibility, "democracy can become a dangerous kind of government." In other words, with the strong reminder of the recently ended era of McCarthyism still in mind, ER adamantly argued that the president must create a climate for rational discussion and calm dissent or the nation could slip back into the politics of reaction.[15]

When Kennedy published *Profiles in Courage*, praising the leadership skills ER saw him lacking, the irony was too strong to overlook. At first, she simply refused to discuss the senator as a viable candidate. Then, in November 1957, a nationwide television audience saw her discount the senator by avoiding Mike Wallace's repeated attempts to get her to place Kennedy in the same league with Stevenson, Symington, and Michigan Governor G. Mennen Williams. After Kennedy won the Pulitzer Prize for his *Profiles in Courage*, which scholars later determined to have been written by Ted Sorensen, she skillfully continued to challenge his credentials without questioning the value of his subject. In March 1958, she again criticized Kennedy's role in McCarthyism in an article for the *Saturday Evening Post*, and she refused to retract her comments when pressured to do so by Kennedy allies, and her publisher, Cass Canfield, chair of Harper and Row. Next, in an interview that rocked the Democratic hierarchy, she told a college reporter on ABC television exactly why she could not back Kennedy. The senator might be long on charm, she said, but he was short on nerve. He could write about bravery, but she "would hesitate to place the difficult decisions that the next President will have to make with someone who understands what courage is and admires it but has not quite the independence to have it."[16]

"My dear boy: I only say this for your own good."
■ **Kennedy, Stevenson, and the 1960 Convention**

Although Eleanor Roosevelt hoped that she would not have to play as active a role in the 1960 presidential campaign as she had for Stevenson's 1956 effort, she nevertheless realized that there was no way that she could avoid the campaign and still expect to have the party adhere to the liberal principles she championed. After the outbursts against the *Brown* decision in Little Rock and New Orleans, civil rights again threatened to divide the Democratic party. Indeed, the party leadership dreaded the prospect of yet another platform fight during the 1960 convention and had already sought ER's advice on how to reach out to party dissidents. Furthermore, Kennedy's lackluster civil rights record, especially his support of the jury trial amendment to the Civil Rights Act of 1957 and his record number of abstentions on the subject, gave ER one more compelling reason to oppose his candidacy. Not only did his lack of leadership in defending basic civil liberties offend her, but she also worried that he would have many problems attracting enthusiastic support from black and liberal voters, two groups whose support she thought essential to offset the anti-Catholic backlash she anticipated throughout the party's southern wing.[17]

Hence, Kennedy's refusal to confront these two crucial domestic problems only underscored his defense of the status quo. Equivocation might win elections, but it was still bad politics. By avoiding controversial positions, Kennedy promoted a politics of complacency, which distorted America's vision and undermined its foreign policy. The world was changing rapidly and ER worried that the nation was too tied to past suspicions and past stereotypes to prepare for the challenges to come. The nation was mired in a defensive posture that reinforced what democracy opposed rather than what it symbolized. Now, more than ever, the party should choose a candidate who, if he could not change the national policies, could at least inspire a new national mood.[18]

She dedicated a large part of the last two years of her life to seeing that the Democratic party and its presidential aspirants recognize the need for new, vigorous leadership. Whether writing columns, articles, and memoirs; addressing liberal organizations; or lobbying Democratic party leadership, ER asserted that a program would be only as successful as the amount of support the public gave it. Moreover, the public could not be expected to see the advantages to change if the president did not explain to them why change was necessary. Lacking from American politics was a passionate commitment from political leaders to talk to the nation in plain and unmistakable language about the problems confronting them. As she declared to audiences across the nation, only when the president becomes a teacher can he truly lead the country.[19]

In stark contrast to other major party leaders who called for unity, Eleanor Roosevelt maintained that political vision was essential if liberal Democrats wanted to lead America. Painfully aware that the 1960 presidential election would be, as she confided to Trude Lash, her "last canter," ER decided to confront the party on its shortcomings. Carefully exploiting her stature within the party, ER chastized those who valued winning elections more than changing policy, even when the targets of her criticism were old friends and liberal allies.[20]

As he learned in one of the most dramatic moments of the 1959 political year, even Harry Truman was not exempt from her scorn. In mid-October, the Democratic Advisory Council hosted a lavish fundraiser at the Waldorf Astoria in honor of ER's seventy-fifth birthday. Immediately after the event was announced party leaders and presidential aspirants recognized that it was a command performance. Even John Kennedy, who had refused to join the council until a few weeks earlier, flew to New York to promote his candidacy only to find himself overshadowed by the Democrats' clash of titans.

When Truman used his introduction of ER as a forum to defend the Rayburn-Johnson congressional Democrats and castigate "hothouse liberals" and "eggheads" for being "the self-appointed guardians of liberal thinking," an angry ER put aside the speech she had intended to deliver. In a response broadcast nationwide over CBS radio and splashed across the nation's front pages, she threw her support behind those liberals who criticized Congress. Truman was wrong, she declared, when he said that liberals must close ranks. As an individual he was certainly entitled to dislike whomever he chose, but as a liberal leader the former president needed to work with every liberal politician and policy analyst who was willing to work with him. Challenging Truman to follow her example, ER proclaimed that she welcomed every kind of politician into the party who understood liberalism and was determined to work for its implementation.[21]

Turning to face the former president, ER cited Truman's own dramatic efforts to save his own presidency. Deftly recalling Truman's broadside attacks on the "do nothing" 80th Congress, ER skillfully drew a parallel to the upcoming election, arguing that a moderate, cautious candidate was bound to fail. While she recognized that the American public might not respond immediately, she nevertheless argued that the public's reluctance to follow should not interfere with the president's duty to lead. Lack of leadership, more than any other single characteristic, was what was wrong with current political performances. Politicians have been too reluctant to do this and the nation as a whole has suffered. "I think perhaps they've . . . been afraid to tell . . . the truth." ER then challenged Democrats in the audience to follow her lead, proclaiming, "I'm not afraid to tell the American people the truth."

ER hoped that the Democratic party would take the same risks that she did and rededicate itself to liberal reform. However, she recognized that two formidable changes would have to occur for liberals to control the Democratic agenda. First, the party would have to survive the challenges its conservative wing posed to civil rights legislation and other extensions of the welfare state. Second, it would have to recognize that domestic policies had international repercussions.

Yet ER refused to let her commitment to liberal ideals obstruct her political acumen. She also understood that two major changes within the party hierarchy would have to occur before liberals triumphed. The Democrats would "have to prove to [their] own people" that they understand what qualities are necessary to address the future creatively. Then, they could only win the election if they could convince the voters that they had "the courage, the vision, the imagination, [and] the honesty" necessary to design and implement effective reform.[22]

Harry Truman was not the only leading Democrat to endure ER's scorn that year. Indeed, relations with Kennedy were never as tense as the year before Kennedy ran for president. In 1959 these two politicians locked horns twice, both times in extremely public arenas; and in both instances, to Kennedy's increasing frustration, ER stole the show. On January 6, she scolded the candidate in her column for relying on his father's wealth to finance his campaign and repeatedly refused to retract the charges when all the allegations could not be substantiated. When Kennedy finally understood that she would not compromise and abandoned his demands for a complete retraction, she responded, with not a little sarcasm. In a telegram that began "My dear boy, I only say these things for your own good" she offered to discuss the issue further, but hoped that perhaps he could accept that "now was the time to turn the other profile."[23]

The next scene played itself out six months later in the Senate Sub-committee on Labor, which Kennedy chaired. In a room crammed full of reporters, ER testified in support of a minimum wage bill the committee was considering, while Kennedy, with his back turned to her, conversed with his staff throughout her testimony. Moreover, to ensure that she understood this snub, he left the committee room without speaking to her. Not to be outflanked, as the reporters gathered around her after she fin-ished her statement, ER deftly, but politely, chided the young man's con-duct. "Where is Senator Kennedy," she asked no one in particular, "I would have liked to say hello to him?" Consequently, when he tried to make amends for his behavior later in the year by attending events in her honor, such as the DAC testimonial dinner, ER had new reasons to question his character.[24]

Kennedy just could not understand such intransigent opposition. When his emissaries failed, he appealed to her close friend Mary Lasker for advice. "Now why is she so much against me?" Kennedy asked Lasker at a Washington dinner party in late 1959. ER's pronouncements "were a great political worry" to Kennedy and Lasker advised her dinner companion "that the only way to reconcile any differences was for him to talk to her directly." ER will be fair, she assured him. Kennedy followed Lasker's sug-gestion and arranged a meeting, but, as ER later told Lasker, the senator "didn't entirely convince her" that he truly understood or opposed the dam-age McCarthy had done.[25]

As the events of early 1960 show, an angry Kennedy begrudgingly real-ized his mistake and tried to offset the political damage this impulsiveness could cost his career. Yet the senator felt trapped between the political value of mending his relationship with ER and his personal desire to sever all ties with her. Kennedy loyalists tried to run interference only to find out once more that ER was not so easily swayed. In fact, the nearer the election grew, the more resistant ER became to Kennedy's conciliatory efforts.

In late 1959, Kennedy supporters learned that ER was conducting a panel discussion of foreign policy on her television series "Prospects for Mankind" and persuaded ER's producer, Henry Morgenthau III, a college friend of Kennedy's, to invite the senator to join the debate. Only a few days before the January 2, 1960 taping Kennedy learned that he could appear the same day on "Meet the Press." ER's show was taped in Boston. "Meet the Press" was live from Washington. Kennedy wanted to announce his candidacy in Washington and leave his press conference to appear immediately on "Meet the Press." To do this, he would have to cancel his appearance on ER's show in Boston. Kennedy called Morgenthau for "help in getting off the hook with Mrs. R." When Morgenthau said that ER would be disappointed, even though Morgenthau "knew that she could care less," Kennedy rearranged his schedule and flew to Boston to tape ER's show on Saturday.[26]

Despite this gesture, ER still did not show any leniency toward the senator. The press wanted ER to respond to his candidacy rather than to discuss foreign aid. A rigid, indignant ER refused to be lured into a discussion of electoral politics. When Boston television commentator Louis Lyon asked her if there was anything she would like to say on such an "important day," she tartly replied "no" and walked away, leaving the senator standing alone. Clearly Kennedy's wish for a public truce with ER would have to wait.[27]

As the 1960 presidential primaries began, ER's exasperation with the Democratic field increased. If, before the primaries, Kennedy's mediocre domestic record had worried ER, by spring, his lack of experience in foreign affairs reinforced her opposition. By mid-May, the U-2 controversy, the collapse of the Soviet-American summit, the ferocity with which Richard Nixon had begun to campaign, and the likelihood that the New York Prendergast machine would join forces with the Kennedy machine to control the convention worried ER so much that she prepared for one last convention battle.[28]

She remained convinced that Nixon could be defeated, but, as she told her son-in-law, Jim Halsted, she also thought that none of the declared Democratic candidates could beat him. She could not have agreed more with her dear friend Agnes Meyer, who in an earlier letter argued that Nixon was a tough opponent and that "you can't beat somebody with nobody." Moreover, when the primary field narrowed to Hubert Humphrey, who recently had disappointed ER with his increasing affiliation with Lyndon Johnson, Johnson himself, and Kennedy, ER bemoaned the indecisiveness that kept Stevenson out of the primaries.[29]

Yet ER's undoubted devotion to Stevenson did not completely overshadow her political common sense. She knew that he hated primaries, but she clearly understood that the longer he denied that he was a candidate and unrealistically waited for the convention to draft him, the weaker his chances became. She seconded the pleas of Agnes Meyer and Walter

Reuther that he declare his intent quickly and mobilize the forces necessary to stop the well-financed and tightly organized Kennedy onslaught. The longer Stevenson postponed his challenge, she argued, the more political bosses could stack the delegates against him. Furthermore, she had reviewed some private poll results, which showed that Stevenson still commanded a strong following within the party that could derail the Kennedy machine, and which showed an increasing reluctance by Americans to vote for a Catholic president.[30]

Stevenson equivocated. He continued to declare that he was not a candidate; however, he also repeatedly refused to say that he would not accept the nomination if the convention decided to draft him. ER stepped up her criticism of Kennedy and lobbied Reuther and other labor officials to delay announcing their endorsements. Meanwhile Tom Finletter, Agnes Meyer, Senator Mike Monroney, and other key leaders of the Draft Stevenson campaign implored Stevenson to understand that if he did not announce his candidacy soon he would lose the groundswell of support for him provided by the collapse of the Soviet summit after the U-2 spy plane incident.[31]

Stevenson rejected their advice. His criticism of Eisenhower's diplomacy was not an indication that he wanted the nomination, but rather a reflection of his duty as a liberal leader. Frustrated by Stevenson's aloofness and yet increasingly convinced that Kennedy had overestimated his own support among convention delegates, in mid-May key Stevenson supporters appealed to ER to force Stevenson to decide whether he would challenge Kennedy. She agreed.[32]

The situation had changed dramatically since late January when she deliberately avoided Stevenson's pleas for advice on whether or not he should run again. Stevenson had requested a private meeting with ER before he left for a two-month tour of Latin America. ER was so afraid that he would seek her opinion that she immediately invited her close friend and personal physician, David Gurewitsch, and his wife Edna to be at Val-Kill when Stevenson arrived. As she told Edna, "He's really coming in the hope that I will persuade him to run for President. I will not persuade him. I believe that anyone who needs to be urged should not run." Now the tables had turned. Kennedy's apparent victory, the international crisis, and the absence of liberal leadership compelled ER to act.[33]

On June 8 an exasperated ER phoned Adlai Stevenson, interrupted his meeting with journalist Theodore White, and insisted that he declare whether he wanted the nomination. When Stevenson responded to her questions by once again arguing that his position was clear, ER testily fired back that his position was anything but clear. She planned to endorse his candidacy that day unless he specifically forbade her to do so. Her deadline was an hour away and she demanded a response. She would call him back shortly. There is no record of their second conversation but it is safe to assume that he failed to convince ER that he did not want the nomination. The following day, Eleanor Roosevelt endorsed Adlai Stevenson for president.[34]

Seizing on the drama her endorsement generated, the press clamored for a response from the reluctant liberal. Trapped, Stevenson again denied his candidacy. ER rebuffed his disclaimer and announced that she had joined the New York Draft Stevenson Committee as its honorary chair. The next day the front page of the *New York Times* described the conflict in a headline that proclaimed "Stevenson: Not a Candidate; Mrs. R.: Yes, He Is." Clearly, those closest to Stevenson believed without question that Stevenson wanted to run again. As ER cryptically wrote her daughter Anna Halsted the following week, "politics are very active . . . and now I have to go out to the convention."[35]

Ultimately, Eleanor Roosevelt succeeded in her mission. Stevenson did enter the race, albeit at the eleventh hour. Yet, much to her chagrin, mobilizing Stevenson's participation in his own campaign proved as difficult a task as forcing Kennedy to state his true opinion of McCarthy had been. When Stevenson finally yielded to ER's demands and declared that he would in fact accept the nomination if the party offered it, new convention battle lines were drawn. While the press treated Stevenson's comments primarily as aspects of a Stevenson-Kennedy rivalry, Kennedy and his confidants understood that it was another replay of the Roosevelt-Kennedy imbroglio.[36]

Kennedy prepared carefully for both battles. Believing that the key to derailing Stevenson was to divide his supporters, Kennedy aides circulated copies of a full-page advertisement that had appeared in the *New York Times* a month before the convention praising Kennedy's qualifications for office. Signed by such former Stevenson advisors as Arthur Schlesinger, Jr., John Kenneth Galbraith, Joe Rauh, Henry Steel Commager, and James MacGregor Burns, this endorsement rather than overcoming ER's objections, only enraged her and fueled her opposition to Kennedy.[37]

As Stevenson's most famous and unquestioned advocate, the media treated Eleanor Roosevelt as though she was Stevenson's de facto campaign manager. Her press coverage increased the closer it got to convention time. Moreover, when she announced that she would go to Los Angeles after all and lobby for Stevenson, each action she took on his behalf became front page news. Consequently, when ER descended from the American Airlines gangplank and greeted the reporters assembled in the Los Angeles airport, the fight became as much a three-way contest among Eleanor Roosevelt, Adlai Stevenson, and John Kennedy for the soul of the Democratic party as it was a battle among John Kennedy, Adlai Stevenson, and Lyndon Johnson for the presidential nomination.[38]

Eleanor Roosevelt failed to secure the nomination for Stevenson. Just as clearly, however, failure to stir the convention rests squarely upon his, rather than her, shoulders. Immediately after deplaning, she launched into the campaign—addressing an assembly of women delegates, holding three press conferences, courting fifteen state leaders, and pressuring Stevenson to enter the convention floor fights. At a luncheon held in her honor she lectured Stevenson on why he must work for the nomination. She debated former Stevenson supporters who had joined the Kennedy campaign so thoroughly that Schlesinger later readily conceded that not only did ER win the debate but also that he "had never been so thoroughly spanked in public." When Walter Reuther and other Stevenson scouts told her that the California and Illinois delegations' support for Kennedy was cracking, she lobbied them until two o'clock in the morning. Half of the delegates deserted Kennedy and endorsed Stevenson. Continually she told anyone within earshot that Kennedy was not ready for the presidency, that Stevenson would be the best candidate to address the current crisis, and—pragmatic as ever—that the best ticket the party could possibly offer would be a Stevenson-Kennedy ticket. And she helped coordinate a massive floor demonstration, which disrupted the convention for sixteen minutes.[39]

Yet even after ER had gone to the mat for Stevenson a second time and risked her reputation within the party to criticize Democratic leadership in the midst of its presidential convention, Stevenson remained so aloof and ambivalent about the nomination that his behavior undermined all her efforts on his behalf. She was bitterly disappointed in him. If he truly did not want the nomination, he should have told her so up front. He should have ordered the draft committees to stop their campaign. Stevenson's indecisiveness infuriated ER so much that she felt he had betrayed her trust in him. Their relationship would never be the same. As Agnes Meyer later told Stevenson's biographer John Bartlow Martin, "Mrs. Roosevelt and I sat there—we and Finletter had worked hard for the demonstration—we had the applause there—but then he went up on the platform and throws it out the window. . . . I could have murdered him. I could see Bobby Kennedy running around on the floor trying to hold his delegates. He should have told us he wouldn't fight."[40]

Despite the respect ER elicited from the delegates, despite the six-minute ovation the delegates gave her when she first entered the convention hall, the convention rejected her pleas for a Stevenson-Kennedy ticket and, after fierce floor negotiations between Robert Kennedy and several delegations, nominated John Kennedy on the first ballot. After the votes were tallied, Eleanor Roosevelt quickly left the convention arena, returned to the residence where she stayed during the proceedings, and prepared to leave Los Angeles that evening. Immediately, rumors about her abrupt exit began to circulate among the delegates—she had left weeping, she had left embittered, she had left furious with Kennedy, she had left determined to sit out the election.[41]

Although ER was extremely disappointed when she left the Los Angeles Arena, none of these depictions accurately reflect ER's state of mind July 14, 1960. Contrary to some news reports, she did not flee the auditorium in tears. She was too experienced a campaigner and too accustomed to controversy to be hurt so easily by defeat or to display such private emotion in such a public forum. She accepted Kennedy's nomination; after all, she was one of the party's most loyal followers. What she did not accept, and what compelled her to reassess her decision about the 1960 campaign, was the lackluster performance of the party leaders and Stevenson liberals.

Eleanor Roosevelt mourned for the future of the party and wondered whether the energies she and other liberal activists had expended throughout the fifties to promote reform had been spent in vain. As she watched the party revert to a more mainstream agenda and endorse a candidate whom she assessed to be long on style and short on substance, she could not help but feel disappointed by the Democrats' selection. She believed that despite all the lip service the party paid to developing a primary process that would reflect accurately the sentiments of local Democrats, it had abandoned its pronouncements and endorsed a primary system in which the candidate with the most funds received the most backing. She watched the urban political machines, which constituted the backbone of Kennedy's campaign, dwarf the party's professed opposition to boss rule.[42]

But above all, Eleanor Roosevelt left the convention dismayed as much by Stevenson's ambivalence as by Kennedy's ambition for the White House. Stevenson's refusal to be pragmatic undermined what little chance he had to derail Kennedy. Yet, as disappointed as ER was with Stevenson, that was only part of her dejection. She also feared for the future because she believed that Stevenson had a better chance of defeating Richard Nixon, the politician she most detested, and worried that, if elected, John Kennedy would be more a hindrance to, rather than a proponent of, vitally needed reform.[43]

■ "The raft at Tilsit."
Kennedy, Stevenson, and the Election of 1960

Once he became the party's standard bearer and rumors of ER's opposition persisted, it became obvious to Kennedy that he needed Eleanor Roosevelt's endorsement more than ever. Campaign officials in New York, California, and Illinois continually reported that Kennedy would lose those states unless every possible Democratic voter supported him. Stevenson had strong support in those states. If the Stevenson state organizations would help the Kennedy campaign, then Kennedy's chances improved dramatically. In addition, Kennedy did not want to become affiliated with the conservative wing of the party. As he confided to aide Arthur Schlesinger, Jr., "I want to be nominated by the liberals . . . I don't want to depend on those Southern bastards." One way to secure this support was to gain the approval of Stevenson's most loyal champion.[44]

Although ER had told the press before the convention that she would support the party's nominee, her hostility to Kennedy was so well known that it overshadowed the lukewarm endorsement she subsequently gave him in the spirit of party loyalty. And her comments immediately following the convention encouraged the media to report her disappointment. For example, when ER praised the platform more than the candidates at a Democratic fundraiser the week after the convention, the *New York Times* not only headlined its story, "She'll Back Democratic Ticket Despite Some Misgivings," but began it by quoting ER that although she was "not well satisfied" with the ticket, she would support it and thought it could win. Rumors promoted by anti-Kennedy pundits suggested that ER would sit out the election rather than vote for either of the two men she so disliked. With such negatives to overcome, Kennedy had to tread lightly in his courtship of ER. He needed her because he knew her active support would keep most Stevenson loyalists and liberal activists in line. But, as much as he needed her, he feared an additional tongue lashing from her could further divide the party and tip the scales in Nixon's direction. In short, Kennedy knew that he needed as much party unity as he could muster to win a very close election and that Eleanor Roosevelt's support was crucial if he was to mobilize doubting Democrats.[45]

Consequently, after winning the Democratic nomination, Kennedy immediately began to court ER assiduously. Once again she proved to be a difficult target. She instructed friends with whom she stayed during the convention to say that she was not in when he called. Later she refused to take his call when he tried to reach her at the Los Angeles airport. In fact, she was so intent on avoiding the conversation that she only took the call after the campaign sent a mutual friend to the airport to intercede on Kennedy's behalf. Even then, she proved a hard sell. Her plane did not leave for an hour, Abba Schwartz pleaded. Would she please take the senator's call since it would not inconvenience the other passengers? Trapped, she yielded, but even then she was curt and noncommittal. Choosing her words carefully, she told the candidate that while she would support him, she would not campaign for him. He "didn't have to worry about her," she replied. If he wanted to talk to her, just talk to her sons, they would pass on any information she needed. In light of their past history, ER's message was unmistakable. He was the party's candidate and while she would not work against him, he could not count on her to campaign for him.[46]

Throughout the summer, ER kept her word and her distance. She was cordial to Kennedy and refrained from criticizing him in ways that might cost him votes. However, her silence created a vacuum, interpreted in different ways. James Roosevelt, an avid Kennedy supporter, tried to exploit his mother's "vacation from the campaign" by reading endorsement messages from ER, which she neither prepared nor supported, at Kennedy dinners. Some staunch Stevenson loyalists, such as Mary Lasker, Agnes Meyer, and Walter Reuther, hoped that ER was jockeying with the campaign team so that she could ensure Stevenson's appointment as Secretary of State. Still other friends, such as Estelle Linzer and Tom Finletter, thought she was so irritated with Kennedy's affiliation with New York's Carmine De Sapio and other political bosses that she wanted to focus on local elections, especially the campaign against De Sapio she helped organize for the New York Committee for Democratic Voters.[47]

Kennedy interpreted the withdrawal differently. He believed that Eleanor Roosevelt was testing him, waiting to see how he would respond to the challenges a national election presented. This was a chance for him to make amends for his past behavior as well as an opportunity to overcome the final stumbling block he needed to mobilize party activists. As Kennedy headquarters continued to receive reports from the field confirming the candidate's fears that the election's outcome was very much in doubt, ER's public and active work on his behalf took on added importance. Especially, he worried that he might not carry New York, California, and Illinois against Richard Nixon, and thought appearances by ER on his behalf in those states could make the difference.

Once again Kennedy knew that he must ask for her support. This time, however, he knew that he must change his approach. Having slighted her in their last two public encounters, Kennedy understood that he must play to her if he expected her to work for him. Furthermore, ever mindful of the public shellacking she had given him in her crowded hotel room in 1956, he knew that he needed to confer with her in private. He would gladly come to her, Kennedy told his advisers, if she would just set a time and place.[48]

Remembering the hostility with which she had met his airport overtures, Kennedy once again turned to an intermediary to plead his case. Kennedy aide Theodore Sorensen asked ER's friend Hyman Bookbinder to arrange a meeting. ER, who still refused to lend her name to Kennedy's New York campaign committee, knew from her contacts throughout the country that "he was in trouble" in other states as well. She wanted to help the party, to help Stevenson and Chester Bowles, who had been defeated when he sought reelection as governor of Connecticut in 1956, find positions within the administration, but she also knew that this was her last campaign. She was beginning to tire easily and the prospect of a protracted campaign effort did not excite her as it once did. Moreover, she knew that if he won the election her counsel would not be as valued in 1964 as it was in 1960. If she was going to influence his behavior, this was her last chance. She agreed to Bookbinder's request. There would be a ceremony at the Roosevelt Library on August 14 commemorating the twenty-fifth anniversary of the Social Security Act, ER told Bookbinder. She would gladly see Kennedy then.[49]

Kennedy knew that there would be a price for this visit. He assumed that she would press for Stevenson's appointment as Secretary of State, a concession Kennedy did not wish to make. Therefore he approached ER with more than his usual trepidation. He wanted her in his camp but not at the expense of a cabinet appointment for a rival he did not like, especially in a position in which he intended to appoint a man who would act as a stand-in for the White House. He approached the meeting as guardedly as he later would prepare for a superpower summit. When his lifelong friend William Walton tried to back out of accompanying the candidate, Kennedy urged him to stay the course. "This is the raft at Tilsit," referring to the meeting between Napoleon and Czar Alexander I, where the emperor not only accepted the czar's surrender, but also persuaded the Russian to support his campaign to conquer Europe. Kennedy recognized that the Hyde

Park meeting was his last chance to recruit her and he wanted the best counsel available. What he did not anticipate were the conditions ER would exact for her endorsement.[50]

Most accounts of Kennedy's pilgrimage to Val-Kill emphasize the statement that ER and Kennedy jointly released to the press and ER's letters to Mary Lasker and Agnes Meyer discussing her assessment of the candidate's performance. Furthermore, Fuchs, Lash, and Schlesinger all emphasize ER's refusal to insist that Stevenson be appointed Secretary of State and argue that a mutual fondness seemed to emerge from the luncheon. While these accounts provide valuable insight into the changing Roosevelt-Kennedy association, they are nevertheless incomplete assessments that focus on personality rather than results. Missing from these accounts is a discussion of what topics were debated and an assessment of the changes this discussion had on the conduct of Kennedy and ER.[51]

Although no written record exists of the talk held in the far alcove of ER's Val-Kill living room, a fairly comprehensive account may be spliced together from oral histories, ER's correspondence, and the memoirs of various Kennedy aides. This reconstruction depicts a firm, but polite Eleanor Roosevelt, determined to leave her mark on John Kennedy, the last Democratic presidential aspirant with whom she expected to have contact, and a determined but wary John Kennedy struggling to make a final appeal for support without tarnishing his own charisma.[52]

Kennedy prepared for this summit carefully. After convincing Walton to accompany him to Hyde Park, he lobbied Stevenson to draft a statement discussing their collaboration on foreign policy. Kennedy hoped that if Stevenson acknowledged his role in the Kennedy inner circle before Kennedy met with ER, then maybe ER would not make a cabinet appointment for Stevenson a condition for campaigning. Finally, still concerned that this paper collaboration was not enough to dissuade ER from predicating her endorsement on Stevenson's appointment, Kennedy tried to squelch the rumors that Chester Bowles's withdrawal from the Connecticut Senate race was really an indication that Bowles was Kennedy's choice for Secretary of State.[53]

ER did not prepare for the meeting. She had nothing to lose and realized that Kennedy was coming to her "with his political hat in his hand." Indeed, all she wanted was for the tete-a-tete to be over. Her favorite granddaughter had died suddenly the day before and that only intensified her desire to keep the conference short and to the point. Consequently, when ER greeted Kennedy at the door of her Val-Kill cottage, she wasted no time on pleasantries. After listening to his solicitations, she once again caught

Kennedy by surprise. He had expected a full court press for Stevenson. Instead, she declared that only the candidate should pick his cabinet and proceeded to instruct him on how to hold the Democratic coalition together.[54]

To win the election, Kennedy had to keep two groups in line, devout Stevensonians, and black Americans who doubted his commitment to civil rights. If Kennedy had any chance at all of carrying California and New York, he must do more than announce that Adlai was chairing his task force on foreign policy. That was "not enough," ER said tartly. Bluntly she advised the candidate to quote Stevenson in his campaign speeches and invite him to appear on the platform with him. In short, if Kennedy wanted to win California and New York, he would have to share the limelight.[55]

Furthermore, Kennedy might as well recognize that he could not carry the South; therefore he must recruit the black and northern urban votes he needed to offset the defection of southern white voters. He could not do this unless he stopped trying to appease the South and articulated his civil rights positions more forthrightly. Kennedy agreed, saying that he only recently had come to understand how deeply the party was split along North-South lines. Although we can only speculate about ER's reaction to this admission, it is certainly safe to assume that she could have told him that years ago and that his lack of knowledge about this basic rift only reinforced her assessment that he was not ready to lead the nation.

Immediately after ER and Kennedy posed for photographs and the candidate drove away, ER wrote a brief description of the meeting for her friends. Although she tried to put a positive spin on the conversation, she could not hide her doubts about his ability and commitment. "I gather that his understanding of the difficulty of the campaign that faces him has matured him in a short time." She was pleased to see that Kennedy was "willing to learn" and had "a quick mind," but she still worried that he would make important decisions too impulsively. "I liked him better than I ever have before because he seemed so little cocksure," she concluded, but she still wished that had a "more judicial type of mind."

Clearly, the candidate eased some of her uneasiness, but large doubts still loomed. Kennedy had the drive that Stevenson lacked, but he lacked Stevenson's intelligence. That bothered ER immensely. Nevertheless, ER agreed to serve as honorary co-chair of the New York Committee for Kennedy. As she told Mary Lasker, he would have to earn her support. "Whether I will take any trips or become more involved will depend on whether or not I am happy with the way he progresses as a person in the campaign."[56]

Ultimately ER did join the Kennedy campaign. After the candidate promised to ban racial discrimination in federal housing late that summer, ER began to believe that Kennedy would take some political risks. And when he suddenly appeared at a civil rights conference in Harlem to receive the recommendations from ER and Adam Clayton Powell adopted at that gathering, she hoped that he would continue "his willingness to learn" after he moved into the White House. She raised funds to sponsor a televised discussion of civil rights featuring Kennedy, New York Senator Herbert Lehman, and herself, and hosted the opening of the Kennedy-Johnson headquarters in New York City. She traveled to hotly contested precincts in California, and to Indianapolis and Chicago for his campaign; and, she taped radio and television ads urging his election. She spent the Sunday night before the election campaigning with Kennedy and Johnson in Manhattan. By early November, she was beginning to think that Kennedy would grow with the presidency and hoped that he would be worthy of the admiration he evoked from the crowds who thronged around him.[57]

■ "Nobody makes sense."
Politics and Death

Eleanor Roosevelt spent election night in her East 74th Street apartment. While she celebrated the outcome, she knew that her influence within the Kennedy administration would be minimal. A polite Kennedy had asked for her reactions to his policies, but she understood the protocol that lay behind his solicitations. He must form his own administration with his own appointments to the cabinet. She would comment on policies and speeches, and serve when called, but she had had her frontier. Consequently, ER refused Kennedy's invitation to sit with his family in the presidential box. Instead, while Lou Hoover and Bess Truman accepted Kennedy's offer to join his family, seventy-six-year-old Eleanor Roosevelt watched the inauguration of forty-four-year-old John Kennedy as she sat on the bleachers in snow-covered Washington, wrapped in an old army blanket.[58]

Kennedy's inaugural address thrilled ER. With his emphasis on service, human rights, and democratic values, Kennedy addressed all the major points with which the president should challenge the nation. And she became an enthusiastic advocate of the Peace Corps, a concept she had promoted since the late 1950s, eagerly accepting a seat on its advisory board and praising it in her columns and speeches. She hoped that his foreign policy would emphasize democratic initiatives rather than focus solely on military containment. And she was quick to criticize when Kennedy diplomacy veered off that track. Appalled by the Bay of Pigs, "that unfortunate raid" as she euphemistically called it, ER reprimanded the president for his impulsive actions and immediately agreed to chair the Tractors for Freedom Committee. She questioned Kennedy's commitment of troops to Vietnam, lobbied against the Taylor-Rostow Report on Indochina, pleaded for a nuclear test ban treaty, and lamented America's support of apartheid.[59]

When Kennedy refused to appoint more than nine women to federal postions within the first three months of his administration, ER met with the president in the Oval Office and presented him a three-page list of women qualified for executive positions. Kennedy responded by asking her to chair his Presidential Commission on the Status of Women. Ever aware of the limits of her energy, ER knew that she would probably not live to see the commission present its findings. In mid-1960 her close friend and physician David Gurewitsch had diagnosed her fatigue and recurrent flu as a result of aplastic anemia. As the anemia and pneumonia she had battled throughout early 1961 took its toll, ER daily encountered new signs that her health was failing rapidly. She knew that she could not fight much longer.[60]

Her illness notwithstanding, she accepted the position and skillfully arranged for her friend of twenty-five years, Pauli Murray, the "firebrand" civil rights attorney, to help draft the commission's study. Perhaps Murray's appointment reassured ER that the commission would not rubber stamp the administration's hiring policies. ER had long valued Murray's audacity as well as her commitment to civil rights for women and black Americans and fully expected the attorney to challenge the administration to correct its discriminatory practices.

Yet Kennedy's avoidance of civil rights—the domestic matter closest to her heart—angered her the most and she aggressively criticized his timer-ousness. When Kennedy delayed his executive order integrating federally financed housing, ER refrained from attacking the president in public and instead doggedly lobbied Attorney General Robert Kennedy to persuade his brother to act. But she soon changed tactics. She chastised the president directly in correspondence and in her column for not making the House Agricultural Committee address the plight of migrant farm workers. When Kennedy, worried that a continuing public association with Martin Luther King, Jr., would alienate core Democrats, refused to invite the leader to the inauguration and excluded him from a White House meeting with other civil rights leaders, she worked to keep King's positions before the president. When King appealed to her to apply "the necessary pressure and persuasion" to bring his proposals to Kennedy, she not only sent the civil rights leader's articles to the president under her own signature and but also seconded King's call for executive intervention in voting rights disputes and physical intimidation of civil rights workers. She gave her very public endorsement to SNCC's "Jail/No Bail" campaign and helped the SCLC solicit funds to run SNCC's training programs.[61]

When ER returned from Europe in February 1962, where she had taped three interviews for her television program, and learned that the Kennedy administration still refused to protect the Freedom Riders or to censor white federal judges whose decisions endorsed violent white resistance, she was incensed. She increasingly pressured the administration to act. Prodding Kennedy, she wrote columns, sent letters of endorsement to arrested activists, and joined national civil rights organizations in criticizing the violent, racist responses to the bus campaigns. When the administration continued to equivocate for fear of alienating the southern power block in the Senate, ER's patience wore out. Speeches were fine, and while ER thought Kennedy's address on the rights of the Freedom Riders good, she scolded the administration for its reliance on rhetoric rather than results.[62]

Perhaps the parallel with FDR's civil rights strategy was too striking for her to overlook. Almost thirty years had passed and the White House was still presenting the same arguments for patience and congressional consensus. When The Reverend Russell R. Bletzer of Deerfield, Illinois, asked her help in securing a federal injunction blocking the county's attempt to label park land recently purchased for an integrated housing development "condemned" property, she invited King to her apartment to meet with other organizers determined to stop "the hysteria." Two months later she agreed to a request issued from Norman Thomas, SNCC, and CORE to chair a public inquiry into the blatant judicial disregard of the Freedom Riders' civil rights and civil liberties, where, in one of her last public appearances, she angrily criticized the Kennedy administration and the Democratic Congress for avoiding their duties. Nor did she moderate her demands when the party continued its silence. After King was arrested in Albany in July, she urged the Justice Department to intercede on King's behalf and used her column to call for his safe treatment and quick release.[63]

After chairing the Commission on the Inquiry into the Freedom Struggle in the South in May 1962, an exhausted ER returned to Val-Kill. She continued to write her column and give an occasional interview; however, most of her energy was spent trying to complete her last book, *Tomorrow Is Now*. The previous summer, she argued that social and economic complacency had killed the American dream and blamed "the older generation" for telling young people to "take a job that will give you security." That position was self-defeating. "You can have no security unless you live bravely," "unless you can choose a challenge instead of a competence." *Tomorrow Is Now* continued her "tooth and nail" fight against political lethargy. An assessment of the political, social, and economic problems facing the nation, the monograph also was ER's last passionate call for individual action. Angered by the "growing tendency among Americans" who "skirt" making choices, "hesitate" expressing opinions, and "take comfort in being part of the herd," she demanded that Americans "determine [their] position, state it bravely and then *act boldly*." The nation must not "blindly leave" difficult decisions to the government. "Without the individual as the steering point, nothing really can be accomplished."[64]

Friends attempted to convince her to cancel all public appearances, and she tried to comply. But she could not bear to spend the last months of her life sitting out the fights that meant the most to her. She wanted "to shock the conscience of America and bring a realization of where we stand in the year 1962 in the United States." Keenly aware of students risking their lives for racial justice, she pushed herself to keep the obligations she felt most important. Nowhere is this more clear than in her struggle to keep her appointments in the black precincts within the borough of Queens for the New York Democratic party. When the driver came to her New York City apartment to pick her up, against the wishes of her friends, an exhausted ER struggled to keep her commitment. She warned her young black escort, "my head is heavy and you'll have to steady me when I get out." Yet she was pleased that she made the effort because at her second stop a young black girl stood in the front of the crowd, arms filled with fresh flowers for her. "You see I had to come," she confided to her driver. "I was expected."[65]

By mid-July, the tuberculosis took control of her life and a tired ER prepared to die. She focused most of her energy on finishing *Tomorrow* and meeting her daily deadline for "My Day." She battled nausea and her gums and throat bled. By the end of the month, she could not hold the pen to edit the drafts of the manuscript her aide had typed for her review. Since she had a committee meeting later that day with the New York Board of Education and her physician was out of town, ER agreed to see a different doctor in the city. He immediately ordered a blood transfusion. The next day her fever reached 105.5 degrees. A delirious ER did not recognize Gurewitsch or her son John when they came to the hospital to visit.[66]

Although she occasionally regained consciousness and tried to respond to the various political demands placed on her, ER never completely recovered from that attack. After she left the hospital, she tried to plan a restful vacation. Friends took her for a brief stay at the Roosevelt lodge at Campobello. With great effort, ER made eagerly awaited visits with dear friends from the New Deal wars, Molly Dewson and Esther Lape. But ER tired easily and fought off fevers and nausea throughout the journey.

Knowing that she would die soon, ER returned to Val-Kill determined to complete *Tomorrow*. In early September, despite a high fever, she stayed up until eleven talking politics with Walter and May Reuther, who had stopped over at Val-Kill on their way back from taking their daughter to school in Vermont. Inspired by their conversation, she asked if she could use his idea about containing communism with economic rather than military aid in the final chapters of the book. Yet the next morning, her exhaustion returned. She could not eat or hold her tea cup; and, confiding in her old colleague, ER told Reuther exactly how sick she felt and asked his help. Would Reuther also please explain to her friends in labor why she could not come to the United Brotherhood of Electrical Workers convention and help Jim Carey run for president?[67]

After the Reuthers left, her secretary took her temperature. The thermometer registered a temperature of 101 degrees, and ER knew that she would probably not recover. She became even more forthright than usual. When Emmanuel Celler, the seventy-four-year-old congressman from Brooklyn, called to say that he was nominating her for the Senate, she blisteringly rebuffed Celler and his plan, saying to the Democrat, "Of course not, I don't believe in old people running." As the fever lowered slightly over the next few days (it would not return to nomal), she determinedly fulfilled the few commitments she made—attending a two-hour session for the American Association of the United Nations and hosting a delegation of Israelis at Hyde Park.[68]

However, the escalating violence in the South so disturbed ER that she tried to rally for one last fight. The night she had dined with the Reuthers, the Klan burned two black churches in Sasser, Georgia. Two days later, shotgun blasts wounded two SNCC workers as they stood in their Ruleville, Mississippi, living room. While she sat on the dias for the AAUN, three white men burned a black church near Dawson, Georgia. September 20, the day the Israelis visited Hyde Park, Mississippi Governor Ross Barnett blocked James Meredith's admission to the University of Mississippi. The following day, she asked King if he would join her in two weeks to discuss these issues on television. He agreed; however, ER collapsed in mid-week and the interview never occured.[69]

September 26, ER entered the hospital for the last time. Her family came and, suspicious of Gurewitsch's diagnosis, requested that new physicians examine her. She was now diagnosed as suffering from bone-marrow tuber-culosis. ER did not care what the cause of her illness was; she just wanted it to end. She refused all visitors, even Stevenson. She confided to Gurewitsch that she was tired of fighting the pain, that she had fulfilled her responsi-bilities, and that she wanted to die. He refused her plea for euthanasia, but he did arrange for her to go home to her New York City apartment. Three days after she returned home, the Cuban Missile crisis erupted. Gurewitsch tried to read the papers to her. She turned away, refusing to listen. Lash tried next. ER responded, "Nobody makes sense. All I want is to be turned over."[70]

Eleanor Roosevelt died November 7, 1962, three weeks after she left the hospital. Three days later, on November 10, she was buried in a plain pine casket in the rose garden of the Roosevelt estate at Hyde Park. Truman, Eisenhower, and Kennedy all attended her funeral. Ten days later, November 20, two weeks after her death, John Kennedy finally signed the executive order banning discrimination in federally financed housing.[71]

■

CONCLUSION
In the Shadow of ER

Power came to Eleanor Roosevelt gradually. Furthermore, as the account of her early years in politics demonstrates, it took her many years to develop the skills necessary to promote her agenda effectively. Throughout the twenties, ER tested her own political skills by devoting most of her time to Democratic party politics and numerous progressive reform organizations. She began to enjoy her independence, and tried to balance her own interests with her husband's political aspirations. This often proved a very difficult assignment.

But ER was an astute observer as well as an increasingly savvy politician. She learned from the successes and mistakes that she, her associates, and her husband made. She understood that one of the fastest ways to political power was to let others take credit for one's successes and project blame for their failures. Never having really desired the glory that motivated other political leaders, ER never became discouraged when she was not credited with a particular victory.

ER was more concerned with results than publicity. By the early thirties, she had not only developed her own political agenda but had also dedicated herself to building the contacts and promoting the officials who would see to it that the reforms she championed so diligently would be implemented. As first lady of New York, she continued to edit the Democratic party newsletter, train lobbyists, and conduct classes in registering voters and managing campaigns. She developed a network which delivered valuable information, helped her articulate policy, provided a vast pool of skilled volunteers dedicated to party politics, and gave her the ammunition necessary to derail her critics.

ER understood that the media should be her friend. Working alongside Louis Howe, she learned how to use the press to diffuse criticism and to increase support for controversial programs. She learned to give a speech without notes and not be afraid. Traveling with Lorena Hickok, she cultivated support among the male and female press corps and responded to their queries graciously and judiciously. She began to enjoy being good copy.

By the time ER moved into the White House, she was a practical politician in her own right. She had confronted Tammany Hall successfully, helped coordinate a national campaign, testified before state and national governmental committees, and forced the New York general assembly to rewrite legislation. She discovered that she did not simply like politics; she was good at it.

But she was also a passionate reformer who walked the delicate line between a wavering faith in public character and an unyielding commitment to democratic politics. She tried to balance her belief in the goodness of the American people against her experiences as the target of American segregationists, xenophobes, and rabid anti-communists. Moreover, she tried to protect her hard-won personal freedom and continue her own career while she promoted her husband's political agenda.

Often this was an amazing exercise in arbitration. Aware that FDR always wanted the limelight, she nevertheless refused to live in his shadow. The New Deal became their battleground. More than his conscience, ER became FDR's in-house rival, arguing that government has a responsibility to make the economic and political system more democratic. Her style alienated some of his core advisers and frequently irritated the president. But FDR understood political power and he knew that his wife was a powerful woman with her own constituency. He wanted that constituency in his coalition.

The war changed that balance of power and forced ER to find new ways to exert influence. Foreign policy and war preparations now consumed FDR's calendar. ER found herself increasingly denied access to FDR, Hopkins, and other key presidential advisers. Frustrated by FDR's abandonment of reform, ER became more a columnist than a White House insider. By late 1939, she learned to use "My Day" as her own call to arms and with an increasing frequency tried to mobilize her readers to take her place pressuring both her husband's administration and his critics. The press rewarded her popularity with a five-year contract, even though her husband's political future was not yet known.

By 1940, despite the venom with which she was treated in some quarters, Gallup polls showed that she was more popular with the public than her husband. She had proof that support of the controversial issues surrounding African Americans, Popular Front student groups, writers, artists, and other "other Americans" did not erode her popularity. She developed a new network and began to lobby unceasingly for an economic bill of rights and against suppression of political dissent. Neither of which proved popular with "Dr. Win the War."

If the war curtailed ER's influence in the White House, it expanded her understanding of American racism and the politics of fear. Never forgiving herself for her acquiescence to FDR's internment policies, ER left the White House more committed to racial justice issues than when she entered it in 1932. In mid-1945, she joined the NAACP board of directors and chaired a national commission investigating white on black violence in Columbia, Tennessee. Despite her intense commitment to the United Nations, ER threw herself into the battle against the poll tax, literacy tests, and other discriminatory voting, housing, and employment policies.

Moreover, her position on civil rights changed over time. By the early 1950s, ER was an active supporter of integration and a champion of integrated schools, housing projects, labor unions, and neighborhoods. As civil rights moved more to the forefront of the domestic agenda, her stature within the civil rights community enhanced her stature within the Democratic party. She moderated platform fights at national conventions, advised candidates and civil rights organizations on the most effective ways to shore up their constituencies, and continually used her column and lecture tours to educate a recalcitrant public on the inherent dangers of a racist society. Now completely comfortable in her own limelight, ER challenged average Americans to follow her lead and attacked politicians who protected their careers at the expense of American justice. Impatient with the politics of avoidance, ER perfected her own version of the politics of confrontation and urged Democrats to keep what her husband called their rendezvous with destiny.

Much to their dismay, vital center liberals were not exempt from ER's public and private rebuke. Although she repeatedly criticized the communist philosophy, she unceasingly defended the rights of Americans to join the Communist party. Refusing to follow public opinion and moderate her opposition to the Smith Act and the House Un-American Activities Committee, ER instead often took the lead in criticizing those politicians and pundits who embraced zealous anti-communism. She refused to condemn Alger Hiss and publicly chastised those who succumbed to peer pressure and endorsed his conviction. She questioned Richard Nixon's character and opposed Joseph McCarthy's grandstanding before any other national leader found it politically safe or chic to do so. She was unceasing in her efforts to educate the public about the inherent dangers of political exclusion and the Democratic party about the idiocy of running on a conservative platform.

These actions did not increase her popularity, but throughout America her stature increased. The Ku Klux Klan offered a reward to a local chapter if they could kidnap her. Senator Bilbo and Representative Fish wanted her deported as a traitor. Dwight Eisenhower refused to invite her to the White House and Republicans often made her an issue in state and national elections. Her refusal to be cowed by her critics often made consensus Democrats uncomfortable. She spared no effort in reprimanding party leaders whose actions failed to live up to their professed principles, even when those leaders were very dear to her. Party leaders appreciated her political clout and decided that it was better to have her be part of the group than the leader of the loyal in-house opposition and asked her to join Americans for Democratic Action, the National Issues Committee, and the Democratic Advisory Council.

When Adlai Stevenson was defeated for the second time in 1956, ER launched an all-out campaign within the party to have those pragmatic politicians who were also true liberals placed in strategic positions. She then took her case to the public and used her columns, articles, autobiographies, and lecture tours to bring Democrats who voted for Eisenhower back to their party. And as her eight-year reproval of John Kennedy clearly illustrates, she also refused to forsake her convictions to win an election. To her death she insisted that integrity was an essential ingredient of political success and that the actions one took after an election were just as important as the positions one advocated during a campaign.

As she aged, she saw democracy in broader terms and used a variety of tactics to implement her vision. As a politician, she tirelessly campaigned for local, state, and national leaders; raised money for political and social reform organizations; and mediated fractious internal disputes which threatened to divide coalitions she worked to build. As a journalist, she dedicated her work to explaining controversial issues, mobilizing grassroots support for political and economic reform, and holding politicians accountable for their actions. As an activist, she chaired investigative committees, embraced confrontation, and raised money for legal challenges. And finally, as both a mother confessor and political sage to liberal leaders and party officials, she provided the perfect example of politics and honor.

Clearly, Eleanor Roosevelt introduced a new level of compassion and integrity to American politics. For many years she was the true conscience of the nation. But she was also much more than that. She was a consummate political realist who goaded, prodded, inspired, lectured, and cajoled American liberals and moderates into action. Not only was she the symbol of America's potential, she was also the target of America's conservatism. More than any of her contemporaries, she defined the liberal agenda that would emerge in the decade after her death and that is so seriously attacked today—quality public and low-cost housing, public education, affirmative action, universal health care, government support of the arts and the United Nations, regulation of corporate development, and serious consideration of other cultures and political philosophies. Thus, two years before his death, Nixon told a colleague that Hillary Rodham Clinton, the Democrat who most represented ER's legacy, was "what we used to call a 'red-hot' in the 1930s—a real lefty like Eleanor Roosevelt."[1]

In his study of postwar presidential politics, *In the Shadow of FDR*, William Leuchtenburg writes that FDR "proved to be an especially tough act to follow." His thirteen years in the White House, his unparalleled legislative record of the First 100 Days, his institutionalization of domestic reform, and his leadership in wartime "cast so long a shadow" that all his successors were left asking "what is there left to do?" If these politicians would study ER's politics with the same scrutiny they applied to her husband, they could answer that question.[2]

Eleanor Roosevelt was a woman, not a saint. She was a power broker, not an elected official. Nevertheless she cast a long shadow across the nation. As Martin Luther King, Jr., wrote, "the impact of her personality and its unwavering dedication to high principle and purpose cannot be contained in a single day or era."[3] She set standards by which all future first ladies will be judged and played a key role in defining American liberalism and Democratic idealism. Just as she was not a sap, she was not a martyr. Better than most, she understood the personal price one pays for confronting a reluctant, disapproving constituency. But once she learned how to survive, she rarely backed away from a fight and she never gave much thought to herself during the process. A pragmatic politician, she embraced coalitions and championed compromise, but she always tried to "compromise up."

■

NOTES

■ INTRODUCTION

1. Arthur M. Schlesinger, Jr., *The Vital Center* (Boston: Houghton Mifflin, 1949), x.

2. Eleanor Roosevelt to Lorena Hickok, April 19, 1945, Anna Eleanor Roosevelt Papers, Franklin D. Roosevelt Library, Hyde Park, New York (FDRL).

■ 1. LEARNING TO BE INDEPENDENT

1. See Blanche Wiesen Cook, *Eleanor Roosevelt, Volume One, 1884–1933* (New York: Viking Press, 1992) for the most accurate interpretation of ER's life before the White House, and Joseph P. Lash, *Eleanor and Franklin* (New York: Norton, 1970).

2. E. Roosevelt, *This is My Story* (New York: Harper and Brothers, 1937), 171.

3. Roosevelt, *This Is My Story*, 176; Ruby Black, *Eleanor Roosevelt: A Biography* (New York: Duell, Sloan and Pearce, 1940), 27.

4. Roosevelt, ibid., 176.

5. Black, *Eleanor Roosevelt*, 39; Cook, 201–235; Lash, *Eleanor and Franklin*, 215; and Roosevelt, *This is My Story*, 244–272.

6. Roosevelt, ibid., 252.

7. The commission agreed with Mrs. Roosevelt's assessment of the hospital and urged that St. Elizabeth's be awarded larger appropriations. Lash, *Eleanor and Franklin*, 218; Roosevelt, ibid., 258–260; and Ruby Black, 38.

8. Roosevelt, ibid., 310, 314, 316; Ruby Black, 45; Alfred B. Rollins, Jr., *Roosevelt and*

1. Learning To Be Independent

Howe (New York: Alfred Knopf, 1962), 159; Maurine H. Beasley, *Eleanor Roosevelt and the Media* (Urbana: University of Illinois Press, 1987), 10.

9. Roosevelt, ibid., 323–324; Joseph P. Lash, *Love, Eleanor: Eleanor Roosevelt and Her Friends* (New York: Doubleday and Company, 1982), 81; Elisabeth Isabels Perry, "Training for Public Life: ER and Women's Political Networks in the 1920s," in Hoff-Wilson and Lightman, *Without Precedent,* 28; and Cook, 338–381.

10. Eleanor Roosevelt, *This I Remember* (New York: Harper and Brothers, 1949), 22; and S. J. Woolf, "A Woman Speaks Her Political Mind," *New York Times Magazine,* April 8, 1928, 3.

11. Ruby Black, 46; Roosevelt, *This Is My Story,* 324–325; Lash, *Eleanor and Franklin,* 360–261; Lois Scharf, "ER and Feminism," in Hoff-Wilson and Lightman, *Without Precedent,* 227; Hilda Watrous, *In League with Eleanor: Eleanor Roosevelt and the League of Women Voters, 1921–1962* (New York: Foundation for Citizen Education, 1984), 2–4.

12. Ruby Black, 46; Roosevelt, *This is My Story,* 325;

13. James Roosevelt, *My Parents: A Differing View* (Chicago: Playboy Press, 1976), 79.

14. Lash, *Love, Eleanor,* 81–82; Roosevelt, *This is My Story,* 344; Eleanor Roosevelt, *This I Remember,* 30–33. Watrous, page 6, discusses ER's articles "The Fall Election" and "Organizing County Women for a Political Party" that appeared in summer issues of the *Weekly News.* Ruby Black, 53.

Black recounts an episode illustrating ER's tenacity in lobbying county chairmen who were opposed to women being equally represented on state and county commit-tees. ER and a colleague tried to visit an especially hostile chairman only to be told by his wife that he was not home. "The two women," according to Black, "had reason to believe that the gentleman was in the house. They sat. His wife again came out to warn the determined ladies that she did not know when her husband would return." ER smiled and replied that their time was not important because they had no other press-ing business. Chagrined, the chairman came out to see them. For articles representing ER's contribution to the *Women's Democratic News,* see Women's Democratic News folder 1920–1933, Speech and Article File, 1933, AER papers, FDRL.

15. Perry, "Training for Public Life," 28–30, 33, 38, 41.

16. Letter from Josephus Daniels to Franklin D. Roosevelt, May 8, 1924 and Franklin D. Roosevelt to Josephus Daniels, May 26, 1924 quoted in Lash, *Eleanor and Franklin,* p. 287.

17. ER did regret this and later felt very guilty for participating in such negative cam-paigning. Roosevelt, *This is My Story,* 355–356; Black, 57; Susan Ware, "ER and Democratic Politics," in *Without Precedent,* 49; Rollins, 217; Eleanor Roosevelt, "Why I Am a Democrat," Junior League *Bulletin,* November 1923.

18. Ruby Black, ibid.; Eleanor Roosevelt's 1928 election cycle articles include "What I Want Most Out of Life," *Success Magazine,* March 1927; "Women Must Learn to Play the Game as Men Do," *Redbook,* March 1928; "Why Democrats Favor Smith," *North American Review,* November 1927; and "Jeffersonian Principles the Issue in 1928," *Current History,* June 1928.

19. Roosevelt, *This I Remember,* 38–41; Black, 55–56; Ware, ibid., 49, 51; James Roosevelt, *My Parents,* 120–122; Hickok, *Reluctant First Lady* (New York: Dodd Mead, 1962), 9; Alfred E. Steinberg, *Mrs. R.: The Life of Eleanor Roosevelt* (New York: Putnam,

1958), 146; Lash, *Eleanor and Franklin,* 317–319; and Woolf, *New York Times Magazine,* April 8, 1928, 3.

20. Roosevelt, *This I Remember,* 39; Eleanor Roosevelt, "Why Democrats Favor Smith;" and James Roosevelt, *My Parents: A Differing View* (New York: Playboy Press, 1976), 122.

Although ER fully recognized the limitations of Smith's commitment to women in politics, she argued that he was infinitely preferable to Hoover because "Governor Smith has done more than fill offices with women" and because "he pays women the compliment of considering them citizens and voters exactly as he does the men." Acknowledging to the public that they "have sometimes disagreed," she had "always been able to believe in the courage of his convictions." See Eleanor Roosevelt, "Women in Politics" and "Why I Believe in Governor Smith," Speech and Article File, 1917–1930, 1928 campaign, AER papers, FDRL.

21. The Reminiscences of Anna Roosevelt Halstead, Oral History Research Office, Columbia University (OHRO), 1975.

22. Eleanor Roosevelt, "What Is a Wife's Job Today? An Interview with M. K. Wisheart," *Good Housekeeping* 91 (August 22, 1930): 34–35, 166, 169–173.

23. Although FDR served as contractor for the cottages and was a frequent and enthusiastic visitor, Val-Kill became ER's sanctuary. For a discussion of the construction of Val-Kill see *This I Remember,* 32–35 and Geoffrey C. Ward, "Eleanor Roosevelt draws her strength from a sanctuary called Val-Kill," *Smithsonian Magazine,* vol 15, no 7, October 1984, 62–73. ER's increasing emotional separation from FDR is documented in a letter from Anna Roosevelt to Eleanor Roosevelt, ca. 1931, in Bernard Asbell, ed., *Mother and Daughter: The Letters of Anna and Eleanor Roosevelt* (New York: Coward, McCann and Geoghegan, 1982), 50; Roosevelt, *This is My Story,* 346–347, 364; Lash, *Love, Eleanor,* 110, 106.

24. Roosevelt, *This I Remember,* 52; Roosevelt, *This Is My Story,* 173. ER's agent, Thomas L. Stix, revealed this conversation when Lash interviewed him for *Eleanor and Franklin.* The quote is cited on page 348.

25. Marion Dickerman interview recited in Kenneth S. Davis, *F.D.R.: The New York Years: 1928–1933* (New York: Knopf, 1985), 24.

26. *The New York Times,* November 8, 1928.

27. Tamara Hareven, *Eleanor Roosevelt: An American Conscience* (Chicago: Quadrangle Books, 1968), 37; Davis, ibid., 183; James Farley, *Behind the Ballots* (New York: Harcourt Brace and Company, 1938), 54, 62–66, 160, 354; Susan Ware, *Partner and I: Molly Dewson, Feminism and New Deal Politics* (New Haven: Yale University Press, 1987), 170; F.D.R. to James Jackson, January 21, 1929, in Elliot Roosevelt, *F.D.R.: His Personal Letters,* Vol. I, 22; For examples of ER's covert contributions to *Women's Democratic News* see the following: untitled editorial dated 1/22/29, untitled article dated 2/14/29 on FDR and Advisory Commission on Agriculture, and undated untitled article on the bond issue in Women's Democratic News folder, Speech and Article File, 1929–1933, AER papers, FDRL.

28. Cooke, "The Political Career of Anna Eleanor Roosevelt," 116; Eleanor Roosevelt to John J. Raskob, July 6, 1929, Politics folder, General Correspondence 1928–1932, AER papers, FDRL; Franklin D. Roosevelt, "Written for the Record," April 6, 1938 in Elliott

1. Learning To Be Independent

Roosevelt, *F.D.R.: His Personal Letters, 1928–1945*, Vol. 2, 772; Davis, *FDR: The New York Years*, 52; Rollins, 316, 320; Steinberg, 158; John Morton Blum, *From the Morgenthau Diaries*, Vol 1 (Boston: Houghton Mifflin Company, 1959), 19.

29. Davis, ibid.; Eleanor Roosevelt to Franklin D. Roosevelt, November 13, 1928, FDR papers, ER-FDR Correspondence, FDRL; Perkins quote is from the Frances Perkins Oral History Collection, Book 3, which is quoted in George Martin, *Madame Secretary: Frances Perkins* (Boston: Houghton Mifflin Co, 1975), 204.

30. ER wrote in *This I Remember* that she regretted her time away from Albany because it cut her off from making more lasting friendships in the state capital. William Leuchtenburg argued, *In the Shadow of FDR* (Ithaca: Cornell University Press, 1983) page x, that ER protected FDR's legacy "with the tenacity of a Chinese empress dowager." For accounts of ER's testimony see Steinberg, 164 and Lash, *Eleanor and Franklin*. Articles published by Eleanor Roosevelt in those years include "What I Want Most Out of Life," *Success Magazine*, Vol. 2 (May 1927): 16–17,70; "Servants," *Forum* 83 (Jan. 1930): 24–28; "What Is a Wife's Job Today? An Interview with M. K. Wisehart," *Good Housekeeping* 91 (Aug. 1930), 34–35, 166, 169–173; "What Do Ten Million Women Want?" *Home Magazine* 5 (Mar. 1932): 19–21, 86; and "What I Want To Leave Behind," *Pictorial Review* vol. 34 (April 1933): 4, 45–46. Ida Tarbell, "Portrait of a Lady," *The Delineator* 119 (October 1931): 19; and *The New York Times*, April 9, 1929.

31. Lash, *Eleanor and Franklin*, 335.

32. Roosevelt, *This Is My Story*, 364.

33. Tarbell, "Portrait of a Lady, 19, 47–50; "Mrs. Roosevelt Tireless Worker," *The Washington Evening Star*, October 13, 1932; and "Wives of the Candidates: Mrs. Roosevelt is Strenuous Worker with Many Projects," *The Sunday Star*, June 12, 1932.

34. Hickok, 2–3; Associated Press News Copy, New York, Nov. 9–11, 1932, box 14, Lorena Hickok Papers (hereafter referred to as LAH papers).

35. Two comments by ER stirred up immediate controversy. The first occurred during her last paid radio broadcast in which she explained her positions as a dry who favored the repeal of prohibition and the second was when she was misquoted as canceling FDR's inaugural. For articles discussing ER's comments on young women and moderate alcohol consumption, see "Drys Hail Attack on Mrs. Roosevelt," *The New York Times*, January 15, 1933; "Mrs. Roosevelt Encounters Kansas," *Decatur* (Ill.) *Herald*, December 12, 1932; "After Mrs. Roosevelt: Frank Facts," *New Orleans Tribune*, December 20, 1932; and "To the Ladies," *The Boston Herald*, December 22, 1932. "Mrs. Roosevelt Would Scrap Outworn Social Traditions," *The Washington Star*, July 4, 1932; "Mrs. Roosevelt Tireless Worker," *The Washington Evening Star*, October 13, 1932; untitled article, *The Springfield Union*, December 22, 1932.

36. For examples of articles supporting ER's activities see "Mrs. Roosevelt's vocation," *Wheeling West Virginia Register*, December 29, 1932 and untitled editorial in *Albany* (Ga.) *Herald*, January 14, 1933. *The Baltimore Evening Sun*, February 4, 1932; *The Hartford Courant*, quoted in "Mrs. Roosevelt's Activities," *The Springfield* (Mass.) *Evening News*, December 22, 1932. For articles criticizing ER's actions, see "Mrs. Roosevelt Has Many Jobs," *Selma* (Ala.) *Times-Journal*, December 22, 1932 and other clippings AER papers, Miscellaneous Clippings Related to Eleanor Roosevelt, 1929–1932, FDR Library.

37. Lorena Hickok, Associated Press News Copy, New York, February 4, 1933, LAH papers, FDRL; Beasley, *Eleanor Roosevelt and the Media*, 34; Hickok, 85; "Mrs. Roosevelt to Abandon Many Activities in March," clipping, February 5, 1933, Miscellaneous Newspaper Clippings re: ER 1933–1945, AER papers, FDRL; and Hickok, 87.

38. While including this quotation in the last of her three-part preinaugural coverage of the first lady, Hickok, in the words of media historian Maurine Beasley, "depicted Eleanor Roosevelt as a new kind of first lady who would refuse to give up her individuality in the White House, in spite of social convention." Increasingly sympathetic to ER's dilemma and aware of the potential repercussions of such statements, Hickok in her Associated Press piece portrayed ER as upbeat and confident: "The prospective mistress of the White House thinks people are going to get used to her ways, even though she does edit *Babies-Just Babies*, wears $10 dresses, and drives her own car."

Hickok, 3; Beasley, 32; and Associated Press news copy, New York, New York, November 11, 1932, box 14, LAH papers.

39. Roosevelt, *This I Remember*, 74–75.

40. For complete listing of all the offices ER held as first lady, see Miriam Teichner, "Mrs. Roosevelt is Fatalist and Husband's Campaign Holds No Thrills for Her," *New York Evening World*, December 2, 1930. Untitled clipping, *New York Evening Post*, February 4, 1933, Miscellaneous Clippings Related to ER, 1929–1932, AER papers, FDRL. For a more extensive discussion see Lash, *Eleanor and Franklin*, 356–68; Hickok, Chapter 8; and Beasley, 32–37.

■ 2. COMING INTO HER OWN

1. Roosevelt, *This I Remember*, 76.

2. Roosevelt, ibid., 76, 89.

3. "Mrs. Roosevelt to Abandon Many Activities in March," February 4, 1933, *New York Times*; Jean E. Collins, *She Was There: Stories of Pioneering Women Journalists* (New York: Messner, 1980), 36–37, and Beasley, 55.

4. Eleanor Roosevelt to Lorena Hickok, May 31, 1933, Lorena Hickok Papers, FDR Library. Cook, *Eleanor Roosevelt*, 477–500.

5. Roosevelt, *This I Remember*, 76, 80–82; Lorena Hickok, "Nation's 'First Lady' Outlines Plans As She Begins White House Residence," *The New York Times*, March 5, 1933; Bess Furman, *Washington By-Line* (New York: Alfred Knopf, 1949), 150–52; and Beasley, 51–67.

6. By mid-April, the first lady inspected poverty-stricken Appalachia and the new bonus army encampment, hosted a Gridiron widows party for the female press corps, and delivered two commencement addresses. By June first, she had traveled over 40,000 miles as FDR's ambassador. Cooke, "The Political Career of Anna Eleanor Roosevelt," 138. For ER's comments on the need for reform, see Roosevelt, Speech to Chatauqua Institute. For ER's comments on political issues see Eleanor Roosevelt, *The White House Press Conferences of Eleanor Roosevelt*, ed. Maurine Beasley (New York: Garland Publishing, Inc., 1983) 6–9.

7. Emma Bugbee interview cited in Lash, *Eleanor and Franklin*, 363.

8. Beasley, *Press Conferences*, 67 and Furman, 194.

9. Eleanor Roosevelt, "I Want You to Write to Me," *Women's Home Companion*,

2. Coming Into Her Own

(August 1933): 4; Eleanor Roosevelt, "Mail of a President's Wife," unpublished article, c. 1939, Speech and Article File, AER papers, FDRL; and Alan Brinkley, *Voices of Protest: Huey Long, Father Coughlin and the Great Depression* (New York: Vintage, 1983), 70. For an extensive discussion of ER's attitude about her mail see Frances M. Seeber, " 'I Want You to Write to Me': The Papers of Anna Eleanor Roosevelt," *Prologue* 19 no. 2 (Summer 1987): 95–105.

10. Richard Lowitt and Maurine Beasley, *One Third of A Nation: Lorena Hickok Reports on the Great Depression* (Urbana: University of Illinois Press, 1981).

11. Eleanor Roosevelt, "What I Want to Leave Behind." Eleanor Roosevelt, "The Ideal Education," *Woman's Journal* (October 1930): 9.

12. Eleanor Roosevelt, "Good Citizenship," *Pictorial Review* (April 1930): 4.

13. Eleanor Roosevelt, "Chatauqua Speech," July 12, 1932, Speech and Article File, AER Papers, FDRL; *New York Times*, January 12, 1933; *New York Times*, July 26, 1935; Eleanor Roosevelt, "My Day," March 17, 1936, My Day Collection, AER papers.

14. Eleanor Roosevelt, "The Ideal Education;" Eleanor Roosevelt, *The Moral Basis of Democracy* (New York: Howell Soskin, and Company, 1940), 14.

15. For historians who emphasize Arthurdale as the clearest example of ER's activism see Lash, *Eleanor and Franklin*, chapter 37; Scharf, *Eleanor Roosevelt*, 102–103; William Leuchtenburg, *Franklin D. Roosevelt and the New Deal* (New York: Harper and Row, 1963), 136–137, 185; Arthur M. Schlesinger, Jr., *The Coming of the New Deal* (Boston: Houghton Mifflin, 1959), 366–367; and Frank Freidel, *FDR: Launching the New Deal* (Boston: Little, Brown, 1973), 296–297. Eleanor Roosevelt to Bernard Baruch, June 13, 1934, Personal Correspondence, AERP.

16. Eleanor Roosevelt, "The Unemployed Are Not a Strange Race," *Democratic Digest* 13, no.6 (June 1936): 19.

17. Winifred D. Wandersee, "ER and American Youth: Politics and Personality in a Bureaucratic Age," in Hoff-Wilson and Lightman, *Without Precedent*, 65; Richard A. Reiman, *The New Deal and American Youth: Ideas and Ideals in the Depression Decade* (Athens: University of Georgia Press, 1992), 35; *New York Times*, May 7, 1934; and R. Black, 211.

18. Reiman, 44.

19. For discussion of ER's opposition to the military aspects of the CCC, see Lash, *Eleanor and Franklin*, 357–340; and Fulton Oursler, *Behold the Dreamer* (Boston: Little, Brown, 1964), 424–425. Eleanor Roosevelt to Harry Hopkins, March 24 and October 5, 1934, Correspondence with Government Agencies, AER Papers; Eleanor Roosevelt to Henry Goddard Leach, January 1934, Miscellaneous Correspondence, AER papers; ER discusses Martin's Progressive Education in "My Day," December 30, 1935, My Day Series, AER papers.

20. For works supporting ER's position as originator of the NYA see Lash, *Eleanor and Franklin*, ibid.; R. Black, chapter 15; Mildred W. Abramowitz, "Eleanor Roosevelt and the National Youth Administration 1935–1943: An Extension of the Presidency," *Presidential Studies Quarterly* 14 (Fall 1984): 569–558. For works arguing ER was a "midwife" to the agency see John A. Salmond, *A Southern Rebel: The Life and Times of Aubrey Williams 1890–1965* (Chapel Hill: University of North Carolina Press, 1983); James R. Kearney, *Eleanor Roosevelt: The Evolution of a Reformer* (Boston: Houghton Mifflin Company, 1968), 22–29. Kearney, ibid, 29.

21. Lash, ibid.; R. Black, ibid.; Wandersee, ibid.; Reiman, 221; and Memo, ER to FDR, undated, Charles Tausig folder, 1936, President's Personal File 1644, FDRL.

22. Roosevelt, "My Day," May 26, 1937, My Day Series, AER Papers. For representative "My Day" references see the following columns: June 5, 1936; June 8, 1936; June 22, 1936; September 20, 1937; April 27, 1939. *This I Remember*, 162–163.

23. Eleanor Roosevelt, "The New Governmental Interest in Art," Speech and Article File, AER papers.

24. Olin Downs, "The New Deal's Treasury Art Program: A Memoir" in Francis O'Connor, ed. *New Deal Art Projects: An Anthology of Memoirs* (Washington: Smithsonian Institution, 1972); William F. MacDonald, *Federal Relief Administration of the Arts* (Columbus: Ohio State University Press, 1969), 363; Richard D. McKinzie, *The New Deal for Artists* (Princeton: Princeton University Press, 1973), 10.

25. Roosevelt, "The New Governmental Interest in Art;" Downs, ibid.; Edward Lansing, "The New Deal Mural Projects," in O'Connor, *The New Deal Art Projects*, 105; James Michael Newell interview in O'Connor, ibid.

26. Edward Bruce to Eleanor Roosevelt, n.d., Correspondence with Government Departments, AER papers; Eleanor Roosevelt to Edward Bruce, May 18, 1935, Miscellaneous Correspondence, AER papers; McDonald, *Federal Relief Administration and the Arts*, 208; Monty Noam Penkhower, *The Federal Writer's Project* (Chicago: University of Illinois Press, 1977), 26–27.

27. Penkhower, *The Federal Writers Project*, 48–49; McKinzie, *The New Deal for Artists*, 84; McDonald, *Federal Relief Administration and the Arts*, 362; Martha H. Swain, "ER and Ellen Woodward: A Partnership for Women's Work Relief and Security," in Hoff-Wilson and Lightman, *Without Precedent*; and Susan Ware, *Beyond Suffrage: Women and the New Deal* (Cambridge: Harvard University Press, 1981), 109, 117, 120, 132, and 137.

28. McDonald, 64–65, 75, 171, and 501.

29. McDonald, *Federal Relief for the Arts*, 413, 501; Gwendolyn Bennett, "The Harlem Community Art Center," in Francis V. O'Connor, ed., *Art for the Millions: Essays from the 1930s by Artists and Administrators of the WPA Federal Art Program* (Greenwich: New York Graphic Society, 1973), 217. Located at Lenox Avenue and 125th Street, the Harlem Community Art Center later was renamed the Schomburg Center for African American Culture.

30. Unnamed correspondent, *Harper's* to Eleanor Roosevelt, February 10, 1938 and Eleanor Roosevelt to *Harper's*, March 4, 1938; Richard Wright to Eleanor Roosevelt, August 22, 1938 and Eleanor Roosevelt to Richard Wright, August 29, 1938, Personal Letters, AER papers.

31. McDonald, *Federal Relief Administration for the Arts*, 501.

32. For detailed discussion of the evolution of ER's civil rights agenda, see Allida M. Black, "A Reluctant But Persistent Warrior: Eleanor Roosevelt and the Early Civil Rights Movement," in Rouse et al, ed., *Women in the Civil Rights Movement: Trailblazers and Torchbearers, 1941–1965* (Brooklyn: Carlson Publishing Inc., 1990). Nancy J. Weiss, *Farewell to the Party of Lincoln: Black Politics in the Age of FDR* (Princeton: Princeton University Press, 1983); 120; Harvard Sitkoff, *A New Deal for Blacks* (New York: Oxford University Press, 1978), 60–65, 128–132, 135, 264, 294, 311–312, and 325–327; and Paul Conkin, *The New Deal* (Arlington Heights, Illinois: Harlan Davidson, 1975), 73.

33. Eleanor Roosevelt's efforts to get FDR to urge the passage of the Costigan-Wagner anti-lynching bill are discussed in detail in the following works: Weiss, ibid; Sitkoff, ibid; Joanna Schneider Zangrando and Robert L. Zangrando, "ER and Black Civil Rights," in Hoff-Wilson and Lightman, *Without Precedent*; Robert L. Zangrando, *The NAACP Campaign Against Lynching, 1909–1950* (Philadelphia: Temple University Press, 1980; Mildred Wilder Abramowitz, "Eleanor Roosevelt and the federal responsibility and responsiveness to youth, the Negro and others in time of depression," Ph.D. diss, (New York University, 1970); Walter White, *A Man Called White* (New York: Viking Press, 1948); and Poppy Cannon White, *A Gentle Knight: My Husband Walter White* (New York: Viking Press, 1956). For works discussing ER's relationship with the Black Cabinet, see Carl Rowan, "The Life of Eleanor Roosevelt," *New York Post*, March 20, 1958; Howard Odum, *Race and Rumors of Race: Challenge to American Crisis* (Chapel Hill: University of North Carolina Press, 1943); Rackhan Holt, *Mary McLeod Bethune: A Biography* (Garden City: Doubleday, 1964) and Robert C. Weaver, "Eleanor and L.B.J. and Black America," *The Crisis* 79, no. 6 (July 1972): 186–193 and "The Black Cabinet," in *The Making of the New Deal: The Insiders Speak*, Katie Louchheim, ed. (Cambridge: Harvard University Press, 1983), 262; Ralph Bunche, "A Critique of New Deal Social Planning as it Affects Negroes," *Journal of Negro Education* 5 (January 1936): 58–62; and Pauli Murray, *Song in a Weary Throat* (New York: Harper and Row, 1988). For a detailed review of ER's legislative work to end discriminatory practices in education, housing, employment and voting see chapter 4.

34. Lillian Rogers Parks, *The Roosevelts: A Family in Turmoil* (Englewood Cliffs: Prentice-Hall, 1981), 32–34.

35. Lash, *Eleanor and Franklin*, 519–521; Barry Bingham to Marvin McIntyre, August 29, 1934 and Eleanor Roosevelt to Barry Bingham, September 4, 1934, Personal Correspondence, AER papers.

36. Walter White to Eleanor Roosevelt, August 28, 1934 and Eleanor Roosevelt to Walter White September 7, 1934, Personal Correspondence, AER papers; Beasley, *The Press Conferences of Eleanor Roosevelt*, 42–44, 49; Eleanor Roosevelt to Walter White, June 15, 1935, Personal Correspondence, AER papers; Weiss, *Farewell to the Party of Lincoln*, 126.

37. Lady Bird Johnson, "The National Youth Administration" in Louchheim, *Inside the New Deal*, 304.

38. Eleanor Roosevelt, "In Defense of Curiosity," *The Saturday Evening Post* 208 (August 24, 1935): 8 and "Responsibility to fellow human beings," Speech and Article file, AER papers.

39. Eleanor Roosevelt, "The Negro and Social Change," *Opportunity: The Journal of Negro Life* (January 1936): 22; *The Georgia Women's World* piece is referred to in a *New York Times*, November 8, 1936 clipping in ER's Miscellaneous Clipping file, AER papers; M. Hornaday, "Mrs. Roosevelt, a Campaign Issue," *The Christian Science Monitor*, June 24, 1936, p. 5; and Editorial, *Baltimore Afro-American*, May 23, 1936, p. 4.

40. Freidel, 279–281; and John Egerton, *Speak Now Against the Day: The Generation Before the Civil Rights Movement in the South* (New York: Knopf, 1994), 179–180.

41. Egerton, 181. Linda Reed, *Simple Decency and Common Sense: The Southern Conference Movement, 1938–1963* (Indianapolis: Indiana University Press, 1991), 10, 12;

and "The Reminiscences of Lucy Randolph Mason," the Southern Historical Collection, University of North Carolina (hereafter SHC).

42. "The Reminiscences of Virginia Durr," interviewed by Sue Thrasher, Oral History Research Office, Columbia University, (hereafter, OHRO); "The Reminiscences of Virginia Durr," interviewed by John Egerton, SHC; "The Reminiscences of Jessie Daniel Ames," interviewed by Pat Watters, SHC; "The Reminiscences of George Stoney," interviewed by John Egerton, SHC; Interview with Dorothy Height; Egerton, 190; Reed, 12. ER to Hickok, November 23, 1938.

43. Egerton, 193.

44. For a complete discussion of the events surrounding the Constitution Hall debate and Marian Anderson's eventual performance at the Lincoln Memorial, April 9, 1939, see Allida M. Black, "Championing a Champion: Eleanor Roosevelt and the Marian Anderson 'Freedom Concert'," *Presidential Studies Quarterly* 20, no. 4 (Fall 1990): 719–737.

45. Ibid., 724.

46. "My Day," February 26, 1939, My Day drafts, AER papers.

47. "Mrs. Roosevelt to Present Spingarn Medal to Marian Anderson at N.A.A.C.P. Conference," April 28, 1939, NAACP Papers, Group I, Annual Conference, Announcements April 25–29, 1939, Library of Congress; Dr. J.M. Tinsely to Walter White, April 29, 1939, NAACP Papers, Group I, Annual Conference, May 1–4, 1939, Library of Congress; Walter White to Dr. Ransome, April 24, 1939, NAACP Papers, Group I, Annual Conference, Announcements 25–29, 1939, Library of Congress; Walter White to Eleanor Roosevelt, June 13, 1939, AER Papers, Series 100, 1939, FDR Library; Walter White to Eleanor Roosevelt, June 20, 1939, NAACP Papers, Group I, Annual Conference, June 20–21, 1939, Library of Congress.

48. See the Gallup Polls of January 15, 1939 and March 19, 1939 cited in *The Washington Post*, March 19, 1939. ER's pro-civil rights image in the South was so indelible by April 1939 that her support of Anderson did little to add to the active anti-New Deal coalition.

49. Beasley, *Eleanor Roosevelt and the Media*, 133.

50. Eleanor Roosevelt to Maude Gray, October 17, 1940, quoted in Lash, *Eleanor and Franklin*, 629.

51. Frances Perkins interview, OHRO; Eleanor Roosevelt interview, Graff papers, FDR Library; *Washington Post*, July 19, 1940; and Goodwin, *No Ordinary Time*, 130–133.

52. *New York Times*, July 19, 1940.

53. George Norris to Eleanor Roosevelt, July 19, 1940, Personal Correspondence, AER papers. For a thorough discussion of ER's role at the convention, see Kirkendall, "ER and the Issue of FDR's Successor," 178–180; Lash, *Eleanor and Franklin*, 622–625; Joseph Lash, *Eleanor Roosevelt: A Friend's Memoir* (New York: Doubleday, 1964), 131–139; Perkins, *The Roosevelt I Knew* (New York: Viking Press, 1946); Farley, *Jim Farley's Story* (New York: McGraw-Hill, 1948), 299–307; and Goodwin, ibid. Farley wrote that ER supported Jesse Jones over Henry Wallace because Jones would bolster business support and increase party contributions. ER disputed this. "I expressed no preference for any candidate and I think the account of the convention which Jim Farley gave in his book

2. Coming Into Her Own

. . . was his impression of what I said rather than what I actually said." Roosevelt, *This I Remember*, 216.

54. *New York Times*, November 9, 1933; Eleanor Roosevelt to David Gaines, November 15, 1933; Joseph P. Lash, *Eleanor and Franklin*, 384–5; Alice Roosevelt Longworth, "The Ideal Qualifications of a President's Wife," *Ladies Home Journal*, February 1936; *New York Times*, November 8, 1936. The Bingay quote is cited in George Wolfskill and John A Hudson, *All But the People: Franklin D. Roosevelt and His Critics* (New York: Macmillan, 1969), 38. Chapter Three "We don't Like Her Either" is devoted to public criticism ER received.

55. Rexford Tugwell, *The Brains Trust* (New York: Macmillan, 1968), 54. Alexander refused to take this advice and, when reviewing his experiences in Washington, wrote, "I . . . trusted Mrs. Roosevelt [and her judgment] more than anybody I ever saw." Ickes recorded his displeasure with the first lady in his diary:

"I am very fond of Eleanor Roosevelt. She has a fine social sense and is utterly self-less, but as the President has said to me on one or two occasions, she wants to build these homesteads on a scale that we can't afford because the people for whom they are intended cannot afford such homes. The President's idea is to build an adequate house and not even put in plumbing fixtures, leaving that sort of thing to be done later by the homesteader as he can afford them. He remarked yesterday that he had not yet dared say this to the people (undoubtedly meaning Eleanor Roosevelt) who wanted the houses built with all modern improvements."

Harold L. Ickes, *The Secret Diary of Harold L. Ickes, Vol. I* (New York: Doubleday, 1953), 227. For an extensive account of Mrs. Roosevelt's commitment to the Arthurdale project, see Lash, *Eleanor and Franklin*, chapter 38. Alexander recounts his conversation with Wallace in his unfinished autobiography, *A Southern Rebel*, in the Will Alexander Papers, FDRL.

56. For firsthand accounts of Mrs. Roosevelt's lobbying efforts within the White House and the reasons for her successes and failures see the following transcripts, in which interviewees discuss the division of White House staff into "camps" supporting and opposing Mrs. Roosevelt's efforts. James Halstead, interview by Emily Williams, May 17 and 22, 1979, transcript, Eleanor Roosevelt Oral History Project (EROHP), FDRL. Anna Rosenberg Hoffman, interview by Thomas Soapes, October 13, 1977, transcript, EROHP, FDRL. James Rowe, interview by Emily Williams, July 12, 1978, transcript, EROHP, FDRL. Jonathan Daniels, interview by Emily Williams, November 16, 1979, EROHP, FDRL. Eleanor Roosevelt, *This I Remember*, 279; Rexford Tugwell, "Remarks," *Roosevelt Day Dinner Journal*, Americans for Democratic Action, January 31, 1963.

57. Lash quoted in Doris Kearns Goodwin, *No Ordinary Time*, 104.

58. The following analyses of the New Deal discuss in a somewhat cursory manner ER's role as both "the conscience of the administration" and as a political player in her own right: Leuchtenburg, *Franklin D. Roosevelt and the New Deal*; Conkin, *The New Deal*; James MacGregor Burns, *The Crosswinds of Freedom* (New York: Alfred Knopf, 1989); Frank Freidel, *FDR: Launching the New Deal* (Boston: Little, Brown, 1973); Joseph Alsop, *F.D.R.: A Centenary Remembrance* (New York: Viking, 1982) as well as the Miller, Perkins, Davis, and Ware biographies of FDR previously cited in the notes.

Katharine Hepburn, *The Making of the African Queen* (New York: New American Library, 1987), 82.

59. Raymond Clapper, "The Ten Most Powerful People in Washington," *Reader's Digest* 38 (May 1941): 48 (condensed from *Look*, January 28, 1941); "Mrs. Roosevelt's Role as White House Advisor," *U.S. News*, December 12, 1940, 9–10; D. W. Brogan, "Mrs. Roosevelt as a Political Force," *Spectator* 169 December 30, 1942, 403; Dorothy Dunbar Bromley, "The Future of Eleanor Roosevelt," *Harper's Magazine* 180 February 1940, 129–139. Arthur Krock's *New York Times* article is quoted in Bromley, page 131. "The Fortune Survey: XXX," *Fortune* 21 (1940): 159–160. For another assessment of ER's political prowess see "Mrs. Roosevelt's Role As White House Advisor," *U.S. News* (December 20, 1940): 9–10.

■ **3. HOLDING TRUMAN ACCOUNTABLE**

1. Eleanor Roosevelt to Maude Gray, July 4, 1944; Eleanor Roosevelt to Joe Lash, April 19, 1945 and Eleanor Roosevelt to Lorena Hickok, April 19, 1945, AER papers.

2. Genevieve Reynolds, "Packing Done, Mrs. Roosevelt Holds Farewell Press Meeting," *Washington Post*, April 20, 1945, A1; "The Story Is Over," *Newsweek* 25 (April 30, 1945): 44–45.

3. Lorena Hickok to Eleanor Roosevelt, "Memos and notes on your activities in 1945," Book and Manuscript File: On My Own, AER papers; Harold L. Ickes to Eleanor Roosevelt, May 21, 1945, General Correspondence, AER papers; Eleanor Roosevelt, "My Day," April 19, 1945, My Day Drafts, AER papers; Joseph and Stewart Alsop, "Candidate Truman's Magic Brew," *Saturday Evening Post* (December 31, 1949): 12.

4. Not all of ER's friends believed her capable of making such important decisions alone. Major Harry Hooker and film producer John Golden proposed setting up a committee in which Hooker would review job options and Golden would provide "whatever showmanship is necessary." Laughingly, ER rebuffed their offer. "Look my dears, I love you both dearly. But you can't run my life. I would probably not like it at all." Roosevelt, *On My Own* (New York: Harper, 1958), 6–7.

For events discussed in the paragraph itself, see John Morton Blum, *From the Diaries of Henry Morgenthau, Jr.*, Vol. 3 (Boston: Houghton Mifflin, 1967), 424; Lorena Hickok to Eleanor Roosevelt, April 13, 1945, Eleanor Roosevelt-Lorena Hickok Correspondence, LAH papers; "Mrs. Roosevelt Will Continue Column; Seeks No Office Now," *The* (Washington) *Evening Star*, April 19, 1945, A1.

5. Justine Wise Polier, interview by Thomas Soapes, December 8, 1977, EROHP; Trude Lash, interview by Thomas Soapes, November 21, 1977, EROHP; James Roosevelt, interview by Thomas Soapes, December 8, 1977, EROHP.

6. Roosevelt, *On My Own*, 2, 4, 12; Elliott Roosevelt and James Brough, *Mother R:* (New York: Putnam, 1977), 43, 104; Joseph P. Lash, *Eleanor: The Years Alone* (New York: Norton, 1972), 38; Elliott Roosevelt, interview by Marilyn Williams, June 20, 1979, EROHP; Eleanor Roosevelt, "My Day," May 8, 1945, My Day Drafts, AER papers.

7. In a December 18, 1943 press conference, FDR told reporters, "The remedies that old Dr. New Deal used were for internal trouble. But at the present time, obviously the principal emphasis, the overwhelming emphasis should be on winning the war." Once victory is at hand, reform would again take center stage. "[But] we don't want to con-

fuse people by talking about it now." ER did not second this approach. Responding to questions for the *New York Times*, ER declared that she did not store New Deal programs "away in lavender." While she agreed that the New Deal had "become rather old, rather stable and permanent, . . . in many ways," she nevertheless believed that America needed more than programs designed to "win-the-war." Franklin D. Roosevelt, Franklin Delano Roosevelt, Personal Papers and Addresses, 1943, 569–575; Eleanor Roosevelt press conference reported in the *New York Times*, January 3, 1944. See also, Joseph P. Lash, *Dreamers and Dealers: A New Look at the New Deal* (New York: Doubleday, 1988), 463 and Lash, *Eleanor and Franklin*, 695–696.

8. John Morton Blum, "Portrait of a Diarist," in Henry A. Wallace, *The Price of Vision*, 9–10.

9. ER wanted Henry Wallace kept on the ticket but as her influence waned in the war years, the southern Democrats increased their opposition to FDR's programs, and Wallace's public feud with Jesse Jones convinced FDR and Hopkins that Wallace should be replaced. Richard S. Kirkendall argues that Wallace believed that ER's support hurt him more than it helped because ER intractably pursued reform at a time when FDR thought such a pursuit detrimental to war aims. Kirkendall, however, also speculates that "the unhappy condition of the Roosevelt marriage" contributed to Wallace's demise. Richard S. Kirkendall, "ER and the Issue of FDR's Successor," in Hoff-Wilson and Lightman.

"I would have preferred Mr. Wallace," ER wrote Walter White. Eleanor Roosevelt to Walter White, August 3, 1944, Miscellaneous Correspondence, AER papers. Harry S. Truman, Diary entry, April 12, 1945 in *Off the Record: The Private Papers of Harry S. Truman*, ed. Robert H. Ferrell (New York: Harper, 1980), 15; Harry S. Truman, *Memoirs*, 2 volumes, (Garden City: N.Y.: Doubleday, 1955–56), 1: 4–5; James Byrnes, *All in One Lifetime* (New York: Harper and Row, 1963), 373.

10. As the vice presidential nominee, Truman echoed the liberal demands for postwar economic conversion. During the 1944 campaign he advocated that factories built by the government for military equipment should be converted to private facilities charged with producing consumer goods, promoted a national unemployment insurance program, and supported New Deal agricultural policies.

For an extensive evaluation of Truman's standing with Democratic liberals see chapter 2: "Wallace, Truman, the Liberals, and the Politics of World War II, in Alonzo L. Hamby, *Beyond the New Deal: Harry S. Truman and the Future of American Liberalism* (New York: Columbia University Press, 1973) and Richard H. Pells, *The Liberal Mind in the Conservative Age: American Intellectuals in the 1940s and 1950s* (New York: Harper, 1985), 56–63. Freda Kirchwey, "The Battle of Chicago," *The Nation* 159 (July 29, 1944), 119; and "President Truman's Task," *The New Republic* 112 (April 23, 1945), 540.

11. For ER's criticism of Truman see Eleanor Roosevelt to Joseph Lash, July 29, 1944, Joseph P. Lash Papers (hereafter cited as JPL papers), FDRL; Eleanor Roosevelt to Lorena Hickok, July (n.d.) 1944, LAH papers, FDRL; Margaret Marshall, "Portrait of Truman," *The Nation* 160 (April 21, 1945), 439; I. F. Stone, *The Truman Era* (Boston: Little, Brown, 1953, 1988), xxi; Truman's assessment of the professional liberal intellectual is quoted in Hamby, *Beyond the New Deal*, 83.

12. Whatever liberal moves Truman might have made on behalf of his constituents,

ER believed, were done for purely electoral ends rather than with any desire to change policy. As Hamby notes, HST did retain the major liberal New Deal symbols, Wallace and Ickes, in his cabinet; however, his initial overtures toward his old conservative and machine allies displeased ER. (Byrnes to ER was everything that a public official should not be: arrogant, greedy for power, anti-New Deal, and a racist.) Harry S. Truman, diary entry, April 13, 1945, in Ferrell, *Off the Record*, 13–14; notes by Trude Lash, April 15, 1945, Trude Lash-Joseph Lash Correspondence, JPL papers; Hamby, *Beyond the New Deal*, 55–58. Robert Clayton Pierce, "Liberals and the Cold War: Union for Democratic Action and Americans for Democratic Action, 1940–1949" (Ph.D. diss., The University of Wisconsin-Madison, 1979), 122.

13. Trude Lash, notes, April 15, 1945, Joseph Lash-Trude Lash Correspondence, JPL papers.

14. The ER-HST relationship, although it has fascinated many historians, is traditionally viewed in the three theories developed by Alonzo Hamby, Michael Massey, and James McGregor Burns. Hamby believes that Truman was "ambivalent" toward liberals because he was more committed to political process than he was to liberal goals; consequently by 1945, "the liberal movement and Truman each held serious reservations about the other" which "degenerate[d] into mutual suspicion and hostility." As the pro-Wallace progressive resurgence of 1946 divided the liberal movement, ER had no choice but to support Truman. While agreeing with Hamby that HST was a quasi-liberal, Massey argues that ER was so focused on ends that Truman had to educate her about effective means. Because these two symbols were so opposite, "the administration became more liberal while the American liberal movement became more pragmatic. [ER was] an important liberalizing influence on Truman, while the President helped educate [ER] in the necessities of pragmatism in politics." Burns equivocates between accepting Massey's view of ER as unrealistic and Hamby's portrait of ER as frustrated by the lack of electable liberal politicians. Burns begins discussing ER as "an impractical politician" who because of her "greatness of character and goodness of heart" became HST's "ally and protagonist." As Truman and Wallace "spun away from each other, she was left isolated in the void between them." Because she had always believed in working within the party, Burns concludes that she had no choice but to support Truman. Consequently, ER shows her capacity "to shift almost overnight from a posture of gracious serenity to that of a hardheaded machine politician" who transcended the divisions within the party to maintain productive relationships with all its leaders. By the mid-1950s, ER is Burns's "consummate politician" who was only kept from higher office because of her sex. Hamby, *Beyond the New Deal*, 48–51; Michael J. Massey, "Relations Between Harry S. Truman and Eleanor Roosevelt: A Constructive Friendship" (senior thesis, University of Indiana, 1985), 1; Burns, *The Crosswinds of Freedom*, 219, 83, 235, 288.

15. Goodwin, *No Ordinary Time*, 59; and ER quoted in Lash, *Eleanor Roosevelt*, 67.

16. Henry Wallace, "The Price of Free World Victory," in *The Price of Vision: The Diary of Henry A. Wallace, 1942–1946* (Boston: Houghton Mifflin, 1973), 636–640. Eleanor Roosevelt agreed with the social gospel approach to Christianity. Christ was a figure whose behavior we should emulate in order to achieve social cooperation and practice what she termed "the moral basis of democracy." For an extensive discussion of ER's views of politics and religion see *The Moral Basis of Democracy*.

3. Holding Truman Accountable

After HAW delivered this address, the vice president and the first lady developed a close and confidential working relationship, often dining alone and discussing political strategy and public policy. Wallace recalled in his diary entry of October 17, 1943 that during dinner with ER she said that both she and FDR "would be for me as the logical one to carry out the policies of the President." Quoted in Joseph P. Lash, *A World of Love: Eleanor Roosevelt and Her Friends, 1943–1962* (New York: Doubleday, 1984), 86–87.

17. Eleanor Roosevelt to Joe Lash, March 1944, JPL papers.

18. Eleanor Roosevelt, review of *The American Presidency: An Interpretation*, In *Harvard Law Review* 54 (Winter 1941): 1413–1414; Eleanor Roosevelt, "Henry Wallace's Democracy," *The New Republic* 7 (August 7, 1944): 165–166; Eleanor Roosevelt to Henry Wallace, April 17, 1945, General Correspondence, AER Papers.

19. For liberal definitions of presidential leadership see I.F. Stone, "The Truman Program," *The Nation* (September 15, 1945) reprinted in I. F. Stone, *The War Years, 1939–1945* (Boston: Little, Brown, 1988), 273–275 and Hamby, *Beyond the New Deal*, 53–55; Cooke, "The Political Career of Anna Eleanor Roosevelt," 160; and Roosevelt, "My Day," April 19, 1945, My Day Collection, AER Papers.

20. Wallace, ibid., 411; James G. Patton, "A Plan for Propserity," *New Republic*, 111 (November 6, 1944): 586–587.

21. Hamby, *Beyond the New Deal*, 10–12; Chester Bowles, *Promises to Keep: My Life in Public Office, 1941–1969* (New York: Harper, 1971), 117–119; Zevin, ibid., 387–397, 421–438; Wallace, ibid., 410.

22. Hamby, ibid., 4–6, 59; I. F. Stone, *The Truman Era*, xxii; James G. Patton, "A Plan for Prosperity," *New Republic* 111 (November 6, 1944): 586–88. "The Reminiscences of Chester Bowles," 1963, OHRO/CU; Bowles, *Promises to Keep*, 122. For ER's response to the UDA plea see "News Flash on Full Employment," No. 4, October 25, 1945, UDA headquarters, attached to Eleanor Roosevelt to Harry Truman, November 1, 1945; and Lash, *Eleanor: The Years Alone* 34; Eleanor Roosevelt, "My Day," October 27, 1945, My Day Drafts, AER papers; and Agnew Bahnson, Jr. to Eleanor Roosevelt, February 3, 1942, Frank Porter Graham Papers, SHC/UNC.

23. During its debate the previous summer on the Murray-Kilgore Reconversion Bill, Congress, while rejecting Patton's demand for increased public spending and RFC loans as the means to full employment, agreed to study whether current levels of public and private expenditures would maintain full employment. Norman D. Markowitz, *The Rise and Fall of the People's Century* (New York: The Free Press, 1973), 141–143. Jesse Jones was no stranger to internal disputes and successfully stripped the RFC and the Federal Home Loan Board from under Wallace's control—thereby ensuring that the Commerce Department would have very limited authority over the reconstruction effort. See Hamby, p. 30, for a complete description of this powerplay. For a discussion of liberals' postwar hopes see Eric F. Goldman, *Rendezvous with Destiny* (New York: Random House, 1977), 312.

24. Hamby, ibid., 60–62; Wallace, ibid., 404; Markowitz, 141–143; Pierce, "Liberals and the Cold War," 107; and John Morton Blum, *V Was for Victory* (New York: Harcourt, 1976), 328–330. For a complete discussion of the legislative and economic history of the Full Employment Bill see Stephen A. Bailey, *Congress Makes a Law: The Story Behind the Employment Act of 1946* (New York: Columbia University Press, 1950).

25. Markowitz, ibid. 144; Pierce, "Liberals and the Cold War," 164; *New York Times*, January 30, 1945; and James Loeb and James G. Patton, "The Challenge to Progressives," *New Republic*, 112 (February 5, 1945): 187–206.

26. Wallace writes, "Veblen's message seems to me to be decidedly worthwhile, and an excellent antidote if one tends to take the classical analysts too seriously," Blum, "Portrait of a Diarist," 8; Wallace, ibid., 638. For Theodore Veblen's influence on Wallace, see in "Seminar in Economics" and "The Power of Books"in Henry A. Wallace, *Democracy Reborn* (New York: Reynal and Hitchcock, 1944). Wallace, "Broadcast to the Little Businessmen on the Nation," in *Democracy Reborn*, 263–268. See also Wallace's "Lincoln" Speech in the same volume for another example of his championing of full employment principles.

27. In May 1945, when he wrote Senator Robert Wagner praising his efforts to secure passage of S. 380, Wallace lamented that if the government had known how to apply fiscal policy to create employment and consumer demand at the onset of the depression, by now both the private and public sectors would be clamoring for cooperative government-industrial planning. Markowitz, 142.

Henry A. Wallace, *Sixty Million Jobs* (New York: Simon and Schuster, 1945). Wagner correspondence is quoted in Markowitz, 142. In opposition to Markowitz's argument see Steven Bailey's argument in *Congress Makes a Law* that Wallace and FDR were reluctant to make full employment an issue until Dewey introduced it as a campaign issue.

28. Alonzo L. Hamby, *Liberalism and its Challengers: F.D.R. to Reagan* (New York: Oxford University Press, 1985), 57–60; Harry S. Truman, *Memoirs: Years of Decision*, 1: 491.

29. Wallace, *The Price of Vision*, April 27, 1945 entry. After FDR delivered his call for sixty million jobs HAW wired him October 29, 1944, "I glory in your daring." See ibid., page 389.

30. Trude Lash to Joseph Lash, April 15, 1945, Trude Lash-Joseph Lash Correspondence, JPL papers.

31. Eleanor Roosevelt to Grace Tully, April 1945, General Correspondence, AER papers; Eleanor Roosevelt to Robert Hannegan, June 3, 1945, General Correspondence, AER papers.

32. Truman, *Memoirs: Years of Decision*, 492–493; and Hamby, *Beyond the New Deal*, 60–62. Richard L. Stout, writing as TRB, opines Truman "has to choose sides . . . he has got to stop writing nice notes to Congress on crucial domestic issues that divide conservatives from liberals and begin throwing his weight around." T.R.B., "Transition to Peace," *New Republic* 113 (August 27, 1945): 239–240; I.F. Stone, "The Truman Program" and "The Same Old Codgers," in I.F. Stone, *The War Years*, 314–316, 280–282. Eleanor Roosevelt to Lorena Hickok, June 11, 1945, LAH papers. Hamby identifies TRB in *Beyond the New Deal*, 6.

33. Eleanor Roosevelt, "My Day," October 27, 1945, My Day drafts, AER papers.

34. By the time ER offered direct political advice to Truman, the bill was bottlenecked in the House Committee on Expenditures chaired by the Alabama archconservative Carter Manasco who was adamantly opposed to both the budget and expenditure components. Meanwhile economists forecasted an unemployment high of 12 to 19 million. For accounts of Truman's speech see Truman, *Memoirs: Years of Decision*, 463 and

3. Holding Truman Accountable

Hamby, *Beyond the New Deal,* 63. For the text, see U.S. President, *Public Papers of the Presidents of the United States* (Washington, D.C.: Office of the *Federal Register,* National Archives and Records Service, April 12 to December 31, 1945), Harry S. Truman, 1945.

35. Harry Truman to Eleanor Roosevelt, November 6, 1945, Harry Truman-Eleanor Roosevelt Correspondence, AER papers.

36. For Harry S. Truman to John McCormack, October 29, 1945, see Truman, *Memoirs: Years of Decision,* 492; Wallace, *The Price of Vision,* notes on Cabinet Meeting, December 14, 1945, 531; Hamby, *Beyond the New Deal,* 60–64; Markowitz, 144–145; and Bailey, 155–78, 222–27.

37. For accounts of the Truman-Byrnes conversation see Leuchtenburg, *In the Shadow of FDR,* 10–11 and Byrnes, *All in One Lifetime,* 373. Labor agreed to wage controls as part of their defense contracts and had depended on overtime pay to augment lower hourly wages. With defense production scaling back by 1945 and an almost obsessive prediction of high unemployment rates, union membership feared that when price controls were lifted, wage controls would remain in place. Reacting to postwar inflation, rumors of strikes abounded. See John Patrick Diggins, *The Proud Decades: America in War and Peace, 1941–1960* (New York: Norton, 1989), 99–101 ; Barton J. Bernstein, "The Truman Administration and Its Reconversion Wage Policy," *Labor History* 6 (Fall 1965): 214–231; and Hamby, 66.

38. Roosevelt, *On My Own,* 12; Lorena Hickok to Eleanor Roosevelt, "Memo on Enclosed Copies of your Column Written during Spring, Summer, and Autumn of 1945," and "Memo on Activities of ER during Spring, Summer and Autumn of 1945, in Addition to those Recorded in her Column," Book and Manuscript File, *On My Own,* AER papers; Roosevelt, "My Day," September 19, 1945, My Day Drafts, AER papers. ER wrote Joe Lash that Hillman's offer "left me torn in my mind." She knew that NCPAC could influence both parties and "they needed to be swayed" but she worried that she could control those who were opposed to the liberal agenda. Eleanor Roosevelt to Joseph P. Lash, July 20, 1945, JPL papers; Eleanor Roosevelt to Sidney Hillman, July 27, 1945, General Correspondence, AER Papers. For an extended discussion of ER and the NCPAC offer see Lash, *Eleanor: The Years Alone,* 32.

39. Walter White to Eleanor Roosevelt, July 19, 1944 and August 9, 1944, Miscellaneous Correspondence, AER papers; memo from Mary McCleod Bethune, Channing Tobias, and Walter White to FDR, September 28, 1944, attached to Walter White to ER, October 4, 1944, Miscellaneous Correspondence, AER papers; Robert E. Sherwood, *Roosevelt and Hopkins* (New York: Harper 1948), 831. Wallace, *The Price of Vision,* 390–391. Nancy J. Weiss argues that although the tie between African Americans and the Democratic Party "proved to be remarkably enduring," economic advancement was the cement which held the bond together and that by 1940, African American voters had developed, in Ralph Bunche's words, "a much keener sense than formerly of the uses to which the ballot can be put." Weiss, 299.

40. Eleanor Roosevelt to Robert Hannegan, June 3, 1945, General Correspondence, AER papers.

41. Ibid. See "Memo on your activities," ibid. Eleanor Roosevelt to Lorena Hickok, June 11, 1945, Eleanor Roosevelt-Lorena Hickok Correspondence, LAH papers. Two months later, ER presented a similar critique to David Dubinsky, president of the

International Ladies' Garment Workers Union. See David Dubinsky to Eleanor Roosevelt, August 24, 1945 and Eleanor Roosevelt to David Dubinsky, August 27, 1945, General Correspondence, AER papers. Eleanor Roosevelt to Harry S. Truman, June 3, 1945, ER-HST Correspondence, General Correspondence, AER papers. For an extensive discussion of ER's role as political adviser to Democratic party officials and candidates, see chapters 4 and 6..

42. For historians who disagree with this interpretation, see Cooke, Massey, and Leuchtenburg. Cooke believes ER wrote Hannegan to "establish herself as a knowledgeable advisor in her own right rather than continue to be thought of as simply a bereaved widow to whom sentimental deference must be paid." Cooke, "The Political Career of Anna Eleanor Roosevelt," 156. Massey argues that the HST-ER relationship was "based on mutual need" and she was reluctant to confront him earlier because ER "and the liberals need presidential support and guidance for liberal policies and appointments." Massey, "Relations Between Harry S. Truman and Eleanor Roosevelt," 4. Leuchtenburg sees it only as ER's attempt to protect FDR's legacy. Eleanor Roosevelt to Harry Truman, ibid.

43. Although the following discussion of compromise refers to the San Francisco planing sessions for the United Nations, it applies to ER's assessment of the full employment situation as well.

"Compromises are never satisfactory. They are always the half-way measures which really please no one. Nevertheless, if they must be made in order to establish the machinery through which we are going to build confidence in each other, then we must look upon them as steps to our ultimate objectives. Confidence will be built eventually by our adherence to our highest standards in dealing with others, and by our own refusal to accept from others any lower standards.

"We will have to wait for the final reports and clarifications on what our representatives have accomplished to understand the whole picture. I think we are moving forward, and, as private citizens, we owe our chosen delegates the confidence and backing that we can only give by believing that they never lose sight of the ultimate objectives."

Eleanor Roosevelt, "My Day," May 8, 1945, My Day Drafts, AER Papers.

For the impact the passage of the Employment Act of 1946 had on one specific liberal interest group see R. C. Pierce's argument that the Union for Democratic Action focused so completely on the passage of the Full Employment Bill that when it failed to pass as they wanted "a disintegration of the liberal's purposes" followed. Pierce, "Liberals and the Cold War," 123. Goodwin, *No Ordinary Time*, 314, 451, and 559.

44. Robert A. Taft, "The Fair Deal is Creeping Socialism," *Harry S. Truman and the Fair Deal*, ed. Alonzo Hamby (Lexington, Mass: D.C. Heath, 1974) 42–52. For anti-price control sentiments of the organizations cited see documents in chapter 2, "Inflation and Politics," *The Truman Administration: A Documentary History*, eds. Barton J. Bernstein and Allen J. Matusow, (New York: Harper and Row, 1966), 46–86. John Morton Blum, *V Was for Victory*, 325–326.

45. ER had recommended Bowles for the OPA position because of his strong commitment to full and fair employment practices and firmly believed in the former advertising executive's ability to state his case to the administration and the public in clear, forthright terms. Bowles, *Promises to Keep*, chapter 9, "My Relations with FDR." Bowles

had never met FDR although he was very close to Eleanor Roosevelt, who lobbied diligently for his OPA appointment. In this chapter, Bowles recounts his efforts to convince Samuel Rosenman, FDR's close aide, to push FDR to deliver a speech detailing his postwar economic plans. Rosenman instructed Bowles to "put it in a memo" and he would deliver it to FDR. Although FDR waited months to respond to Bowles's call for a "Second Bill of Rights," he did adopt it in his State of the Union address and later rounded off Bowles's estimate of the need for 57 million jobs in his famous "60 million jobs" speech. When FDR regularly balked at introducing legislation to implement these demands, Bowles sought ER's counsel. Following her advice, Bowles redrafted his memo. Although FDR did not respond immediately to his advice, he did offer Bowles a new position, "the first Secretary of the new government department I plan to set up after the war—the Department of Public Welfare, which would also include health and education." See Bowles, ibid., 29, 121–123. Dorothy Bowles, interview by Emily Williams, December 9, 1977, EROHP.

46. For a discussion of the various positions staked out by members of the Truman administration see Wallace's notes on the October 19, 1945 Cabinet meeting on price controls in Wallace, *The Price of Vision*, 494–496. Chester Bowles to Harry S. Truman, January 24, 1946 reprinted in Bernstein and Matusow, *The Truman Administration*, 63–66. In a memorandum to FDR entitled "Democratic Senatorial and Congressional Candidates—Whether Victorious or Not," Edwin Pauley wrote FDR that the losses the party had suffered in the 1942 election occurred because either the voters had stayed home or cast their votes against policies they resented, rather than for candidates they supported. Blum, ibid., 233.

47. Chester Bowles, *Tomorrow Without Fear* (New York: Simon and Schuster, 1946) and *Promises to Keep*, 162–163.

48. Ibid.

49. Hamby, *Beyond the New Deal*, 66; Harry S. Truman, "Wage and Price Address, October 30, 1945," reprinted in "Truman's Wage-Price Program," in Bernstein and Matusow, *The Truman Administration*, 52–56; and Chester Bowles to Harry S. Truman, December 17, 1945, reprinted in same.

50. This was the second directive letter ER sent HST that month. Clearly she did not believe that Truman had the wherewithal to handle congressional rebuke and again prodded him to stay the course. For an example of Lash's efforts as reporter and intermediary, see Joseph Lash to Eleanor Roosevelt, January 20, 1946, JPL papers. Eleanor Roosevelt to Harry S. Truman, November 20, 1945, ER-HST Correspondence, AER papers.

51. Yet she was on record as being a strong supporter of wage increases before the labor disputes erupted; therefore, Truman should not have been completely surprised when she opposed his proposal to amend the Railway Labor Act. Eleanor Roosevelt to Harry S. Truman, ibid.; Bernstein and Matusow, 56; *The New York Times*, September 20, 1945; *New York Times*, October 7, 1945; "My Day," December 10, 1945, My Day Drafts, AER papers.

52. Eleanor Roosevelt, "My Day," December 13, 1945, My Day Drafts, AER papers. ER's definition of production was not limited to production of goods.

"What do we mean when we talk about production? We do not mean . . . merely creating things that have no value. We must produce things that people really need. Or, when you go beyond actual needs, production must be justified through its contribution to better living and the enjoyment of the finer things in life.

"For production to have real value, it must come up to certain standards. Just to multiply the things in the world, unless they meet the needs for which they are produced, would be a rather stupid procedure . . . . I think that, if we remember that in every field quality is as important as quantity, it will help us not go astray."

"My Day," March 22, 1946, ibid.

53. Chester Bowles to Harry S. Truman, December 17, 1945.

54. Chester Bowles to Harry S. Truman, January 24, 1946 quoted in entirety in Bernstein and Matusow, 61–66.

55. While Bowles confessed to the public that "for weeks [he] had been deeply concerned over the possibility—the very real possibility—that your country and my country is stumbling toward economic disaster . . . [t]onight this danger seems closer than ever." Office of Economic Stabilization press release, April 17, 1946 reprinted in Bernstein and Matusow, 71–72. For Truman's new policy directive see "Third Wage-Price Program," in the same anthology.

56. Roosevelt, "My Day," February 23, 1945, My Day Drafts, AER papers.

57. Roosevelt, "My Day," March 25, 1946, April 23, 1946, and April 30, 1946, My Day Drafts, AER papers.

58. The Taft and Wherry amendments to the Price Control Bill that allowed each processor who contributed to a product's manufacture and distribution to raise prices created, in Truman's words, "a choice between inflation with a statute and inflation without one." Bowles urged him to veto the bill and ER praised his act in her column. Ironically, however, when Truman signed the re-amended bill later the next month, he accepted most of the tenets he had vetoed earlier and ER once again lamented that his policy "would have less meaning than before." Roosevelt, "My Day," April 23, 1946 and June 15, 1946, My Day Drafts, AER papers; Truman, *Year of Decision*, 490–491; Markowitz, 148; Bowles, *Promises to Keep*, 138–142; and Wallace, *Price of Vision*, 582–583.

59. Although ER was no fan of John L. Lewis and agreed that the strike was ill-timed, she nonetheless supported the rights of the miners to a health and retirement fund. Roosevelt, "My Day," November 29, 1946 and June 30, 1947, My Day Drafts; Herbert Parmet, *The Democrats: The Years After FDR* (New York: Oxford University Press, 1976), 60–72. Truman, *Years of Decision*, 500–505.

60. While she recognized that "the old right to strike does not hold good when your job is one that affects the people of the world and the great mass of people in your country," ER still hoped that government would appreciate the dilemmas workers faced and act aggressively to solve the disputes. Roosevelt, My Day, May 25, 1946; Eleanor Roosevelt to Harry Truman, May 27, 1945, ER-HST Correspondence, AER papers; Elliott Roosevelt, *Mother R:*, 98; Roosevelt, "My Day," May 27, 1946, My Day Drafts, AER papers.

61. Burns, *The Crosswinds of Freedom*, 235–239; Lash, *Eleanor: The Years Alone*, 138–154. In this chapter, which Lash subtitles "A New Party—Not a Third Party," Lash astutely traces ER's involvement with party leadership but never seems to make the point he introduced with this phrase. If he had, there would be no reason to criticize his interpretation of the 1948 election.

62. Lash, *Eleanor: The Years Alone*, 141; Joseph P. Lash to Eleanor Roosevelt, June 9, 1947 and Eleanor Roosevelt to Joseph P. Lash, June 14, 1947, JPL Papers; Eleanor Roosevelt to Fiorello La Guardia, April 11, 1947, Miscellaneous Correspondence, AER papers.

63. Roosevelt, "Why I Do Not Choose to Run," *Look* 10 (July 9, 1946): 24–25; Arthur M. Schlesinger, Jr., *The Vital Center* (Boston: Houghton Mifflin, 1949); and Roosevelt, Address to the New York State Democratic Convention, 1946, Speech and Article File, AER papers.

The major issue confronting liberal political groups like the Union for Democratic Action, the Progressive Citizens of America and other liberal interest organizations discussed in Pierce and Gillon's histories was whether or not Americans with communist sympathies and/or allegiance should be allowed to participate in liberal organizations. Roosevelt, "My Day," September 2, 1948, My Day Drafts, AER papers.

64. For a thorough discussion of Wallace's foreign policy actions, see Edward L. and Frederick H. Schapsmeier, *Prophet in Politics: Henry A. Wallace and the War Years: 1940–1965* (Ames, Iowa: The Iowa State University Press, 1970), 142–162; Wallace, *The Price of Vision*; Roosevelt, "My Day," September 17, 1946, My Day Drafts, AER papers. Richard Norton Smith, *Thomas E. Dewey and His Times* (New York: Simon and Schuster, 1982), 468–543.

65. Roosevelt, "My Day," September 17, 20, 21, and 23, 1946, My Day Drafts.

66. Roosevelt, "My Day," January 25, 1947, My Day Drafts, AER papers.

67. For ER's stance on Truman's loyalty program see chapter 5, and Roosevelt, "My Day," March 25, 27, and 29, 1947, My Day Drafts. Eleanor Roosevelt to Harry S. Truman, November 13, 1947, and Harry S. Truman to Eleanor Roosevelt, November 26, 1947, ER-HST Correspondence. For ER's position on Taft-Hartley, see "My Day," June 10, 14, 26, August 28, September 6, 15, November 20, 1947 and Eleanor Roosevelt to Alfred Harris, September 8, 1947, Miscellaneous Correspondence, AER papers. Eleanor Roosevelt to Harry S. Truman, September 3, 1947, HST-ER Correspondence. Jack Redding, *Inside the Democratic Party* (Indianapolis: Bobbs-Merrill, 1958), 90–93.

68. For an account of ER's support of the Marshall Plan see George C. Marshall to Eleanor Roosevelt, July 23, 1947, Miscellaneous Correspondence, AER papers; Roosevelt, "My Day," September 18, 1947; Eleanor Roosevelt to George C. Marshall February 10, 1948, Miscellaneous Correspondence, AER papers, and Lash, *Eleanor: The Years Alone*, 95–106. For her stance on Israel see Lash, ibid., 108–137; Truman, *Memoirs*, 2: 163; Eleanor Roosevelt to Adlai Stevenson, April 28, 1948, and Eleanor Roosevelt to David Gurewitsch, May 26, 1948, Miscellaneous Correspondence, AER papers.

69. Roosevelt, "My Day," January 2, 1946, My Day Drafts. Eleanor Roosevelt to Harry S. Truman, December 23, 1947, ER-HST Correspondence, AER papers.

70. Roosevelt, "My Day," January 14, 15, July 31, 1947. The quotation is from "My Day," July 2, 1947, My Day Drafts, AER papers.

71. "I hope," she wrote Truman, "that you are going to make a real fight for every one of the social things that you mentioned in your message." Eleanor Roosevelt to Harry S. Truman, January 16, 1948, ER-HST Correspondence, AER papers. *Public Papers of the President: Harry S. Truman, 1948* (Washington: United States Government Printing Office, 1964), 122. For an extensive discussion of the electoral rationale for this

address, see William C. Berman, *The Politics of Civil Rights in the Truman Administration* (Columbus: Ohio State University Press, 1970), 70–135. See also James Loeb interview, EROHP, FDR Library.

72. Roosevelt, "My Day," February 21 and July 16, 1948, My Day Drafts.

73. Roosevelt, "My Day," July 19, 1948, My Day Drafts; Eleanor Roosevelt to Harry S. Truman, March 26, 1948, ER-Truman Correspondence, and Eleanor Roosevelt to George C. Marshall, March 27, 1948, Miscellaneous Correspondence, AER papers; Lash, *Eleanor: The Years Alone*, 154–159; Pierce, "Liberals and the Cold War," 360–363; Eleanor Roosevelt to Chester Bowles, June 23, 1948, Miscellaneous Correspondence, AER papers; and Eleanor Roosevelt to David Gurewitsch, July 1, 1948 quoted in Lash, *A World of Love*, 268–9.

74. "My Day," August 11, 1948, and September 10 and 11, 1948, My Day Drafts, AER papers.

75. Eleanor Roosevelt to Frances Perkins, October 4, 1948, Miscellaneous Correspondence, AER papers.

76. Eleanor Roosevelt to May Craig, May 5, 1948, Miscellaneous Correspondence, AER papers; Massey, "The Political Career of Anna Eleanor Roosevelt," 53; Eleanor Roosevelt to Harry S. Truman, October 14, 1948; Eleanor Roosevelt to Bernard Baruch, October 4, 1948, AER papers. For a through discussion of ER's election correspondence see Lash, *Eleanor: The Years Alone*, 138–154; and Harry Truman, "The Truman Tapes: Harry S. Truman Speaking Frankly with Ben Gradus," Caedman, 1960.

77. TRB, "Washington Wire, *New Republic* 119 (November 8, 1948): 3–4, and November 15, 1948; Roosevelt, My Day, September 2, and November 2, 1948, My Day Drafts, AER papers.

∎ **4. CHAMPIONING CIVIL RIGHTS**

1. *Amsterdam News*, November 24, 1962, page 1.

2. For an example of those who argue that there was no substantial change in ER's civil rights positions see, Joanna Schneider Zangrando and Robert L. Zangrando, "ER and Black Civil Rights," in Hoff-Wilson and Lightman, *Without Precedent*, 88–107. For a discussion of ER's response to private appeals see Allida Black, "A Reluctant but Persistent Warrior."

3. Eleanor Roosevelt, *Tomorrow Is Now* (New York: Harper and Row, 1963), 19.

4. "It is to be noted that the files, especially with respect to the negro situation in other parts of the country, reflect numerous complaints, especially with regard to the First Lady." FBI memorandum to J. Edgar Hoover, October 14, 1943. Eleanor Roosevelt, *If You Ask Me* (New York: D. Appleton-Century, 1946) 68.

5. "Memorandum for the Director," October 14, 1943.

6. Lloyd C. Stark to ER, February 2, 1940 and ER's reply, February 10, 1940, General Correspondence, AER papers; and Evans C. Johnson Interview, SHC.

7. Eleanor Roosevelt to Evans C. Johnson, September 18, 1942, attached to Johnson Interview, SHC.

8. Ralph J. Bunche, "Memo on Interview with Mrs. Franklin D. Roosevelt at the White House, May 15, 1940," Myrdal Study, Senate Interviews File, Ralph J. Bunche papers, Special Collections, University of California at Los Angeles. See also "Memoran-

dum presenting suggestive notes on 'The Negro Worker and the Struggle for Economic Justice,'" Prepared for Miss Thompson, attached to Ralph J. Bunche to Malvina Thompson, September 11, 1940, personal property of Ben Keppel of UCLA.

9. Eleanor Roosevelt, *The Moral Basis of Democracy*, 43; "The Issue Is Freedom," *New Republic* 107 (August 3, 1942): 147–148; Draft, "What are We Fighting For?" *The American Magazine*, July 1942, and "Broadcast, National Democratic Forum," February 24, 1945, Speech and Article File, AER papers.

10. Eleanor Roosevelt, "Freedom: Promise or Fact," *Negro Digest* October 1943, 8–9.

11. Eleanor Roosevelt, "Tolerance," attached to George Bye to Eleanor Roosevelt, February 27, 1945, and "Building for Peace," Speech and Article File, AER papers.

12. For representative press coverage of the article see UPI release, dateline Chicago, October 11, 1943; Doxey Wilkerson "If She Were a Negro," *Daily Worker*, October 20, 1943; and "First Lady Urges Negroes to Fight for Full Equality," *Louisiana Weekly*, October 2, 1943. Letter to J. Edgar Hoover, re: Mrs. Roosevelt's article "If I were a negro," October 13, 1943, FBI file # 100–0–19681, FOIPA request by author.

13. "Race Riots," n.d., Record Group 44–802–167, FBI Files, FOIPA request by author.

14. John Morton Blum, *V Was for Victory* (New York: Harcourt, 1975), 200–201; and Goodwin, *No Ordinary Time*, 326–327.

15. Blum, 202–203; Goodwin, *No Ordinary Time*, 444; ER to Trude Pratt, June 28, 1943, JPL papers.

16. "The Reminiscences of Virginia Durr," February 6, 1990, Southern Historical Collection, University of North Carolina (hereafter known as SHC); "The Reminiscences of Henry A. Wallace," August 28, 1943, ORHO; and ER to Josephus Daniels, July 23, 1943, AER papers.

17. Lash, *Eleanor and Franklin*, 654; and ER to Doris Fleeson, October 4, 1943, AER papers.

18. See folder 190.1, Criticism of the Negro Question, AER papers.

19. Eleanor Roosevelt, "For the Joint Commission on Social Reconstruction," October 1945, and "The Minorities Problem," attached to William Scarlett to Eleanor Roosevelt, March 19, 1946, Speech and Article File, AER papers; Roosevelt, untitled radio address, August 16, 1943, Speech and Article file, and audio tape file, AER papers.

20. For ER interventions on behalf of Walter White see, the Walter White folders, 1935–1945, General Correspondence; for Mary McLeod Bethune (MMB) see Mary McLeod Bethune to Eleanor Roosevelt, November 22, 1941 and ER's response of November 27, 1941, and MMB to Malvina Thompson, March 18, 1943, Correspondence with Government Officials, AER papers; for A. Philip Randolph and Odell Waller see Black, "A Reluctant but Persistent Warrior;" for military camps see John A. Lapp to ER, August 12, 1942, Malvina Thompson to MMB, n.d., and MMB's reply, August 29, 1942, General Correspondence, AER papers. Bunche, "Memorandum." Jonathan Daniels Interview, March 22, 1972, SHC; The Reminiscences of Jonathan Daniels, Southern Intellectual Series, ORHO, 1972.

21. Pauli Murray, *Song in a Weary Throat*, chapters 13–14; Pauli Murray interview by Dr. Thomas Scopes, February 3, 1978, transcript, EROHP; Clark Foreman, "The Decade of Hope," in *The Negro in Depression and War*, ed. Berhard Sternsher (Chicago:

Quadrangle Books, 1969), 150–166; Eleanor Roosevelt to Pauli Murray and Murray's responses, 1940, 1941, 1942 folders, General Correspondence, AER papers; Kate Hubell to Dear Friend, February 27, 1941, FBI file N 100–14597–0, FOIPA request by author; Sylvia Bethscher to Dear Friend, November 19, 1942, FBI file 100–135–53–44, FOIPA request; and Guy Hottel to J. Edgar Hoover, April 3, 1943, National Committee to Abolish the Poll tax file, FOIPA request.

22. ER to Governor Darden, June 2 and 22, 1942 and his response, June 23, 1942, AER papers; Murray Interview; Murray, *Song in a Weary Throat*, ibid.; Eleanor Roosevelt to A. M. Kroeger, August 20, 1942, Personal Correspondence, AER papers; Memorandum on the Waller Case, Group II B 54, Odell Waller—1941, NAACP papers; "Urge Roosevelt to Fix Waller's Fate," *New York Times*, July 2, 1941; "Darden Rules Waller Must Die," *The New York Times*, July 1, 1941; "The Case of Odell Waller," a memorandum prepared by the Workers Defense League, Group II B Legal File B54, Odell Waller folder, 1942, NAACP papers.

23. Murray, *Song in a Weary Throat*, 173; Allida Black, "Reluctant but Persistent Warrior."

24. APR source, FBI files, April 19, 1944, clipping from Baltimore conference. Evidence of FDR's reluctance to praise NAACP actions can be found in the note attached to Franklin D. Roosevelt to Arthur P. Spingarn, October 1, 1943; President's Personal File (PPF), Franklin D. Roosevelt Papers, Hyde Park. "Miss Tully brought this in. Says the President doesn't think too much of this organization—not to be to[o] fulsome—tone it down a bit." Lash, *Eleanor and Franklin*, 709.

25. Wilson sent a friend a poem criticizing ER's "nose-rubbing" greeting with a Maori woman and FDR's pursuit of a fourth term. The poem ended with a Maori woman pondering, "just rubbed a Roosevelt nose, will it keep on running?"

26. Pearl D. Burnette to Eleanor Roosevelt, November 10, 1944, General Correspondence, AER papers; Alfred Steinberg, *Mrs. R: The Life of Eleanor Roosevelt* (New York: Putnam, 1958) 303; Carl Sferrazza Anthony, *First Ladies* (New York: Morrow, 1990), 506; and *The Alabama Sun*, April 28, 1944.

27. Eleanor Roosevelt to M. M. Moulthrop, August 3, 1942, General Correspondence, AER papers; "First Lady Defines Social Equality," *New York Times*, September 7, 1944, p. 25.

28. Pauli Murray, "Social Equality Needs Definition, Writer." *L.A. Sentinel*, September 14, 1944, attached to Eleanor Roosevelt to Pauli Murray, October 3, 1944; Eleanor Roosevelt to Pearl Burnette, November 24, 1944, AER papers; and Murray Interview, EROHP.

29. Gunnar Myrdal, *An American Dilemma: The Negro Problem and Modern Democracy* (New York: Harper, 1944), 797; "For Manhood in National Defense," *Crisis* 47 (December 1940): 375; Mary McLeod Bethune to Eleanor Roosevelt, July 12, 1940, Correspondence with Government Departments, AER papers; and Richard M. Dalfiume, "The 'Forgotten Years' of the Negro Revolution," in *The Negro in Depression and War: Prelude to Revolution, 1930–1945*, ed. Bernard Sternsher (Chicago: Quadrangle Books, 1969) 298–316.

30. For an extensive discussion of the FEPC from 1945 through its demise in 1946 see Merle E. Reed, *Seedtime for the Modern Civil Rights Movement: The President's*

4. Championing Civil Rights

Committee on Fair Employment Practice 1941–1946 (Baton Rouge: Louisiana State University Press, 1991), 321–343.

31. Oliver W. Harrington, *Terror in Tennessee: The Truth about the Columbia, Tennessee Outrages* (New York: The National Committee for Justice in Columbia Tennessee, 1946), 3, NAACP papers, Record Group II B-9, National Committee for Justice in Columbia, Tennessee, Manuscript Division, Library of Congress; Dorothy Beeler, "Race Riot in Columbia, Tennessee," *Tennessee Historical Quarterly* 39 (Spring 1980): 50–51.

32. "Stenographic Notes taken at Committee Meeting, March 4th, re situation at Columbia Tennessee," NAACP Papers, Record Group II B-9, National Committee for Justice in Columbia, Tennessee. Beeler, ibid.

33. For a representative United Press release see "Kill 2 in Freedom Dash," *The Meridian Star*, Friday March 1, 1946, 1 and *The Nashville Tennessean*, March 1–3, 1946; "Pogrom in Tennessee—and the Part Politics Plays," *The New Republic* 114 (April 29, 1946): 429; Guy B. Johnson, "What Happened in Columbia, *New South* 1 (May 1946): 1–8; Mary McLeod Bethune to ER, March 23, 1946, General Correspondence, AER papers.

34. Walter White to George Marshall, April 1, 1946, NAACP papers, Group II A 199, Columbia Tennessee Riot: SCHW, LOC.

35. "National Committee for Justice in Columbia Tennessee," Minutes of Meeting held April 4, 1946, NAACP Group II B 9, National Committee for Justice in Columbia, Tennessee, NAACP papers, LOC.

36. Ibid.

37. ER to Tom Clark, September 23 and November 6, 1946, and his replies of October 8, and November 26, 1946, General Correspondence, AER papers; Thurgood Marshall to Eleanor Roosevelt, October 28, 146, and Thurgood Marshall to Tom Clark, December 27, 1946, General Correspondence, AER papers.

38. W. E. B. DuBois et al., "A Statement on the Denial of Human Rights to the Minorities in the Case of Citizens of Negro Descent in the USA and an Appeal to the United National for Redress Prepared for the NAACP . . . ," General Correspondence, NAACP file, AER papers; Lash, *Eleanor: The Years Alone*, 68; Minnie Finch, *The NAACP: Its Fight for Justice* (Metuchen, N.J.; The Scarecrow Press, 1981), 119–120.

39. Walter White to Eleanor Roosevelt, October 20 and 21, 1947 and ER's response, October 22, 1947, General Correspondence, AER papers.

40. Walter White to Eleanor Roosevelt, October 21 and October 25, 1947, General Correspondence, AER papers.

41. Eleanor Roosevelt to Walter White, ibid.

42. "Russian Says U.S. Condones Slavery, Mrs. Roosevelt Denies Charge," *New York Times*, December 9, 1947.

43. W.E.B. DuBois to Walter White, July 1, 1948, attached to W.E.B. DuBois to ER July 1, 1948, General Correspondence, AER papers.

This hostility did not go unnoticed by the NAACP Board of Directors. When Walter White was appointed observer to the forthcoming UN session in Geneva and asked DuBois to prepare a report detailing the foreign policy issues with which he should be familiar, DuBois balked at the assignment and indicted ER in his refusal. W.

E. B. DuBois to Walter White and the Board of Directors of the NAACP, September 7, 1948, General Correspondence, AER papers.

44. Finch, *The NAACP*, 120; "Marshall Plan for NAACP," *Daily Worker*, September 16, 1948, 9.

45. Jack Greenberg, *Crusaders in the Courts* (New York: Basic Books, 1944), 70. See the following correspondence in the NAACP folder, General Correspondence file, AER papers: Oliver Harrington to Eleanor Roosevelt, May 7, 1947; Charles E. Levy to Eleanor Roosevelt, July 12, 1948 and ER's reply, n.d.; Ruby Hurley to Malvina Thompson, June 9, 1948, July 6 and 9, 1948 and Malvina Thompson's reply of July 6, 1948; Daniel E. Byrd to Eleanor Roosevelt, August 25, 1948 and ER's response August 31, 1948.

46. M. Glen Johnson, "The Contribution of Eleanor and Franklin Roosevelt to the Development of International Protection of Human Rights," *Human Rights Quarterly* 9 (1987): 39; Dean Rusk to George C. Marshall, August 23, 1948 with Attachments and Durward Sandifer to Eleanor Roosevelt, September 9, 1948, AER papers; and Eleanor Roosevelt, "The Struggle for Human Rights," September 28, 1948, Speech and Article File, AER papers.

47. "Memorandum of Conference of the Secretary with Mrs. Eleanor Roosevelt at their New York Home," March 1, 1945, Group I, NAACP Papers; My Day, July 31, 1945, My Day drafts, AER papers.

48. The Wagner-Ellender-Taft Housing Bill was to provide low-interest government loans to companies engaged in slum clearance projects and construction of low-income housing. It committed the government to invest $133,00 over a six-year period and "was aimed not only at the immediate emergency but also at long-range solutions."

Eleanor Roosevelt to Howard Smith, March 30, 1945, General Correspondence, AER papers; "My Day," March 7, 12, 13, 1946, My Day Drafts, AER papers; Hareven, *Eleanor Roosevelt: An American Conscience*, 193.

49. Eleanor Roosevelt, "My Day," March 12, 1946, My Day drafts.

50. Eleanor Roosevelt, "Housing and Community Relations—One Approach to Intercultural Relations," Workshop for Democracy of the Downtown Community School folder, Speech and Article File, AER papers. For further discussion of ER's evaluation of the Detroit disturbance see Lillian Smith to ER, June 20, 1944 and ER's reply, June 26, 1944, General Correspondence, AER papers. *New York Times*, October 3, 1945.

51. FBI report, unknown field correspondent to J. Edgar Hoover, memorandum re: The War Worker, January 1946, FBI file, The War Worker, FOIPA request; *Baltimore Afro-American*, August, 1949; and "Full Justice for Minorities Urged by Mrs. Roosevelt," *Washington Evening Star*, September 7, 1949.

52. "Support of NAACP Program Asked by Mrs. Roosevelt," December 3, 1953, NAACP II A, Board of Directors, Eleanor Roosevelt 1946–1955, NAACP Papers; Caroline Shirley to Eleanor Roosevelt, n.d. 1947 and Barry Bingham to Eleanor Roosevelt, February 20, 1948, General Correspondence, AER papers.

53. Memorandum to J. Edgar Hoover from SAC, New York, FBI file No. 100–13534–457 and Memorandum, August 24, 1945, Southern Conference for Human Welfare file, FBI file No. 100–10355.

4. Championing Civil Rights

54. Eleanor Roosevelt to Pauli Murray, March 9, 1944, General Correspondence, AER papers; Murray Marder, "Segregation Ban at Airport To Face Court Test Monday," *Washington Post*, March 11, 1949.

55. Eleanor Roosevelt, "My Day," April 22, 1949, My Day Drafts, and ER to David Sarnoff, April 20, 1949, General Correspondence, AER papers.

56. "U.S. Beset by Fear and Unnatural Hate, Mrs. Roosevelt Says," *Washington Star*, November 22, 1953.

57. Frances Lide, "Mrs. Roosevelt Counsels Interracial Conference," *Washington Star*, November 17, 1956, A-7.

58. "Housing Integration in North Proposed," *Washington Post and Times Herald* November 20, 1956, A7; Eleanor Roosevelt, If You Ask Me, February 1959 and March 1959, If You Ask Me file, AER papers.

59. "Contribution to Democracy," NAACP 1950 folder, General Correspondence, AER papers; Henry Lee Moon to Eleanor Roosevelt, June 27, 1949, General Correspondence; Marian Anderson and Ruth Bryan Rohde to Eleanor Roosevelt, December 8, 1950, General Correspondence; Eleanor Roosevelt to David Sarnoff, April 20, 1949 and his reply, April 27, 1949, General Correspondence; J. Claude Hudson to ER, October 10, 1950, General Correspondence; Roy Wilkins to ER, February 6, 1950, General Correspondence; and Walter White to Eleanor Roosevelt, November 21, 1950, General Correspondence, AER papers. See also NAACP Board of Directors Minutes, 1946–1952, Group III, NAACP papers, Library of Congress. "My Day," July 29, 1946, My Day Drafts.

60. Oliver Harrington to ER, May 7, 1947, General Correspondence. Although she could not attend the meetings, she carefully read all the proposals and made her opinions known to the rest of the committee. Roy Wilkins to ER, February 6, 1950, and ER's notes on the document, General Correspondence, AER papers.

61. Walter White to ER, November 21, 1950, and ER to George F. Baker, Jr., December 1950, and Walter White to ER, December 18, 1953 and January 13, 1954, General Correspondence, AER papers.

62. Notes attached to Walter White to Eleanor Roosevelt, March 14, 1950; Walter White to ER July 19, 1950; Walter White to Dave Niles, July 19, 1950; Walter White to ER, undated telegram, 1950 and Memorandum to Eleanor Roosevelt and Walter Reuther, December 12, 1950, and the attached report "Tentative Draft of Statement by Subcommittee appointed at Breakneck Hill," General Correspondence, AER papers.

63. Minutes, NAACP Board of Directors, April 10, 1950, 3–4, NAACP Minutes, NAACP II-144, Administrative File, Board of Directors, NAACP papers; Walter White to Eleanor Roosevelt, March 14, 1950, May 11, 1950, and July 14, 1950, General Correspondence, AER papers; Roy Wilkins to Eleanor Roosevelt, March 21, 1940 and ER's response, April 4, 1950, General Correspondence, AER papers.

64. For general overviews of the 1956 election that argue that ER and Stevenson sold out the more liberal civil rights activists, see the following: Lash, *Eleanor: The Years Alone*, 245–265; Parmet, *The Democrats*, 130–141; Arlene Lazarowitz, "Years in Exile: The Liberal Democrats, 1950–1959 (Ph.D. diss., University of California Los Angeles, 1982), 309–388; and Martin, *Adlai Stevenson and the World*, 301–302, 315–317, and 341–349.

65. When questioned by a black minister on whether or not he would support sending in federal troops if school districts did not desegregate within the next six months, Stevenson responded:

"I think that would be a great mistake. This is exactly what brought about the difficult Civil War and division of the Union. Now, we will go about these things gradually, because it will be the spirit of man that will make the laws successful and make it possible to enforce them continuously. It will not be troops or bayonets. We will have to proceed gradually. You do not upset the habits and traditions that are older than the Republic overnight. There is, however, a question of what is tolerable to bring about the family of man in this country. We have been a hundred years almost—it will be a hundred years on January 1, 1963. It will be almost a hundred years from the Emancipation [Proclamation] to the time when I think the spirit of that decision will be enforced. That is a long, long time."

John Barlow Martin, *Adlai Stevenson and the World: The Life of Adlai Stevenson* (New York: Doubleday, 1977), 248–266; Lash, *Eleanor: The Years Alone*, 245–246; Robert Frederick Burk, *The Eisenhower Administration and Black Civil Rights* (Knoxville: University of Tennessee Press, 1984), 168–169.

66. Eleanor Roosevelt to Adlai Stevenson, June 13 and his reply, June 15, 1956; and Adlai Stevenson to Eleanor Roosevelt, August 9 and her response August 28, 1956, Adlai Stevenson-Eleanor Roosevelt Correspondence, General Correspondence, AER papers.

67. Eleanor Roosevelt to Pauli Murray, February 22, 1956, Pauli Murray Papers, Small Collections, FDR Library.

68. Richard Bolling to Eleanor Roosevelt, January 10, 1956 and her reply, January 20, 1956, General Correspondence, AER papers.

69. Stevenson wanted ER to write an article for *Look* explaining his civil rights stance but she refused, arguing that she would be more effective negotiating in person with black leaders. Adlai Stevenson to Eleanor Roosevelt, June 4, 1956, Stevenson-Roosevelt folder, and Eleanor Roosevelt to Roy Wilkins, n.d., and Roy Wilkins to ER, April 2, 1956, Eleanor Roosevelt to Channing Tobias, April 26, 1956, General Correspondence, AER papers. Lash, *Eleanor: The Years Alone*, 246–250.

70. Eleanor Roosevelt to Adlai Stevenson, June 13, 1956, Adlai Stevenson folder, General Correspondence, AER papers. Agnes E Meyer to Eleanor Roosevelt, January 25, 1956, Eleanor Roosevelt folder, and Agnes E. Meyer to Walter Reuther, July 17, 1956, Walter Reuther folder, Agnes E. Meyer papers, Library of Congress.

71. ADA representative Joe Rauh recommended a plank that would reiterate "the 1952 platform on civil rights and the majority rule with the additional statement that the Supreme Court's decision on school desegregation is morally right and must be implemented with all deliberate speed by the executive and legislative branches of government." Joseph Rauh to Eleanor Roosevelt, July 24, 1956, General Correspondence, AER papers. Alex R. Preston, "Virginia Caucus Told by Battle of School Plank," *The Evening Star*, August 12, 1956; "Mrs. Roosevelt Cautions Convention to Resolve Differences, " *New York Times*, August 14, 1956.

72. Eleanor Roosevelt to Adlai Stevenson, June 13, 1956, Stevenson-Roosevelt Correspondence, and Paul Butler, June n.d., 1956, General Correspondence, AER

4. Championing Civil Rights

papers and her reply, July 2, 1956; Joseph Rauh, Jr., to Eleanor Roosevelt, August 2, 1956 and her reply, July 30, 1956, General Correspondence, AER papers.

73. Martin, *Adlai Stevenson and the World,* 348.

74. Lash, *Eleanor: The Years Alone,* 263–265.

75. Martin, *Civil Rights and the Crisis of Modern Liberalism,* chapter 8; Edith Evans Asbury, "Democrats Open Sessions Today; Bitter Fight Due," "Truman is Rebutted by Mrs. Roosevelt," and "Liberals and Conservatives Near an Agreement," *The New York Times,* August 13, 1956; Alex R. Preston," Virginia Caucus Told by Battle of School Plank" and J. A. O'Leary, "Mrs. Roosevelt Reported Asking Rights Harmony," *Washington Evening Star,* August 13, 1956; "Mrs. Roosevelt Cautions Convention to Resolve Differences," *New York Times,* August 14, 1956; J. A. O'Leary, "Stevenson Nearly 'Over Top;' Mild Rights Plank Revealed," *Washington Evening Star,* August 13, 1956; and "Democrat 'Loyalty Oath' Headed for Graveyard," *Washington Evening Star,* August 15, 1956.

76. *Official Proceedings of the Democratic National Convention 1956,* Mrs. Ruth All and Dr. Daniel M. Odgen, Jr., editors (Richmond: Beacon Press and the Democratic National Committee, 1956), 231–232.

77. Joseph Rauh interview, EROHP.

78. When ER was asked during her "Meet the Press" appearance about "her feelings" for Nixon, she replied:

"I know how I feel . . . . I am told that Mr. Nixon is a very fine young man by many Republican people whom I know, particularly young people, and that he has matured and grown in many ways. I happen to remember very clearly his campaign for the Senatorship. I have no respect for the way in which he accused Helen Gahagan Douglas of being a communist because he knew that was how he would be elected, and I have no respect for the kind of character that takes advantage and does something they know is not true. He knew that she might be a Liberal but he knew quite well, having known and worked with her, that she was not a Communist. I have always felt that anyone who wanted an election so much that they would use those means, did not have the character that I really admired in public life." Transcript, Stevenson folder, 1956, General Correspondence, AER papers.

79. A. O'Leary, "Mrs. Roosevelt Reported Asking Rights Harmony," *Washington Star,* August 13, 1956.

80. *Washington Star,* August 14, 1956; "Democratic Keynote Assails Nixon as 'Hatchet Man' of G.O.P.; Lays 'Indifference' to President: Mrs. Roosevelt Urges Unity—Stevenson is Still Leading," *New York Times,* August 14, 1956; "Mrs. Roosevelt Cautions Convention to Resolve Differences: Urges Delegates to Keep Party Young," *New York Times,* August 15, 1956.

81. Bertram Russell, *Power: A New Social Analysis* (London: Unwin Books, 1960), 25; Doris Fleeson, "Truman's Political Motives," *Evening Star,* August 13, 1956.

82. "Eleanor, Backing Adlai, Says Ike Is Failure as a Leader," *The Columbus Citizen,* October 14, 1956, attached to Katie Loucheim to Eleanor Roosevelt, October 15, 1956, General Correspondence, AER papers; "Luncheon Meeting—Beckley, West Virginia" notes, October 1, 1956, Speech and Article File, AER papers; "Civil Rights Lag Scored at Rally," *New York Times,* May 25, 1956, p.8; "Mrs. Roosevelt Puts Case for Integration," *New York World Telegram,* May 25, 1956, 10.

83. Pauli Murray to Eleanor Roosevelt, November 1, 1956, General Correspondence, AER papers.

84. Roosevelt, "I Sorrow for Our Last Three Years," *Washington News*, April 30, 1957.

85. Lyndon Johnson to Eleanor Roosevelt, August 12, 1957 and her reply, August 17, 1957, Famous Names File, LBJ papers; "I Sorrow for Our Last Three Years;" and Roosevelt, "My Day," 9, 1957.

86. Robert Fredrick Burk, *The Eisenhower Administration and Black Civil Rights* (Knoxville: University of Tennessee Press, 1984), 147; and Roosevelt, ibid.

87. A. H. Belmont to L. V. Boardman, "Drew Pearson Radio Broadcast," January 14, 1957, Record Group 948350838, FBI papers, FOIPA request; "The Disease is Spreading," Chicago Defender, June 4, 1957, p. 11; A. H. Belmont to L. V. Boardman, May 2, 1959, FBI File No. 100–7801–3864 and "U.S. Klans, Knights of the Ku Klux Klan, Inc. (Tennessee)," June 28, 1958, FBI File No. 100–7801–3924, FOIPA request.

88. Burk, 174. To ER, Daisy Bates, despite her bitterness, was the true hero of Little Rock. She faced death threats, the loss of her newspaper, and constant verbal and physical assault with "such courage" that ER "paid her homage in [her] thoughts many times and [she wanted] to tell her again how remarkable I think she was through these horrible years."

Eleanor Roosevelt, "Faubus Seems to Lack Scruples," *Washington News*, September 3, 1958 and foreword to *The Long Shadow of Little Rock* by Daisy Bates, Manuscripts and Article Drafts, AER papers.

89. Eleanor Roosevelt, "My Day," February 23, 1956.

90. Eleanor Roosevelt, "Salute to Montgomery," *Liberation*, 1 (December 1956): 1; Eleanor Roosevelt, *India and the Awakening East* (New York: Harper, 1953), 196–207; "The Reminiscences of Bayard Rustin, OHRO, 1988; Interview with Dorothy Height, July 27, 1994.

91. "Southern Conference Education Fund," October 1, 1951, File No. 100–759, FBI papers, FOIPA.

92. "Southern Conference Education Fund," October 1, 1951; and Irwin Klibaner, *Conscience of a Troubled South: The Southern Conference Education Fund, 1946–1966* (New York: Carlson Publishing Inc., 1989), 110.

93. *Southern Patriot*, February 1956; Klibaner, 112–113; Eleanor Roosevelt to William Langer, February 1956, AER papers.

94. Klibaner, 115; "School Board Hears Desegregation Plea," *The Times Picayune*, September 13, 1955; Roy Wilkins to Maxwell E. Foster, Jr., March 27, 1956, SCEF folder; James Dombrowksi to ER, May 12, 1954 and September 15, 1955, AER papers.

95. Klibaner, 147–148; Anne Braden, *The Wall Between* (New York: Monthly Press, 1958) and "The Reminiscences of Anne Braden," July 1979, ORHO.

96. Conrad J. Lynn, *There Is A Fountain: The Autobiography of a Civil Rights Lawyer* (Westport: Lawrence Hill and Company, 1979), 116–118; Braden, dustjacket.

97. Klibaner, 149; "The Reminiscences of Anne Braden." For a thorough discussion of ER's response to Melish's appointment see NYSECF folder, box 20, folder 8, and Rockland Committee folder, box 91, folder 19, SCEF files, James Dombrowski papers, Wisconsin State Historical Society.

98. Lynn, 142–157; and Conrad J. Lynn, interview by author, June 2, 1994.

99. Roosevelt, "My Day," July 9, 1957.

4. Championing Civil Rights

100. Denton L. Watson, *Lion in the Lobby: Clarence Mitchell, Jr.'s Struggle for the Passage of Civil Rights Laws* (New York: William Morrow, 1990), 360–394; and "My Day," August 9, 1957.

101. Eleanor Roosevelt to Lyndon Johnson, January 29, 1960, Famous names file, Lyndon B. Johnson papers, LBJ Library, Austin, Texas.

102. Roosevelt, "My Day," March 3, 1960.

103. Roosevelt, "My Day," April 7, 1960.

104. Myles Horton, *The Long Haul* (New York: Doubleday, 1990), 189–190; Joe Rauh to Joe Lash, May 18, 1959, General Correspondence, Joseph P. Lash Papers, FDR Library; Lillian Smith to Eleanor Roosevelt, June 20, 1944, September 30, 1954, July 11, 1954, August 15, 1956, March 3, 1957, October 31, 1961, General Correspondence, AER papers; and Pauli Murray to ER, June 16 and July 4, 1958, General Correspondence, AER papers. See also, Roosevelt, Foreword, *In the Shadow of Little Rock.*

105. AP wire release, "Racial Inquiry," May 25, 1962, Committee of Inquiry into the Administration of Justice in the Freedom Struggle, CORE papers.

Maureen Corr interviewed by Emily Williams, October 29, 1978, EROHP. For a sample of ER's association of segregation with apartheid see "My Day," March 26, 1960; Roosevelt, "What Has Happened to the American Dream," 47. Eleanor Roosevelt to CORE solicitation list, n.d., Committee on Inquiry into the Administration of Justice, Reel 5, frame 500, CORE papers. Roosevelt, *The Moral Basis of Democracy,* 57.

106. Marvin Rich to Eleanor Roosevelt, December 22, 1959, Reel 5, Section 201, and Eleanor Roosevelt to Ralph McGill et al., n.d., Congress of Racial Equality Papers, Reel 5, Manuscript Room, LOC. For ER's early endorsement of the CORE-SNCC sit-ins see "My Day," February 18, 1960.

107. Eleanor Roosevelt to Carl Rachin, April 26, 1962, Reel 5, frame 498, CORE papers.

108. Eleanor Roosevelt to Ralph McGill et al., ibid.

109. The Committee was comprised of Norman Thomas, Roger Baldwin, Dr. Kenneth Clark, John Bolt Culbertson, Joe Rauh, Boris Shiskin, Rev. Gardner Taylor, and Telford Taylor. The Committee Counsels were Rowland Watts (ACLU) and Carl Rachin (CORE).

"Justice," Core pamphlet, series 5, reel 45. Marvin Rich, Memo, "Advance Information Not For Publication," n.d., Committee of Inquiry into the Administration of Justice in the Freedom Struggle, CORE papers; Clarence Hunter, "Panel Hears How South Harassed Rights Groups," *Washington Evening Star,* May 26, 1962.

110. "Justice," a pamphlet transcript of the Committee of Inquiry into the Administration of Justice in the Freedom Struggle, Series 5 Reel 45, folder 474, Congress of Racial Equality papers, Library of Congress.

111. Roosevelt, *Tomorrow Is Now,* 51, 65.

112. Martin Luther King, Jr., to Eleanor Roosevelt, February 15, 1961, General Correspondence, AER papers: "Mrs. Roosevelt never went around the world talking about her husband, Franklin. Mrs. King cannot open her mouth without talking about her dead husband, Martin. Mrs. Roosevelt got herself involved in all kinds of causes for the betterment of mankind, and Mrs. King runs a mausoleum dedicated to Martin in Atlanta. There is a difference, and therefore, she will make mistake after mistake and

look as if she's a person of no convictions, although I think she has some." "The Reminiscences of Bayard Rustin"; Lynn interview.

∎ **5. CONFRONTING THE VITAL CENTER**

1. For ER's views on the Constitution and the Bill of Rights, as well as her criticism of Jefferson on sedition, see her American history notebooks in The Todhunter File, AER papers.

2. For samples of the criticism ER faced for her positions see Wolfskill and Hudson, *All But the People*, 37–46; Westbrook Pegler, "Fair Enough," *Washington Times Herald*, January 2, 1951; "Communists: Dr. Gilbert Assails Radical Educators," *Herald Express*, January 11, 1946; "Eleanor Set Right," *Washington Times Herald*, November 1, 1949; Elizabeth Gurley Flynn, "Life of the Party," *The Daily Worker*, January 1, 1949; Mike Gold, "Change the World," *The Worker*, June 24, 1945; and William F. Buckley, *Up from Liberalism* (New York: Stein and Day, 1959, 1984), xiii.

3. Reinhold Niebuhr, *The Children of Light and The Children of Darkness: A Vindication of Democracy and a Critique of Its Traditional Defense* (New York: Scribner's, 1944); Arthur M. Schlesinger, Jr., "The U.S. Communist Party," *Life* 21 (July 29, 1946): 84–96; Eleanor Roosevelt, "My Day," March 27, August 14, October 7, 1946 and January 11, September 5, and, December 30, 1947, My Day Drafts, AER papers.

4. Gerald W. Johnson quoted in Wolfskill and Hudson, *All But the People: F. D. Roosevelt and His Critics*, 37.

5. Unsigned editorial, *Counterattack*, June 4, 1948; "Mrs. Roosevelt and Her Record," *Counterattack*, March 18, 1955; "All for American to F.B.I.," September 14, 1950, FOIPA request; unknown to Bureau of Investigation, September 25, 1947, FOIPA request; and Wolfskill and Hudson, 43.

6. "Leaders Aid Reds Charge," *The Herald Tribune*, January 11, 1946; "Communists: Dr. Gilbert Assails Radical Educators," *Herald Express*, January 11, 1946; pamphlet, "Danger! Warning! White Man Awaken," attached to Eleanor Roosevelt to J. Edgar Hoover, June 143, 1946, FBI papers, FOIA request; Wolfskill and Hudson, 43; and Memo, SAC Oklahoma City to J. Edgar Hoover, November 20, 1950, FBI file 62–43818–1015, FOIA request.

7. Roosevelt, *The Autobiography of Eleanor Roosevelt* (New York: Harper, 1961), 264; *Tomorrow Is Now*, 52; "My Day," May 6, July 5, and August 17, 1946, January 28 and February 2, 1949, and January 6, 1950, My Day Drafts, AER papers.

8. Buckley, *Up from Liberalism*, 36, 40–43, 63; James Burnham, review of *India and the Awakening East*, quoted in Buckley, 43*n*; "Mrs. FDR Expresses Alarm at New Orleans Witchunt," *The Daily Worker*, March 28, 1954, p. 3; and Roosevelt, *Tomorrow Is Now*, 121.

9. Ibid., 131. Roosevelt, Todhunter files, AER papers. See also Roosevelt, *The Moral Basis of Democracy*.

10. Horton, 190; Robert Griffith, *The Politics of Fear: Joseph R. McCarthy and the Senate* (Lexington: University of Kentucky Press, 1970), chapter 1. See also, Richard Hofstader, *The Paranoid Style of American Politics and Other Essays* (New York: Knopf, 1965).

11. Leo P. Ribuffo, "*U.S. v. McWilliams*: The Roosevelt Administration and the Far Right," in Michal R. Belknap, ed., *American Political Trials* (Westport: Greenwood

5. Confronting the Vital Center

Press, 1981), 201–205; Leo P. Ribuffo, *The Old Christian Right* (Philadelphia: Temple University Press, 1983), 179–185; Geoffrey S. Smith, *To Save a Nation: American 'Extremism,' the New Deal, and the Coming of World War II* (Chicago: Ivan Dee, 1992), 90; and Frances Biddle, *In Brief Authority* (Garden City: Doubleday, 1962), 234–238.

12. Eleanor Roosevelt, "Fear is the Enemy," *The Nation*, February 10, 1940, 3.

13. Roosevelt, "Civil Liberties—The Individual and the Community," address to the Chicago Civil Liberties Committee, March 14, 1940, pamphlet, Speech and Article File, AER papers.

14. Ibid.

15. Roosevelt, *This Is My Story*, 242–253; Roosevelt, *The Autobiography of Eleanor Roosevelt*, 85–98; Roosevelt, *This Troubled World*; Cook, *Eleanor Roosevelt*, 213–236; Blanche Wiesen Cook, "Turn Towards Peace," in Hoff-Wilson and Lightman, *Without Precedent*; Cook, "Eleanor Roosevelt and Human Rights: The Battle for Peace and Planetary Decency" in *Women and American Foreign Policy*, ed. Edward Crapol (New York: Greenwood Press, 1987); 91–119; and Lash, *Eleanor and Franklin*, 638–653. ER alludes to her efforts in *This I Remember*, 207–209, and 230–235.

16. Cook, "Eleanor Roosevelt and Human Rights," 90–96; ER to Lewis Chamberlain, February 19, 1938, AER papers; ER to Mrs. Graham, February 2, 1938; and Lash, *Eleanor and Franklin*, 555–556.

17. Roosevelt, *The Autobiography of Eleanor Roosevelt*, 230.

18. Carola von Schaeffer-Bernstein to Eleanor Roosevelt, January 3, 1936 and ER's reply, January 28, 1936, Carola von Schaeffer-Bernstein to Eleanor Roosevelt, December 13, 1936, General Correspondence, AER papers; Lash, *Eleanor and Franklin*, 722–741; *The New York Times*, June 3, 1937. Eleanor Roosevelt to Pearl Buck, May 23, December 14, December 18, 1941 and March 13, 1942, General Correspondence. See also Roosevelt, Address to American Youth Congress, February 21, 1939, Speech and Article File, AER papers.

19. Roosevelt, "My Day," September 23, 1938, My Day Drafts, AER papers. Lash, ibid., 638; Lash, Diary, February 27, 1941, JPL papers; Roosevelt, *This I Remember*, 239.

20. Lash, ibid., and Cook, "Eleanor Roosevelt and Human Rights," 90–97.

21. Roosevelt, Radio Broadcast, February 22, 1942, Tape Collection, Speech and Article File, AER papers; Hareven, *Eleanor Roosevelt*, 145–162; FBI Memoranda, "Internal Security—I, November 15, 1951, file 100–2862, FOIPA request; and F. L. Welch to Mr. Ladd, May 24, 1943, FBI file 100–168918–98, FOIPA request. ER did discuss pro-Nazi activity with Attorney General Biddle and FBI Director Hoover, but only when she feared that such sentiment could lead to espionage.

22. Since the ACLU objected to this procedure and ER was very close to ACLU Executive Director Baldwin and an active contributor and public spokesperson for the group, it is possible that Baldwin did discuss the case with her. It is reasonable to assume that ER objected to the trial procedures. However, no records of such an appeal exist either in AER files, the Justice Department papers, or Baldwin's records. Eleanor Roosevelt to Clarence Pickett, June 17 and 18, 1944, Correspondence with Government Officials, AER papers.

23. Roosevelt, "Freedom of Speech," October 14, 1941 broadcast, Tape File, Speech and Article File, AER papers; Hareven, *Eleanor Roosevelt*, 164.

24. Fiorello La Guardia, WYNC radio broadcast, February 15, 1942, FDR Library; "Mrs. Roosevelt Berlin Target," *The New York Times*, November 18, 1941; "Mrs. Roosevelt Is Cited in Japan as Bad Example," *The New York Times*, February 27, 1942.

A precursor to JFK's Peace Corps, the program ER so wholeheartedly endorsed dispatched graduates skilled in health care and construction to China, the Philippines and other war-torn arenas. Lawrence Burd, "Mrs. Roosevelt's Plan to Train War Objectors Abandoned," *Washington Star*, July 9, 1943. Nevertheless, after the CPS rejected her appeals for wages, ER did not fight for the objectors to be paid for their CPS labor.

25. Eleanor Roosevelt, "My Day—Discussing Place of Conscientious Objectors in War," *Memphis Press Scimitar*, June 20, 1944. See also boxes of "My Day Responses" for April, May, and June 1944, My Day Responses, AER papers. Roosevelt, "My Day," June 21, 1944, My Day Drafts, AER papers.

26. Ibid. ER continued to defend COs after the war. "As long as the conscientious objector exists in relation to majority opinion," she wrote April 5, 1947, "he illustrates the point that we must preserve the right of individuals to be different. And we must carefully guard against legal proceedings under which human beings can be punished for holding different ideas from the majority of their fellows." Roosevelt, "We Must Preserve the Individuals [sic] Right to Be Different," *Washington News*, April 5, 1947.

27. Goodwin, *No Ordinary Time*, 323.

28. "Mrs. Roosevelt Greeting American Born Japanese," *The New York Times*, December 15, 1941; Francis Biddle, *In Brief Authority* (Garden City: Doubleday, 1962), 214; Roosevelt, "My Day," December 15, 1941, My Day Drafts, AER papers.

29. Yet the ACLU's record at this time was not much better than ER's. Eleanor Roosevelt to Francis Biddle, November 5, 1941 and his response, December 5, 1941; ER to Biddle, January 2, 1942 and his response, January 3, 1942; ER to Biddle, February 25, 1942; Secretary to Mrs. Roosevelt to Francis Biddle, March 3, 1942; and ER to Biddle, May 8, 1942 and his response, May 5, 1942, Correspondence with Government Officials, AER papers; Steinberg, 283–284; and Pamphlet, American Civil Liberties Union, "Freedom in Wartime," Washington, D.C., 1943.

30. Biddle, 219; Peter Irons, *Justice at War: The Inside Story of the Japanese American Internment* (New York: Oxford University Press, 1983); and Roger Daniels, *The Decision to Relocate the Japanese Americans* (Melbourne, Florida: Kreiger, 1981).

31. *Washington Star*, December 17, 1942; Eleanor Roosevelt to Francis Biddle, December 5, 1941, January 2, February 25, and March 3, 1942, and June 16, 1943 and Francis Biddle to Eleanor Roosevelt, May 2, 1942, Correspondence with Government Officials; Secretary to Mrs. Roosevelt to Clarence Pickett, October 25, 1943, AER papers.

32. Secretary to Mrs. Roosevelt to Mrs. Clark, January 5, 1944; Janet Fukushima to Eleanor Roosevelt, November 13, 1943, General Correspondence; Eleanor Roosevelt to Colonel Oveta Hobby, May 6, 1943, Correspondence with Government officials; Eleanor Roosevelt to George Marshall, May 24, 1943 and FDR to Mrs. Roosevelt, May 19, 1943 (attached), AER papers.

33. Harold Ickes to FDR, April 13, 1943, Harold Ickes papers, LOC; and Goodwin, *No Ordinary Time*, 427–429.

34. ER's silence on Japanese-American induced violence was limited to actions that occurred stateside. When news that the Japanese had executed some American aviators

reached her, ER immediately, in the words of one reporter, "went on record opposing reprisals." "For the sake of our own souls," the first lady told reporters, "we should live up to the way of doing things that we believe is the right and civilized thing to do." "Opposes Any Reprisals," *The New York Times*, May 11, 1943. Roosevelt, "My Day," April 26 and 27, 1943, My Day Drafts, AER papers; "Mrs. F. D. Roosevelt Visits: Urges Wise Resettlement and Admires Evacuee Fortitude," *Gila Courier*, April 24, 1943, War Relocation Authority Files, Record Group 210, 4 (b), Box 32, National Archives.

35. ER to Joe Lash, April 22, 1943, AER papers; and Roosevelt, "A Challenge to American Sportsmanship," *Collier's* (October 16, 1943): 21, 71.

36. Ibid., 71. [name concealed] to ER, January 1944. I am grateful to Shelly Jacobsen for sharing this letter with me.

37. Goodwin, *No Ordinary Time*, 323.

38. Eleanor Roosevelt, "My Day," May 12, 1942; Eleanor Roosevelt to Flora Rose, June 6, 1942, General Coorespondence, AER papers; Eleanor Roosevelt, "My Day," June 2, 1942; and Goodwin, 430–431, and 514.

39. Ibid., 71. Togo Tanaka to Eleanor Roosevelt, January 26, 1942, and her reply, February 12, 1942, General Correspondence AER papers.

40. Roosevelt, "Japanese Relocation Camps," attached to Dillon Meyer to ER, May 13, 1943, AER papers.

41. Eleanor Roosevelt, "My Day," *Washington News*, April 5, 1947; "My Day," November 2, 1943, My Day Drafts, and "Untitled Speech in Human Rights," Speech and Article File, 1945–1948, AER papers. For a brief discussion of ER's criticism of Truman's Loyalty Program, see chapter 3.

42. Eleanor Roosevelt, "My Day," December 1, 1949 and August 13, 1947, My Day Drafts, AER papers.

43. Eleanor Roosevelt to Mrs. Deane, June 7, 1934, Miscellaneous Correspondence, AER papers. Eleanor Roosevelt to Emma Goldman, n.d. 1934, Emma Goldman papers, University of California, Berkeley [I am grateful to Candace Falk of the Emma Goldman Project for sharing this information with me]; Anna Louise Strong to Eleanor Roosevelt, January 29, 1935, and ER's reply, February 13, 1935; Anna Louise Strong to ER, February 13, 1947 and ER's reply, February 24, 1937; and ER to Anna Louise Strong, October 25, 1939, Miscellaneous Correspondence, AER papers. Lash, *Eleanor and Franklin*, 594.

44. ER's support of the American Youth Congress so distressed J. Edgar Hoover that in January 1942, he ordered FBI agents to break into the AYC's office in New York City to photocopy ER-AYC correspondence. When the Washington office received these documents, Hoover ordered them "carefully reviewed and analyzed." To safeguard these records and to prevent any public disclosure of the Bureau's investigation of the first lady, Hoover ordered the report written under the guideline of a Do Not File procedure and then stored it in Assistant Director Louis Nichols's Official and Confidential File. References to this appear throughout the AYC file I obtained during my FOIPA request. However, the full description of this break-in appears in Athan G. Theoharis, *Beyond the Hiss Case: The FBI, Congress and the Cold War* (Philadelphia: Temple University Press, 1982), 7. For ER's version, see *This I Remember*, 200–205. For Lash's version, see *Love, Eleanor*, 445–491.

45. Roosevelt, *The Autobiography of Eleanor Roosevelt*, 208–211. For a detailed discussion of ER's belief in the students see Roosevelt, "Why I Still Believe in the Youth Congress," *Liberty*, 17 (April 20, 1940): 30–32.

46. Reflecting on her strategy before the committee, ER wrote in 1961, "just what the questioner thought I was going to do I do not know, but my action had the effect I desired." Roosevelt, *Autobiography of Eleanor Roosevelt*, 209.

Roosevelt, *This I Remember*, 201–203. For extensive accounts of ER's efforts at these hearings, see Winifred D. Wandersee, "ER and American Youth: Politics and Personality in a Bureaucratic Age," in Hoff-Wilson and Lightman, *Without Precedent*. 63–87; Lash, *Eleanor and Franklin*, 463–464, 591–602; Martin Dies, *The Martin Dies Story* (New York: Bookmailer, 1963); Walter Goodman, *The Committee: The Extraordinary Career of the House Committee on Un-American Activities* (New York; Farrar, Straus, 1968), 77–80. Goodman also argues that ER's intervention in the immigration request of German-born film composer and lyricist Hans Eisler sparked the HUAC's fury and eventually led to the committee's investigation of the Hollywood Ten.

47. Eleanor Roosevelt to Bernard Baruch, Dember 2, 1939 and December 12, 1939, Personal Correspondence, AER papers.

48. G. C. Burton to Mr. Ladd, FBI Internal memorandum, December 31, 1943, Eleanor Roosevelt, FBI papers, FOIPA request; Lash, *Love, Eleanor*, 460–461; Curt Gentry, *J. Edgar Hoover: The Man and the Secrets* (New York: Plume Books, 1992), 385; and Gene Fowler, *Minutes of the Last Meeting* (New York: Viking Press, 1954), 56–59.

49. Roosevelt, "An FBI Agent Asks Me About John Foster Dulles," *Washington News*, November 29, 1952, notation in Hoover's handwriting, ER file, FBI papers; J. Edgar Hoover to [name deleted], January 4, 1960, File 62–1–5–78 and J. Edgar Hoover to [name deleted], October 23, 1959, File 62–62735, FOIPA request; and Ted Gup, "Eleanor and Edgar: 'Hoot Owl' vs. the 'Gestapo', *Washington Post*, July 6, 1982; and Athan Theoharis, "J. Edgar, Eleanor and Herbert, Too?" *The Nation*, vol. 234, no. 7, 200.

50. Eleanor Roosevelt to J. Edgar Hoover, April 12, 1951, and his reply, April 17, 1951, AER file, FBI papers, FOIPA request.

51. Hareven, *Eleanor Roosevelt*, 202 and Eleanor Roosevelt, "My Day," February 24, March 9, May 27, and June 1948, My Day Drafts, AER papers.

52. Roosevelt, "My Day," November 5, 1947, My Day Drafts, AER papers and Eleanor Roosevelt, "No Art Flourishes on Censorship and Repression," *Washington News*, November 5, 1947.

53. Carl Levin, "State Dept. Assails Attack on Aide Over His Leftish Second Cousin," *New York Herald Tribune*, March 11, 1948.

54. *Chicago Sun*, May 22, 1947; FBI memorandum, addressee and author deleted, June 23, 1947, 100–351157–1, FOIPA request; and "Mrs. Roosevelt Decries 'Fear' of Communism," *New York Herald Tribune*, June 25, 1952.

55. The SCEF objected to the execution of the Martinsville Seven, seven black men who were sentenced to death for raping a white woman. The men also had the active support of the Civil Rights Congress and the Communist party of the United States. To members of the press and HUAC investigators, this proved that the SCEF was a communist front. "Southern Conference Education Fund," FBI internal memo, ibid.

5. Confronting the Vital Center

Jim Dombrowski to ER, April 27, 1954 and ER et al. to Senator William Langer, attached to Dombrowski to ER; Virginia Durr to ER, March 31, 1954; and Aubrey Williams to ER, May 12, 1954, General Correspondence, AER papers.

56. As David Shannon argued, communists enjoyed less ill will from the American public in the immediate postwar years. In 1946, less than fifty percent of the country favored outlawing membership in the CPUSA. This was a substantial decline from a 1940 poll, which showed a 74 percent support for criminalization.

David A. Shannon, *The Decline of American Communism: A History of the Communist Party of the United States Since 1945* (New York: Harcourt, Brace and Company, 1959), 190. See also Guenter Lewey, *The Cause that Failed: Communism in American Political Life* (New York: Oxford University Press, 1990), 76–82.

57. Roosevelt, "My Day," June 21, 1945, My Day Drafts.

58. The Alien Registration Act of 1940 quoted in Shannon, *Decline of American Communism*, 193–194.

59. Although the Smith Act was promoted as a means to regulate the activities of the communist left, by the time the bill became law, the far right was increasingly becoming its target. However, when Hitler invaded Russia, the left, resurrected as a new Popular Front, was placed on a cold back burner. FDR was much more interested in prosecuting the right than he was the left.

Blanche Wiesen Cook, "Turn Toward Peace," in Hoff-Wilson and Lightman, *Without Precedent*, 119; Eleanor Roosevelt, "My Day," May 21, 1941, My Day Drafts; and Roosevelt, "War Brings Curtailment of Rights," Draft article for *American Laborite*, Speech and Article File, 1941, AER papers; excerpt from *The People's World*, August 24, 1940 cited in SAC to Director, FBI, May 20, 1948, FBI Papers, FOIPA request; and Roosevelt, "Humanitarian Democracy," draft, Speech and Article File, 1940, AER papers.

60. Although there is no written record of ER's response to the initial Smith Act prosecutions of the radical right, such as *U.S. vs. McWilliams* and the prosecution of two American civilians for sedition in a military court, ER's intervention on behalf of Harry Bridges, Earl Browder, and other anti-interventionists as well as her public defense of the right to lampoon her, make it safe to assume that ER questioned these judicial maneuvers with both the attorney general and her husband.

61. Roosevelt to Francis Biddle, January 14, 1941, Correspondence with Government Officials, AER papers; Abram Sachar interviewed by Thomas Soapes, November 10 and 15, 1978, EROHP; Eleanor Roosevelt to J. Edgar Hoover, June 13, 1949 and April 12, 1951, ER file, FBI papers, FOIPA request; Michal Belknap, *Cold War Political Justice* (Westport: Greenwood Press, 1977), 25–27; Pells, 204.

62. Michal R. Belknap, "Cold War in the Courtroom: The Foley Square Communist Trial," in Belknap, *American Political Trials*, 233–262; Shannon, 201–233; Pells, ibid., and Lewey, 76–90.

63. Although twelve were initially indicted, one of the defendants, William Z. Foster, was dropped from the final indictment due to illness. Belknap, ibid., Shannon, ibid. For a complete transcript of the trial see *Dennis v. United States*, 341 U.S. 494 (1951).

64. Eleanor Roosevelt, "My Day," July 13, 1950, and February 15, and June 26, 1951, My Day Drafts, AER papers. William O. Douglas, *The Autobiography of William O.*

Douglass: The Court Years: 1939–1975 (New York: Random House, 1980), 92–94; and "Mrs. Roosevelt Voices Fear of Smith Act Ruling," *The Daily Worker,* June 27, 1951.

65. Lewey, 84; Shannon, 200; Pells, 281–282; Sidney Hook, "Does the Smith Act Threaten Our Liberties?" *Commentary* 15 (January 1953): 63–72; Arthur M. Schlesinger, Jr., "The Right to Loathsome Ideas," *Saturday Review of Literature* 32 (May 14, 1949), 17, 18, 47 and *The Vital Center,* 207; and "The U.S. Communist Party," *Life* 21 (July 29, 1946): 84–96; and Gillon, 82.

66. Roger Baldwin, "Liberals and the Communist Trial," *New Republic,* 115 (January 31, 1949): 8; James Wechsler, *The Age of Suspicion* (New York: Donald I. Fine, 1953), 324; and Gillon, 78–82.

Weschler did initially object to the *Dennis* decision and drafted, with Joseph Rauh, a statement for Americans for Democratic Action declaring that "freedom of speech ought never to be a political football." However, when the ADA National Board objected to this position, and Arthur Schlesinger, Jr. was unable to mediate a compromise between Weschler and ADA Chair Francis Biddle, Weschler refrained from further criticism.

67. Douglas, *Autobiography,* 207.

68. "Mrs. Roosevelt Decries Negative Fight on Reds," *New York Post,* October 4, 1954.

69. Eleanor Roosevelt, *The Wisdom of Eleanor Roosevelt: Eleanor Roosevelt Writes About Her World* (New York: McCalls Corporation, 1962), 12.

70. A. J. Muste et al., "A Petition to the President of the United States On Amnesty for Smith Act Victims and postponement of Trials," December 1955, FBI Papers, FOIPA request.

71. In addition to ER, Niebuhr, Muste, and Thomas, the most noted signers were Henry Steel Commager, Paul Lens, and Lewis Mumford. The vast majority were theology professors and clergy.

Norman Thomas to Eleanor Roosevelt, October 4, 1956, and her reply, n.d., General Correspondence; Eleanor Roosevelt, "My Day," July 14, 1945, My Day Drafts, AER papers; "A Petition to the President of the United States for Smith Act Victims and Postponement of Trials," December 1955, FBI file 100–392–047–III, FOIPA request.

72. Eisenhower refused the demands of the petitioners. However, in 1957, the Supreme Court reversed the contempt conviction of John T. Watkins and overturned the conviction of five Californians indicted under the Smith Act.

In her defense of the *Watkins* decision, ER also explained the logistical technicalities the justices used to reach their conclusion to her readers. She carefully explained how the statue of limitations effected the case. "The court held that the Communist party had been organized in its present form in 1945 at the latest and that, in 1951 when the indictment was brought against the leaders, the three-year statute of limitations had run out."

Eleanor Roosevelt, "I'm Glad Over Recent High Court Decisions," *Washington News,* July 10, 1957; and "My Day," July 10, 1957, My Day Drafts, AER papers.

73. Roosevelt, "My Day," July 14, 1945, My Day Drafts, AER papers. For additional explanations on why she opposed Smith and signed the clemency petition see Roosevelt, "If You Ask Me," May 1956, Speech and Article file, AER papers.

74. Hamby, *Liberalism and Its Challengers*, 287–288; Kenneth O'Reilly, *Hoover and the Un-Americans: The FBI, HUAC, and the Red Menace* (Philadelphia: Temple University Press, 1983), 104. For an extensive account of Nixon's 1946 campaign, see Stephen E. Ambrose, *Nixon, Volume I: The Education of a Politician, 1913–1962* (New York: Simon and Schuster, 1987), 117–140.

75. Mildred Kahler Geare, "Communism in the U.S. No Menace—Mrs. Roosevelt," *The Baltimore News Post*, January 11, 1949.

76. Ambrose, *Nixon*, 160; Richard M. Nixon, *RN: The Memoirs of Richard Nixon* (New York: Grosset and Dunlap, 1978), 47–48; and *Appendix to Congressional Record, House*, 94, Pt. 5 (May 1948): A643–645.

77. Ambrose, *Nixon*, 160–161; *Appendix to Congressional Record, House*, 94, Pt. 9 (February 3, 1948): A643–645. Nixon, 47–50.

78. Alan D. Harper, *The Politics of Loyalty: The White House and the Communist Issue, 1946–1952* (Westport: Greenwood Press, 1969), 145, 153; and Hamby, *Liberalism and Its Challengers*, 288; Nixon, ibid.

79. Ambrose, *Nixon*, 162–163; *Congressional Record, House*, 94, Pt. 5, (May 1948): 6104, 6145–6146; Nixon, *Memoirs*, 46–47. For an examination of the reasons why the House supported the bill see Mary McAuliffe, *Crisis on the Left: Cold War Politics and American Liberals, 1947–1954* (Amherst: University of Massachusetts Press, 1978), 48–51.

80. Eleanor Roosevelt, "My Day," June 1, 1948, My Day Drafts, AER papers. ER also editorialized against the bill in her June 8, 1948 column. But perhaps the best description of her motivation occurred eight years later. "It is only one step from the control of expression to accusing people for what they may think." Roosevelt, "If You Ask Me," May 1956, Speech and Article File, AER papers.

81. Ibid.

The Senate refused to pass the bill. However, most of the provisions that Nixon proposed were eventually incorporated into the McCarran Internal Security Act. ER also vehemently opposed this legislation and praised the efforts of those who turned to the courts to test its constitutionality. By the time the McCarran Act was adopted, Nixon had defeated Helen Gahagan Douglas and was serving in the Senate. This just reinforced ER's assessment that he would do anything to get elected. Clyde Tolson to L. B. Nichols, November 21, 1950, FBI File No. 62–62735–36, FOIPA request; and ER to J. Edgar Hoover, January 17, 1951, ER File, FBI, FOIPA request.

82. Ambrose, *Nixon*, 166; George Nash, *The Conservative Intellectual Movement in America Since 1945* (New York: Harper, 1979), 99.

83. Kenneth O'Reilly correctly argues that the Hiss case "graphically symbolizes the altered perspective of American liberal intellectuals in the fifties." After 1950 many liberals used Hiss's conviction to argue that popular front cooperation was political suicide and shifted more toward the vital center. This shift was so pervasive that by 1950 O'Reilly believed that liberals' concern with combating "internal security threats" made their actions "virtually indistinguishable from the conviction of Cold War conservatives." Kenneth O'Reilly, "Liberal Values, the Cold War, and American Intellectuals: The Trauma of the Alger Hiss Case, 1950–1978," in Theoharis, *Beyond the Hiss Case: The FBI, Congress and the Cold War*, 309; and untitled article, "The Washington Times

Herald loudly pointed out that . . . ," *Washington Times Herald,* January 28, 1950, AER file, FBI papers, FOIPA request.

84. Alger Hiss, *Recollections of a Life* (New York: Seaver Books, 1988), 138–145, and chapters 3 and 4; Morton Levitt and Michael Levitt, *A Tissue of Lies: Nixon v. Hiss* (New York: Stein and Day, 1979), Introduction; Eleanor Roosevelt to Anna Roosevelt Halstead, January 2, 1946, Anna Roosevelt Halstead Papers, FDR Library.

85. Eleanor Roosevelt to blacked out correspondent, October 27, 1953, ER file, FBI Papers, FOIPA request; and "Mrs. Roosevelt Not Convinced of Hiss' Guilt," *New York Times Herald* [sic], January 29, 1950.

86. William F. Buckley, *The Committee and Its Critics: A Calm Review of the House Committee on Un-American Activities* (New York: Putnam, 1962), 151; and Roosevelt, "My Day," August 19, 1948, My Day Drafts, AER papers.

87. When confronted with ER's comments, Chambers responded, "I think that Mrs. Roosevelt, like some other people, is too inclined to consider this a contest between Alger Hiss and Whittaker Chambers. She overlooks the fact that the jury did not reach its verdict merely on the basis of the two stories of the two men. There were corroboration from many witnesses and from other forms of evidence. . . . I believe the American people still accept the verdicts of the duly selected juries rather than the personal opinion of any well-meaning individual, no matter how highly placed that individual may be." *New York Times Herald,* January 29, 1950.

As she responded to a reader's request to clarify her position, although she knew during the trial that "Hiss was not telling the truth," she was convinced that he was "not guilty of the things Whittaker Chambers accused him of." She did not interpret Hiss's effort to conceal his actions as proof of sedition and she held no respect for those who were willing to make such a rush to judgment. "I dislike extremely our proneness to accept as gospel truth whatever a reformed communist hands us and certainly you cannot believe that Chambers is a good man." Furthermore, even if she was wrong and he was guilty, it is a minor point. "Hiss was judged . . . and he is paying the price for whatever mistakes he made. I am quite sure that he did no harm at Yalta and he certainly did no harm while he was Dulles' advisor." ER to Mr. McDonald, n.d. [probably 1950], General Correspondence, AER papers. See also Jason Berger, *A New Deal for the World: Eleanor Roosevelt and American Foreign Policy* (New York: Social Science Monographs, 1981), 81–82.

88. "To Clear 'Rumors' Lie Detector Test Offered by Chambers," *Washington Post,* January 20, 1950; George Sololsky, "These Days," *New York Times Herald,* July 28, 1949; "Mrs. Roosevelt Not Convinced of Hiss' Guilt," *New York Times Herald,* January 29, 1950; "Chambers Invites Lie Test on Motives in Accusing Hiss," *Washington Star,* January 29, 1950; and untitled clipping, *Washington Times Herald,* January 28, 1950, FBI files, FOIPA request.

For a concise appraisal of the evidence presented against Hiss and summary of the conservative and liberal reaction to it, see Earl Latham, *The Communist Controversy in Washington: From the New Deal to McCarthy* (Cambridge: Harvard University Press, 1966), 184–196. See also Athan Theoharis, "Unanswered Questions: Chambers, Nixon, the FBI, and the Hiss Case," in Theoharis, *Beyond the Hiss Case,* 270–283.

89. Adlai Stevenson's response to Hiss's conviction is typical of the pains liberal politicians took to distance themselves from their earlier endorsement. When Hiss was

initially indicted for perjury, Stevenson gave a deposition attesting to Hiss's good character. He rebuked those who criticized this action by declaring, "it seems to me that it will be a very sad day for Anglo-Saxon justice when any man, and especially a lawyer, will refuse to give honest evidence in a criminal trial for fear the defendant in an action may eventually be found guilty." However, once that defendant was found guilty, Stevenson's tone changed dramatically. While he defended his deposition as part of his civic duty, he still strove to distance himself from Hiss by saying that he and Hiss were not close friends, that they had a brief friendship, and that "he had never entered my house and I never entered his." When this still did not satisfy his critics, Stevenson proclaimed that he "never doubted the verdict of a jury." Norbert Muhlen, "The Hysteria of the Hisslings," *The New Leader*, May 13, 1950; Allen Weinstein, *Perjury: The Hiss-Chambers Case* (New York: Alfred A. Knopf, 1978), 511–512; Gillon, 84; Roosevelt, "My Day," January 25, 1959; "Enough is Enough," *Washington Post*, January 29, 1950.

90. ER also worried that the media frenzy surrounding the trial could pressure the juries to discount what ER saw as flimsy evidence. As she wrote a conservative Buffalo journalist, "even juries have been known to be wrong when the evidence has been largely circumstantial."

Eleanor Roosevelt to Burt Drummond, October 27, 1953 and his reply, November 2, 1953, General Correspondence, AER papers; and Burt Drummond, "Everybody's Column," *Buffalo Evening News*, October 1, 1953.

91. Interview with Elizabeth Matheson, February 25, 1995.

92. Eleanor Roosevelt to Burt Drummond, October 27, 1953 and his reply, November 2, 1953, General Correspondence, AER papers; and Burt Drummond, "Everybody's Column," *Buffalo Evening News*, October 1, 1953.

93. Ibid.

94. Eleanor Roosevelt to Arthur C. Grafflin, December 3, 1953, General Correspondence, AER papers.

95. Deftly, Nixon positioned himself as the only leader capable of correcting Truman's mistakes. As he announced to the press the day Hiss was found guilty, "I believe the President will have further reason to regret his . . . remark." By the end of the week he delivered a ninety-minute address to the House extolling his role in unravelling the Hiss conspiracy and indicting those who failed to challenge Hiss as "disloyal." Declaring that "this Nation cannot afford another Hiss case," he demanded a complete "overhaul [of] our system of checking the loyalty of Federal employees" and "wholehearted support" for HUAC. To make sure that the media gave his address proper attention, Nixon sent copies of it to editors of all the nation's major papers.

Nixon statement to *the New York Times* is quoted in Ambrose, *Nixon*, 206. *Congressional Record, House*, 96, Pt. 1 (January 26, 1950): 999–1007. For an extensive account of Nixon's use of Hiss as the groundwork for his 1950 Senate campaign, see Ambrose, *Nixon*, 196–209.

96. Ambrose, *Nixon*, 215–217; Helen Gahagan Douglas, *A Full Life* (Garden City: Doubleday, 1982), 268–282 and 306–309; Nixon, *Memoirs*, 74–77.

97. Douglas, 310–313; Ambrose, ibid.; and David Oshinsky, *A Conspiracy So Immense: The World of Joe McCarthy* (New York: Free Press, 1983), 177.

98. Douglas, 89–143; Helen Gahagan Douglas interviewed by Emily Williams,

January 22, 1979, EROHP, AER papers; Helen Gahagan Douglas to Lorena Hickok, [n.d.] [probably December 1950, January 1951], Lorena Hickok papers.

99. Ambrose, *Nixon*, 216; and Bela Kornitzer, *The Real Nixon: An Intimate Biography* (Chicago: Rand McNally, 1960), 187.

100. When Douglas sent ER a copy of the Votes for Nixon flyer which airplanes had dropped over major California cities and which implied that a vote for Nixon might be worth a Proctor Silex appliance, ER was indignant and urged Lorena Hickok to go to California to determine if charges of voter fraud could be filed against him.

Nixon steadfastly denies these charges. In his memoirs, after rebuking Douglas for not publicly congratulating him on his victory, he describes his election as follows:

"The 1950 campaign became highly controversial because of the 'rocking, socking' way in which I was said to have waged and won it. Mrs. Douglas and many of her friends and supporters claimed that I had impugned her loyalty and smeared her character, thus depriving the voters of the opportunity to make an honest choice.

"Anyone who takes the trouble to go back through newspapers and other sources of the period, however, will find that things happened as I have described them here.

"Helen Gahagan Douglas waged a campaign that would not be equaled for stridency, ineptness, or self-righteousness until George McGovern's presidential campaign twenty-two years later. In the long run, however, even this probably made little difference. Helen Douglas lost the election because the voters of California in 1950 were not prepared to elect as their senator anyone with a left-wing voting record or anyone they perceived as being soft on or naive about communism. She may have been at some political disadvantage because she was a woman. But her fatal disadvantage lay in her record and her views." Nixon, *Memoirs*, 77. Nixon mentions ER only once in this record and it is only a passing reference made by a friend who describes seeing ER abroad. Yet the aforementioned inference to Douglas's "friends" is an unmistakable reference to her.

101. "Statement for Stevenson," September 21, 1952, ER-Stevenson file, General Correspondence, AER papers.

102. Dorothy Kenyon, a former New York City municipal judge who had received an honorary appointment to the United Nations Commission on the Status of Women from 1947 to 1949, was the first State Department official McCarthy labeled a "security risk." Her testimony to counter these allegations was so strong that the press turned against McCarthy, with *Life* assessing her testimony as "convincing" and *The Washington Post* publishing a cartoon on the editorial page, which depicted the senator hiding in the cloakroom while the judge testified. Kenyon did have a considerable track record of joining organizations that had communists in their ranks, but when they began to struggle to control the agenda her record of opposing the groups was just as strong as her initial endorsements. McCarthy emphasized her membership while never discussing her resignations. Oshinsky, *Conspiracy So Immense*, 120–122; and Richard Rovere, *Senator Joe McCarthy* (New York: Harper, 1959), 147; Roosevelt, "My Day," March 11, 1950, My Day Drafts, AER papers; and Berger, *New Deal for the World*, 80–84.

103. ER did lend support to Kenyon outside of her column. She agreed to co-sponsor a "Hear the People v. McCarthy" rally, at which Dorothy Kenyon was the special honored guest, at Hunter College later that month. McCarthy refused to let the Kenyon allegations drop, even after attacks against him increased. In fact, he escalated the alle-

gations, declaring to the *Chicago Tribune* in June 1954 that she was in fact a communist and that ER had befriended her while both worked with the State Department. "Hear the People v. McCarthy" flyer, May 20, 1954, FOIPA request, FBI papers; *Chicago Tribune*, June 28, 1954; Roosevelt, "My Day," August 15, 1954; "Faces in the News," *Life* March 27, 1950, 34; and *The Washington Post*, March 13, 1950; and Roosevelt, "My Day," March 11, 1950, My Day Drafts, AER papers.

104. ER was so angered by Jenner's attack on Marshall that she devoted most of her September 18, 1950 column to his lack of professional ethics. By refusing to hold their colleague accountable for this abuse of power, the Senate acquiesced to "the type of intemperate and scandalous character-smearing which is occasionally attempted by irresponsible and, usually, little-known representatives in the legislative branches of our government." Roosevelt, "My Day," September 18, 1950, My Day Drafts, AER papers; Berger, *New Deal for the World*, 82; and *New York Times*, September 16, 1950.

105. In 1947, ER defended the ADA position of anti-communist liberalism while she also admitted that the policy saddened her.

"I would like to see all progressive groups work together. But since some of us prefer to have our staffs and policy-making groups free of any American Communist infiltration, while others have not quite as strong a feeling on this subject, it is natural that there should be two set-ups. That does not mean that the force of all liberals may not go to some of the same objectives, and I certainly hope this will be the case.

"While in our democracy, I feel that Americans who believe in democracy should lead. While other beliefs must exist and I would fight for the rights of others to their beliefs, I must work with those who hold to the fundamental beliefs which I consider sound and true." "Mrs. FDR Speaks," *New Republic* 116 (February 3, 1947): 8.

106. Roosevelt, "Address to Americans for Democratic Action," April 2, 1950, Speech and Article File, AER papers.

Lash argued that this speech indicated how committed ER was to the ADA record of anti-communist liberalism. Following his lead, most ER historians concur that this is intended to reinforce ADA policy rather than to admonish them for not practicing what they preach. Clearly when this speech is examined in the whole context of ER's philosophy of pragmatic politics and democratic ideals, she is rebuking the organization that she helped found for not sufficiently supporting the rights of free speech and political association. Once again, these words place her outside the vital center.

107. Roosevelt, "My Day," April 14, 15; May 26, 28, 29 1952; "If You Ask Me," July 1953, September and November 1954; and Berger, *New Deal for the World*, 87.

108. Berger, *New Deal for the World*, 83 and 88; and Roosevelt, "My Day," October 11, 1951, My Day Drafts.

109. Rovere, 139.

110. Roosevelt, "My Day," February 8, 1951, My Day Drafts, AER papers.

ER was a vehement opponent of literary censorship. From the publication of *Ulysses* to the banning of *The Nation*, she continually argued that the public had a right to read whatever they wanted to read and that banning a publication only heightened public awareness of its contents. Roosevelt, "If You Ask Me," September 1954.

111. "Mrs. Roosevelt Says McCarthy is Menace," *New York Times*, September 21, 1951; "Mrs. Roosevelt Calls McCarthy a Menace," *New York Herald Tribune*, September 21,

1951; and Roosevelt, "Address to the Democratic National Convention," Speech and Article File, AER papers.

112. Roosevelt, "My Day," August 29, 1952, My Day Drafts, AER papers. For hundreds of letters ER received on this issue and how she responded see My Day Correspondence: McCarthy file, My Day Drafts, AER papers.

113. Roosevelt, "If You Ask Me," *McCall's*, June 1953.

114. Buckley, *Up From Liberalism*, 42–43 and James Burnham, book review of *India and the Awakening East*, cited in Buckley, ibid. and Burnham, *Suicide of the West* (New York: John Day, 1964).

115. Joe Rauh interview, EROHP; *New York Post*, May 25, 1953; Berger, *New Deal for the World*, 104; Allen Drury, "ADA Blasts McCarthy Again; G.O.P. Chairman Defends Him," *Washington Star*, May 25, 1953; Arthur Schlesinger, interviewed by author, June 23, 1994.

116. Stevenson supported the Truman loyalty program, praised the Smith Act prosecutions, and agreed that communist faculty should be fired. All three were stances in direct opposition to ER's positions. See John Bartlow Martin, *Adlai Stevenson: Man from Illinois*, 744; Rovere, *Senator Joe McCarthy*, 7, 12–17; Thomas Reeves, editor, *McCarthyism* (Malabar, Florida: Robert E. Krieger Publishing, 1989).

117. The Senate passed the legislation unanimously. Eleanor Roosevelt to James Doyle, September 4, 1954, Americans for Democratic Action papers, Historical Society of Wisconsin. See also, Parmet, *The Democrats*, 104.

■ 6. CHALLENGING THE PARTY

1. Robert Benjamin, interviewed by Thomas Soapes, December 13, 1977, EROHP; Roosevelt, *On My Own*, 163–164; Oshinsky, *Conspiracy So Immense*, 490–491; Elliott Roosevelt, *Mother R*, 233–234; and Lash, *World of Love*, 519. For an extensive account of JFK's anti-communist activism on the House Education and Labor Committee see Herbert S. Parmet, *JFK: The Struggles of John F. Kennedy* (New York: The Dial Press, 1983), 175–84.

2. Eleanor Roosevelt to Trude Lash, July 18, 1952, and Eleanor Roosevelt to John Roosevelt, July 9, 1953, AER papers.

3. Roosevelt, *Tomorrow is Now*, xvi.

4. Eleanor Roosevelt to Mary Lasker, August 15, 1960, Personal Correspondence, AER papers; and Roosevelt, *The Autobiography of Eleanor Roosevelt*, 436.

5. Eleanor Roosevelt to Mary Lasker, ibid.; and Henry Morgenthau III interview, EROHP.

6. For example see, Arthur M. Schlesinger, Jr., *A Thousand Days* (Boston: Houghton Mifflin Company, 1965) and *Robert Kennedy and His Times* (Boston: Houghton Mifflin, 1978); Parmet, *JFK*; Theodore Sorensen, *Kennedy* (New York: Harper and Row, 1965); Theodore White, *The Making of the President 1960* (New York: Atheneum, 1961); and Benjamin Bradlee, *Conversations with Kennedy* (New York: Norton, 1975).

7. For those Kennedy biographers who argue that ER overcame her opposition to become a champion of his policies see: Schlesinger, *A Thousand Days*; Bradlee; Sorensen, *Kennedy*; White; and Parmet. For those ER historians who argue that the relationship became one of mutual respect and friendship, see Lash, *Eleanor: The Years Alone*;

Lawrence Fuchs, "The Senator and the Lady," *American Heritage*, 25 no. 6 (October 1974): 57–61, 81–83; Cooke, "The Political Career of Anna Eleanor Roosevelt," and Hareven. See also the memoirs of ER's sons, James Roosevelt, *My Parents: A Differing View*, and Elliott Roosevelt, *Mother R*.

8. In July 1949 ER, who opposed legislation that would give federal aid to Catholic schools, editorialized against the proposal in her column. Cardinal Francis Spellman, who disagreed with almost all of ER's other social policies, launched a broadside attack on her, suggesting that the priests in his diocese question her character in their sermons. His strategy backfired when an outraged public supported ER. An embarrassed Vatican ordered the cardinal to apologize for his conduct and a very chagrined Spellman drove to Val-Kill to do so. Later both ER and Spellman tried to defuse the public outcry by releasing their correspondence to the press. For a detailed discussion of this power play see Philip A. Grant, "Catholic Congressmen, Cardinal Spellman, Eleanor Roosevelt and the 1949–1950 Federal Aid to Education Controversy," *Records of the American Catholic Historical Society of Philadelphia* 90 (December 1979): 3–13 and Spellman Controversy file, AER papers. Most historians who focus on John Kennedy rather than ER believe that her suspicion of Catholics was the real reason she disliked JFK. Joseph Lash also argued that JFK's Catholicism was a major factor. "Somewhere deep in her subconscious was an anti-Catholicism which was a part of her Protestant heritage." Although she had unreservedly supported Al Smith in the 1920s as governor and as presidential candidate, "her fear of the church as a temporal institution was reawakened from time to time by its political operations. The clash with Cardinal Spellman had left its scars." Lash, *Eleanor: The Years Alone*, 282.

However, oral histories of those who knew ER and to whom she confided her true feelings about the young senator just as adamantly suggest different motivations. See Fuchs and also the following interviews in the Eleanor Roosevelt Oral History Project to substantiate this claim: Robert Benjamin, Estelle Linzer, James Roosevelt, Henry M. Morgenthau III, Mary Lasker, and Abba Schwartz. See also, Michael Beschloss, *Kennedy and Roosevelt* (New York: Norton, 1980), 229.

9. Although he attacked the electrical workers first, the issue that generated the most press for JFK was his attack on the leaders of Local 248 of the United Auto Workers Union in the Allis-Chalmers manufacturing controversy. Furthermore, Kennedy disliked Helen Gahagan Douglas and supported Richard Nixon in the infamous 1950 California Senate race. Although the record is unclear as to whether or not ER knew the extent of JFK's involvement, Hollywood celebrities played a major role in Douglas's campaign, and with Joe Kennedy's Hollywood connections silent on Douglas's behalf, ER probably knew that his relationship with Douglas was not smooth.

Parmet, *JFK*, 175–178; U.S., Congress, House, *Hearings Before the Committee on Education and Labor*, 80th Cong., 1st session, 1947, 1: 3577; and Nixon, *Memoirs*, 44–45.

10. Roosevelt, *On My Own*, 163–164; and Victor Lasky, *J.F.K.: The Man and the Myth* (New Rochelle: Arlington House, 1963), 238–239.

11. Lasky, ibid., and Eleanor Roosevelt, "Of Stevenson, Truman, and Kennedy," *Saturday Evening Post*, 230, March 8, 1958, 72–73.

12. James Roosevelt and Franklin D. Roosevelt, Jr., were active Kennedy supporters in 1956. Elliott Roosevelt, *Mother R*, 234; Elliott Roosevelt and James Roosevelt interviews, EROHP, FDR Library; Lazarowitz, "Years in Exhile," 361–364; and Lasky, 240.

13. ER refused to become a regular member of the group because United Features Syndicate told her that to do so would make her columns serve as "a mouthpiece for the committee." Furthermore, she had, as she told Paul Butler, "already lost a number of column customers due to political activities" and she worried that she would "lose a certain amount of influence" if the public perceived her as speaking for the group rather than herself. Eleanor Roosevelt to Paul Butler, December 6, 1956; Eleanor Roosevelt to Doris Fleeson, December 6, 1956; and Roosevelt, "If You Ask Me," March 1957, AER papers.

14. Instead, in addition to Stevenson and Humphrey, she praised Wayne Morse, G. Mennen Williams, Joseph Clark, Edmund Muskie, and Chester Bowles. Later, she dejectedly admitted that Hubert Humphrey was the only young senator in her mind who showed "the spark of greatness" necessary to be president. Transcript, "Meet the Press," September 9, 1956, Speech and Article File, AER papers; ER to Lyndon Johnson August 17, 1957, AER papers; "Mrs. Roosevelt Lauds Humphrey," *New York Times*, December 8, 1958, 8; and "Humphrey Favored as '60 Candidate," *Washington Star*, December 8, 1958.

15. Roosevelt, "On Truman, Kennedy and Stevenson," 74; and Roosevelt, *The Autobiography of Eleanor Roosevelt*, 357–358.

16. Undeterred, she continued to air her assessments in public, responding to allegations against her made by Kennedy supporters in a sardonic footnote to her discussion of her 1956 meeting with Kennedy in *On My Own*:

" . . . I began to be visited by a number of people who told me that the Senator felt I had misquoted him or incorrectly understood his position. I certainly had not intended to misquote him and I usually understand people and at least am able to gather what they mean, but in this case I may well have misunderstood the Senator. He has recently said that he had made statements upholding the code of the Senate but this is not exactly what I think is called for. I believe that a public servant must clearly indicate that he understands the harm that McCarthyism did to our country and that he opposes it actively, so that one would feel sure he would always do so in the future."

Transcript, Mike Wallace, "The Mike Wallace Interview, Guest: Eleanor Roosevelt," November 23, 1957, Speech and Article File, AER papers; Roosevelt, "On Truman, Stevenson and Kennedy"; Roosevelt, *On My Own*, 164; Transcript, "College New Conference," December 7, 1958, Speech and Interview Tape File, AER papers.

17. Eleanor Roosevelt to Agnes Meyer, June 6, 1960, General Correspondence, AER papers; Eleanor Roosevelt to Joseph Lash, June 6, 1960, JPL papers.

As Bruce Miroff thoroughly demonstrates, Kennedy's civil rights record was a true profile in avoidance. While he refused to endorse the Southern Manifesto, he defended the rationale the senators used in drafting the document. While he supported the Civil Rights Act of 1957, he also voted in favor of the amendment that would order that violators be tried before juries. This basically stripped the law of its most powerful enforcement tool. While the easiest interpretation of his actions on civil rights is to say that he diligently strove to avoid alienating major voting blocks, that is only a peripheral analysis. Kennedy "lacked understanding of the urgency of the struggle, and of the great passion it brought forth." Bruce Miroff, *Pragmatic Illusions: The Presidency of John F. Kennedy* (New York: McKay, 1976), 223–270. For a contrasting view see Carl M. Brauer, *John F. Kennedy and The Second Reconstruction* (New York: Columbia University Press, 1977).

6. Challenging the Party

As she commented to the press during the 1960 convention, ER also doubted Kennedy's ability to hold the black vote he needed to offset the anti-Catholic sentiment she expected to undermine the party's traditional southern support. See N. R. Howard, untitled clipping, *The Cleveland Plain Dealer*, July 13, 1960, Clipping file, AER papers.

18. Roosevelt, "What are we for?" in *The Search for America*, ed. Huston Smith (New York: Spectrum Books, 1959), 3–12; Roosevelt, *The Autobiography of Eleanor Roosevelt*, 410–418; "Mrs. Roosevelt Hits Leadership," *The Evening Star*, October 1957, A-15; Roosevelt, *Tomorrow is Now*, 8–19; and Roosevelt, "My Day," October 23, 1959, April 11, June 8, and November 2, 1960, My Day Drafts, AER papers.

19. Leo Egan, "Democrats Fear Split on Liberals," *New York Times*, December 9, 1959; Eleanor Roosevelt correspondence, Democratic Advisory Committee, Topical File, AER papers; Eleanor Roosevelt to John F. Kennedy, August 27, 1960 and July 22, 1961, AER papers.

20. Lash, *A World of Love*, 511.

21. Leo Egan, "Mrs. Roosevelt Disputes Truman on Liberals' Role," *New York Times*, December 8, 1959, A1.

22. Ibid. This was not the only time Eleanor Roosevelt challenged Democratic officials and liberal leaders to redefine their goals and to propose inventive, rather than reactive, solutions to problems facing the nation. The exchange with Truman was unique not because ER differed with leading Democrats but because it was the most public challenge she issued to liberal and Democratic party leadership. Only three months before the DAC gathering, she joined with Massachusetts Institute of Technology philosopher Huston Smith to insist in the introduction to *The Search for America*, an anthology of essays by such noted American liberals as Paul Tillich, Reinhold Niebuhr, Margaret Mead, Benjamin Mays, and Harry Ashmore, that American progress was impeded because the nation no longer understood its purpose.

In the introduction to this volume, ER boldly challenged her readers to recognize that "our security is in jeopardy" because "our principles are on the defensive." Moreover, she resolutely believed that unless the nation regained its vision of its rightful place in the world, it would buckle under the tremendous strain of raging civil rights conflicts, labor-management disputes, and North-South rivalries placed on the national character. Now more than ever, America must understand that refusing to deal with these problems only plays into the hands of our rivals and undermines the practice of democracy at home and its symbolic value abroad. "What remains lacking," she concluded, "is a leader with imagination great enough to see the convergence of our national interest with world welfare defined in terms of peace, autonomy, prosperity, and democracy, and who possesses the leadership ability to translate his vision into concrete policies that will carry the support of the people."

23. Roosevelt, "Of Truman, Stevenson and Kennedy"; Roosevelt, "My Day," January 6, 1959, My Day Drafts, AER papers; John Kennedy to Eleanor Roosevelt, December 11, 1958 and her reply, December 18, 1958; John Kennedy to Eleanor Roosevelt, December 29, 1958, and her reply, January 6, 1959; John Kennedy to Eleanor Roosevelt, January 10, 1959 and her reply, January 20, 1959; John Kennedy to Eleanor Roosevelt, January 22, 1959, Miscellaneous Correspondence, AER papers.

24. Lasky, 243; Roosevelt, "Statement by Mrs. Franklin D. Roosevelt of Behalf of the

National Consumers League before the Subcommittee on Labor of the Committee on Labor and Public Welfare, May 11, 1959," Speech and Article file, AER papers; Joe McCarthy, *The Remarkable Kennedys* (New York: The Dial Press, 1961), 171–172; and *Washington Star*, May 12, 1959.

25. "The Reminiscence of Mary Lasker," 1966, OHRO.

26. Henry Morgenthau III, interviewed by Emily Williams, August 30, 1978, EROHP, FDR Library.

27. Kennedy did the show and after dining with Morgenthau and Arthur Schlesinger, returned to Washington to film "Meet the Press." Henry Morgenthau III interview, EROHP; and "Kennedy Says He'd Like Aid of Mrs. Roosevelt," *Washington Star*, January 3, 1960.

28. Michael Prendergast chaired the New York State Democratic Committee and personified the type of old-line boss rule that ER believed corrupted the Democratic party, controlled the party's slate and sabotaged reform. Prendergast reciprocated the dislike, arguing that ER represented the kind of mushy-headed liberal who would undermine party unity and divide the constituency. Indeed Prendergast disliked ER so strongly that he refused to allow her to attend the 1960 national convention as a super-delegate.

Roosevelt, *The Autobiography of Eleanor Roosevelt*, 421–427; Lash, Diary, February 21, April 12, and April 23, 1960, JPL papers.

29. Although ER avoided Stevenson earlier in 1959 when he wanted her advice about seeking the nomination, arguing that a candidate who had to be coaxed to run didn't deserve the nomination, a year later she had changed her mind. Two events that occurred before the Democratic convention and pushed ER to actively urge Stevenson to run again were the U-2 incident and the collapse of the Soviet-American summit.

Adlai Stevenson to Lady Barbara Jackson, June 21, 1960, Adlai E. Stevenson Papers, Princeton University; Eleanor Roosevelt, Statement to the Press, June 12, 1960, Speech and Article File, AER papers; and Agnes Meyer to Eleanor Roosevelt, August 19, 1958, Eleanor Roosevelt folder, Box 26, Agnes E. Meyer Papers, Library of Congress; Lash, *A World of Love*, 513; and Eleanor Roosevelt to Jim Halstead, February 1960, AER papers.

30. Agnes E. Meyer to Walter Reuther, May 21 and May 17, 1960, Walter Reuther file, AEM papers; Eleanor Roosevelt to Joe Lash, June 15, 1960, JPL papers; Agnes Meyer to Walter Reuther, May 12, 1960, Reuther folder, AEM papers; and Mary Lasker interview, EROHP.

31. Martin, *Adlai Stevenson and the World*, 491–493; Porter McKeever, *Adlai Stevenson* (New York: William Morrow, 1989), 448–450; White, *The Making of the President 1960*, 139–142; Robert Benjamin, interview by Thomas Soapes, December 13, 1977, EROHP, FDR Library; ER to Joe Lash, June 15, 1960, JPL papers; Agnes Meyer to Walter Reuther, February 23, 1960 and May 12 and 17, 1960, Reuther folder, AEM papers; Stevenson to Agnes Meyer, March 10, 1960, reprinted in *The Papers of Adlai Stevenson*, 5: 430–432.

32. Agnes Meyer to Eleanor Roosevelt, August 19, 1958, AEM papers; William Atwood interview, EROHP, FDR Library; Adlai Stevenson to ER, January 10, 1960, AES papers; Cooke, "Political Career," 256–258; and small collection entitled "Stevenson for President Draft Movement, 1960," Manuscript Room, Syracuse University.

33. Lash, *A World of Love*, 513.

34. White, ibid., 3.

35. "Stevenson: Not A Candidate; Mrs. R., Yes He Is," *New York Times*, June 12, 1960; and Eleanor Roosevelt to Anna Boettinger, July 17, 1960, Anna Boettinger papers, FDR Library.

36. *New York Post*, editorial, June 29, 1960; *New York Times*, Anthony Lewis editorial, July 9, 1960; Transcript, "Face the Nation," July 10, 1960, Speech and Article File, AER papers; Newton Minow interview by John B. Martin, used in Martin, *Adlai Stevenson and the World*, 522–535; Schlesinger, *A Thousand Days*, 37.

37. "Text of Letter to Liberals on Kennedy," and "Stevenson Group Backing Kennedy," *New York Times*, June 17, 1960.

ER thought this display of disloyalty "unconscionable" and had not kept her opinion a secret. All five men understood the extent of her displeasure. For example, see John Kenneth Galbraith, marginalia, John Kenneth Galbraith, "March of the Kennedy Men," *The Observer*, August 21, 1960, 10, attached to J.K.G. to James Rowe, Personal Correspondence File, 1060, James H. Rowe papers, FDR Library; Joseph Rauh Interview, EROHP; and Roosevelt, *The Autobiography of Eleanor Roosevelt*, 422.

38. Roosevelt, "My Day," July 10, 1960; *New York Post*, July 29, 1960; Eleanor Roosevelt: June 13, 1960, reprinted in *Congressional Record*, June 16, 1960, A5118–A5119; Roosevelt, "My Day," July 14, 1960; May Craig, "Mrs. Roosevelt Got Right to the Point," *Portland Press Herald*, June 22, 1960; Eugene Patterson, "Kennedy Power is Cracking, Foes say in Last Minute Push," *Atlanta Constitution*, July 14, 1960; and Lawrence E. Davies, "Mrs. Roosevelt Notes Issue of Religion," *New York Times*, July 12, 1960.

39. McKeever, *Adlai Stevenson*, 455–459; "Stevenson Wins Double Triumph," *New York Times*, July 13, 1960; Lash, *Eleanor: The Years Alone*, 293; interview with Arthur Schlesinger, June 23, 1994; John Bartlow Martin, *The Papers of Adlai Stevenson*, 5: 535–538; and Martin, *Adlai Stevenson and the World*, 525.

40. Roosevelt, *The Autobiography of Eleanor Roosevelt*, 421–427; McKeever, *Adlai Stevenson*, 457–461; Eleanor Roosevelt to Joseph and Trude Lash, June 19, 1960; Lash, *World of Love*, 523; White, *Making of the President 1960*, 186; and the following EROHP interviews: Morgenthau, Lasker, Benjamin, Linzer, and James Roosevelt.

41. Roosevelt, *The Autobiography of Eleanor Roosevelt*, 427; Lash, *Eleanor: The Years Alone*, 295; David E. Lilienthal, *The Journals of David Lilienthal*, (New York: Harper and Row, 1971), 5: 103; Roosevelt, "My Day," July 20, 1960, My Day Drafts, AER papers.

42. Roosevelt, *The Autobiography of Eleanor Roosevelt*, ibid.; *Official Proceedings of the Democratic National Convention, 1960* (Washington: National Document Publishers, 1964), 60–63; and Cooke, "Political Career," 269.

43. Joseph P. Lash, Diary, July 17, 1960, JPL papers.

ER worried that Nixon would win the election regardless of who his Democratic rival was, but she thought that a Stevenson-Kennedy ticket would increase the party's chance for victory. Trude Lash to Joseph Lash, June 2, 1960, JPL papers; *New York Times*, July 9, 1960; and Eleanor Roosevelt to Joseph Lash, June 7, 1960, ER papers.

44. Schlesinger Journal entry May 22, 1960 quoted in McKeever, *Adlai Stevenson*, 496; Bradlee, 31; Lasky, 457; James Rowe interview, EROHP.

45. "Mrs. Roosevelt's View: She'll Back Democratic Ticket Despite Misgivings," *New York Times*, July 24, 1960; Schlesinger, *A Thousand Days*, 9–19; Victor Lasky, *JFK:*

The Man and the Myth, 242–244; Sorensen, *Kennedy,* 154–156; and McKeever, *Adlai Stevenson,* 449.

46. See the following interviews in the EROHP: Mrs. H. (Tiny) Martin, Robert Benjamin, Henry Morgenthau, and Abba Schwartz. See also; Lash, *Eleanor: The Years Alone,* 296–297; Fuchs, 81; and Lasky, 415–416.

47. Agnes Meyer to Walter Reuther, May 12, 1960, Reuther folder, AEM papers; Fuchs, ibid., Lash, *World of Love,* 525; Morgenthau, Schwartz, Lasker, and Meyer interviews, EROHP; and Abba Schwartz, "Confidential Memorandum of Conversation with Mrs. FDR in New York, November 18, 1960," Matters re Eleanor Roosevelt, 1960, Abba Schwartz, Small Collections, FDR Library.

48. William Walton, *Conversation with Kennedy,* ed. John K. Jessup (New York: privately printed ,1965), 88.

49. Fuchs, 82; Eleanor Roosevelt to Adlai Stevenson, August 10, 1960, General Correspondence, AER papers; Herbert Lehman interview [excerpts], information on date and interviewer not available, Columbia Oral History Project, Small Collections, FDR Library; Hyman Bookbinder, interviewed by Thomas A. Soapes, EROHP.

50. Walton, *Conversation with Kennedy.*

51. Fuchs, "The Senator and the Lady"; Lash, *Eleanor: The Years Alone;* Lash, *ER: A Friend's Memoir;* Schlesinger, *A Thousand Days;* Schlesinger, *Robert Kennedy and His Times;* and Sorensen, *Kennedy.*

52. If Kennedy was not sufficiently aware of the seriousness with which ER approached this meeting, when she refused to cancel the meeting after her favorite granddaughter died suddenly the day before, he certainly must have recognized the grave importance she placed on their talk.

53. Martin, *Adlai Stevenson and the World,* 535.

54. Lasky, *JFK,* 415–416; William Walton, *Conversation with Kennedy,* 88.

55. Eleanor Roosevelt to Mary Lasker, August 15, 1960 and Eleanor Roosevelt to Agnes Meyer, August 15, 1960; Fuchs, ibid.; McKeever, *Adlai Stevenson,* ibid., and Lasker interview, EROHP.

56. Other historians have quoted ER's final assessment of JFK differently because they have referred to the typed draft of ER's letter to Lasker. I have instead quoted the letter to include the notations ER made in the margin after she reviewed the draft. Mary Lasker et al., August 15, 1960, Lasker folder, General Correspondence, AER papers; Eleanor Roosevelt to Agnes Meyer, August 15, 1960, Agnes Meyer papers; and Lasky, *JFK,* ibid.

57. Eleanor Roosevelt to Dear Friends, n.d., Democratic National Convention 1960 folder, Group IIIA, NAACP papers; Abba Schwartz to Raymond Cory, Material Relating to ER, 1960, Abba Schwartz papers, Small Collections, FDR Library; "My Day," November 2, 1960, My Day Drafts, AER papers; and Schlesinger, *A Thousand Days,* 76.

58. Whether her animosity toward Joe Kennedy, her disappointment that Stevenson was not asked to join the Cabinet, or her desire to let the president have all the limelight was the reason for her decision is difficult to determine. Lash, *Eleanor: The Years Alone,* 300. See also Abba Schwartz, "Memorandum of Conversation with Mrs. F.D.R. in New York, November 23, 1960, Special Collections, AER papers.

59. Eleanor Roosevelt to Adlai Stevenson, April 19, 1961; Eleanor Roosevelt to John Kennedy, February 19, March 14, April 10, July 22, and November 2, 1961; John Kennedy to Eleanor Roosevelt, April 28, July 28, and November 21, 1961, Eleanor Roosevelt-John Kennedy Correspondence, AER papers. [Scholars who wish to pursue this correspondence should note that the JFK Library has a more complete collection of the ER-JFK correspondence than does the FDR Library.] Roosevelt, "My Day," May 29, 1962, My Day Drafts, AER papers; Cook, "Eleanor Roosevelt and Human Rights," 113–117; and Lash, *Eleanor: The Years Alone*, 317–320.

60. Pauli Murray and Justine Wise Polier interviews, EROHP; Murray, *Song in a Weary Throat*, 347; Lois Sharf, "ER and Feminism," in Hoff-Wilson and Lightman, *Without Precedent*, 248–252; "List of Women Eligible for Appointment," Commission on the Status of Women files, AER papers; *New York Times*, May 8, 1961; and Commission on the Status of Women to Eleanor Roosevelt, October 29, 1962.

By early 1962 she started sending checks for her usual charitable and personal contributions six months early.

61. Roosevelt, "My Day," May 29, 1962, My Day Drafts, AER papers; Eleanor Roosevelt to John Kennedy, September 10, 1961, Roosevelt-Kennedy folder, AER papers; Martin Luther King, Jr., to Eleanor Roosevelt, February 15, 1961 and March 24, 1961; and, Robert Kennedy to Eleanor Roosevelt, December 19, 1961, AER papers; Schlesinger, *Robert Kennedy and His Times*; Benjamin, Murray, and Rauh interviews, EROHP.

62. See discussion in chapter 4 on the Committee of Inquiry into the Scope of Justice in the Freedom Struggle for a thorough description of these actions.

63. Eleanor Roosevelt to Martin Luther King, Jr., March 31, 1962, AER papers. King could not attend because of scheduling reasons.

64. Roosevelt, *Tomorrow Is Now*, 120–121.

65. Lash, *Eleanor: The Years Alone*, 323; Maureen Corr and Anna Roosevelt interviews, EROHP.

66. Lash, Diary, September 20, 1962; and Elinore Denniston, "A Recollection," in Roosevelt, *Tomorrow Is Now*, x.

67. Lash, *Eleanor: The Years Alone*, 327; Lash, Diary, November 5–9, 1960; Eleanor Roosevelt to Lorena Hickok, September 14, 1962; and Lash, *World of Love*, 559–575.

68. Lash, Diary, September 20, 1962, JPL papers; and Denniston, ibid.

69. Eleanor Roosevelt to Martin Luther King, Jr., September 21, 1962, Martin Luther King, Jr. Papers, Stanford University.

70. A. David Gurewitsch to Joseph P. Lash, December 15, 1962, JPL papers; Jim Halstead to James Roosevelt, March 25, 1966, JPL and James Roosevelt papers; Lash, Diary, September 20, 1962; Lash, *Eleanor: The Years Alone*, 330; and James Halstead and Anna Roosevelt interviews, EROHP.

71. Asbell, *Mother and Daughter*, 354–355.

■ CONCLUSION

1. R. W. Apple, Jr., "For Clinton and Nixon, A Rarefied Bond," *The New York Times*, April 25, 1994, A1.

2. Leuchtenburg, *In the Shadow of FDR*, 239–240.

3. Martin Luther King, Jr., "Epitaph for a First Lady," MLK Papers.

■

Bibliography

INTERVIEWS:
Dorothy Height, Washington, D.C.
Conrad J. Lynn, Ponoma, New York
Elizabeth Matheson, Hillsborough, North Carolina
Joseph Rauh, Hyde Park, New York
Arthur Schlesinger, Jr., New York

MANUSCRIPT COLLECTIONS:
The Federal Bureau of Investigation:
main file, Anna Eleanor Roosevelt
reference file, Anna Eleanor Roosevelt

Franklin Roosevelt Presidential Library:
Molly Dewson Papers
Democratic National Committee Papers, 1932–1945
Doris Faber Papers
Anna Roosevelt Halstead Papers
Lorena Hickok Papers
Esther Lape Papers
Joseph P. Lash Papers
Eleanor Roosevelt Oral History Project

Bibliography

Eleanor Roosevelt Papers
Franklin D. Roosevelt Papers
Franklin D. Roosevelt Junior Papers
Henry Wallace Papers

Harry S. Truman Presidential Library:
India Edwards Papers
Thomas K. Finletter Papers
Charles S. Murphy Papers
Harry S. Truman Papers

John F. Kennedy Presidential Library:
Democratic National Committee Papers, 1945–1963
John F. Kennedy Papers
Robert F. Kennedy Papers

Lyndon B. Johnson Presidential Library:
Lyndon B. Johnson Papers

Manuscript Division, Library of Congress:
Congress on Racial Equality Papers
Democratic Study Group Papers
William O. Douglas Papers
Harold Ickes Papers
Agnes E. Meyer Papers
National Association for the Advancement of Colored People Papers
Joseph Rauh Papers

Martin Luther King, Jr. Center for Nonviolent Social Change:
Martin Luther King, Jr. Papers

Mary McLeod Bethune Archives:
Mary McLeod Bethune Papers
National Council of Negro Women Papers

National Archives:
War Relocation Authority Records

*Oral History Research Office, Columbia University,
The Reminiscences of:*
Anne Braden
Jonathan Daniels
Virginia Durr
Anna Roosevelt Halstead
Harry Hopkins
Gardner Jackson

Herbert Lehman
Thurgood Marshall
Frances Perkins
Eleanor Roosevelt
Bayard Rustin
Henry Wallace
Aubrey Williams

Princeton University:
Adlai E. Stevenson Papers

Southern Historical Collection, University of North Carolina:
Frank Porter Graham Papers
Evans C. Johnson Papers
Allard K. Lowenstein Papers

Southern Oral History Program, University of North Carolina
Interviews with:
Jessie Daniel Ames
Jonathan W. Daniels
Virginia Foster Durr
Alexander Heard
Calvin and Elizabeth Kytle
Hilda Worthington Smith
Olive Mathews Stone
George Stoney
Adolphine Fletcher Terry
Louise Young

Stanford University:
Martin Luther King, Jr., Papers

University of California at Berkeley:
Emma Goldman Papers

University of California at Los Angeles:
Ralph J. Bunche Papers

University of Georgia:
Lillian Smith Papers

Wisconsin State Historical Society:
James Dumbrowski Papers

Yale University:
Walter White Papers

NEWSPAPERS CONSULTED:
Alabama Sun
Albany (Ga.) Herald
Amsterdam News
Atlanta Constituion
Baltimore African-American
Baltimore Evening Sun
Baltimore News Post
Boston Herald
Buffalo Evening News
Chicago Defender
Christian Science Monitor
Cleveland Plain Dealer
Columbus Citizen
Daily Worker
Decatur, Illinois, Herald
Hartford Courant
LA Sentinel
Louisiana Weekly
Memphis Commercial Appeal
Meridian Star
Nashville Tennessean
New Orleans Times Picayune
New Orleans Tribune
New York Evening Post
New York Evening World
New York Herald Tribune
New York Times
New York World Telegram
Portland Press Herald
Selma Times-Jounral
Springfield (Mass.) Evening News
Springfield Union
Washington Post
Washington Star
Washington Times Herald
Wheeling, West Virginia, Register

■ **Primary Source Publications:**

Alsop, Joseph. *FDR: A Centenary Remembrance.* New York: Viking Press, 1982.
Alsop, Joseph and Stewart. "Candidate Truman's Magic Brew," *Saturday Evening Post* (December 31, 1949): 12.
Asbell, Bernard. *Mother and Daughter: The Letters of Anna and Eleanor Roosevelt.* New York: Coward, McCann, and Geoghegan, 1982.

Aull, Ruth and David M. Ogden, Jr. *Official Report of the Proceedings of the Democratic National Convention.* Richmond, Virginia: Beacon Press, 1956.

Bain, Richard C. and Judith H. Parris. *Convention Decisions and Voting Records.* 2nd edition. Washington: Brookings Institution, 1973.

Baldwin, Roger. "Liberals and the Communist Trial," *New Republic* 115 (January 31, 1949) 8.

Bates, Daisy Gatson. *The Long Shadow of Little Rock: A Memoir.* Foreword by Eleanor Roosevelt. New York: David McKay, 1962.

Beasley, Maurine, ed. *The White House Press Conferences of Eleanor Roosevelt.* New York: Garland Press, 1983.

Bell, Daniel. *The End of Ideology.* New York: Free Press, 1962.

Biddle, Francis. *In Brief Authority.* Garden City: Doubleday, 1962.

Black, Ruby. *Eleanor Roosevelt: A Biography.* New York: Duell, Sloan and Pearce, 1940.

Blum, John Morton. *From the Morgenthau Diaries.* Boston: Houghton Mifflin, 1959, 1967.

Bowles, Chester. *The Conscience of a Liberal,* edited by Henry Steele Commanger. New York: Harper and Row, 1962.

Bowles, Chester. *Promises to Keep: My Years in Public Life, 1941–1969.* New York: Harper and Row, 1971.

Bowles, Chester. *Tomorrow Without Fear.* New York: Simon and Schuster, 1946.

Bradlee, Benjamin. *Conversations with Kennedy.* New York: W. W. Norton, 1975.

Braden, Anne. *The Wall Between.* New York: Monthly Review Press, 1958.

Bray, William J. and Venice T. Spraggs, ed. *Official Report of the Proceedings of the Democratic National Convention.* Democratic National Committee, 1952.

Brogan, D.W. "Mrs. Roosevelt as a Political Force," *Spectator* 169 (December 30, 1942), 403.

Bromley, Dorothy Dunbar. "The Future of Eleanor Roosevelt," *Harpers Magazine* 180 (February 1940) 129–139.

Brynes, James A. *All in One Lifetime.* New York: Harper and Row, 1958.

Buckley, William F. *Up from Liberalism.* New York: Stein and Day, 1959, 1984.

Bunche, Ralph. "A Critique of New Deal Social Planning As It Affects Negroes." *Journal of Negro Education* 5 (January 1936), 58–62.

Burnham, James. *Suicide of the West.* New York: John Day, 1964.

Chambers, Whitakker. *Witness.* New York: Random House, 1952.

Clapper, Raymond. "The Ten Most Powerful People in Washington," *Reader's Digest* (May 1941), 48.

Debnam, W.E. *Weep No More, My Lady: A Southerner Answers Mrs. Roosevelt's Report on the "Poor and Unhappy" South.* Raleigh, N.C.: The Graphic Press, 1950.

Dies, Martin. *The Martin Dies Story.* New York: Bookmailer, 1963.

Douglas, Helen Gahagan. *A Full Life.* Garden City: Doubleday, 1982.

Douglas, Paul H. *In the Fullness of Time.* New York: Harcourt Brace Jovanovich, 1972.

Douglas, William O. *The Court Years: The Autobiography of William O. Douglas, 1939–1975.* New York: Random House, 1980.

Douglas, William Orville. *Being an American.* New York: J. Day Company, 1948.

Durr, Virginia Foster. *Outside the Magic Circle: The Autobiography of Virginia Foster Durr.* New York: Simon and Schuster, 1985.

Farley, James. *Behind the Ballots.* New York: Harcourt Brace, 1938.

Bibliography

Farley, James. *The Jim Farley Story.* New York: McGraw-Hill, 1948.

Flynn, Edward Joseph. *You're the Boss: The Practice of American Politics.* Foreword by Eleanor Roosevelt. New York: Collier Books, 1962.

Fowler, Gene. *Minutes of the Last Meeting.* New York: Viking Press, 1954.

Furman, Bess. *Washington By-Line.* New York: Knopf, 1949.

Galbraith, John Kenneth. *A Life in Our Times.* Boston: Houghton Mifflin, 1981.

Gladney, Margaret, editor. *How Am I To Be Heard: The Letters of Lillian Smith.* Chapel Hill: University of North Carolina Press, 1993.

Goldman, Eric F. *Rendezvous with Destiny.* New York: Random House, 1977.

Handlin, Oscar. "Party Maneuvers and Civil Rights Realities." *Commentary* 14 (September 1952), 197–205.

Hepburn, Katharine. *The Making of the African Queen.* New York: New American Library, 1987.

Hickok, Lorena. *Eleanor Roosevelt: Reluctant First Lady.* New York: Dodd Mead, 1962.

Higham, John. "The Cult of the `American Consensus'," *Commentary* 27 (February 1959), 93–99.

Hiss, Alger. *Recollections of a Life.* New York: Seaver Books, 1988.

Hook, Sidney. "Does the Smith Act Threaten Our Liberties?" *Commentary* 15 (January 1953), 63–72.

Hornaday, Mary. "Eleanor Roosevelt: The Woman Nobody Understands." *Look* December 28, 1943, 40–44.

Horton, Myles. *The Long Haul.* New York: Doubleday, 1990.

Huie, William Bradford. "How Eleanor Roosevelt Let Our Generation Down." *Today's Woman* 28 (July 1953), 27, 40–42.

Humphrey, Hubert Horatio. *The Education of a Public Man: My Life and Politics.* Garden City: Doubleday, 1976.

Ickes, Harold L. *The Secret Diary of Harold L. Ickes.* New York: Doubleday, 1953.

Johnson, Guy. "What Happened in Columbia," *New South* 1 (May 1946), 1–8.

Johnson, Walter and Carol Evans, ed. *The Papers of Adlai E. Stevenson.* 7 volumes. Boston: Little Brown, 1972–1979.

Johnson, Walter. *How We Drafted Adlai Stevenson.* New York: Alfred Knopf, 1955.

Key, V. O. *Southern Politics.* New York: Alfred Knopf, 1949.

Keyserling, Leon. "Eggheads and Politics." *New Republic* 139 (October 27, 1958), 13–17.

Kirchway, Freda. "The Battle of Chicago," *The Nation* 159 (July 29, 1944), 119.

Lash, Joseph P. *Eleanor Roosevelt: A Friend's Memoir.* New York: Doubleday, 1964.

Lash, Joseph P. *Love, Eleanor: Eleanor Roosevelt and Her Friends.* New York: Doubleday, 1982.

Lash, Joseph P. *A World of Love: Eleanor Roosevelt and Her Friends, 1943–1962.* New York: Doubleday, 1984.

Lilienthal, David E. *The Journals of David Lilienthal, Volumes III-V.* New York, Harper and Row, 1977.

Loeb, James and James G. Patton. "The Challenge to Progressives," *New Republic* 112 (February 5, 1945), 187–206.

Longworth, Alice Roosevelt. "The Ideal Qualifications of a President's Wife." *Ladies Home Journal* (February 1936), 33.

Louchheim, Katie, ed. *The Making of the New Deal: The Insiders' Speak.* Cambridge: Harvard University Press, 1983.

Lowenstein, Allard K. *Brutal Mandate: A Journey to Southwest Africa.* Foreword by Eleanor Roosevelt. New York: Macmillan, 1962.

Lynn, Conrad J. *There Is a Fountain: The Autobiography of a Civil Rights Lawyer.* Westport: Lawrence Hill and Company, 1979.

Marshall, Margaret. "Portrait of Truman," *The Nation* 160 (April 21, 1945), 439.

McCarthy, Joe. *The Remarkable Kennedys.* New York: The Dial Press, 1961.

Miller, Merle. *Plain Speaking: An Oral Biography of Harry Truman.* New York: Putnam and Sons, 1974.

Muhlen, Norbert. "The Hysteria of the Hisslings," *The New Leader* (May 13, 1950).

Murray, Pauli. *Human Rights U.S.A.: 1948–1966.* Cincinnati: Service Center, Board of Missions, Methodist Church, 1967.

Murray, Pauli. *Song in a Weary Throat.* New York: Harper and Row, 1988.

Myrdal, Gunnar. *An American Dilemma: The Negro Problem and Modern Democracy.* New York: Harper and Brothers, 1944.

Niebuhr, Reinhold. *Children of Light and Children of Darkness: A Vindication of Democracy and a Critique of Its Traditional Defense.* New York: Scribner's, 1944.

Niebuhr, Reinhold. *Reinhold Niebuhr: His Religious, Social and Political Thought,* edited by Charles W. Kegley and Robert W. Bretall. Mew York: MacMillan, 1961.

Nixon, Richard M. *RN: The Memoirs of Richard Nixon.* New York: Grosset and Dunlap, 1978.

Nixon, Richard M. *Six Crises.* Garden City: Doubleday, 1962.

O'Connor, Francis V. *Art for the Millions: Essays form the 1930s by Artists and Administrators of the WPA Federal Art Program.* Greenwich: New York Graphic Society, 1973.

O'Connor, Francis V. *New Deal Art Projects: An Anthology of Memoirs.* Washington: Smithsonian Institution, 1972.

Oursler, Fulton. *Behold the Dreamer.* Boston: Little Brown, 1973.

Parks, Lillian Rogers. *The Roosevelts: A Family in Turmoil.* Englewood Cliffs: Prentice-Hall, 1981.

Patton, James G. "A Plan for Prosperity." *New Republic* 109 (November 6, 1944), 586–88.

Pearson, Drew. *Diaries, 1949–1959,* edited by Tyler Abell. New York: Holt Rinehart and Winston, 1974.

Perkins, Frances. *The Roosevelt I Knew.* New York: Viking Press, 1946.

Redding, Jack. *Inside the Democratic Party.* Indianapolis: Bobbs-Merrill Company, 1958.

Rollins, Alfred B., Jr., *Roosevelt and Howe.* New York: Alfred A. Knopf, 1962.

Roosevelt, Anna Eleanor. *The Autobiography of Eleanor Roosevelt.* New York: Harper, 1961.

Roosevelt, Eleanor and Lorena Hickok. *Ladies of Courage.* New York: G.P. Putnam's Sons, 1954.

Roosevelt, Eleanor. "Abolish Jim Crow." *New Threshold* 1 (August 1943), 4, 34.

Roosevelt, Eleanor. "The American Presidency: An Interpretation." *Harvard Law Review* 54 (Winter 1941), 1413–1414.

Roosevelt, Eleanor. "Before the Democratic National Convention." *Representative American Speeches* (1956/1957), 109–113.

Roosevelt, Eleanor. "A Challenge to American Sportsmanship," *Collier's*, October 16, 1943.

Roosevelt, Eleanor. "Civil Liberties - The Individual and the Community." *Reference Shelf* 14 (1940), 173–182.

Roosevelt, Eleanor. "Domestic Order: The Minorities Question" in *Toward a Better World*, edited by William Scarlett. Philadelphia: John C Winston, Company, 1946.

Roosevelt, Eleanor. "Fear Is the Enemy," *The Nation* (February 10, 1940), 3.

Roosevelt, Eleanor. "Freedom: Promise or Fact," *Negro Digest* (October 1943), 8–9.

Roosevelt, Eleanor. "Good Citizenship," *Pictorial Review* (April 1930), 4.

Roosevelt, Eleanor. "Henry Wallace's Democracy." *New Republic* 7 (August 7, 1944), 165–166.

Roosevelt, Eleanor. "How to Take Criticism," *Ladies Home Journal* 61 (November 1944), 155, 171.

Roosevelt, Eleanor. "Human Rights and Human Freedom." *New York Times Magazine* (March 24, 1946), 21.

Roosevelt, Eleanor. *The Human Factor in the Development of International Understanding*. Hamilton, N.Y.: Colgate University Press, 1949.

Roosevelt, Eleanor. "I Want You to Write to Me," *Women's Home Companion* (August 1933), 4.

Roosevelt, Eleanor. "The Ideal Education," *Woman's Journal* (October 1930), 9.

Roosevelt, Eleanor. *If You Ask Me*. New York: Appleton-Century, 1946.

Roosevelt, Eleanor. "In Defense of Curiosity," *Saturday Evening Post* 208 (August 24, 1935), 8–9, 64.

Roosevelt, Eleanor. "In the Service of Truth." *Nation* 181 (July 9, 1955), 37.

Roosevelt, Eleanor. *India and the Awakening East*. New York: Harper, 1953.

Roosevelt, Eleanor. "The Issue Is Freedom." *New Republic* 107 (August 3, 1942), 147–148.

Roosevelt, Eleanor. *It Seems to Me*. New York: Norton, 1954.

Roosevelt, Eleanor. *It's Up to the Women*. New York: Frederick A. Stokes, Co., 1933.

Roosevelt, Eleanor. "Jeffersonian Principles the Issue in 1928," *Current History* (June 1928), 354–357.

Roosevelt, Eleanor. "Keepers of Democracy." *Virginia Quarterly Review* 15 (January 1939), 1–5.

Roosevelt, Eleanor. *The Moral Basis of Democracy*. New York: Howell, Soskin, and Company, 1940.

Roosevelt, Eleanor. "The Negro and Social Change," *Opportunity: The Journal of Negro Life* (January 1936), 22.

Roosevelt, Eleanor. "Of Stevenson, Truman, and Kennedy," *Saturday Evening Post*, 230 (March 8, 1958), 72–76.

Roosevelt, Eleanor. *On My Own*. New York: Harper, 1958.

Roosevelt, Eleanor. "Race, Religion and Prejudice." *New Republic* 106 (May 11, 1942): 630.

Roosevelt, Eleanor. "Salute to Montgomery," *Liberation* 1 (December 1956), 1.

Roosevelt, Eleanor. "Social Responsibility for Individual Welfare," in Russell, James Earl editor, *National Policies for Education, Health, and Social Services*. Garden City: Doubleday, 1955.

Roosevelt, Eleanor. "Some of My Best Friends are Negro." *Ebony* 8 (February 1953), 16–20, 22, 24–26.

Roosevelt, Eleanor. *This I Remember.* New York: Harper and Brothers, 1949.

Roosevelt, Eleanor. *This Is My Story.* New York: Harper and Brothers, 1937.

Roosevelt, Eleanor. *This Troubled World.* New York: Kinsey, 1938.

Roosevelt, Eleanor. *Tomorrow Is Now.* New York: Harper and Row,1963.

Roosevelt, Eleanor. "The Unemployed Are Not a Strange Race," *Democratic Digest* 13 no. 6 (June 1936), 19.

Roosevelt, Eleanor. "What Are We Fighting For?" *The American Magazine* (July 1945).

Roosevelt, Eleanor. "What are we for?" in *The Search for America*, Huston Smith, ed. New York: Spectrum Books, 1959, 3–12.

Roosevelt, Eleanor. "What Do Ten Million Women Want." *Home Magazine* (March 1932), 19–21, 86.

Roosevelt, Eleanor. "What Has Happened to the American Dream," in *Modern Composition*, edited by Wallace Earle Stegner. New York: Holt Rinehart and Winston, 1965.

Roosevelt, Eleanor. "What I Want Most Out of Life." *Success Magazine*, May 1927, 16–17, 70.

Roosevelt, Eleanor. "What I Want to Leave Behind." *Pictorial Review* 34 (April 1933), 4, 45–46.

Roosevelt, Eleanor. "What Is a Wife's Job Today? An Interview with M.K. Wiseheart, *Good Housekeeping* (August 22, 1930), 34–35, 166, 169–173.

Roosevelt, Eleanor. "What Liberty Means to Me" in *The Liberty Years, 1924–1950*, edited by Allen Churchill. Englewood Cliffs, N.J.: Prentice-Hall, 1969.

Roosevelt, Eleanor. "Where I Get My Energy." *Harper's Magazine* 45 (January 1959), 45–47.

Roosevelt, Eleanor. "Why Democrats Favor Smith," *North American Review* (November 1927), 472–475.

Roosevelt, Eleanor. "Why I Am a Democrat." *Junior League Bulletin* (November 1923).

Roosevelt, Eleanor. "Why I Do Not Choose to Run." *Look*, July 9, 1946, 24–25.

Roosevelt, Eleanor. "Why I Still Believe in the Youth Congress." *Liberty* 17 (April 20, 1940) 30–32.

Roosevelt, Eleanor. *The Wisdom of Eleanor Roosevelt: Eleanor Roosevelt Writes About Her World.* New York: McCalls Corporation, 1962.

Roosevelt, Eleanor. "Women in Politics." *Good Housekeeping* 110 (January, March, and April 1940), 18–19, 150; 45,46; 202–203.

Roosevelt, Eleanor. "Women Must Learn to Play the Game as Men Do." *Redbook* (April 1928), 78–79, 141–142.

Roosevelt, Elliot. *F.D.R.: His Personal Letters.* New York: Duell, Sloan and Pearce, 1948.

Roosevelt, Elliott and James Brough. *Mother R: Eleanor Roosevelt's Untold Story.* New York: Putnam, 1977.

Roosevelt, Franklin Delano. *Nothing to Fear: The Selected Addresses of Franklin Delano Roosevelt, 1932–1945*, edited by B. D. Zevin. Boston: Houghton Mifflin, 1946.

Roosevelt, James with Bill Libby. *My Parents: A Differing View.* Chicago: Playboy Press Book, 1976.

Bibliography

Rovere, Richard. *Senator Joe McCarthy.* New York: Harper, 1959.

Russell, Bertrand. *Power: A New Social Analysis.* London: Unwin Books, 1960.

Schapsmeier, Edward L. and Frederick H. *Prophet in Politics: Henry A. Wallace and the War Years: 1940–1965.* Ames, Iowa: The Iowa State University Press, 1970.

Schlesinger, Arthur M. Jr. *The Coming of the New Deal.* Boston: Houghton Mifflin, 1973.

Schlesinger, Arthur M. Jr. "The Future of Liberalism." *Reporter* 15 (May 3, 1956), 8–11.

Schlesinger, Arthur M. Jr. *The Politics of Hope.* New York: Houghton Mifflin, 1963.

Schlesinger, Arthur M. Jr. "The Right to Loathsome Ideas," *Saturday Review of Literature* 32 (May 14, 1949), 17, 18, 47.

Schlesinger, Arthur M. Jr. "Stevenson and the American Liberal Dilemma." *Twentieth Century* 158 (January 1953), 24–29.

Schlesinger, Arthur M. Jr. *The Vital Center: The Politics of Freedom.* Boston: Houghton Mifflin, 1949.

Schlesinger, Arthur M. Jr. "The U.S. Communist Party," *Life* 21 (July 29, 1946), 84–96.

Sherwood, Robert. *Roosevelt and Hopkins.* New York: Harper, 1948.

Smith, Lillian., *How Am I To Be Heard: The Letters of Lillian Smith*, edited by Margaret Rose Gladney. Chapel Hill: University of North Carolina Press, 1993.

Smith, Lillian. *Killers of the Dream.* New York: Norton, 1961.

Smith, Lillian. *Strange Fruit.* New York: Norton, 1944.

Smith, Lillian. *The Winner Names the Age: A Collection of Writings by Lillian Smith*, edited by Michelle Cliff. New York: Norton, 1986.

Sorensen, Theodore. *Kennedy.* New York: Harper and Row, 1965.

Steinberg, Alfred E. *Mrs. R: The Life of Eleanor Roosevelt.* New York: Putnam, 1958.

Stevenson, Adlai E. *The Papers of Adlai E. Stevenson.* Walter Johnson, ed. Boston: Little Brown, 1972–1979.

Stone, I. F. *The Haunted Fifties.* Boston: Little Brown, 1963.

Stone, I. F. *The Truman Era.* Boston: Little Brown, 1953, 1988.

Stone, I. F. *The War Years.* Boston: Little Brown, 1946.

T.R.B. "Transition to Peace," *New Republic* 113 (August 27, 1945), 239.

Tarbell, Ida M. "Portrait of a Lady," *The Delineator* 119 (October 1931), 19.

Truman, Harry S. *Memoirs.* 2 volumes. Garden City: Doubleday, 1955–1956.

Truman, Harry S. *Off the Record: The Private Papers of Harry S. Truman*, edited by Robert H. Ferrell. New York: Harper and Row, 1980.

Truman, Harry S. *The Public Papers of the President, Harry S. Truman: 1945–1953.* 8 volumes. Washington, D.C.: U.S. Government Printing Office, 1961–1966.

Truman, Harry S. "The Truman Tapes: Harry S. Truman Speaking Frankly with Ben Gradus," Caedman Recording Company, 1960.

Truman, Margaret. *Harry S. Truman.* New York: Morrow, 1972.

Tugwell, Rexford. *The Brains Trust.* New York: Macmillan, 1968.

Tully, Grace. *F.D.R.: My Boss.* New York: Scribner's, 1949.

Wallace, Henry A. *Democracy Reborn.* New York: Reynal and Hitchcock. 1944.

Wallace, Henry A. *The Price of Vision.* Boston: Houghton Mifflin, 1973.

Wallace, Henry A. *Sixty Million Jobs.* New York: Simon and Schuster, 1945.

Walton, William. *Conversation with Kennedy.* John K. Jessup, ed. New York: 1965.

Weschler, James. *The Age of Suspicion.* New York: David I. Fine, 1953.

White, Poppy Cannon. *A Gentle Knight: My Husband Walter White.* New York: Viking Press, 1956.

White, Theodore. *The Making of the President 1960.* New York: Antheneum, 1961.

White, Walter. *A Man Called White: The Autobiography of Walter White.* New York: Viking Press, 1948; Indiana University Press paperback, 1980.

SECONDARY SOURCE PUBLICATIONS:

Abramowitz, Mildred W. "Eleanor Roosevelt and the Federal Responsibility and Responsiveness to Youth, the Negro, and Others in Time of Depression." Ph.D. dissertation: New York University, 1971.

Ambrose, Stephen E. *Nixon: Volume I - The Education of a Politician, 1913–1962.* New York: Simon and Schuster, 1987.

Anthony, Carl Sferrazza. *First Ladies, Volume I.* New York: William Morrow and Company, 1990.

Ashmore, Harry S. *Hearts and Minds: The Anatomy of Racism from Roosevelt to Reagan.* New York: McGraw Hill, 1982.

Atwell, Mary Welek. "Notes and Comments: Eleanor Roosevelt and the Cold War Consensus." *Diplomatic History* 3(1) (1979), 99–113.

Bailey, Stephen A. *Congress Makes A Law: The Story Behind the Employment Act of 1946.* New York: Columbia University Press, 1950.

Beasley, Maurine. *Eleanor Roosevelt and the Media.* Urbana: University of Illinois Press, 1987.

Beeler, Dorothy. "Race Riot in Columbia, Tennessee," *Tennessee Historical Quarterly* 39 (Spring 1980), 31–61.

Belknap, Michal R., ed. *American Political Trials.* Westport: Greenwood Press, 1981.

Belknap, Michal R. *Cold War Political Justice.* Westport: Greenwood Press, 1977.

Berger, Jason. *A New Deal for the World: Eleanor Roosevelt and American Foreign Policy.* New York: Social Science Monographs, 1981.

Berman, William C. *The Politics of Civil Rights in the Truman Administration.* Columbus: Ohio State University Press, 1970.

Bernstein, Barton. *Politics and Policies of the Truman Administration.* Chicago: Quadrangle Books, 1970.

Bernstein, Barton J. "The Truman Administration and Its Reconversion Wage Policy," *Labor History* 6 (Fall 1965), 214–231.

Bernstein, Barton J. and Allen J. Matusow. *The Truman Administration: A Documentary History.* New York: Harper and Row, 1966.

Beschloss, Michael. *Kennedy and Roosevelt.* New York: Norton, 1980.

Bilsborrow, Eleanor Janice. "The Philosophy of Social Reform in the Speeches of Eleanor Roosevelt." Ph.D. dissertation: University of Denver, 1957.

Black, Allida M. "Championing A Champion: Eleanor Roosevelt and the Marian Anderson Freedom Concert," *Presidential Studies Quarterly* (Fall 1990),

Black, Allida M. "A Reluctant but Persistent Warrior: Eleanor Roosevelt and the Early Civil Rights Movement," in *Women in the Civil Rights Movement: Trailblazers and*

Bibliography

Torchbearers, 1941–1965, edited by Jacqueline Rouse, et al, Brooklyn: Carlson Publishing, Inc., 1990.

Blum, John Morton. *V Was for Victory*. New York: Harcourt Brace and Jovanovich, 1979.

Branch, Taylor. *Parting the Waters*. New York: Simon and Schuster, 1988.

Brauer, Carl M. *John F. Kennedy and The Second Reconstruction*. New York: Columbia University Press, 1977.

Brinkley, Alan. *Voices of Protest: Huey Long, Father Coughlin and the Great Depression*. New York: Vintage Books, 1983.

Brock, Clifton. *Americans for Democratic Action*. Washington: Public Affairs Press, 1962.

Buckley, William F. *The Committee and Its Critics: A Calm Review of the House Committee on Un-American Activities*. New York: Putnam, 1962.

Burk, Robert Frederick. *The Eisenhower Administration and Black Civil Rights*. Knoxville; University of Tennessee Press, 1984.

Burke, Fran. "Eleanor Roosevelt, October 11, 1984 - November 7, 1962—She made a difference." *Public Administration Review* 44 (September/October 1984), 365–372.

Burns, James MacGregor. *The Crosswinds of Freedom*. New York: Knopf, 1989.

Cochran, Burt. *Harry Truman and the Crisis Presidency*. New York: Funk and Wagnalls, 1973.

Collins, Jean E. *She Was There: Stories of Pioneering Women Journalists*. New York: Messner Publications, 1980.

Conkin, Paul. *The New Deal*. Arlington Heights: Harlan Davidson, 1975.

Cook, Blanche Wiesen. *Eleanor Roosevelt, Vol. I, 1884–1933*. New York: Viking Press, 1992.

Cook, Blanche Wiesen. "Eleanor Roosevelt and Human Rights: The Battle for Peace and Planetary Decency" in *Women and American Foreign Policy*, edited by Edward Crapol. New York: Greenwood Press, 1987.

Cook, Blanche Wiesen. "Eleanor Roosevelt, Power and Politics: A Feminist Perspective" in *Eleanor Roosevelt: An American Journey*, edited by Jess Flemion and Colleen O'Connor. San Diego: San Diego University Press, 1987.

Cooke, Robert John. "The Political Career of Anna Eleanor Roosevelt: A Study of the Public Conscience." Ph.D. dissertation: Syracuse University, 1965.

Davis, Kenneth S. *F.D.R.: The New York Years, 1928–1933*. New York: Knopf, 1985.

Davis, Kenneth S. *The Politics of Honor*. New York: Putnam, 1967.

Daniels. Roger. *The Decision to Relocate the Japanese Americans*. Melbourne, Florida: Kreiger Press, 1981.

Diggins, John Patrick. *The Proud Decades: America in War and Peace, 1941–1960*. New York: Norton, 1989.

Egerton, John. *Speak Now Against the Day: The Generation Before the Civil Rights Movement in the South*. New York: Knopf, 1994.

Elshtain, Jean Bethke. "Eleanor Roosevelt as Activist and Thinker: The Lady, the Life of Duty." *Halycon* 8 (1986), 93–114.

Erikson, Joan M. "Nothing to Fear." *Deadalus* 93 (Spring 1964), 781–801.

Faber, Doris. *The Life of Lorena Hickok: E.R.'s Friend*. New York: William Morrow, 1980.

Finch, Minnie. *The NAACP: Its Fight for Justice*. Metuchen, N.J.: The Scarecrow Press, 1981.

Foucault, Michel. *Power/Knowledge: Selected Interviews and Other Writings, 1972–1977.* New York: Pantheon, 1980.

Freidel, Frank. *FDR: Launching the New Deal.* Boston: Little Brown, 1973.

Gardner, Richard N. "Enduring Human Rights Legacy of Eleanor Roosevelt." *Congressional Record,* February 22, 1985, S1900-S1903.

Gentry, Curt. *J. Edgar Hoover: The Man and the Secrets.* New York: Plume Books, 1992.

Gillon, Steven M. *Politics and Vision: The ADA and American Liberalism, 1947–1985.* New York: Oxford University Press, 1987.

Goodman, Walter. *The Committee: The Extraordinary Career of the House Committee on Un-American Activities.* New York: Farrar, Straus and Giroux, 1968.

Goodwin, Doris Kearns. *No Ordinary Time: Franklin and Eleanor Roosevelt and the Home Front in World War Two.* New York: Simon and Schuster, 1994.

Gorman, Joseph Bruce. *Kefauver: A Political Biography.* New York: Oxford University Press, 1971.

Graham, H. Davis. "The Paradox of Eleanor Roosevelt: Alcoholism's Child." *Virginia Quarterly Review* 63 (Spring 1987), 3–26.

Grant, Philip A. Jr. "Catholic Congressmen, Cardinal Spellman, Eleanor Roosevelt and the 1949–1950 Federal Aid to Education Controversy." *American Catholic Historical Society of Philadelphia Records* 90 (December 1979), 3–13.

Greenberg, Jack. *Crusaders in the Courts.* New York: Basic Books, 1994.

Griffith, Robert. *The Politics of Fear: Joseph R. McCarthy and the Senate.* Lexington: University of Kentucky Press, 1970.

Hamby, Alonzo L. *Beyond the New Deal: Harry S. Truman and American Liberalism.* New York: Columbia University Press, 1973.

Hamby, Alonzo L. *Harry S. Truman and the New Deal.* Lexington: D.C. Heath and Company, 1974.

Hamby, Alonzo L. *Liberalism and Its Challengers: FDR to Reagan.* New York: Oxford University Press, 1985.

Harper, Alan D. *The Politics of Loyalty: The White House and the Communist Issue, 1946–1952.* Westport: Greenwood Press, 1969.

Hareven, Tamara K. *Eleanor Roosevelt: An American Conscience.* Chicago: Quadrangle Books, 1968.

Herberg, Will. *Catholic, Protestant, Jew.* Garden City: Western Reserve Historical Society, 1965.

Hoff-Wilson, Joan and Marjorie Lightman, eds. *Without Precedent: The Life and Career of Eleanor Roosevelt.* Bloomington: Indiana University Press, 1984.

Hofstader, Richard. *The Paranoid Style in American Politics and Other Essays.* New York: Knopf, 1965.

Holt, Rackhan. *Mary McLeod Bethune: A Biography.* Garden City: Doubleday, 1964.

Irons, Peter. *Justice at War: The Inside Story of Japanese American Internment.* New York: Oxford University Press, 1983.

Isenberg, Nancy G. "Eleanor Roosevelt: Joseph Lash's 'Eternal Mother,'" *Biography* 10(2) (1987), 107–115.

Isserman, Maurice. *If I Had a Hammer: The Death of the Old Left and the Birth of the New Left.* New York: Basic Books, 1987.

Bibliography

Johnson, M. Glen. "The Contributions of Eleanor and Franklin Roosevelt to the Development of International Protection of Human Rights." *Human Rights Quarterly* 9 (1987), 19–48.

Katz, Michael B. *In the Shadow of the Poorhouse: A Social History of Welfare in America.* New York: Basic Books, 1986.

Kearney, James R. *Anna Eleanor Roosevelt: The Evolution of a Reformer.* Boston: Houghton Mifflin, 1968.

Kertzer, David I. *Ritual, Politics, and Power.* New Haven: Yale University Press, 1988.

Klibaner, Irwin. *Conscience of a Troubled South: The Southern Conference Education Fund, 1946–1966.* New York: Carlson Publishing, Inc., 1989.

Klibaner, Irwin. "The Travail of Southern Radicals: The Southern Conference Education Fund, 1946–1976." *Journal of Southern History* 49 (May 1983), 179–202.

Kluger, Richard. *Simple Justice: The History of Brown v. Board of Education and Black America's Struggle for Equality.* New York: Random House, 1975.

Kornitzer, Bela. *The Real Nixon: An Intimate Biography.* Chicago: Rand McNally, 1960.

Krueger, Thomas A. *And Promises to Keep: The Southern Conference on Human Welfare, 1938–1948.* Nashville: Vanderbilt University Press, 1967.

Lasch, Christopher. *The New Radicalism in America.* New York: Knopf, 1965.

Lash, Joseph P. *Dreamers and Dealers: A New Look at the New Deal.* New York: Doubleday, 1988.

Lash, Joseph P. *Eleanor and Franklin: The Story of Their Relationship Based on Eleanor Roosevelt's Private Papers.* New York: Norton, 1970.

Lash, Joseph P. *Eleanor: The Years Alone.* New York: Norton, 1972.

Lasky, Victor. *J.F.K.: The Man and the Myth.* New Rochelle: Arlington House, 1963.

Latham, Earl. *The Communist Conspiracy in Washington: From the New Deal to McCarthy.* Cambridge: Harvard University Press, 1966.

Lazarowitz, Arlene. "Years in Exile: The Liberal Democrats, 1950–1959." Ph.D. dissertation: University of California Los Angeles, 1982.

Leuchtenburg, William E. *Franklin D. Roosevelt and the New Deal.* New York: Harper and Row, 1963.

Leuchtenburg, William E. *In the Shadow of FDR: From Harry Truman to Ronald Reagan.* Ithaca: Cornell University Press, 1983.

Lewey, Guenter. *The Cause that Failed: Communism in American Political Life.* New York: Oxford University Press, 1990.

Loveland, Anne. *Lillian Smith: A Southerner Confronting the South.* Baton Rouge: LSU Press, 1986.

Lowitt, Richard and Maurine Beasley. *One Third of a Nation: Lorena Hickok Reports on the Great Depression.* Urbana: University of Illinois Press, 1981.

Lubell, Samuel. *The Revolt of the Moderates.* New York: Harper and Row, 1956.

MacDonald, William. *Federal Relief Administration of the Arts.* Columbus: Ohio State University Press, 1969.

Markowitz, Norman D. *The Rise and Fall of the Peoples' Century: Henry Wallace and American Liberalism, 1941–1948.* New York: Free Press, 1973.

Martin, George. *Madame Secretary: Frances Perkins.* Boston: Houghton Mifflin, 1975.

Martin, John Bartlow. *Adlai Stevenson of Illinois*. New York: Doubleday and Company, 1976.

Martin, John Bartlow. *Adlai Stevenson and the World*. New York: Doubleday and Company, 1977.

Martin, John Fredrick. *Civil Rights and the Crisis of Liberalism: The Democratic Party, 1945–1976*. Boulder: Westview Press, 1979.

Massey, Michael J. "Relations Between Harry S. Truman and Eleanor Roosevelt: A Constructive Friendship." Senior Thesis: Indiana University, 1985.

McAuliffe, Mary. *Crisis on the Left: Cold War Politics and American Liberals, 1947–1954*. Amherst: University of Massachusetts Press, 1978.

McCoy, Donald and Richard Ruetten. *Quest and Response*. Lawrence: University of Kansas Press, 1973.

McCullough, David. *Truman*. New York: Touchstone Books, 1992.

McKeever, Porter. *Adlai Stevenson: His Life and Legacy*. New York: William Morrow. 1989.

McKinzie, Richard C. *The New Deal for Artists*. Princeton: Princeton University Press, 1977.

Miroff, Bruce. *Pragmatic Illusions: The Presidency of John F. Kennedy*. New York: McKay, 1976.

Mower, Alfred Glenn. *The US, the UN, and Human Rights: The Eleanor Roosevelt and Jimmy Carter Eras*. Westport, Conn: Greenwood Press, 1979.

Nash, George. *The Conservative Intellectual Movement in America Since 1945*. New York: Harper and Row, 1979.

Nevins, Allan. *Herbert H. Lehman and His Era*. New York: Scribner's, 1973.

O'Reilly, Kenneth. *Hoover and the Un-Americans: The FBI, HUAC, and the Red Menace*. Philadelphia: Temple University Press, 1983.

Odum, Howard. *Race and Rumors of Race: Challenge to American Crisis*. Chapel Hill: University of North Carolina Press, 1943.

Oshinsky, David. *A Conspiracy So Immense: The World of Joe McCarthy*. New York: Free Press, 1983.

Ottenberg, James M. *The Lexington Democratic Club Story*. New York: Lexington Democratic Club, 1959.

Overmeyer, Deborah Ann. "'Common Ground' and America's Minorities, 1940–1949: A Study in the Changing Climate of Opinion." Ph.D. Dissertation, University of Cincinnati, 1984.

Parmet, Herbert. *The Democrats: The Years After FDR*. New York: Oxford University Press, 1976.

Parmet, Herbert S. *Eisenhower and the American Crusades*. New York: Macmillan, 1972.

Parmet, Herbert S. *JFK: The Presidency of John F. Kennedy*. New York: Dial Press, 1983.

Pells, Richard H. *The Liberal Mind in a Conservative Age: American Intellectuals in the 1940s and 1950s*. New York: Harper and Row, 1985.

Penkhower, Noam. *The Federal Writer's Project*. Chicago: University of Illinois Press, 1977.

Pierce, Robert Clayton. "Liberals and the Cold War: Union for Democratic Action and Americans for Democratic Action, 1940–1949." Ph.D. dissertation, University of Wisconsin, Madison, 1979.

Reed, Linda. *Simple Decency and Common Sense: The Southern Conference Movement, 1938–1963.* Indianapolis: Indiana University Press, 1991.

Reed, Merle. *Seedtime for the Modern Civil Rights Movement: The President's Committee on Fair Employment Practice, 1941–1946.* Baton Rouge: Louisiana State University Press, 1991.

Reeves, Thomas, ed. *McCarthyism.* Malabar, Florida: Robert E. Krieger Publishing, 1989.

Reiman, Richard A. *The New Deal and American Youth: Dreams and Ideals in the Depression Decade.* Athens: University of Georgia Press, 1992.

Ribuffo, Leo P. *Left, Center, Right: Essays in American History.* Rutgers: Rutgers University Press, 1991.

Ribuffo, Leo P. *The Old Christian Right.* Philadelphia: Temple University Press, 1983.

Salmond, John. *A Southern Rebel: The Life and Times of Aubrey Williams 1890–1965.* Chapel Hill: University of North Carolina Press, 1983.

Schlesinger, Arthur M. Jr. *Robert Kennedy and His Times.* Boston: Houghton Mifflin, 1978.

Schlesinger, Arthur M. Jr. *A Thousand Days.* Boston: Houghton Mifflin, 1965.

Schmidt, Karl M. *Henry A. Wallace: Quixotic Crusade 1948.* Binghampton, N.Y.: Syracuse University Press, 1960.

Seeber, Frances M. "'I Want You to Write to Me:' The Papers of Anna Eleanor Roosevelt," *Prologue* 2 (Summer 1987), 95–105.

Shannon, David A. *The Decline of American Communism: A History of the Communist Party of the United States Since 1945.* New York: Harcourt Brace, 1959.

Sitkoff, Harvard. *A New Deal for Blacks.* New York: Oxford University Press, 1978.

Smith, Geoffrey S. *To Save a Nation: American 'Extremism,' the New Deal, and the Coming of World War II.* Chicago: Ivan T. Dee, 1992.

Smith, Richard Norton. *Secrecy and Power: The Life of J. Edgar Hoover.* New York: Free Press, 1987.

Smith, Richard Norton. *Thomas E. Dewey and His Times.* New York: Simon and Schuster, 1982.

Sternsher, Berhard, ed. *The Negro in Depression and War.* Chicago: Quadrangle Books, 1969.

Sundquist, James. *Politics and Policy: The Eisenhower, Kennedy and Johnson Years.* Washington: The Brookings Institution, 1968.

Theoharis, Athan G. *Beyond the Hiss Case: The FBI, Congress and the Cold War.* Philadelphia: Temple University Press, 1982.

Theoharis, Athan. "J. Edgar, Eleanor and Herbert, Too?" *The Nation,* 234 (7), 200.

Ward, Geoffrey C. "Eleanor Roosevelt Draws Her Strength from a Sanctuary Called Val-Kill." *Smithsonian Magazine* 15 (7) (October 1984), 62–73.

Ware, Susan. *Beyond Suffrage: Women and the New Deal.* Cambridge: Harvard University Press, 1981.

Ware, Susan. *Partner and I: Molly Dewson, Feminism and New Deal Politics.* New Haven: Yale University Press, 1987.

Watrous, Hilda. *In League with Eleanor.* New York: Foundation for Citizen Education, 1984.

Watson, Denton L. *Lion in the Lobby: Clarence Mitchell, Jr.'s Struggle for the Passage of Civil Rights Laws.* New York: William Morrow, 1990.

Weaver, Robert C. "Eleanor and L.B.J. and Black America." *Crisis* 79 (6) (1972), 186–193.

Weinstein, Allen. *Perjury: The Hiss-Chambers Case.* New York: Knopf, 1978.

Weiss, Nancy J. *Farewell to the Party of Lincoln: Black Politics in the Age of FDR.* Princeton: Princeton University Press, 1983.

White, Theodore H. *America in Search of Itself: The Making of the President, 1956–1960.* New York: Harper, 1982.

Wilson, James Q. *The Amateur Democrats: Club Politics in Three Cities.* Chicago: University of Chicago Press, 1962.

Wolfskil, George and John A. Hudson. *All But the People: Franklin D. Roosevelt and His Critics.* New York: Macmillan, 1969.

Yarnell, Allen. *Democrats and Progressives: The 1948 Election as a Test of Postwar Liberalism.* Berkeley: University of California Press, 1974.

Zagrando, Robert L. *The NAACP Campaign Against Lynching, 1909–1950.* Philadelphia: Temple University Press, 1980.

Index

Abraham Lincoln Brigade, 138
Adams, Josephine Truslow, 152
Addsco shipyard, 92
African-Americans, *see* Black Americans
The African Queen (film): ER as model for, 48
Alabama, 86, 127
The Alabama Sun (newspaper), 95
Alcohol consumption: girls and, 20, 25, 208*n*35
Alexander I, Czar of Russia, 189
Alexander, Will, 47, 93, 214*n*55
Alien Registration Act, *see* Smith Act
Allen, George, 65
Allenswood Academy: influence on ER, 7, 131
Allied Powers, 59, 139
Allis-Chalmers Manufacturing Company, 248*n*9
Alsop, Joseph and Stewart, 52

America First Committee (AFC), 140
American Association of the United Nations (AAUN), 196
American Broadcasting Company (ABC), 178
American Civil Liberties Union (ACLU): internment and, 143; Smith Act and, 153, 236*n*22, 237*n*29
An American Dilemma (Myrdal): ER interviewed for, 88
American Farm Bureau Federation, 69
American Federation of Artists, 33–34
American Friends Service Committee: ER and, 137
American Labor party, 122, 153
American Legion: wartime lobbying of, 141
American Liberty League: ER attacked by, 46
The American Magazine, 89

American Progress: ER's concerns re, 26
Americans for Democratic Action
    (ADA): anti-communist position of,
    246*m*05; Civil Rights Act and, 124;
    ER's criticism of, 165; on free speech,
    241*n*66; McCarthy and, 165, 169; 1956
    Democratic platform and, 113; Rauh
    on, 126; SCEF and, 122; voting drive
    of, 76; H. Wallace and, 79, 81; men-
    tioned, 120, 202
American Student Union: and HUAC
    hearings, 148
American Veterans Committee: and
    Columbia, Tn riot, 98, 99
American Youth Congress (AYC), 139:
    HUAC investigation of, 148, 149–150,
    152, 238*n*44
Amityville (L.I.): struggle to integrate,
    104
Anderson, Clinton: ER's opposition to,
    79
Anderson, Marian: ER's support of, 41–
    44, 97, 213*n*48
Andrew Rankin Memorial Chapel: ER's
    speech in, 104
Antibusiness sentiment, *see* Business
    interests
Anti-Catholic sentiment: against JFK,
    175, 178, 183, 248*n*8, 250*n*18, *see also*
    Catholics
Antilynching legislation: ER's support of,
    37, 38, 39, 41, 81, 93

Baltimore Afro-American: on ER and civil
    rights, 39
Baltimore Sun: ER lampooned by, 20, 21
Barnett, Ross: and James Meredith, 196
Baruch, Bernard: ER and, 72, 149
Bates, Daisy: and Little Rock Central
    High School, 118, 233*n*88, *see* Civil
    rights
Baton Rouge (La.): and Weldon
    Rougeau, 127
Battle, John S.: segregation policies of,
    113, 120
Battle of the Bulge, 120

Bay of Pigs Invasion: ER's criticism of,
    193
Beasley, Maurine, 25, 209*n*38
Belle Isle (Detroit): race riots in, 91
Benjamin, Robert: on ER and JFK, 175
Bethune-Cookman College: ER's sup-
    port of, 93, 107
Bethune, Mary McLeod: ER as advocate
    for, 93, 94; Columbia riot and, 98;
    ER, NYA and, 32–33, 107; SCEF and,
    120; postwar concerns of, 96
Bible, 117
Biddle, Francis: internment and, 136, 143,
    144, 236*n*21, 241*n*66
Bigelow, Albert, 128
Bilbo, Theodore: ER's deportation urged
    by, 133, 202
Bill of Rights: ER's interpretation of, 131,
    137
Bingay, Malcolm, 46
Bingham, Barry: and civil rights, 37–38,
    104–5
Birmingham (Ala.): 1938 SCHW confer-
    ence and, 40–41, 119
Black, Hugo, 40
Black, Ruby, 11, 24, 206*n*14
Black Cabinet, 37
Black Americans: anticommunists on,
    133; as artists, 36; Democratic party
    and, 220*n*39; as farmers, 87, 93–94;
    FDR and, 37, 68, 91, 92, 93; JFK and,
    178, 191, 192–194, 250*n*17; in New
    Deal era, 37–44; in Queens, 195;
    Republican party and, 94, 125;
    Truman and, 66; youth and, 33, 36;
    women, 93 *see Brown v. Topeka*, black
    veterans, civil rights, racism,
    Southern blacks
Black Muslims, 119
Black veterans: discrimination against,
    93, 96, 97
Bletzer, Russell R., 194
Block, Herbert (Herblock): on
    McCarthy, 169
Blum, John Morton, 70
Bok Peace Prize Committee, 137

Bolling, Richard: ER and Powell amendment and, 111
Bonus Army: ER's visit to, 25, 209n6
Bookbinder, Hyman: JFK and ER and, 189
Book burning: Eisenhower's duplicity on, 167
Bowles, Chester, 76; FDR and, 221–22n45, 249n14; departure of, 79; on "economic bill of rights," 60; JFK and, 189, 190; job creation proposal of, 61; pessimism of, 223n55; wage-price control issue and, 70–71, 72, 73–74, 75
Boycotts: ER's support of, 122, 127
Braden, Anne: and SCEF, 121–22, 123, 126
Braden, Carl: and SCEF, 121–22, 123
Brain Trust, 47
Brecht, Bertolt, 139
Bricker Amendment: ER's campaign against, 166
Bridges, Harry, 240n60
Britain: foreign policy of, 109, 119; wartime policy of, 139
British royalty: Marian Anderson and, 42, 43
"Broadcast to Little Businessmen" (H. Wallace), 62
Browder, Earl, 240n60
Brownell, Herbert, Jr.: and Civil Rights Act of 1957, 117
Brown v. Topeka Board of Education, 106, 109–18, 121; Bradens and, 122; civil rights legislation and, 125; 1956 Democratic platform dispute and, 109–115; ER's support of, 106–108, 121; implementation of, 118; NAACP finances and, 108; Southern response to, 178
Bruce, Edward: and PWAP, 34–35
Bryn Mawr College, 48
Buck, Pearl, 139
Buckley, William: criticism of ER by, 168–69
Budget Bureau, 103

Bugbee, Emma, 26
Bunche, Ralph: ER interviewed by, 88, 89: on Stevenson's "gaffe," 111; quoted, 220n39
Burnette, Pearl, 96
Burnham, James, 169
Burns, James MacGregor, 76, 184, 217n14
Business interests, 1; *see also* Industrial interests
Butler, Paul: and Democratic Advisory Council, 177: 1956 Democratic convention and, 112, 113
Byrnes, James F.: ER's opinion of, 56, 57, 66, 67, 78

Cahill, Holger, 35
Cain, Harry, 142
California: Japanese Americans in, 144; 1950 Senatorial race in, 162–64, 245n100, 248n9; 1960 presidential campaign and, 185, 187, 188, 191, 192; Smith Act and, 156, 241n72
Campobello lodge, 196
Canfield, Cass: JFK and, 178
Cannon, Poppy: ER's support for, 109
Carey, James: ER's support for, 72, 196
Carnegie Foundation for Peace: Hiss and, 159
Caster-Knot Electric Appliance store, 97
Catholicism: as campaign issue, 175, 183, 248n8: ER and Cardinal Spellman debate, 178, 249n17
Catt, Carrie Chapman: ER's respect for, 137–38, 139
Celler, Emmanuel, 196
Censorship, 140, 246n110, *see* civil liberties
Central High School (Little Rock): integration of, 86, 118, 124, 178
Chamberlain, Lewis, 138
Chambers, Whittaker: accusations of, 159–61, 243n87
Chautauqua Institute: ER's speech to, 27
Chiang Kai-shek, 154
Chicago Civil Liberties Committee: ER's speech to, 137

Index

Chicago Sun: ER's ad in, 151

Chicago Tribune, 246*n*103

China: and U.S. foreign policy, 138, 154, 166, 237*n*24

Christianity, 58, 117, 217*n*16; *see also* Catholics

Conscientious objectors, 140–42, 237*n*26

Christian Nationalist Crusade: ER ridiculed by, 134

Christian Press Association, 133

Christian Science Monitor, 39

Churchill, Winston, 83; "Iron Curtain" speech of, 139

Civil Aeronautics Administration: ER and, 105

Civil disobedience: ER's support of, 119, 127; *see also* Boycotts

Civil liberties: 131–170; AYC and, 148–149; anticommunist movement and, 152, 170; conscientious objectors and, 140–142; ER's philosophy of, 131–136, 201; FBI and, 149–150; Hiss and, 159–161; HUAC and, 147–152, 157, 159; Humphrey and, 169; of Japanese Americans 142–147; JFK and, 173–176, 177, 178; McCarthyism as threat to, 164–170; Mundt-Nixon bill and, 157–159; Smith Act and, 152–156; Stevenson on, 247*n*116

Civil rights: anti-communist movement and, 152, 170; civil disobedience and, 119, 122, 127–129: Eisenhower and, 116, 118, 126, 153; ER and, 2, 4, 30, 85–129, 201; and 1960 election, 178; Japanese American internment and, 144, 147; Harriman and, 110, 112; Height and, 119; LBJ and, 124–126; JFK and, 175, 177, 178, 191, 193–94, 249*n*17; kissing case and, 123–124; in New Deal era, 37–44; New Deal officials and, 47; Rustin and, 119, 129; televised discussion of, 192; Truman and, 80–81, 83, 97; voting rights and, 125–126; Williams and, 32, 40, 94, 120, 121, 122; for women, 193; *see* M. Anderson; antilynching legislation;

Brown v. Topeka: ER, and civil rights; CORE; DuBois; Housing; NAACP: SCEF; SCHW: specific legislation; W. White; R. Wilkins

Civil Rights Act (1957): ER's support for, 116–17; ER vs. moderates on, 124–25; ER vs. JFK on, 177, 178, 249*n*17

Civil Rights Act (1960): ER on 125–126

Civil Rights Congress: and SCEF, 120, 239*n*55

Civil War: Richard Russell as throwback to, 124, 231*n*65

Civil Works Administration (CWA), 34

Civilian Conservation Corps (CCC): ER's position on, 31, 34

Civilian Public Service: ER's support of, 141, 237*n*24

Clapper, Raymond: on ER, 48

Clark, Clifford: quoted by Truman, 82

Clark, Joseph: ER on, 249*n*14

Clark, Kenneth: and CIFS, 234*m*109

Clark, Tom: ER lobbied by, 99

Clinton, Hillary Rodham: compared to ER, 203

Coggs, Pauline Redmond: ER on, 103

Cohn, Roy: book burning by, 167

Cold War: civil liberties and, 132, 147, 148; ER on, 3, 4–5, 135; First Red Scare and, 152; foreign policy in, 79, 138, 154, 163, 166, 237*n*24; liberal reform and, 77; literature and, 167; major political figures of, 157; in Truman era, 79; H. Wallace on, 78; *see* China; Soviet Union

College of the City of New York (CCNY): Young Democrats of, 167–68

College students: in civil rights movement, 127, 195; ER and, 31; McCarthyism and, 166, 167–68; NYA and, 30; in Popular Front, 201; *see* American Youth Congress; College of the City of New York

Columbia (Tenn.): race riot in, 97–99, 108, 129, 201

Columbia University: ER's speech to, 104

Commager, Henry Steele, 184, 241*n*71

Commission on the Inquiry into the Freedom Struggle (CIFS): ER as chair of, 128–29, 194, 234*n*109

Committee on Economic Conditions in the South: and SCHW, 40

Committee on Economic Development: Bowles' criticism of, 70–71 Committee on Public Information (CPI): and Cold War, 139

Common Sense: quoted by ER, 135

Communist Control Act (1954): ER's opposition to, 169–70, 247*n*117

"Communist League of Negro Women": Nixon and, 163

Communist party (CPUSA): AYC and, 152; defended by ER: 132, 201–2; Hiss and, 159; Martinsville Seven and, 239*n*55; public opinion on, 240*n*56; SCEF and, 120, 121; Smith Act and, 153–157; Soviet Union and, 158; H. Wallace and, 77; *Watkins* case and, 241*n*72; *see also Dennis vs U.S.*; Popular Front; Communism, allegation of: 135, 148, 171; in civil rights movement, 95, 119, 136, 152; in Detroit, 91; FBI on, 150; fundamentalists on, 133–34; Hiss and, 159; HUAC and, 148–152; JFK and, 175; in labor movement, 67; McCarthy and, 164–70, 245*n*102, 245–46*n*103; in NAACP, 101; *Negro Digest* and, 90; Nixon and, 159, 163, 164, 232*n*78, 245*n*100; in SCEF, 122, 239*n*55; in SCHW, 105; vital center Democrats and, 79

Communists: civil liberties of, 148; economic containment of, 196; fear of, 2, 132, 148, 154, 161; free speech debate and, 132, 170; Kenyon and, 245*n*102; liberals and, 77, 224*n*63, 246*n*105; Mundt-Nixon Bill and, 159; NYA and, 32; Smith Act and, 152–157; Stevenson on, 247*n*116; in UN, 100, 152, 168; wartime investigations of, 136; *see also* First Red Scare

Condon, Edward: ER's defense of, 151

Conformity, dangers of, 135

Congress: Alien Registration Act and, 148; anti-lynching legislation and, 41; Civil Rights Act and, 117, 125–26, 172, 177; civil rights and, 30, 92, 194; communists and, 153; Condon investigation and, 151; conscientious objectors and, 141; "do nothing," 180; Employment Act and, 69; Freedom Riders and, 128; Full Employment Bill and, 64, 65, 66; Howard University and, 38; interviews of, 10; liberal criticism of, 179; Murray-Kilgore Reconversion Bill and, 218*n*23; Powell amendment and, 111; public housing proposals and, 103; slum clearance and, 91; Truman addresses to, 57, 59, 64, 66, 72, 80–81; wage-price controls and, 71, 73, 75; Wallace nomination and, 61

—House, 74, 75, 103, 158, 244*n*95

—House Agricultural Committee, 193

—House Committee on Expenditures, 66, 70, 219*n*34

—House Education and Labor Committee: ER's testimony before, 175

—House Judiciary Committee, 124

—House Subcommittee on Appropriations, 35, 36

—House Un-American Activities Committee (HUAC): ER's opposition to, 2, 4–5, 147–52, 153, 202; civil rights organizations and, 122; H. G. Douglas on, 163; Eisler and, 239*n*46; FBI and, 160, 162; FTP and, 35; JFK and, 175; Nixon and, 157–58, 159–60, 161, 244*n*95; SCEF and, 120, 239*n*55

—Senate: Bilbo on ER and, 133; ER on Bricker Amendment and, 166; California campaign for, 162–64, 245*n*100, 248*n*9; Civil Rights Act of 1960 and, 125, 126; Communist Control Act and, 170, 247*n*117; 1960 Connecticut campaign for, 190; D.C. housing and, 106; ER nominated for, 196; HUAC and, 152; McCarthy cen-

sured by, 172; 1952 Massachusetts campaign for, 172–73; Mundt-Nixon Bill and, 242*n*81; munitions industry and, 138; professional ethics of, 246*n*104; Southern power block in, 194; Wagner campaign for, 13; Wherry compromise and, 109
—Senate Banking and Currency Committee, 70
—Senate Commerce Committee, 61
—Senate Committee on Foreign Relations, 165, 166
—Senate Internal Security Subcommittee, 121, 152
—Senate Judiciary Committee, 117, 124, 152
—Senate Subcommittee on Human Rights, 121
—Senate Subcommittee on Labor, 181
Congressional conservatives: in postwar era, 53; reconversion policy and, 68; Truman and, 58–59; H. Wallace and, 61, 62; in World War II era, 47, 57; *see also* Southern Democrats
Congressional elections: *1942*: 222*n*46; *1946*: 68, 78; *1948*: 76, 82; *1950*: 162–64, 245*n*100, 248*n*9; *1952*: 172–73; *1960*: 190
Congressional Record, 10, 151
Congress Makes a Law (Bailey), 219*n*27
Congress of Industrial Organizations (CIO): 40; ER and, 67, 92–93, 109
Congress of Industrial Organizations Political Action Committee CIO-PAC), 62, 67, 98, 99, 157
Congress of Racial Equality (CORE): ER's support of, 119, 122, 127, 128, 194; *see also* CIFS; Freedom Riders
Connor, Eugene ("Bull"): and SCHW, 41
Conscientious objectors; ER's position on, 140–42, 237*n*26
Conservatives: Catholic, 175; civil libertarianism and, 135; criticism by, 2, 168–69, 203; fears of, 133; free speech debate and, 132; Mundt-Nixon Bill and, 159; "One Third of a Nation"

and, 35; price control policies and, 69–70; wartime investigations of, 136; youth and, 30; *see also* Congressional conservatives; Democratic conservatives; Republican party
Constitution, 88, 119, 143, 164, 170; Bill of Rights, 131, 137; First Amendment, 154, 167; Fourteenth Amendment, 102
Constitution Hall (D.C.), 42
Cook, Blanche Wiesen, 3, 138
Cook, Nancy: ER and, 11, 15, 21, 24
Cooke, Robert John, 221*n*42
Coolidge, Calvin: and election of 1950, 10
Corcoran Gallery: ER's visit to, 34
Corr, Maureen: ER and, 127
Costigan-Wagner Bill: ER's support for, 38
Coughlin, Charles E.: ER's concerns re, 26, 140
Council on Soviet-American Friendship, 122
Counterattack (periodical): ER attacked by, 133
Cox, James M.: FDR and, 9–10
"Cracking the Color Line" (CORE): ER's introduction to, 127
Craig, May: ER confides in 82
Creel Committee: ER's opinion of, 139
Crisis (periodical): DuBois and, 99, 100
Cuban Missile Crisis: ER's disinterest in, 197
Culbertson, John Bolt, 234*n*109
Current History (periodical): ER and, 13

Daniels, Jonathan: on ER, 93
Daniels, Josephus: on ER, 9, 12
Darden, Clement: lobbied by ER, 94
Darkness at Noon (Koestler): ER's review of, 167
Dartmouth College, 167
Daughters of the American Revolution (DAR), and Marian Anderson concert, 42–44
Davis, John W.: Al Smith and, 12

Davis, Kenneth S.: Marion Dickerman and, 16

Dawson (Ga.): arson in, 196

Death penalty: blacks and, 120

Declaration of Human Rights, *see* United Nations

Deficit spending: FDR and, 60

Democracy, ER on: accountability in, 27, 86; Christianity and, 58, 117, 217*n*16; civil rights and, 88, 89, 93, 102, 127, 129; communism and, 148, 155, 156, 168, 246*n*105; defensive mentality and, 178–79; freedom protections and, 136; HUAC and, 151; implementation of, 115, 134; international perceptions of, 74, 104, 164; Mundt-Nixon Bill and, 158, 159; in post-World War II era, 55; presidential responsibilities and, 177; public character and, 200; school desegregation and, 111; self-expression and, 137, 141; social egalitarianism and, 96; tolerance and, 28–29; youth commitment to, 30, 31

Democracy Reborn (H. Wallace), 58

Democratic Advisory Council (DAC): Benjamin and, 175; ER and, 177, 202, 249*n*13; Truman-ER debate before, 179–80, 181

Democratic coalition, 3–4; JFK and, 191; Truman and, 56, 66, 68, 71

Democratic conservatives: *Brown v. Board of Education* and, 115; civil rights legislation and, 117, 180; Eisenhower and, 202; JFK and, 187; Truman and, 56; *see also* Southern Democrats

Democratic electoral campaigns: *1920*: 9–10; *1928*: 14; *1946*: 78; *1948*: 79, 82–83; *1950*: 162–64; see also Douglas; Kennedy; Stevenson; Truman

Democratic National Committee (DNC), 22, 79, 114

Democratic National Conventions: ER and: *1924*: 12; *1940*: 44–45, 58; *1944*: 94–95; *1948*: 81; *1952*: 168; *1956*: 112–14, 115; *1960*: 178, 182, 183, 185–87, 251*n*28

Democratic party: black electorate and, 220*n*39; *Brown v. Board of Education* and, 109–18; civil rights and, 86, 125, 126, 177, 178, 201; communism and, 169–70; "crisis of the New Order" and, 77; in Eisenhower era, 4; ER's criticism of, 5, 79, 202; ER's loyalty to, 19, 59, 83–84, 174; ER's vision for, 1, 2, 5, 199, 201–203; JFK and, 175; labor organizations and, 67; North-South split in, 191; postwar domestic policy of, 55–56; principles of, 67–68; shortcomings of, 172; *see also* Democratic coalition; Democratic conservatives; Democratic party leadership; Dixiecrats; New York State Democratic party (NYSDP); Southern Democrats

Democratic party leadership: ER and, 48, 85, 202, 250*n*22; FDR legacy and, 84; 1948 election and, 76; 1960 election and, 180; temerity of, 171, 172; Truman and, 64; vision of, 179–181

"Democratic Senatorial and Congressional Candidates" (Pauley), 222*n*46

Democratic Women's Committee (DWC), 15, 16–17; *see also* New York State Democratic Committee Division

Dennan, William, 147

Dennis v. United States: Smith Act and, 153, 154, 155, 156, 241*n*66

Department of Commerce, 61, 62, 63, 70, 218*n*23

Department of Justice: Civil Rights Act and, 117, 124, 126; civil rights division of, 81; Columbia riots and, 99; Japanese Americans and, 143, 144; M. L. King and, 194; Mundt-Nixon Bill on, 158; Julius and Ethel Rosenberg and, 166

Department of Public Welfare (proposed), 222*n*45

Department of State: Communist China and, 166; DuBois statement and, 100, 101; McCarthy and, 165, 245*n*102, 246*n*103; Sorbonne address and, 102

Depression, *see* Great Depression

De Sapio, Carmine: ER's criticism of, 188

Desegregation, *see* Civil rights

Des Moines, 93

Detroit: race riot in, 91–92

Detroit Free Press: ER satirized in, 46

Dewey, Thomas: Democratic policy and, 81; gubernatorial campaign of, 68, 78; Drew Pearson on, 82; presidential campaign of, 60, 219*n*27

Dewson, Molly: ER and, 17, 196

Dickerman, Marion: politics of, 11; partners with ER, 15; on ER and FDR, 16, 21, 24

Dictatorships, *see* Totalitarianism

Dies, Martin, 35, 148; see also Congress, HUAC

Discrimination, *see* Racism

District of Columbia, *see* Washington, D.C.

District of Columbia Citizens Council for Community Planning, 103

District of Columbia School Board: Marian Anderson and, 42

Dixiecrats, 113

Dombrowski, Jim: and SCEF, 121, 152

Domestic policies: ER's legacy on 203; *see* civil rights; civil liberties; economic policies; education; full employment; Fair Deal; New Deal; wage and price controls

Domestic workers: Eleanor clubs and, 87

Douglas, Helen Gahagan: election of 1950 and, 163–64, 232*n*78, 242*n*81, 245*n*100, 248*n*9

Douglas, Paul, 169

Douglas, William O., and *Dennis vs. US*, 154, 155

Downey, Sheridan, 162

Downtown Community School (N.Y.C.): ER's speech before, 103–4

Draft Stevenson campaign (1960): ER's role in, 183, 184

Drummond, Burt: on ER and Hiss, 162

Dubinsky, David, 220–21*n*41

DuBois, W. E. B.: intercession for, 93; ER's rift with, 101, 102, 109, 228*n*43; "Statement on the Denial of Human Rights to Minorities," 99–100, 103; on World War II, 96

Dulles, John Foster: FBI and, 150; Hiss and, 160, 243*n*87

Dunjee, Roscoe, 105

Eastland, James: White Citizens Council and, 117, 121

"Economic Bill of Rights": FDR on 55, 60; Truman on, 63, 66; ER on, 201

Economic opportunity, 89, 220*n*39

Economic policies: ER's views on, 4, 28, 40, 51–76, 83; *see also* Consumers; Full employment policies; New Deal; Production; Wage-price controls

Education: federal aid to 30, 110, 116, 175, 248*n*8; *see* Schools; Vocational training; NYA

Edward Bok Peace Prize Committee, 137

Eisenhower, Dwight D., 4; candidacy of, 81; civil rights and, 116, 118, 126, 153; Democratic supporters of, 202; diplomacy of, 183; ER on, 116; at ER's funeral, 197; "kissing case" and, 123–24; McCarthy and, 167; Nixon and, 114, 164; reelection of, 116; Smith Act and, 156, 241*n*72; Stevenson vs., 110

Eisenhower, Milton: WRA policies and, 144

Eisler, Hans, 239*n*46

Eleanor Clubs: and FBI, 87

Electrical workers: strike of, 73, 248*n*9

Elk Lodge, 134

Ellis (Mississippi judge): civil rights and, 127

Emancipation Proclamation: legacy of, 80, 110; Stevenson on, 125, 231*n*65

Emergency Peace Committee: ER's support of, 137

Employment, *see* Full employment poli-
cies; Labor; Unemployment; FEPC
Employment Act (1946): legacy of, 69,
221*n*43; *see also* Full Employment
Employment Service: Truman and, 80
England, *see* Britain
"Ethiopia" (play): FTP and, 35
Executive Order 9066: 143

Fair Deal: ER's praise of, 80
Fair Employment Practices Commission
(FEPC): postwar plans for, 54, 55; C.
Houston and, 66, 97; investigations
by, 93; racial discrimination and, 96;
Reuther and, 72; Truman on, 81
Farley, Jim: ER and, 17, 23, 45, 213–14*n*53
Farmers: ER organizes, 12–13, 17; share-
croppers, 87, 93–94; migrant, 193
Farm Security Administration (FSA), 93
Farm workers: see farmers
Fascism: defeat of, 93; fear of, 137; isola-
tionism and, 138; monitoring of, 136;
New Deal and, 57–58; pacifism and,
142; pro-Allied propaganda and, 139;
Republican accusations of, 48; rise of,
28; Smith Act and, 240*nn*59, 60; U.S.
racism and, 90; *see also* Axis Powers;
Hitlerism; Nazi Germany
Fast, Howard: censorship and, 140
Faubus, Orval, 118
FDR Young Democrats of City College
(organization), 167–68
Federal Art Project (FAP): ER's role in,
35, 36; *see also* Public Works Art
Project (PWAP)
Federal Bureau of Investigation (FBI):
AYC and, 238*n*44; civil rights organizations and, 122; complaints to, 92,
225*n*4; ER dossier of, 87; Goldman
and, 148; Highlander workshop and,
118; HUAC and, 160, 162; internees
and, 144, 145; Lash "affair" and,
149–50; wartime investigations of,
136; on *The War Worker*, 104; *see*
Hoover
Federal Council of Churches: ER and, 98

Federal Emergency Relief Administration
(FERA), 24, 26–27; *see also* Federal
One Programs
Federal government: advocated overthrow of, 153, 154; alleged red infiltration of, 159; arts and, 33–34, 36;
Brown v. Board of Education and, 112,
113, 114; civil rights and, 81, 121, 125,
126, 231*n*65; economic intervention
by, 55, 61, 63, 64, 69; industry cooper-
ation with, 219*n*27; munitions industry and, 138; postwar investment by,
71; women appointees in, 193
Federal Home Loan Board, 218*n*23
Federal One Programs: ER as architect
of, 29–30, 33–36, 37
Federal Theater Project (FTP): ER and,
35–36
Federal Works Agency (FWA): discrimi-
nation and, 91
Federal Writers Project (FWP): ER and,
35, 36
Fellowship of Reconciliation: ER and,
156
Fields, W. C.: and J. Edgar Hoover on
ER, 150
Fieldston School, 107
Fighting Fund for Freedom (proposed),
104
Finletter, Tom: Draft Stevenson cam-
paign and, 183, 185; on ER, 188
Firing Line (periodical): ER criticized in,
121
First Amendment: ER on, 154, 167; *see*
Free expression
First 100 Days: 203; and ER, 24
First Methodist Church (Birmingham,
Ala.): and SCHW, 40–41
First Red Scare, 139, 152
Fish, Hamilton: and ER, 202
Flanagan, Hallie: and FTP, 35–36
Fleming, William, 97
Flynn, Ed: and ER, 52
Ford Motor Company: ER's criticism of,
67, 73
Foreign policy: Churchill and, 83; FDR

Foreign policy (*Continued*)
  and, 131, 200; JFK and, 178, 190, 191,
  192–93; Nixon and, 163; in postwar
  era, 2, 78, 79, 83; segregation as detri-
  ment to, 83–84, 131; Truman and, 83;
  Wallace and, 78–79; *see also* Isolation-
  ism; Marshall Plan; Soviet Union;
  Truman Doctrine
Foreman, Clark: civil rights and, 40, 91,
  98
Fortune (periodical), 48
Forum (periodical), 31
Foster, William Z., 240*n*63
Fourteenth Amendment: ER's interpreta-
  tion of, 102
Franco, Francisco, 137, 138
Freedom of assembly: ER's position on,
  149, 153, 154, 246*n*106
"Freedom Concert": Marian Anderson
  and, 41–44, 97, 213*n*48
Freedom Riders: attacked, 86, 127; ER's
  support of, 85, 86, 118–119, 192; ER on
  JFK and, 129, 194; *see* Committee on
  Inquiry
Freedom Schools, 85
Free expression, 132; ADA and, 241*n*66,
  246*n*106; in art, 33; conscientious
  objection and, 141; *Dennis v. United
  States* on, 154; Nixon on, 158, 159; in
  prewar era, 137; Smith Act and, 153;
  see also Censorship; First Amend-
  ment
Fuchs, Lawrence: JFK and, 174, 190
Full Employment Bill (S. 380): congres-
  sional debate on, 64, 65, 66; ER's
  support of, 64–65; introduction of,
  61; liberal groups and, 62, 69;
  Manasco and, 219*n*34; Truman-
  Wallace interpretations of, 63; UDA
  and, 221*n*43; Wagner and, 219*n*27; *see*
  Employment Act
Full employment policies: ER on, 54,
  60–69, 79, 218*n*23, 219*n*27
Fundamentalists: on ER, 133–34
Furman, Bess, 24, 26
"Fusion" ticket, 77

Gaines v. Canada; ER on, 108
Galbraith, John Kenneth, 184
Gallup polls, 44, 48, 201
Gandhi, Mahatma, 119
Garner, Ettie Rheiner, 23
Garner, John Nance, 23, 45
Gelder, Joe, 40
General Motors Corporation: ER's criti-
  cism of, 71, 72
George, Walter: on ER, 39, 61
The Georgia Woman's World: ER attacked
  in, 39
German American Bund: ER on, 140
German Americans: ER on, 143
Germany: information on, 139; Jews in,
  129; Poland invaded by, 138; press of,
  141; in prewar era, 137; spies of, 140;
  U.S. prisoners of, 120; USSR invaded
  by, 240*n*59
Gila River camp: ER's report on, 145; *see*
  Internment policies
Gilbert, Dan: on ER, 133
Gillette, Guy, 166
Glass, Carter: FDR and, 39
Golden, John, 215*n*4
Goldman, Emma; ER and, 148
Good Housekeeping, 14
Goodwin, Doris Kearns, 3
Go South for Sorrow (Rowan), 117
Grafflin, Arthur C., 162
Graham, Frank Porter; ER and, 40, 60,
  161
Grave, Bibs, 40
Great Depression, ER on: 24, 25, 28; eco-
  nomic causes of, 27; lessons of, 74;
  racism and, 88, 94; H. Wallace on,
  219*n*27
Greece, 163
Griffith, Robert, 136
Guilford (N.C.): ER threatened in, 117
Gurewitsch, David: ER's relationship
  with, 81, 183, 193, 196, 197
Gurewitsch, Edna: ER and, 183, 195
Gurewitsch, John, 195

Halsted, Anna Roosevelt Boettinger: on

ER and Lucy Mercer, 14, 207*n*23; on
ER and 1960 convention, 184

Halsted, Jim, 182

Hamby, Alonzo L., 217*n*12

Hannegan, Robert: as DNC chair, 79;
Cabinet appointment of, 56; ER's
advice to, 68–69; Cooke on, 221*n*42;
rejection of W. White and, 95

Hansen, Alvin: full employment and, 60

Harding, Warren G., 10

Harlem Artists Guild: ER and, 36

Harlem Community Art Center: visited
by ER, 36, 211*n*29

Harmon Foundation, 36

Harper's, 48

Harriman, Averell: NAACP and, 110, 112

Harrington, Oliver, 108

The Hartford Courant (newspaper), 20

The Harvard Lampoon (periodical), 20

Height, Dorothy: ER and, 119

Hellman, Lillian, 139

Hepburn, Katharine: ER as model for,
48

Herrick, Genevieve, 24

Hickok, Lorena: Beasley on, 209*n*38;
ER's confessions to, 2, 20, 21, 22, 24;
as ER's "First Friend," 24; ER introduced to press by, 200; ER teased by,
41; FERA and, 24, 26–27; 1940 Democratic Convention and, 45; Nixon
Senatorial campaign and, 164,
245*n*100; on ER's postwar opportunities, 52; travels with ER, 38, 200;
Truman described to, 65

Highlander Folk School: ER's support of,
107, 118, 126

Hill, Herbert, 104

Hillman, Sidney: NCPAC and, 67,
220*n*38

Hirabayashi case, 147

Hiss, Alger: ER's support of, 2, 5, 159–
162, 243*n*87; Nixon and, 159–62, 175,
244*n*95; O'Reilly on, 242*n*83;
Stevenson and, 161, 243–44*n*89; mentioned, 164, 175, 202

Hitler, Adolf, 88, 137, 139, 240*n*59

Hitlerism: ER accused of, 95

Hitler Youth, 30

Hobby, Oveta, 144

Hodges, Luther, 124

Hohri, Sam, 143

Hollywood Ten, 157, 239*n*46

Holocaust, 1

Hook, Sidney, 155

Hooker, Harry, 215*n*4

Hoover, Herbert, 207*n*20

Hoover, J. Edgar: AYC and, 238*n*44; hostility toward ER, 149–50; memo to re:
ER, 225*n*4; on ER's "Negro blood,"
87; popular appeals to re: ER, 90, 133;
ER confers with, 236*n*21

Hoover, Lou, 192

Hopkins, Harry: black farmers and, 93–
94; Churchill and, 139; Hickok and,
26; public arts programs and, 34, 35;
on Truman, 57; H. Wallace and, 62,
216*n*9; in World War II era, 200;
youth programs and, 31, 32

Horton, Myles, 136, 152

Hospitals, 152

Hotel Watkins (Houston), 118

Hotel Watkins (Los Angeles), 110

House Un-American Activities Commit-
tee, *see* Congress. House Un-
American Activities Committee
(HUAC)

Housing: Amityville, 104; Arthurdale,
103, 214*n*55; civil rights and, 103–
105; D.C., 38, 105–6; Deerfield, 194;
Detroit, 91; ER on, 91–92, 103–4,
106–7, 229*n*48; internment camps
and, 144; JFK and, 192, 193, 197;
Lexington, 104–5; Louisville, 121–22;
McCarran Housing bill, 103; New
York City, 105; riots over, 91–92; substandard, 38, 105–106; shortages of
105, *see Brown*

Houston (Tex.), 117–18

Houston, Charles, 66, 97

Howard University: M. Anderson and,
42; criticized 39; ER's support of, 38,
39, 107

Howe, Louis: ER and disputes with James Farley, 17, 23; on ER as FDR's successor, 49; as friend of ER and FDR and, 14, 25; 1928 gubernatorial campaign and, 14; influence on ER, 9, 14, 200; news media and, 200; 1920 vice presidential campaign and, 9
Humphrey, Hubert: Communist Control Act and, 169–70; ER's criticism of 169–170, 182; ER's praise for, 177, 249*n*14
Hungwai Ching, 144
Hunter College, 245*n*103
Huston, John, 48

Ickes, Harold L.: vs. ER on Arthurdale, 214*n*55; on internment policy, 145, 146; resentment of ER by, 47; urges ER to run for Senate, 52; Truman and, 216–217*n*12
"If You Ask Me" (ER), 87
Independent Citizens Committee of the Arts, Sciences and Professions, 62
India, 119
Indochina, 193
Industrial interests, 71, 72, 73, 74
Industrial strikes, *see* Strikes
Inflation, 70, 75, 223*n*58
Integration, *see* civil rights
Internal Security Act: ER's opposition to, 163, 242*n*81
International Federation of Business and Professional Women, 151–52
International Ladies' Garment Workers Union (ILGWU), 221*n*41
Internment policies: 140, 142–147; as civil rights issue, 144, 147; FDR vs. ER on, 4, 140, 142–43; *see* Japanese Americans
Interracial marriage: ER on, 95, 96
In the Shadow of FDR (Leuchtenburg), 203, 208*n*30
Isolationism: ER's criticism of, 138, 166
Israel: ER's support for, 79–80, 196
Isseis, *see* Japanese Americans
"I Want You to Write to Me" (ER), 26

Jackson, Gardner, 92
Jackson Daily News, 92
Japan, 138, 139, 141, 237–38*n*34
Japanese American Citizens League, 143
Japanese Americans: wartime experiences of, 4, 140, 142–47
Jeffries, Edward, 91
Jenner, William, 165–66, 246*n*104
Jessup, Philip, 166
Johnson, Evans C.: ER defends civil rights to, 87, 88
Johnson, Lady Bird: on ER, 38
Johnson, Lyndon: Civil Rights Act and, 117, 124; ER's criticism of 117, 124–125; Humphrey and, 182; 1960 election and, 185, 192; Truman on, 179
Jones, Jesse: removed from Commerce by FDR, 61, 62; H. Wallace vs., 54, 61, 213–14*n*53, 216*n*9, 218*n*23

Kearney, James, 32
Kefauver, Estes, 110, 176
Kellogg-Briand Treaty: ER's support of, 137
Kennedy, John F.: ER's reproval of, 2, 5, 169, 171–174, 186–192, 193–195, 202; at ER's funeral, 197; Freedom Riders and, 127–28, 129, 194; 1960 campaign of, 171–92; McCarthy and, 169, 175–178; *On My Own* on, 249*n*16; presidency of, 192–94, 197
Kennedy, Joseph P.: ER and, 5, 175, 253*n*58; Hollywood connections of, 248*n*9; McCarthy and, 172–173; wealth of, 180–181
Kennedy, Robert F.: Freedom Riders and, 128, 129; housing integration and, 193; McCarthy and, 169, 172, 176; at 1960 convention, 185–86
Kenyon, Dorothy: attacked by McCarthy, 165, 245*n*102, 245–46*n*103
Keynesianism, 62, 66
King, Coretta Scott: B. Rustin on ER and, 129, 234–35*n*112
King, Martin Luther, Jr.: ER and, 116, 196; on ER, 85–86, 129, 203; JFK and,

193–94; G. Wallace and, 114; *The Wall Between* and, 122

Kipling, Rudyard, 89

Kirchwey, Freda, 56

Kirkendall, Richard S., 216*n*9

"Kissing case," 123–24

Koestler, Arthur: ER on, 167

Korean War, 163

Korematsu case, 147

Krock, Arthur, 48–49

Ku Klux Klan: threats against ER by, 2, 118, 121, 196, 202

Labor: ER's support of, 66–67, 72–73, 75–76; FDR and, 68; legislation re: 18, 181; rights of, 156; Stevenson and, 183; wage-price control issue and, 70, 71, 72, 73, 74, 220*n*37; *see also* J. Carey; FEPC; Miners; W. Reuther; Strikes; Taft-Hartley; Truman

La Guardia, Fiorello, 77

Landis, James, 176

Lane, Franklin, 9

Langer, William, 121, 152

Lansing, Edward, 34

Lape, Esther, 10, 196

Lash, Joseph: on ADA, 76, 246*n*106; correspondence with ER, 51, 58, 640, 220*n*38; hospital visit by, 197; on JFK, 174, 190; McCarthy and, 169; on new party, 77, 223*n*61; on 1956 Democratic platform, 113; Rauh and, 126; Reuther and, 72; on Roosevelt marriage, 19; Starnes and, 149; Stix and, 207*n*24

Lash, Trude: on Byrnes, 57; correspondence of, 92, 179; on ER, 47; teasing by, 53; voice of, 150

Lasker, Mary: on Stevenson-Kennedy rivalry, 181, 188, 190, 191

Leach, Henry Goddard, 31

League of Nations (LN), 137, 138

League of Women Voters (LWV): ER and, 10–11, 13, 17, 22, 206*n*14

Lee, George, 120–21

Lehman, Herbert, 192

Lens, Paul, 241*n*71

Leuchtenburg, William, 203, 208*n*30, 221*n*42

Levenson, Eleanor, 148

Lewis, John L., 75, 223*n*59

Liberalism: anti-communism confused with, 79; communism and, 155, 246*n*105; conservative fears of, 133; "crisis of the New Order" and, 77; Democratic weakness and, 172; ER's vision of, 1–5; Employment Act and, 69; Hiss representative of, 159; in late 20th century, 203; 1960 election and, 180; in postwar era, 2, 3, 55–56, 59, 135

Liberals: anti-communist movement and, 4–5, 148, 165, 169–70; Bowles and, 70; civil rights movement and, 120, 125–26; communists and, 77, 224*n*63, 246*n*105; egotism of, 126, 171; ER's criticisms on, 201–204; electoral politics and, 76, 78, 83, 178, 187; free speech debate and, 132; Hiss and, 5, 161, 242*n*83; postwar policies of, 54; Republican, 68–69; Smith Act and, 154–55, 156; Southern, 40, 87, 88; Truman and, 64, 179–80, 217*n*14, 221*n*42; in vital center, 84, 201; Wallace confirmation and, 61, 62; World War II and, 1; youth and, 30; *see* ADA; JFK; Niebuhr; Schlesinger; Stevenson

Libraries: ER on, 167

Library of Congress, 144

Lincoln, Abraham, 26, 80, 125

Lincoln Memorial (D.C.): Marian Anderson and, 42, 80, 102

Linzer, Estelle, 188

Little Rock (Ark.): and Central High School, 86, 118, 124, 178

Lodge, Henry Cabot, 172

Long, Huey, 26

Longworth, Alice Roosevelt: ER criticized by, 46

Louisville Courier-Journal: B. Bingham and, 37, 104

Loyalist Spaniards, 137

Loyalty oaths: ER's opposition to, 175, 244*n*95, 247*n*116

Lucy, Autherine, 116

Lynchings, 41; *see also* Antilynching legislation

Lynn, Conrad: "kissing case" and, 123, 124, 129

Lyon, Louis, 182

McAllister, Frank, 91

MacArthur, Douglas, 166

McCall's, 156

McCarran Housing Bill: 103, *see* housing

McCarran Internal Security Act, 163, 242*n*81

McCarthy, Joseph: ER's opposition to, 2, 4, 157, 164–70, 202; JFK and, 169, 175, 176, 178, 181, 184, 249*n*16; Kennedy family and, 5, 172–73; Kenyon and, 245*n*102, 245–46*n*103; Wechsler and, 155

McDonald, William, 36

McGovern, George, 245*n*100

McGrath, J. Howard, 79

McIntyre, Marvin, 37

McLaurin v. Oklahoma State Regents, 108

Macomb (Miss.), 126

Manasco, Carter, 66

Manasco Committee, 66, 70, 219*n*34

Mann, Thomas, 139

Manzanar (Calif.), 145, 147, *see also* internment

Mao Tse-tung, 154

Marcantonio, Vito: Nixon and, 153, 163

Marcus, Bernice, 123

Marcus, Sissy, 123

Marian Anderson Citizens Committee, 42

Markowitz, Norman, 63

Marriage: ER on, 95, 96; *see also* Interracial marriage

Marshall, George: ER vs. on race relations, 102; and internment, 144; McCarthy's attack on, 165–66, 246*n*104; *see also* Marshall Plan

Marshall, Margaret, 56

Marshall, Thurgood: ER and, 99, 102, 108

Marshall Plan: 163; ER on, 79, 83

Martin, John Bartlow, 185

Martinsville Seven, 239*n*55

Mason, Lucy Randolph, 40

Massey, Michael, 217*n*14, 221*n*42

Materialism: ER on dangers of, 27

Matthews, J. B., 148–49

Mays, Benjamin, 250*n*22

Mead, Margaret, 250*n*22

Meatpackers, 73

Media, *see* News media

"Meet the Press," ER's appearance on, 182, 232*n*78, 251*n*27

Melish, William Howard, 122

Mercer, Lucy, 7, 14

Meredith, James, 196

Meyer, Agnes: Stevenson campaigns and, 182, 183, 185, 188, 190

Meyer, Dillon, 146

Migrant farm workers, 193

Military intelligence: FDR on, 136; ER and, 144

Military personnel, 141; army, 92, 144, 146; female, 93, 144; navy, 9

Military preparedness: ER on, 138

Military service: ER on 75, 88, 140

Miller, Earl, 24

Miners, 37, 39, 75, 223*n*59

Minimum wage legislation: ER on, 181

Miroff, Bruce, 249*n*17

Mississippi: civil rights in, 41, 86, 121, 127

Mitchell, Clarence, 125

Mixed marriage, 95, 96

Mobile (Ala.), 92

Mobilization for Human Needs: ER and, 32

Monroe (N.C.), 125

Monroney, Mike, 183

The Moral Basis of Democracy (ER), 28, 89

Morgenthau, Elinor, 15, 24

Morgenthau, Henry, 17

Morgenthau, Henry, III: on ER and JFK, 181, 182, 251*n*27

Morgenthau, Henry, Jr., 52, 56

Morse, Wayne, 249*n*14
Moses, Bob, 128
Moses, Robert, 18
Moskowitz, Belle: ER on, 13, 18
Mothers League of Little Rock (MLLR),
   118
Moulthrop, M. M., 95
Mumford, Lewis, 241*n*71
Mundt, Karl, 158
Mundt-Nixon Bill, 158–59, 242*n*81
Munitions industry: ER on, 138
Murray, James, 61
Murray, Pauli: correspondence with ER,
   110, 111; on ER, 96, 116; Presidential
   Commission on the Status of Women
   and, 193; on social equality, 95; Waller
   and, 94
Murray-Kilgore Reconversion Bill,
   218*n*23
Murray-Wagner Full Employment Bill,
   see Full Employment Bill (S. 380)
Muse, Vance, 46
Muskie, Edmund, 249*n*14
Mussolini, Signora Benito, 48
Muste, A. J., 156
"My Day" (ER): circulation of, 48; on
   civil rights legislation, 4, 125; on compromise, 221*n*43; on Condon, 151; on
   conscientious objectors, 141; on DAR,
   42–43, 44; on FDR's restrictions, 60;
   on foreign service, 166–67; on full
   employment, 65, 69; on housing, 103;
   on international aggression, 138; on
   Japanese Americans, 142–43, 144; on
   JFK, 181–182; on labor-management
   disputes, 72, 74, 76; last columns for,
   195; on literature, 167; on McCarthy,
   165; on Mundt-Nixon Bill, 158–59;
   on 1948 campaign, 83; on NYA, 33;
   on production, 222–23*n*52; reader
   response to, 134; renewal contract for,
   44, 201; on responsibility, 28; on
   SCEF, 121; Scripps-Howard chain
   and, 117; on Truman civil rights policy, 80; on H. Wallace, 62, 78; on
   youth concerns, 32

Myrdal, Gunnar: ER interviewed for, 88,
   89, 96

Napoleon I, Emperor of the French, 189
The Nation, 56, 136
National Association for the Advancement of Colored People (NAACP):
   Civil Rights Act and, 124; Columbia
   riot and, 98–99; DAR and, 42; ER
   and, 96–109; FDR and, 38, 39, 95,
   227*n*24; C. Houston and, 66, 97;
   "kissing case" and, 123; Lynn on, 129;
   national conventions of, 38, 39, 43,
   44, 80, 102; 1956 campaign and, 110,
   113; Powell amendment and, 111; rift
   in, 102; SCEF and, 121, 122; UN and,
   101; Waller and, 94; Wherry compromise and, 109; C. Wilson and, 104;
   mentioned, 120; *see* ER, civil rights
   and
—Board of Directors: DuBois and, 99–
   100, 228*n*43; ER and, 95, 96, 97, 112,
   201; mentioned, 86
—Legal Defense and Education Fund:
   ER and, 98, 107, 108, 122–23
—Public Relations Committee: ER and,
   107–8
National Association of Manufacturers
   (NAM): ER's criticisms of, 69, 74, 75
National Broadcasting Company (NBC),
   39, 43
National Bureau of Standards, 151
National Citizens Political Action Com-
   mittee (NCPAC): ER and, 61, 62, 67,
   220*n*38
National Committee for Justice in
   Columbia, Tennessee (NCJCT): ER
   and, 86, 99, 201
National Committee on Segregation in
   the Nation's Capital, 105
National Conference on the Cause and
   Cure of War: ER and, 137
National Consumers League: ER and, 10,
   40
National Council of Negro Women
   (NCNW): ER and, 106

National Democratic forum: ER and, 89

National Farmers Union: ER and, 54, 60, 62

National Guard, 98

National Issues Committee (NIC): ER and, 202

National Lawyers Guild: ER and, 98, 99

National Negro Council, 100

National Resources Planning Board (NRPB): ER and, 60

National Review, 168

National Sharecroppers Week: ER on, 94

National Urban League: ER's speech before, 38, 39

National Youth Administration (NYA): ER's influence on, 29, 30–33, 37, 94, 107

National Youth Conference, 102

Native Son (Wright), 36

Navy Relief, 8

Nazi-Soviet Pact, 153

Negroes: *see* Black Americans

Negro Art Exhibition (Tex.), 36

Negro Digest: ER's article in, 89–90

Nehru, Jawaharlal, 120

Nelson case, 122

Nesbit, Henrietta, 37

New Deal: anticommunist movement and, 132; as ER-FDR battleground, 23, 196, 200; black civil rights and, 37–44, 85, 93; disaffection with, 26; European fascism and, 57–58; free speech debate and, 132; Hiss representative of, 159, 160; housing issue and, 103; idealism in, 29; postwar preservation of, 53–54; rightists vs., 136; Southern congresspersons and, 47; Southern Democrats vs., 40, 216*n*9; Truman and, 56, 57, 217*n*12; youth employment and, 30, 32; women and, 25; World War II and, 138, 140, 215–16*n*7; *see* ER, New Deal Policies and; Second New Deal; specific agencies and legislation

Newell, James Michael, 34

New Frontier, 174

"The New Governmental Interest in Art" (ER): and PWAP, 33–34

New Orleans: 152, 178; schoolboard in, 121

The New Republic: on Columbia riot, 98; on communism, 155; on racism, 89; on Truman, 56, 83, 219*n*32; H. Wallace and, 58, 62

News media: ER and, 2, 200; on Birmingham visit, 41; civil rights movement and, 128, 129; on Columbia riot, 98; on "Eleanor Clubs," 87; in first FDR term, 19–21, 25–26; foreign, 141; in "governorship years," 16, 18–19; Hiss case and, 161, 244*nn*90, 95; McCarthy and, 167, 245*n*102; in 1920s, 10; on 1960 presidential campaign, 187; on Nixon, 164; on race relations, 39, 92–93; on Stevenson, 184; on Truman, 56; in World War II era, 90; *see also* ER, as journalist; individual publications; *New York Times*; Radio broadcasts; Television broadcasts; Women reporters

New South (periodical), 98

New York City Board of Education: ER and, 195

New York City Democratic party: ER's criticism of, 195

New York Committee for Democratic Voters: ER and, 188

New York Committee for Kennedy: ER and, 191

New York Draft Stevenson Committee: ER as chair, 184

The New Yorker: parody of ER in, 39

New York Junior League, 46

New York Post: James Wechsler and, 155, 169

New York State: gubernatorial elections in, 13, 14, 15, 68, 78; labor legislation in, 18; 1960 presidential election and, 187, 188, 189, 191; rural vote in, 12–13, 17

New York State Assembly: ER on, 10, 200

New York State Democratic Committee: ER and, 17, 182, 251*n*28

New York State Democratic Committee Women's Division: ER and, 10, 11, 12; anti-war memoranda and, 137; seed money for, 17; A. Smith campaign and, 13

New York State Democratic party: ER as activist for, 12–13, 15, 17, 206*n*14

New York State Industrial Commission: ER and, 17

New York State Mayor's Conference: ER and, 17

New York State Penal Law: ER and, 12

New York State Senate: FDR and, 7, 8

New York Times: ER interviews with, 16, 19, 28; on 1936 election, 39; on 1960 presidential campaign, 187; on "One Third of a Nation," 35; on presidential succession, 48–49; on Stevenson, 184

New York Times Magazine: ER interviewed by, 13, 30

The New York World (newspaper), 12

New York World Telegram (newspaper), 135

New Zealand, 92

Niebuhr, Reinhold: as Cold War Liberal, 2, 132, 156, 241*n*71, 250*n*22

Nixon, Richard M.: ER on, 114, 157–64, 202, 232*n*78; on H. Clinton, 203; H. G. Douglas vs., 162–64, 245*n*100, 248*n*9; Hiss and, 159, 160, 161, 162, 175, 244*n*95; JFK vs., 174, 182, 187, 189, 252*n*43; McCarran Internal Security Act and, 242*n*81; McCarthy and, 164, 165, 166; Mundt-Nixon bill, 158–159, 242*n*81

No-Foreign War Crusade: ER and, 137

Non-Partisan Legislative Committee: ER and, 22

Norris, George: on ER, 45

North American News Alliance, 20

North American Review, 13

North Carolina, 38

Northern California Conference for Protection of the Foreign Born: ER on, 153

North, the: ER on discrimination in, 106–7, 116, 122, 124

Norton, Mary: and ER, 52

Nuclear test ban treaty: ER on, 193

Nye, George P., 138

O'Connor, Basil("Doc"): on ER, 46–47

O'Day, Caroline: ER and, 11, 15

Office of Economic Stabilization: Bowles and, 70, 71, 73

Office of Minority Affairs: Bethune and, 33

Office of Price Administration (OPA): Bowles and, 61, 70, 71, 79, 221*n*45

Office of Production Management, 69

Office of War Mobilization and Reconversion, 65

O'Mahoney, Joseph, 61

"One Third of a Nation" (play): ER on, 35

On My Own (ER), 53, 249*n*16

O'Reilly, Kenneth, 242*n*83

Paine, Thomas: quoted by ER, 135

Palmer, Charles: housing policies of, 91

Pandit, Madame Vijaya, 120

Parks, Lillian Rogers: on ER, 37

Parks, Rosa: ER's advice to, 136

Parmet, Herbert, 75, 175

Parochial schools: ER on, 175, 248*n*8

Patrick, Luther: antilynching legislation and, 41

Patton, James: and ER, 54, 60, 218*n*23

Pauley, Edwin: ER's opposition to, 56, 222*n*46

Peace Corps: ER's support of, 174, 192, 237*n*24

Peace movement: and ER, 137–38, 139–40, 142

Peace Production Board (proposed): Reuther, ER, and, 69

Pearl Harbor attack: ER's response to, 141, 142, 143

Pearson, Drew, 82
Pegler, Westbrook: on ER, 48, 140, 153–54
Perkins, Frances: ER and, 17, 45, 47, 56, 82
Philippines, 237*n*24
Planned Parenthood: ER and, 133
Plessy v. Ferguson, 102
PM (periodical), 56
Polish Americans, 91
Poll tax, 86, *see* civil rights, voting rights
Popular Front, 148, 201, 240*n*59, 242*n*83
Poston (Ariz.): internment camp and, 145
Powell, Adam Clayton: and ER, 116, 192
Powell Amendment: ER's support of, 110, 111–12, 116
Prejudice, *see* Racism
Prendergast, Michael: ER and political machine of, 182, 251*n*28
Presidential Commission on the Status of Women: ER and, 174, 193
Presidential duties: ER's definition of, 177, 179, 180
Presidential Commission on Civil Rights: Truman and, 80, 81
Presidential elections: *1920*: 9–10; *1928*: 12, 13–14; *1932*: 19–20, 21–22, 23; *1936*: 38–39, 46; *1944*: 47, 95, 216*n*10; *1948*: 76, 77, 79, 83; *1956*: 109; *1960*: 171–97; *see* ER, Presidential Politics and; Democratic national conventions; Democratic party; Republican party
Press, *see* News media
Price, Hampton: kissing case and, 123, 125
Price controls, *see* Wage-price controls
Price Controls Act: Truman, ER on, 73, 75, 223*n*58
"The Price of Free World Victory" (H. Wallace), 58, 218*n*16
Profiles in Courage (JFK): ER on, 177
Progressive Citizens of America: ER, Wallace on, 79, 224*n*63
Prohibition: ER on, 20, 208*n*35
Propaganda, 139

"Prospects for Mankind" (TV series); ER as host of, 181, 182, 251*n*27
Protestant fundamentalists: criticism of ER, 133–34
Public education, *see* Schools
Public housing, *see* housing
Public Works Art Project (PWAP), 34; *see also* Federal Art Project (FAP)

Quakers: as conscientious objectors, 137
Queens (N.Y.); ER's visit to, 195

Rachin, Carl, 127, 234*n*109
Race riots, 88, 92, 98, 104
Racism: in Baton Rouge, 127; in Birmingham, 40–41, 119; in Columbia, TN, 87–99; in D.C., 66, 97, 105–6; in Detroit, 91–92; in education, 39, 102; fascism equated with, 90; in Georgia, 196; in housing, 103–6, 107, 121, 194; literature on, 167; overcoming of, 28–29, 88; in South Africa, 109, 127, 193; *see also* Aryanism; race riots; White supremacists
Radical right, *see* Fascism
Radio Free Europe, 139
Railroad Trainmen and Locomotive Engineers brotherhood, 75, 76
Railway Labor Act: ER and, 73, 222*n*51
Randolph, A. Philip: ER and, 93, 94, 122
Rand School Bookstore, 148
Rankin, John, 151
Rape: and racial violence, 120, 123–24, 152, 239*n*55
Raskob, John, 17
Rauh, Joe: Committee of Inquiry into the Administration of Justice in the Freedom Struggle and, 234*n*109; on free speech, 241*n*66; JFK and, 184; on judges, 128; J. Lash and, 126; McCarthy and, 169; 1956 Democratic platform and, 114, 231*n*71
Rayburn, Sam, 52, 179
Read, Elizabeth, 10
Reconstruction Finance Corporation

(RFC): Commerce Department and, 61, 62, 63, 70, 218*n*23; Jones-Wallace rivalry and, 54

Red-baiting, *see* communism, allegations of

Redbook, 13

Red Cross: ER and, 8–9, 143

Red Scare (1919), 139, 152

Religion, 140; *see also* Christianity

Rent controls, 73

Report on Economic Conditions in the South, 40

Republican party: blacks and, 94, 125; campaigns, 202; *1940*: 44, 45; *1944*: 95; *1946*: 78; *1948*: 81, 82; *1950*: 162; *1956*: 112; *Harper's* on, 48; liberals in, 68–69; McCarthy and, 165; Democratic "outconserving" of, 5, 79; Powell amendment and, 111; Second New Deal and, 57; Southern Democrats and, 68; UN and, 166; wage-price controls and, 69, 71

Reuther, Mary, 196

Reuther, Walter: blacks and, 91; ER and, 67, 72; Peace Production Board proposal of, 69; Stevenson and, 183, 188; Truman and, 66; at Val-Kill, 196

Rich, Marvin, 127

Richmond (Va.): NAACP and, 43

Riots, *see* race riots

Robeson, Paul: ER on, 91

Roosevelt, Alice: on ER, 46

Roosevelt, Anna, *see* Halsted, Anna

Roosevelt, Anna Hall, 7

Roosevelt, Elliott, 81

Roosevelt, Eleanor: communist allegations against, 135–136; criticism of 46–47, 133–134; dual stature of, 133; as first lady of New York, 15–16; health of, 128, 172, 193; leaves White House, 52; New York State politics and, 10–14, 16–19; political development of, 51; political philosophy of, 2–5, 27–29, 135; political skills of, 83–84; popularity of, 48; impact of World War I on, 8–9

—*Civil Liberties and:* accused of communism for supporting, 133–134, 136; American Youth Congress and, 148–149; breaks with vital center on, 84, 201; her critics and, 140; conscientious objectors and, 140–142; W. Douglas and, 154, 155; on role of FBI in, 149–150; Hiss case, and, 158–162; criticism of HUAC on, 148–151; internment and, 142–147; on JFK and, 171–173; on loyalty oaths and, 175, 244*n*95, 247*n*116; McCarthyism and, 164–170; modification of stance on, 4, 131–132, 140; on Mundt-Nixon bill, 158–59; peace movement and, 137–140; as lay philosopher for, 133–135, 147–148, 201–202; differences with FDR over, 131, 132, 136–137, 142–143; on Smith Act, 148, 153–156; on Truman, 175; *see also* Communist; Communism; Communism, allegations of; *Dennis vs. US*; Nixon; SCEF

—*Civil Rights and:* Marian Anderson controversy and, 41–44; antilynching legislation and, 38–39; Bethune and, 32, 33, 93, 94, 96, 98, 107; *Brown vs. Topeka* and, 106–113; civil disobedience and, 118, 126–129; Civil Rights Act of 1957, and, 116–117, 124–125, 177–178, 249*n*17; Civil Rights Act of 1960 and, 125–126; Columbia, Tn riots and, 97–99; criticism received for, 46, 87–88, 90, 118; 1956 Democratic convention and, 109–116; Detroit riots and, 91–92; DuBois and, 99–102; Harriman and, 110, 112; hedges on social equality, 95; D. Height, and, 113; housing and, 38, 91–92, 103–107; C. Houston and, 97; Humphrey and, 177; comparison of Jim Crow to Aryanism by, 88–90, 93, 95, 96; LBJ and, 117, 124–125; JFK and, 127–128, 129, 249*n*17; Coretta King and, 129, 234–235*n*112; M. L. King and, 85–86, 116, 129, 196; KKK and, 118; P. Murray and, 94, 95, 96,

110, 111, 116, 193; NAACP and, 38, 39, 96–107; A. P. Randolph, and, 94; relationship with leaders of, 85, 93–96; B. Rustin and, 119, 129, 234–235*n*112; SCEF and, 86, 118–122, 153; SCHW and, 40–41, 86, 91, 119; Stevenson and, 110–111, 113, 231*n*65; understanding of, 4, 85–86, 88–90; UN and, 99–104; O. Waller and, 94; W. White and, 93, 94–95, 96, 98, 100–101, 109, 140, 144; on White Citizens Councils. 117–118; White House staff and, 37; R. Wilkins and, 110–111; *see also* ER, and Presidential Politics

—*FDR and:* 1920 campaign and, 9–10; 1932 campaign and, 19, 23, 46, 47; death of 3, 51–53, 57; influence on, 30–37; partnership with, 2, 14, 19, 27, 46, 207*n*23; political differences with, 15, 23, 29, 47, 131, 132, 136–137, 200

—*as journalist:* in print, 11, 13, 14, 20, 24, 26, 28,31, 39, 89–90, 98, 115, 117, 135, 136, 144, 151, 156, 167, 178, 200, 206*n*14, 209*n*38, 245*n*102, 250*n*22; on radio, 20, 22, 24, 39, 43, 105; on television, 181–182, 192, 194, 232*n*78, 251*n*27

—*New Deal policies and:* advocates economic relief, 29; begins column, 26; CCC projects and, 34; Federal Artists Project and, 34–35; Federal Theater Project and, 35–36; Federal Writers Project and, 35–36; architect of NYA, 30–33, 37; press conferences during, 25–26; Subsistence Homesteads and, 29, 47, 103, 214*n*55; *see also* ER, Civil Rights and; ER, Civil Liberties, and; ER, FDR and; New Deal

—*Presidential Politics: JFK and:* attends inaugural of, 192; disappointment with, 193–194; doubts re: 5, 171–174, 177–178; 1956 opposition to, 175–176; 1960 campaign reproval of, 179–182; election of 1960 and, 186–192; *see also* JFK; Civil Rights; Civil Liberties;

Foreign Policy; *Stevenson and:* 1960 candidacy of, 182–184; 1960 convention and, 184–186; 1960 election and, 189–191; *see also* Civil Rights; Civil Liberties; Stevenson; *Truman and:* criticism of, 55–58, 76, 79; DAC debate with, 179–180; election of 1948 and, 81–83; election of 1956 and, 110; eventual support of 78–84; *see also* Civil Liberties: Civil Rights; FEPC; Full Employment; and Truman; Wage and Price Controls; *Wallace and:* 1940 convention and, 44–45; as FDR's true successor, 58, 59; as vice president, 57–50; 1948 candidacy of, 76–78, 85; *see also* Eisenhower; Humphrey

—*Reconversion Economics and:* B. Baruch and, 72; C. Bowles and, 70–71, 73–75; vs FDR on 60, 63, 64; lobbyist for full employment, 60–69; labor unrest and, 74–76; supports Murray Wagner Bill, 69; on veto of Price Control Act, 69; Reuther and, 72–73; opposition to Taft-Hartley, 79; vs. Truman on, 60–69, 70–76; ER's vision for, 54–55; wage and price controls and, 69–76; comments on UMW strike, 75–76; *see also* FEPC; Housing; Labor; Strikes

Roosevelt, Franklin D.: Arthurdale and, 214*n*55; Baruch and, 72; blacks and, 37, 68, 91, 92, 93; Bowles and, 76, 221–222*n*45, 249*n*14; CCC and, 31; Cabinet appointment of, 8; Costigan-Wagner Bill and, 38; critics of, 26; death of, 1; free speech issue and, 137; full employment proposals and, 60, 63, 64; funeral for, 51–52, 56–57; governorship of, 17–18; gubernatorial campaign of, 13, 14, 15; J. E. Hoover and, 150; internment policy of, 4, 140, 142–47, 201; Japanese imports and, 139; JFK compared to, 174, 194; marriage of, 14, 19, 207*n*23; NAACP and, 38, 39, 95, 227*n*24; NYA and, 30, 31–32; paralysis of, 11; political heirs of, 49, 58, 81, 218*n*16; political legacy of, 84, 133, 203; popularity of, 48, 57, 201; public housing and, 103; Reuther and, 67; "second Bill of Rights" speech, 70; A. Smith and, 12; Southern Democrats and, 39–40; Soviet invasion and, 240*n*59; Stalin and, 132; tells ER of Polish invasion and, 138; Truman and, 54, 55, 56; vice presidential campaign of, 9–10; H. Wallace and, 44–45, 54, 58–62; Waller and, 94; *see* New Deal; ER, FDR and

Roosevelt, Franklin, Jr.: JFK and, 81, 248*n*12

Roosevelt, James: on ER, 11, 16; and JFK, 188, 248*n*12

Roosevelt, Sara Delano: ER and, 7, 8, 9, 38

Roosevelt, Theodore, 7

Roosevelt, Mrs. Theodore: as first lady, 21–22

Roosevelt, Theodore, Jr., 13

Roosevelt High School (Rotterdam, N.Y.), 123

Rose, Flora, 146

Rosenberg, Ethel and Julius, 166

Rosenman, Sam: on ER, 45, 46–47, 222*n*45

Rougeau, Weldon: ER's support of, 127, 128

Rowan, Carl: ER on, 117

Ruleville (Miss.): murders in, 196

Rusk, Dean, 102

Russell, Richard: ER's criticism of, 117, 124

Rustin, Bayard: and ER, 119; on Coretta King vs ER, 129, 234–35*n*112

St. Elizabeth's Hospital: ER on, 9, 205*n*7

Sakanishi, Shio, 144

San Francisco Press Club: Douglas Nixon debate before, 163

Sarnoff, David, 105

The Saturday Evening Post, 39, 178

Schaeffer-Bernstein, Carola von: ER and, 138–39

Schine, David: bookburning by, 167

Schlesinger, Arthur, Jr.: ADA and, 169, 241*n*66; anti-communist movement and, 132; on ER, 185; on "fighting faith," 2; Hiss and, 5; JFK and, 184, 187, 251*n*27; Smith Act and, 155; on Stevenson, 190; on "vital center," 1

Schomburg Center for African American Culture, 211*n*29

School integration: JFK and, 177; NAACP and, 102; in New Orleans, 121; Powell Amendment and, 111–12, 116; Stevenson on, 110–11, 231*n*65; Supreme Court and, 106–8, 231*n*71; *see* Powell Amendment; *Brown vs. Topeka*

Schools, 39, 102, 175, 248*n*8; *see also* Vocational training

Schwartz, Abba: JFK, ER, and, 176, 188

Schwartz, Nell, 17

Scientific management: Wallace's support of, 62, 63, 71

The Search for America (H. Smith), 250*n*22

Second New Deal, 29, 57

Secret Service protection: ER's refusal of, 145

Sedition, 122, 156, 240*n*60, 243*n*87; *see also* Treason

Segregation, *see* Racism

Selective Service, 141

Senate, *see* Congress. Senate; New York State Senate

Shannon, David, 240*n*56

Sharecroppers: ER and, 87, 93–94

Shirley, Caroline: ER's intervention for, 104–5

Shishkin, Boris, 234*n*109

Simpson, Fuzzy, 123

Sixty Million Jobs (H. Wallace), 63

Slums, *see* Housing

Smith, Al: ER on, 12, 13–14, 17–18, 207*n*20, 248*n*8

Smith, Ed ("Cotton"): and ER, 39

Smith, Gerald L. K.: on ER, 134

Smith, Huston, 250*n*22

Smith, Lamar, 120–21
Smith, Lillian: ER and, 126, 140
Smith Act: ER on, 5, 153–56, 202; Nixon on, 157; passage of, 148; radical right and, 240*n*59; Stevenson and, 247*n*116; *Watkins* case and, 241*n*72
Snyder, John: ER and, 65; H. Morgenthau, Jr. and, 56; price control policy and, 73, 74; Truman and, 70, 72
Social conformity: ER on, 135
Social equality: ER on, 95–96
Social Gospel: and ER, 58, 217*n*16
Socialism, 69, 74, 154, 157
Social Security Act, 189
Sojourner Truth Project (Detroit): ER on, 91
Soldiers, 92, 144, 146; *see also* Army; Veterans
Sorbonne; ER's speech before, 102
Sorensen, Theodore: JFK and, 177, 189
South African apartheid: ER's opposition to, 109, 127, 193
Southern blacks: advocacy of, 93–94; civil rights of, 88, 125, 126, 128; "Eleanor Clubs" and, 87
Southern Christian Leadership Conference (SCLC), 119, 194
Southern Conference Education Fund (SCEF): ER and, 86, 119, 120–22, 153; HUAC and, 152, 239*n*55; Rauh on, 126
Southern Conference for Human Welfare (SCHW): Columbia riot and, 99; ER and, 40–41, 86, 91, 119; first meeting of, 40, 41, 119; founding of, 86; housing program of, 105; rumors in, 91; SCEF and, 120
Southern Democrats: anti-Catholic sentiment among, 178, 50*n*17; *Brown v. Board of Education* and, 112, 113; Civil Rights Act and, 124; FDR and, 38, 39–40; JFK and, 187, 194; New Deal and, 40, 47, 216*n*9; Northern Republicans and, 68; Truman and, 56; *see also* Dixiecrats

Southern Manifesto, 113, 177, 249*n*17
The Southern Patriot (newspaper), 120
Southern Regional Council (SRC), 120
South, the: antilynching legislation and, 41; Eastland leadership of, 117; economic conditions in, 40, 71; "Freedom Concert" and, 44; hospital integration in, 152; national chains in, 122; press of, 92–93; restaurant integration in, 119; voting rights in, 106
Southern Tenant Farmer's Union: ER, Murray and, 94
South Pacific: ER's tour of, 92
Souvestre, Marie: and ER, 7, 131
Soviet-American relations, *see* Cold War
Soviet-American summit (1960), 182, 183, 251*n*29
Soviet Union: Condon and, 151; CPUSA and, 158; DuBois report and, 101; Nazi invasion of, 240*n*59; Rosenbergs and, 166; suspected espionage of, 134; UN delegates of, 152, 168; *see also* Cold War
Spanish Loyalists, 137
Spellman, Francis Joseph: ER's clash with, 175, 248*n*8
Spingarn, Arthur, 98, 102
Spingarn Medal: Marian Anderson and, 42, 43
The Springfield Evening Union, 20–21
Stalin, Joseph, 132, 133
Stark, Lloyd C.: on sharecroppers, 87
Starnes, Joseph: ER and, 149
State Industrial Commission (N.Y.): Perkins, ER and, 17
State Mayor's Conference (N.Y.): ER's recommendations re, 17
"Statement on the Denial of Human Rights to Minorities" (DuBois): ER's position on, 99–100, 103
Stephenson, Gladys, 97
Stephenson, James, 97
Stevenson, Adlai: anti-communist movement and, 247*n*116; civil rights leaders and, 112; defeat of, 177, 202; Hiss and, 5, 161, 243–44*n*89; JFK and, 176; loy-

alists of, 187, 188, 191; McCarthy and, 169; 1956 campaign of, 115, 116, 178; 1960 candidacy of, 182–86, 251*n*29, 252*n*43; on school desegregation, 110–11, 113, 231*n*65; Secretary of State post and, 188, 189, 190, 253*n*58; mentioned, 197, 249*n*14; *see also* ER, Presidential Politics and
Stimson, Henry Lewis, 146
Stix, Thomas L., 207*n*24
Stone, I. F., 56
Stout, Richard L., 219*n*32
Strayer, Martha, 24
Strikes, 70; auto workers, 67, 72, 73; mine workers, 75, 223*n*59; trainmen, 75, 76; *see* Taft-Hartley Act; labor
Strong, Anna Louise, 148
Student Nonviolent Coordinating Committee (SNCC): ER's support of, 122, 194, 196; "Jail/No Bail" campaign, 194
Subsistence Homestead Division: ER and, 94
Subversive Activities Control Board, 158
Supreme Court: civil rights decisions of, 102, 107, 231*n*71; "packing" of, 57; sedition convictions and, 156; Smith Act and, 241*n*72; see also *Brown v. Topeka Board of Education*; *Dennis v. United States*; *Nelson* case; *Plessy v. Ferguson*
Sweatt v. Painter, 102, 108
Symington, Stuart, 176, 177

Taft, Robert, 70, 223*n*58
Taft-Hartley Act: ER and Truman on, 79
Talmadge, Eugene, 46
Tammany Hall, 8, 77, 200
Tanaka, Togo, 147
Tarbell, Ida, 19
Taussig, Charles: ER and, 31, 32
Taylor, Gardner, 234*n*109
Taylor, Myron, 32
Taylor, Telford, 234*n*109
Taylor-Rostow Report: ER on, 193
Teapot Dome scandal: ER's exploitation of, 13

Tenant farmers: ER and, 93–94
Tenerowicz, Rudolph, 91
Texas White Citizens Council, 117–18
Theologians, 241*n*71
Third party (proposed), 4, 68, 77
This I Remember (ER), 10, 21–22, 33, 208*n*30, 213–14*n*53
This Is My Story (ER), 12
This Troubled World (ER), 138
Thomas, Elbert, 61
Thomas, Norman: Commission on the Inquiry into the Freedom Struggle and, 194, 234*n*109; Smith Act and, 155, 156, 241*n*71; ER's support for, 15
Thompson, Dorothy, 48
Thompson, Hanover, 123–24
Thompson, Malvina ("Tommy"), 45
Till, Emmett, 110, 120
Tillich, Paul, 250*n*22
Tilsit (USSR), 189
Time, 48
Tobias, Channing, 98, 112
Todhunter School for Girls: ER and, 15, 16, 21, 22
Tolstoy, Leo, 139
Tomorrow Is Now (ER), 86, 129, 194–95, 196
Toombs, Robert Augustus, 124
To Secure These Rights (Civil Rights Commission), 81
Totalitarianism, 1, 148, 154, 159; *see also* Communists; Fascism
Tractors for Freedom Committee: ER and, 193
TRB (columnist), 83, 219*n*32
Treason: ER accused of, 150; *see also* Sedition
Truman, Bess: ER and, 192
Truman, Harry S.: ER and, 4, 51–84, 174, 250*n*22; civil rights and, 57, 80–81, 83, 97; communists and, 153, 154, 162; at ER's funeral, 197; at FDR's funeral, 52, 56–57; Korean policy of, 166; liberals and, 64, 179–80, 217*n*14, 221*n*42; loyalty program of, 175, 247*n*116; in 1944 campaign, 216*n*10; public hous-

Truman, Harry S.: (*Continued*)
ing and, 103; Stout on, 219*n*32; *see
also* ER, Presidential Politics
Truman Doctrine; ER on, 79, 83, 163
Tugwell, Rexford: on ER and FDR,
46–47
Tully, Grace, 227*n*24
Turkey, 163
Tydings, Millard: on McCarthy, 165, 166

Uncle Tom's Children (Wright): ER's comments on, 36
Unemployment: among artists, 33–36,
46; among defense workers, 96; postwar forecasts of, 60, 219*n*34, 220*n*37;
relief policies for of, 25, 28, 29–30;
among youth, 29, 30–33, 46; *see also*
specific programs
Union County (N.C.), 123
Union for Democratic Action (UDA):
communists and, 224*n*63; FDR employment policies and, 61; Full Employment Bill and, 221*n*43; postwar
economic plans of, 60; Reuther and,
72; H. Wallace and, 62
United Auto Workers Union (UAW):
blacks and, 91; Ford vs., 67, 73; General Motors vs., 71, 72; JFK and,
248*n*9; W. White and, 109
United Brotherhood of Electrical
Workers, 196
United Committee against Police Terror
in Columbia, Tennessee (UCPTCT),
98
United Electrical, Radio and Machine
Workers of America (UERMWA), 175
United Features Syndicate: "My Day"
and, 44, 249*n*13
United Mine Workers (UMW), 75
United Nations (UN): DuBois statement
and, 99–100; ER and, 4, 74, 76, 201;
Geneva session of, 228*n*43; Hiss and,
160, 161; human rights work of, 102;
Israeli delegation to, 196; Jewish
homeland and, 80; Marshall Plan

and, 79; NAACP and, 101, 102; 1948
election and, 77; planning conference
on, 52, 221*n*43; Republicans vs., 166;
Soviet delegation to, 152, 168
—Commission on the Status of Women,
245*n*102
—General Assembly, 101, 103, 166
—Human Rights Commission, 100, 101
—Universal Declaration of Human
Rights: ER's role in, 101, 113
University of Alabama, 116
University of Mississippi, 196
University of Texas Law School, 108
U.S. vs. McWilliams, 240*n*60
U-2 spy plane incident, 182, 183, 251*n*29

Val-Kill (residence), 24; construction of,
15, 207*n*23; as ER's home, 54, 194,
196; furniture factory at, 16; JFK at,
190–91; NAACP institutes in, 102;
Spellman at, 248*n*8
Veblen, Theodore, 219*n*26
Veterans: Bowles on, 70; ER and, 92, 93,
96, 97; on ER
Veterans Administration (VA), 96
Veterans National Liaison Committee, 25
Vietnam: ER on JFK and, 193
Vinson, Frederick Moore, 154
Virgin Islands, 38
Vishinsky, Andrei: ER on, 152
Vocational training, 30, 32
Von Schaeffer-Bernstein, Carola: ER
and, 138–39
Voorhis, Jerry; ER on, 157

Wade, Andrew, 121
Wadsworth, James, 13
Wage-price controls: debate over, 66,
69–76, 79, 220*n*37
Wagner, Robert, 13, 61, 64, 219*n*27
Wagner-Ellender-Taft Housing Bill, 103,
229*n*48
Walker, Jimmy, 17
Wallace, George, 114
Wallace, Henry: ER on, 4, 83, 84; ADA

and, 79, 81; W. Alexander and, 47; C.
Anderson vs., 79; black/labor vote
and, 66; Bowles and, 71; "Broadcast
to Little Businessmen," 62; on cooperative planning, 219*n*27; *Democracy
Reborn*, 58; FDR's death and, 54, 58,
59; on foreign policy, 78; full employment and, 55, 58, 60–62, 66; Hamby
on, 217*m*2; Jones vs., 54, 61, 213–
14*n*53, 216*n*9, 218*n*23; leftists and, 76,
77; 1940 electoral campaign and, 44,
45; Patton and, 60; political ingenu-
ousness of, 59; "The Price of Free
World Victory," 58, 218*m*6; Progressive presidential campaign of, 79, 132,
217*m*14; on racial unrest, 92; *Sixty
Million Jobs*, 63; Stone on, 56; on
Veblen, 219*n*26; Voorhis and, 157;
wage and price controls and, 69–71;
see also ER, Presidential Politics
Wallace, Mike: ER interviewed by, 177
The Wall Between (A. Braden), 122
Waller, Odell: ER's intervention for, 94
Walton, William: JFK's visit to Val-Kill
and, 189, 190
War Department, 141
War Relocation Authority (WRA), 144,
145, 146; *see* internment
Warren, Earl: influence of, 81
The War Worker: on ER, 104
Washington, D.C.: CIO canteen in,
92–93; "Freedom Concert" in, 42–44;
racism in, 66, 97, 105; slums in, 38,
105–6
Washington-National Airport: integra-
tion of, 105
The Washington News, 117
Washington Post, 245*m*102
Washington Post Building, 128
The Washington Star, 20, 115, 144
Watkins, John T.: and *Watkins vs. US*,
241*n*72
Watson, Edwin M.("Pa"), 32
Watts, Rowland, 234*m*109
Webb, Elizabeth Yates, 42

Wechsler, James, 155, 169, 241*n*66
Weekly News (League of Women Voters):
ER and, 13, 206*m*4
Weiss, Nancy J., 220*m*39
West Coast: wartime visit of ER to, 142,
145, 146
Western Democrats, 124
Westinghouse Research Laboratories, 151
Wherry compromise: White's appeal to
ER re, 109, 223*n*58
White, Theodore: on Stevenson and ER,
183
White, Walter: Columbia riot and, 98;
correspondence of, 216*n*9; DuBois
and, 100, 101, 228*n*43; "Freedom
Concert" and, 42; Japanese
Americans and, 140, 144; on legal vic-
tories, 108; marriage of, 109; on 1944
Democratic Convention, 94–95; on
veterans, 96; on Virgin Islands, 38;
mentioned, 93, 102; *see also* Civil
Rights; ER, Civil Rights and; NAAC
White Citizens Councils: ER's opposi-
tion to, 117–18, 121
White House: ER on beer in, 25; con-
certs in, 42, 43; domestic staff in, 37;
farewell tea in, 52; murals displayed
in, 34; youth activists in, 148
White Southerners, 37, 112, 114, 124, 191
White supremacists, 118, 127, 128; *see
also* Ku Klux Klan; White Citizens
Councils
Wilkins, Roy: ER's disagreements with,
109, 110, 111, 112, 114
Williams, Aubrey, 120; in Birmingham,
40; black farmers and, 94; HUAC
and, 152; New Orleans School Board
and, 121; NYA and, 32; *The Wall
Between* and, 122
Williams, G. Mennen: ER on, 177,
249*m*4
Wilson, Clarence, 104
Wilson, Edith, 95, 227*m*25
Wilson, Woodrow, 8, 26, 139
Wiltwyck Academy, 107

Wise, Justine and Samuel, 126
Woman's Home Companion, ER's article
  in, 26, 31
Women: black, 93; drinking by, 20,
  208*n*35; Japanese American, 144; in
  Kennedy administration, 193; New
  Deal and, 25; newspapers and, 25;
  politics and, 206*n*14, 207*n*20; of
  upstate New York, 17; rights of, 193;
  wartime employment of, 70, 93, 144;
  see also Rape
Women reporters: ER and, 24–25, 26, 52,
  209*n*6
Women's Auxiliary Army Corps
  (WAAC), 93, 144
Women's City Club (New York); ER
  and, 10, 12
Women's Democratic News: ER and, 11, 13,
  200
Women's International League of Peace
  and Freedom (WILPF): ER and, 137
Women's Joint Legislative Committee:
  ER and, 10
Women's Trade Union League (WTUL):
  ER and, 10, 22
Woodward, Ellen, 35

Works Progress Administration (WPA):
  ER and, 34, 94; *see also* Federal One
  Programs
World Court: ER on, 137
World War I, 8–9, 139
World War II: civil liberties and, 131, 132,
  136–47; defense purchases in, 71;
  effect on ER, 92, 132–133, 136–142;
  economic planning and, 60, 70; the
  homefront and blacks, 88–96; housing construction and, 103; ER on Jim
  Crow and, 89, 90, 93, 95, 96; immi-
  nent end of, 59, 70, 93; internment
  policies in, 4, 140, 142–47, 201; J. P.
  Kennedy and, 5; liberalism and, 1; *see
  also* antiwar activism; conscientious
  objectors;
Wright, Richard: ER's support for, 36

Yaemitsu Sugimachi, 143
Yalta Conference: Hiss and, 159, 243*n*87
Young Democrats of City College: ER's
  speech before, 167–68
Youth: ER as ombudsman for, 29, 30–33,
  36, 46; ER challenged on civil rights
  by, 39; *see also* College students